Praise for the Book

Christian does a great job of focusing on patterns from a .NET perspective. He explores some very practical patterns and provides .NET specific guidance and code for implementations.

I particularly liked the bubble-up pattern for exception handling as I am a firm believer in top-level exception management. He looks at a broad set of patterns from the presentation tier to the data tier, and does a great job of focusing on XML and XML Web services throughout.

The best part of the book is the fact that Christian's insights come from a real-world experience with patterns and .NET. That's readily apparent by the way he brings it all together in the section on applying patterns to commercial products. He offers something to everyone:

- VB6 developers coming to .NET and beginning to learn OO thinking and patterns

- Experienced OO developers thinking through pattern implementations with .NET

- Advanced pattern connoisseurs

—Stephen Fulcher
Microsoft Regional Director and .NET Trainer

The Software Patterns Series

Series Editor: John M. Vlissides

The Software Patterns Series (SPS) comprises pattern literature of lasting significance to software developers. Software patterns document general solutions to recurring problems in all software-related spheres, from the technology itself, to the organizations that develop and distribute it, to the people who use it. Books in the series distill experience from one or more of these areas into a form that software professionals can apply immediately.

Relevance and *impact* are the tenets of the SPS. Relevance means each book presents patterns that solve real problems. Patterns worthy of the name are intrinsically relevant; they are borne of practitioners' experiences, not theory or speculation. Patterns have impact when they change how people work for the better. A book becomes a part of the series not just because it embraces these tenets, but because it has demonstrated it fulfills them for its audience.

Titles in the series:

Data Access Patterns: Database Interactions in Object-Oriented Applications, Clifton Nock

Design Patterns Explained: A New Perspective on Object-Oriented Design, Alan Shalloway/
    James R. Trott

Design Patterns Java™ Workbook, Steven John Metsker

The Design Patterns Smalltalk Companion, Sherman Alpert/Kyle Brown/Bobby Woolf

The Joy of Patterns: Using Patterns for Enterprise Development, Brandon Goldfedder

The Manager Pool: Patterns for Radical Leadership, Don Olson/Carol Stimmel

.NET Patterns: Architecture, Design, and Process, Christian Thilmany

Pattern Hatching: Design Patterns Applied, John Vlissides

Pattern Languages of Program Design, edited by James O. Coplien/Douglas C. Schmidt

Pattern Languages of Program Design 2, edited by John M. Vlissides/James O. Coplien/
    Norman L. Kerth

Pattern Languages of Program Design 3, edited by Robert Martin/Dirk Riehle/
    Frank Buschmann

Small Memory Software, James Noble/Charles Weir

Software Configuration Management Patterns, Stephen P. Berczuk/Brad Appleton

For more information, check out the series web site at www.awprofessional.com/series/swpatterns

.NET Patterns

Architecture, Design, and Process

Christian Thilmany

✦✦ Addison-Wesley

Boston • San Francisco • New York • Toronto • Montreal
London • Munich • Paris • Madrid
Capetown • Sydney • Tokyo • Singapore • Mexico City

The publisher offers discounts on this book when ordered in quantity for bulk purchases and special sales. For more information, please contact:

> U.S. Corporate and Government Sales
> (800) 382-3419
> corpsales@pearsontechgroup.com

For sales outside of the U.S., please contact:

> International Sales
> (317) 581-3793
> international@pearsontechgroup.com

Visit Addison-Wesley on the Web: www.awprofessional.com

Library of Congress Cataloging-in-Publication Data

A CIP catalog record for this book can be obtained from the Library of Congress.

The art displayed on chapter opening pages is used with the permission of M. C. Escher, "Development I" © 2003 Cordon Art B. V. - Baarn - Holland. All rights reserved.

ISBN: 0-32-113002-2

Text printed on recycled paper

First printing

Contents

Foreword xv

Preface xvii

The Road to .NET and this Book xvii

Book Layout xx

Part I: Building a Framework with .NET xxi
Part II: Creating the Tiers of a Framework xxiii
Acknowledgments xxvi

PART 1 BUILDING A FRAMEWORK WITH .NET

Chapter 1. New Framework, New Model, New Measures   3

Not Another Language—Please Stop! 3

The .NET Framework and a Distributed New World 5

The .NET Framework and the World of OO 8
How Did We Get Here? 11

.NET and XML Web Services 13

XML Web Services Primer   19

    What Is an XML Web Service?   19

    Web Services and SOAP   24

    Security in SOAP?   28

    WSDL   32

    UDDI   33

Highlights of .NET   33

Components of .NET—A Snippet   35

Patterns Explained   35

History and Categorization   39

Categorizing Patterns   40

The Pattern Library   42

    General Framework Patterns   42

    Presentation-Tier Patterns   42

    Middle-Tier Patterns   43

    Persistence-Tier Patterns   43

    Advanced Patterns   43

How to Use the Pattern Library   43

Chapter 2. Framework Patterns: Exception Handling, Logging, and Tracing   **45**

Overview   45

Exception Handling   47

    Application-Specific Exceptions   47

Building a Base Exception Class   53

    Determining Where to Log (Using the Trace Object)   58

    Determining What to Log   59

    Throwing System Exceptions   62

Managing Exception Boundaries   63

    Throwing Exceptions from Web Services   63

Technology Backgrounder—SOAP Faults   65

    Adding SOAP Exception Support to BaseException   71

    Determining When to Log   76

Technology Backgrounder—Trace Switches and Trace Listeners   77

Trace Listeners   77

Boolean and Trace Switches   80

Remote Tracing—Building a Custom Trace Listener   82

Building a Custom Trace Listener   83

Building a Remote Trace Receiver   86

Sending Traces to a Message Queue   87

Sending Traces via Sockets   92

Building a Remote Trace Viewer   94

Summary   104

PART 2 CREATING THE TIERS OF A FRAMEWORK

Chapter 3. Presentation-Tier Patterns   107

Overview   107

Notifying Thread Manager   108

Intent   108

Problem   108

Forces   109

Structure   109

Consequences   110

Participants   110

Implementation   111

Related Patterns   116

Pollable Thread Manager   116

Intent   116

Problem   116

Forces   116

Structure   117

Consequences   117

Participants   118

Implementation   118

Related Patterns   122

MultiSync Thread Manager   122

    Intent   122

    Problem   122

    Forces   123

    Structure   123

    Consequences   124

    Participants   124

    Implementation   124

    Related Patterns   125

Error Cross-Reference Generator   125

    Intent   125

    Problem   125

    Forces   126

    Structure   126

    Consequences   127

    Participants   127

    Implementation   127

    Related Patterns   128

WebForm Template   128

    Intent   128

    Problem   128

    Forces   128

    Structure   129

    Consequences   129

    Participants   130

    Implementation   130

    Related Patterns   131

Dynamic Assembly Loader   132

    Intent   132

    Problem   132

    Forces   133

    Structure   133

    Consequences   133

    Participants   134

    Implementation   134

Stunt Driver Interface   135

    Intent   135

    Problem   135

    Forces   135

    Structure   135

    Consequences   136

    Participants   136

    Implementation   136

    Related Patterns   139

Chapter 4. Middle-Tier Patterns   141

Overview   141

Chained Service Factory   143

    Intent   143

    Problem   143

    Forces   145

    Structure   146

    Consequences   146

    Participants   148

    Implementation   149

    Related Patterns   152

Unchained Service Factory   152

    Intent   152

    Problem   152

    Forces   154

    Structure   155

    Consequences   155

    Participants   157

    Implementation   157

    Technology Backgrounder—.NET Reflection Services   159

    Related Patterns   162

Product Manager   163

    Intent   163

    Problem   163

    Forces   165

Structure   166

Consequences   166

Participants   167

Implementation   168

Related Patterns   171

Service Façade   171

Intent   171

Problem   171

Forces   173

Structure   173

Consequences   174

Participants   174

Implementation   175

Related Patterns   178

Abstract Packet Pattern   178

Intent   178

Problem   179

Forces   180

Structure   181

Consequences   181

Participants   183

Implementation   183

Technology Backgrounder—Boxing/Unboxing   185

Related Patterns   192

Packet Translator   192

Intent   192

Problem   192

Forces   193

Structure   193

Consequences   194

Participants   194

Implementation   196

Related Patterns   200

Chapter 5. Persistence-Tier Patterns   **201**

Overview   201

Technology Backgrounder—Schemas and DataSets   204

    XML Schema   204

    Schemas and DataSets   206

    Creating Typed DataSets   208

    Schema Types   212

    Tables, Columns, and Keys   213

Poly Model Pattern   217

    Intent   217

    Problem   217

    Forces   218

    Structure   219

    Consequences   223

    Participants   226

    Implementation   226

    Related Patterns   231

Schema Field Pattern   231

    Intent   231

    Problem   232

    Forces   233

    Structure   234

    Consequences   235

    Implementation   235

    Related Patterns   245

Schema Indexer   245

    Intent   245

    Problem   246

    Forces   247

    Structure   247

    Consequences   250

    Implementation   251

    Related Patterns   264

Chapter 6. Process Patterns: Applying .NET Patterns to a Commercial Product   265

Overview   265

ProductX and the Commercial Framework   267

What is ProductX?   270
Why Should Consumers or Businesses Use this Type of Product?   271
A .NET Product in the Financial World   272
Electronic Check Web Servicing   275

.NET Technology: A Competitive Advantage   279

Why is .NET a Competitive Advantage?   279

Applying .NET Patterns   291

Applying the Service Façade Pattern   292
Applying the Product Manager Pattern   296
Applying the Unchained Service Factory Pattern   303
Applying the Poly Model Pattern   309

Invoking our framework from the ProductX Web Client   313

Summarizing the Suite   317

Chapter 7. Advanced Patterns   319

Overview   319

Abstract Cache   320

Intent   320
Problem   320
Forces   322
Structure   322
Consequences   322
Participants   325
Implementation   326
Technology Backgrounder—A Look at SOAP Headers   327
Technology Backgrounder—ASP.NET Caching   338
Related Patterns   342

Web Service Interface Pattern   342

Intent   342
Problem   342

Forces   343

Structure   344

Consequences   344

Participants   346

Implementation   347

Loosely Coupled Transactor Server   350

Intent   350

Problem   354

Forces   357

Structure   358

Consequences   359

Participants   362

Implementation   364

Loosely Coupled Transactor Client   380

Intent   380

Problem   380

Forces   380

Structure   381

Consequences   383

Participants   384

Implementation   385

Password Storage   400

Intent   400

Problem   400

Forces   400

Structure   401

Consequences   401

Participants   401

Implementation   401

Index   403

Foreword

Pattern recognition just might be the fundamental operation of human intelligence. Once Christopher Alexander recognized that patterns exist in good buildings, it wasn't long before software developers began talking explicitly about the patterns that exist in good code. What took us so long? Reusing not just code, but also the way we create that code, makes good sense.

One of the most important bodies of reusable code today is the class library that's part of the .NET Framework. This very large set of software provides standard ways to manipulate XML documents, create GUIs, communicate with other systems, and much more. Learning to use at least some parts of this library is a fundamental task for any Windows software developer.

Yet learning this technology alone isn't enough. Understanding how a particular .NET namespace works doesn't automatically give you the intellectual tools necessary to apply this understanding effectively. Figuring out which patterns work best in a given .NET context is a critical part of creating a good solution.

That's where *.NET Patterns: Architecture, Design, and Process* comes in. In this book, Christian Thilmany combines the abstractions of the design patterns world with the concrete development approach embodied in .NET. The result is a collection of ideas—guiding practices as well as more formal patterns—that will be useful for a large set of .NET developers. Some of them are generic enough to be used by anybody working in any software environment. Others depend specifically on some aspect of .NET, which is exactly what you'd expect from a book with this focus. In either case, software professionals working in the .NET world can gain from the experience of those who've gone before.

The design patterns movement has long been a fixture of the Java community. I'm happy to see that with the arrival of .NET, the Microsoft world is also explicitly embracing these ideas. This book is a valuable step down that road.

David Chappell
San Francisco, CA

Preface

THE ROAD TO .NET AND THIS BOOK

Until now, we have been inundated with a melee of material in the areas of software architecture, design, and "professional" principles. The need for design material seems to be always at its peak when either a new language or technology appears in the market. When Java first entered the market, you could hear the squalls of developers as they flooded into the local bookstores to pick up the latest copy of *Learn Java in 10 Minutes*. Not only was Java a new language but it was also a new platform, and it was *the* language for developing rich Internet applications. Not only were developers challenged with a new syntax but they also had to learn the new semantics of this new development medium. For those new to object-oriented technologies, it meant an even greater learning curve. Everything in Java is an object, and it takes another level of discipline to design robust and reusable applications even after mastering the syntax and its base libraries. Having been programming in Java since its inception, I hope I have come to appreciate the things I would like to see in any new technology material offered. This is especially true in the area of architecture and design. This book is the culmination of many of the "do's and don'ts" I would have liked to have had when I was not only learning .NET but trying to master it, as well.

Before returning to Microsoft as a .NET solutions architect and having embraced Java at one point, I truly have tried to hold myself impartial to the technology and language wars that insued between the two giants of Sun and Microsoft. I never prescribed to becoming truly biased in any one direction. Java definitely has its strengths and before .NET, had become my favorite object-oriented language for many reasons. I loved its syntax, threading model, type system, and especially the base class libraries. From someone coming over from C/C++ and Visual Basic, Java was it. No longer did you have to struggle with the C runtime and the myriad of functionality-overlapped external libraries. But Java wasn't perfect, as we all soon found out. "Write once, run everywhere" wasn't quite as seamless as first promised. Developing a custom Java GUI was not straightforward, and there were too many vendor options for code generation. Object orientation also became more mainstream and, with it, the need for design disciplines.

The Microsoft platforms have their strengths, as well. Visual Basic provides a fast development cycle when building rich GUI applications. As Visual Basic matured, it was becoming harder and harder to justify the need to develop specialized code, such as COM components using a lower level language such as C++. Visual Basic (VB) gave you this with much less effort unless, of course, you were writing a commercial product and needed extremely specialized behavior or a very small .DLL footprint. Using VB, business applications could be brought to production in weeks instead of months. Anyone who has done any GUI development in Java versus VB will understand exactly what I'm referring to. From the development viewpoint, I loved Java but it was too painful putting together GUI applications using AWT, Swing, or whatever third-party library I was using. The third parties made it easier as Java matured but you found yourself indicted with almost too many options. Choose one and you risk adopting a technology that becomes either unsupported or unmarketable. That seems to always be the problem when the inventor of the language doesn't also provide the most popular development environment for the language created. This is the case with Java.

In my humble opinion and even before joining Microsoft I feel that it has always built some of the best Integrated Development Environments (IDEs). Sure, there are more powerful editors out there that provide the truly hard-core developer a feeling of being omniscient. However, for the masses, you want a well-designed, tightly integrated, and user-friendly IDE that is not only reliable but also commonplace. What makes *vi* so popular in the UNIX world is what makes Visual Studio so appealing—it can be found everywhere. If a Visual Basic or C++ application is going to be written on Windows 2000, Visual Studio is usually your tool. That is not the case in the world of Java. You have editors by BEA, Borland, Sun, IBM, etc., each with their own means of building GUI applications and code generation. As a Java consultant, I was required to try all of the major vendors because it seemed that no one editor was really predominant. For capitalism, this "open market" idea seems compelling but for engineering it can create convolution.

I thought to myself, "If there were only a platform that combined the best of Java with that of Visual Basic, sprinkled with the power of C++." This is what .NET (especially C#) is. I hope I can say this without making too many folks completely red in the face and wanting to put the book down as we speak. But being on both sides of the language wars, I hope I've earned the right to make such an opinion. The .NET framework is everything I loved about Java and much more. No longer do you have to choose a language and suffer the inconsistencies of the libraries that actually drive the development, not to mention other numerous benefits that I'll cover in this book. Being a first-generation product (version 1.1 of the framework is still first generation in my book), I'm astounded by the amount of functionality we have today, and this is the tip of the iceberg. Hopefully, .NET will continue to improve and become the cross-platform development framework of the future and bring along its benefits to those environments for years to come. Considering the amount of functionality already offered in only version 1.1 of the .NET framework and that offered by Visual Studio .NET, I can only imagine how much further the .NET platform will be two years from now. The rate at which Microsoft has generated this relatively different development environment is amazing and reminds me of the rate at which Internet Explorer blossomed into the predominant browser in the market in such a short period of time. That is not just good marketing but also good delivery. If you are a Java developer, take .NET for a serious spin; I cannot imagine you wanting to go back.

I began this book just after .NET Beta 2 was released in hopes that most of major features of the .NET libraries and its runtime would be complete. A year later, the framework version is due to be released and should be out by the time you pick up the first copy of this book. Thankfully, there has not been much change in that time, which says a lot for the thought that went into the original release and the stability of Beta 2. In fact, if you happen to have an old Beta 2 copy around, you are free to test the code referenced in this book. It should both compile and run. After all, this is a design and architecture best practices book. It is hard enough writing code in an environment that is somewhat of a moving target but even harder when trying to develop best practices during that time. The point was to write code somewhat agnostic to the technology. Using Framework 1.1 as an acid test to this, I was pleased to find out that all was compatible. When this book is finally published, .NET 1.0 will have been released for over a year and thousands of developers will be clamoring for content, sample code, and principles to use. Heck, I was doing that during Beta 2.

I hope to help you enter this different world that is a departure from Microsoft's traditional development platforms. Not only is Microsoft introducing what equates to an entirely new set of languages, but it also is providing those same elements that have attracted Java developers to its world. Microsoft is now introducing the aspect of true object orientation for all of those Visual Basic developers who have begun to taste it but not yet truly experience it. Bottoms up to the new taste of .NET; I'm sure everyone will be satisfied with the cooking.

BOOK LAYOUT

I've divided this book into three major parts. Part I introduces .NET and the elements of design and architecture necessary to begin writing truly sound applications. This includes the lower level plumbing components that most frameworks require. These "framework patterns and practices" apply to all aspects of .NET development, such as exception handling and logging. Part II outlines specific things to do and things not to do in a tier architecture, breaking the pattern classifications up into your three tiers: presentation tier, middle tier, and persistence tier. This highlights not only best practices and implementation patterns but also the more technology-agnostic architecture and design patterns. The final chapter really belongs on its own because it includes more advanced patterns covering topics such as asynchronous behavior, complex threading, and caching. These patterns are needed for many frameworks but are not considered a requirement and, thus, are given their own chapter. Many of the patterns will coincide with the established patterns of the "gang of four," adding to your design tool belt.

In Chapter 1, I will give you a brief technical rundown of XML Web services, the .NET world of object orientation, and a few pattern definitions for those new to this design approach. Throughout the book, I will introduce new .NET topics and some of the features unique to other frameworks that may affect your design and your understanding of the content. I will also begin to plant the seeds of those services supplied by .NET that will be leveraged in the more technology-focused patterns later in the book.

Part I: Building a Framework with .NET

Chapter 1—New Framework, New Model, New Measures

Here I take a brief look at patterns, their classifications, and applying them to the .NET framework. I'll introduce patterns for those of you who have never worked with them in the past and provide a process of how they may be applied. I will also frame what separates this development release from all others coming from Microsoft, such as the incorporation of XML Web services.

This chapter will also take a brief look at the elements of .NET that will be used to exemplify each practice presented. Although many patterns are technology-agnostic, this is not always the case for implementation and architecture patterns. Here I will briefly review those .NET elements required to grasp the more technology-specific patterns. This will also serve as a "crash course" for those new to the .NET base class library (BCL).

Finally, this chapter takes a deeper looks at patterns, their classifications, and their history. This chapter will be especially important for programmers used to more linear style (e.g., Visual Basic, Active Server Pages, etc.) who may be comfortable with component-oriented COM design but less comfortable with OO design. I'll explain what implementation patterns are and how they are different from architecture and design patterns. Here I talk about the good and the bad of .NET design, architecture, and development by presenting a set of best practices and "named" implementation patterns.

I also will provide a .NET primer along the way to acquaint those unfamiliar with the "library hieroglyphics" used in the upcoming pattern diagrams. These "primers" will be only a "tutorial thumbnail" because there is so much material better suited that will cover the background of these topics in depth.

Chapter 2—Framework Patterns: Exception Handling, Logging, and Tracing

Topics such as debugging, error handling, and logging will be covered in this chapter due to their general applicability and importance. This content belongs right up front in the book because I feel it is one of most important elements of a good design and a robust application overall. To begin with a design of any good framework, you can start with these practices and implementation patterns to put together the initial "plumbing" for your application. Again at this point, you should be comfortable with the .NET technology and of patterns in general. These topics overall are what I call *framework patterns* because they make up the backbone of the framework and are vital to any application. This includes exception handling, logging, tracing, and many other practices not categorized as presentation, middle-tier, or persistent-oriented. Although much of this code can be placed at the middle tier, much of is vital to all tiers and is categorized as such.

The principles and patterns covered in detail are:

Exception Handling—Structured error handling with .NET

Exception Logging—Event logging and instrumentation practices

Exception Chaining—"Bubbling up" your errors from tier to tier

Building a Base Exception Class—Creating a foundation for your error handling

Tracing and Trace Listening—Centralizing and simplifying your instrumentation

Error and Call Stacks—Presenting and enriching your presented errors

When, Where, and How to Log—The heuristics of error handling in .NET

SOAP Exceptions and SOAP Faults—Errors in the Web services environment

Interop Exception Handling—Errors in the distributed EAI environment

The following specific implementation patterns will be described in detail:

Remote Tracer—Tracing and error handling across machine boundaries

Custom Soap Exception Handler—Error handling in the Web services environment

System Exception Wrapper—Handling .NET system exceptions

Soap Fault Builder—Preparing errors to be viewed by Web service clients

This part of the book dives right into the catalog of design and architecture patterns typically (but not always) found at specific tier of an application. Some are simply new twists to old familiar patterns, whereas others are unique. Some of the patterns will be technology-agnostic and others exploit some unique framework features of .NET and, thus, are slightly more technology-specific.

Part II: Creating the Tiers of a Framework

Chapter 3—Presentation-Tier Patterns

At this point, you should be comfortable with .NET, Web services, and patterns. Now I delve into the implementation practices for all front-end development. This includes "thin" and "thick" client implementation practices such as screen refreshing, GUI threading, custom control display, and interface template principles. Even more advanced topics, such as asynchronous Web service invocations and client-side threading, will be discussed. If you will be working solely on middle-tier components, you are free to skip this chapter.

As you may surmise, this chapter catalogs patterns found at the presentation tier. This includes:

Notifying Thread Manager—Create a thread and notify a Windows form

Pollable Thread Manager—Create a thread and periodically check status

MultiSync Thread Manager—Combine Notifying and Pollable Thread Managers

Error Cross-Reference Generator—Error ID generator used during exception handling

Web Form Template—Base template class for a quick interface layouts

Stunt Driver—Generic interface for testing a component

Dynamic Assembly Loader—Dynamic loading and caching driver

Chapter 4—Middle-Tier Patterns

In this chapter, I cover six middle-tier or "business"-tier patterns that can really be applied at any level. This catalog contains all of those patterns that are not typically considered "advanced" yet cannot be truly considered related to the tier-2 tiers, presentation or persistence (data). For those designing an architecture that must present a single point of entry, sometimes it makes sense to start here. This can also be considered an opportunity to design the distributed wrapper that will make all components of your middle-ware accessible yet secure to the outside world. Both the framework patterns and these patterns are the very first pieces I recommend be created for any architecture. These patterns, along with those from Chapter 2, provide the essential elements needed to build a truly dynamic and flexible design. These should also insulate your support from change based on user requirements in the future and allow your developers to concentrate on business rules definition and not "plumbing" problems.

The patterns covered here are:

Chained Service Factory—Creating a single entry point for Web services

Unchained Service Factory—A late-bound single entry point for Web services

Product Manager—Handling unmanaged code in a managed way

Service Façade—Delegating complex logic from Web services

Abstract Packet—Handling and passing complex parameter sets

Packet Translator—Translating those complex parameters sets

Chapter 5—Persistence-Tier Patterns

Here I will focus on the persistent-tier architecture and implementation patterns. This includes database access, streaming practices, and XML schema-based I/O. Here I will get into some of .NET's most powerful XML data features and show how you can exploit them. This includes taking advantage of DataSets, XML schemas, automated data-tier code generation, dynamic data modeling, type-strong schemas, and the flexibilities of XML and how to leverage it.

The architecture patterns covered are:

Poly Model—Providing a "dynamic physical data model" using XML schemas

Poly Model Factory—Applying Factory Methods to Poly Models

Schema Field—Persisting schemas, retrieving schemas, and schema management

Schema Indexer—Building dynamic indexes using schema and Poly Models

Abstract Schema—Applying the Abstract Packet pattern in a world of XML schemas

Chapter 6—Process Patterns: Applying .NET Patterns to a Commercial Product

In this chapter, I talk about a real-world .NET commercial application called *ProductX* that I had the pleasure to lead in the design and architecture effort. I will provide some of the practices we applied to this financial services application and how .NET was used as the migration target technology from a traditional C++/COM-based platform. I will also describe how some of the patterns outlined in this book were applied to its implementation. During this product's development life cycle, I "ate my own dog food," so to speak, by using most of the patterns in this book in a live commercial application.

The patterns from this book that I provide a roadmap to in this commercial application are:

Poly Model—Applying the Poly Model composite pattern and integrating it with a product database

Unchained Service Factory—A late-bound single entry point for the Web services used by ProductX for all external access

Product Manager—Providing the business framework by which all financial components were managed in the Commercial Framework.

Service Façade—Delegating complex logic from Web services and defining the framework feature set for financial services

Chapter 7—Advanced Patterns

This chapter goes into those patterns I considered advanced. These can be applied at any level and are not consider essential to an application but extremely useful. When performance becomes an issue, some of these patterns can be applied, such as the addition of caching and asynchronous processing. These can be added to enhance a design but should be used in only specific scenarios and with greater caution. If any of these patterns are implemented or applied incorrectly, they will decrease their overall benefit and defeat any reason for applying them.

The advanced patterns include:

Abstract Cache—Abstracted caching framework using cache object

Web Service Interface—Interface-based Web services

Loosely Coupled Transactor—Abstracted asynchronous business transactions

LCT Server—Server-based Loosely Coupled Transactor

LCT Client—Client-based Loosely Coupled Transactor

For those who are already comfortable with the .NET framework or do not wish to hear another executive retread of this .NET or of Web services, WSDL, or SOAP you can skip the following section. For those new to SOAP and how Web services work, read on.

Acknowledgments

A book is more than the authors who write it. It is a culmination of creative effort from ideas, whiteboard sessions, art work, editing, and most importantly, time. There have been many people explicitly and implicitly involved in this 18-month project. The easiest to forget are those who've contributed those intangible assets such as time and the patience to go along with it. I'd like to thank some of the people who've helped me get from that first blurry idea to design to code to content to production. Not only were people providing their own time to dedicate to the material presented here but there also were those folks who provided me with my own time to use on this project. There were those individuals like Brett Walker who allowed me the time to work on this, even when that time could have been spent elsewhere—time that could have been used for more immediately profitable ventures. So I will thank all those individuals in "chronologically contributing order" from ideas to production.

I want to thank Paul Becker for taking the time to hear my ideas for this book and for seeing the merit of its premise. I want especially to thank John Neidhart for picking up this project at Addison, taking its ideas on trust (with little time to dig in), and reeling me in by rescoping my efforts and providing me a more practical set of deliverables. I want to thank all of the members of the production team (Kyle Howard, Marti Jones, and Patti Guerrieri) for making this first book as painless as possible.

I thank Brett Walker for allowing me to continue this book during my time spent working with him and his company. I was given the ability to synergize my efforts of designing a production application using principles in this book, and

Brett provided me that perfect testing platform. Without this cooperative and synergistic effort, many of the principles in this book may have fallen into an academic pit. Brett Walker, David Mytchak, James Williams gave me the important feedback and creative inspiration for many of these patterns. My ideas would not have made it to fruition during the early months without the help of David Mytchak. Without David's thoughts and James's code, I would have never been able to go against some traditional thinking and created Chapter 5. The Poly Model was your "raw idea" coming to life in these pages.

I also want to thank all those at Microsoft who inherited this book upon my rejoining the company in early spring of 2003. Everyone at Microsoft has been so supportive of this project and has helped me refine the book's message. The material presented here has fit very nicely with Microsoft's own prescriptive branding and its own architecture principles. It just goes to show you that good design is good design, no matter how you brand it. I specifically want to thank the members of the Gulf Coast developer team at Microsoft of which I'm a member: Ed Draper, J Sawyer, Michael Lane Thomas, and John Opalko for helping me get the message out that this book existed—and for adding it to their presentation slides at the last minute.

I want to thank my wife, Hilari. By the time this is published, we will have just returned from our honeymoon. We can now look back and enjoy the fruits of our labor. We can now appreciate all of the weekends and weeknights spent in front of my computer when she had to slip food under my door. Thanks for being patient and understanding with this project. I also want to thank my mother for all those "little favors" that saved me so much time to work on this book.

Finally, I need to thank Brian Eshelman, who saved my backside by being the major contributor of all content for Chapter 3. Those were his ideas, designs, and code. Without them, my deadline would have been in jeopardy—thank you so much, Brian, for being a part of this book. You are a wonderful designer, developer, and friend.

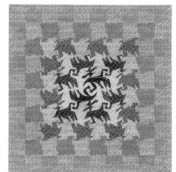

Part 1

Building a Framework with .NET

1

New Framework, New Model, New Measures

NOT ANOTHER LANGUAGE—PLEASE STOP!

Back when Microsoft first announced one of the new languages that would fit into its new .NET framework, I was very skeptical. That language was C# (pronounced *C-Sharp*) and is the primary language that this book uses for its examples. This doesn't mean that those developers choosing other .NET-supported languages (e.g., VB.NET, J#, Managed C++, etc.) cannot use this material. In fact, the primary goal of this book is to provide, as much as possible, a language-agnostic viewpoint of .NET practices. This approach is the very same approach Microsoft has implemented in .NET with its runtime and its language specifications. The focus is on the framework, its design elements, and what best practices and patterns can be extracted from it. The samples happen to be written in C# because that is my personal preference, but each of these ideas can be implemented in VB.NET, J#, or any other supported .NET language. This has to do with the way

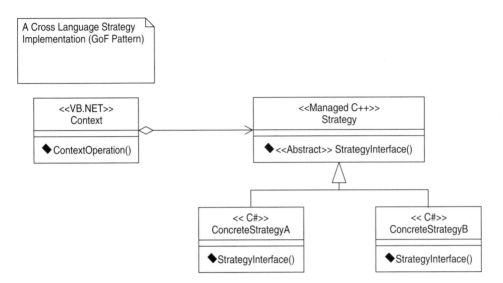

FIGURE 1.1: Shows how a classic design pattern such as Strategy can be implemented in .NET.

Microsoft has architected its framework. This is truly one of the most powerful and unique features of this product. The developer now gets to choose his or her own syntax of choice while still learning all of the common elements from the .NET libraries, along with common design philosophies taught in this book. Using .NET, more common design patterns such as the "strategy" pattern can now be implemented using a multitude of languages. Figure 1.1 uses stereotypes to designate what language each entity of the strategy pattern is implemented in. This is only a simple demonstration of the flexibility cross-language inheritance provides the designer. Even commonly implemented patterns such as the Strategy can be given a new twist with the help of .NET.

If you happen to be at the crossroads of which .NET language to select, I would select C#. This may come as a shock to those Visual Basic programmers who feel that learning VB.NET would be less of a technology leap. Because this framework is so different, the learning curve is not in the syntax but in the environment. For those new to object-oriented technologies, even VB.NET will be quite a leap from the Visual Basic 6.0 world. If you were to learn such a new system, I would suggest picking a language where the most examples could be found. Again, I believe that is C#, although Microsoft has made an incredible effort to show both VB.NET and C# in its documentation and online content. Even though .NET will support any language conforming to the common language infrastructure (CLI), C# is the language of .NET, similar to the way that C is the language of Windows (Dr. GUI, November 20, *MSDN Magazine*). C# was built with .NET in mind from the ground up. Even much of the framework itself was built using this language.

The runtime I keep referring to is called the *common language runtime* (CLR). The type system used by the CLR is referred to as the *common type system* (CTS), and the specification of .NET is called the *common language specification* (CLS)—a mouthful of acronyms, to say the least. Although I assume most readers will have worked with .NET or are familiar with its environment, you will not require any significant .NET design experience to understand the principles in this book. I also assume a familiarity with object orientation, but only a cursory knowledge is required. Understanding the basics of inheritance, abstraction, association, and polymorphism will help you decipher the benefits of the ensuing material. However these patterns are aimed at those new to object orientation, service-orientation, and specifically object-oriented best practices. One of my primary goals is to bridge the gap between service-oriented and object-oriented architectures and not just provide the reader with yet another rehash of common design patterns and practices. Unfortunately, I will not be going deep into the plumbing of the CLR, CTS, CLI, or CLS. However, throughout the book, I will be providing "technology backgrounders" on some of the more specific shared library implementations for those just learning some of .NET's more advanced features. I hope to provide everyone, including those new to this framework, a chance to improve their designs using these patterns and principles. I also hope to provide you with a reference-like resource so that this book does not have to absorbed in its entirety or be "shelved" once it is read. Hopefully, this will serve as a quasi-library of information and a catalog of "named ideas" that can be used again and again.

THE .NET FRAMEWORK AND A DISTRIBUTED NEW WORLD

With .NET and the world of Extensible Markup Language (XML) Web services, we have finally reached a point where it has become not only desirable to employ distributed applications but rather simple, as well. The allure of employing Web services in your design has now become irresistible. Web service consumers can now leverage both intranet and Internet-based Web service providers. No longer does each IT department require the need to reinvent the proverbial "custom software wheel." Services can now be easily used instead of produced. However, this allure comes with some serious considerations. Not only do developers require another level of skillset to produce scalable applications, but the same goes for those supporting its infrastructure. Vendors are also getting into the services business and not just those that consider themselves "application service providers." Traditional application vendors, such as the one covered in Chapter 6, are wrapping their products around a standard Web service layer to give customers features that were previously shrink-wrapped, installed locally, or too difficult to provide.

All of this is possible because of XML Web services and the newly released .NET framework. With .NET, building truly distributed business services is as easy as adding an *attribute* to a method. Alas, this is the benefit *and* the curse. Technology departments must ready themselves for this invasion. They must be ready not only to take full advantage of this opportunity but also to prepare their infrastructures, their teams, and their perspectives. Many times, as you have seen with the likes of Visual Basic, the easier it is to build applications, the greater the tendency is to produce half-baked applications. Distributed applications are hardly the kind of application any business wants to be poorly designed, especially when the opportunity to leverage the applications services now becomes convenient. With XML Web services and the simplicities of .NET come the added responsibility of producing sound designs. This is true now more than it ever has been.

Exploiting the .NET framework in proper object-oriented fashion is only half the story here. As far as design challenges go, this is only the tip of the iceberg. With .NET, you now have to the power to design services not only from object boundaries but from machine or network boundaries, as well. That's the power that an XML Web service provides the developer. With them, object invocation can now easily cross the network, even if that network is the Internet. As mentioned above, this distributed service-based approach to application architecture brings with it entirely new challenges. Design disciplines are always needed but never so much as now. Now you must account for the fact that the objects you are creating may or may not be local or even controlled by your design. You must now account for the fact that your application design may be distributed across the Internet. Does that mean that classic OO principles are not applicable in a "service-based" world? The answer is absolutely not. However, design philosophies must be adjusted. This is another reason why I wanted to take on this book.

Before I go into what areas of the .NET framework require design forethought, let me first run down why this thing is still a positive thing overall. This "thing" I'm referring to is the new world of CLR and the melee of business-specific Web service applications that will soon follow. Aside from all of the hype and maybe even a little skepticism, .NET and XML Web services really do provide distinct advantages and not just from the perspective of your department's local code-nerd. These services finally provide us with a machine-readable contract framework. By properly leveraging the Web Services Description Language (WSDL) specification into your "distributed wrappers," you can finally allow servers to talk to one another in a standard and type-safe fashion. For smaller server-to-server applications, this is a blessing.

No longer do simple applications require expensive "eBusiness" software to manage communications. Web services can be compared with Web servers, but for machines. No longer do we need to rely on protocol-specific proprietary component models to dictate how services can be provided and consumed. Gone are the days when installing one DLL file for one application on your server trounces another's functionality. This "DLL-hell," as it has been called, truly does finally provide you the protection of long-awaited application isolation in Windows. Application deployment can be as simple as a file copy, although more complex applications may require custom installations using Microsoft Installer. Even more importantly, an update to an SML Web service code does *not* require shutting down the server! We can finally put down those registry editors and slowly get used to "*XCOPY*ing" our way to *deployment bliss.*

Can you really begin to provide those distributed architectures where you "design it, build it, and they will consume it?" Can you do this without bringing down your network while providing hundreds of Web services? How many Web services do you need or should you have? Can you provide business logic through Web services as you provide data through data warehousing? Can you do this without all of the proprietary protocols, firewall issues, and deployment headaches? Can you do this in a truly object-oriented way without performance problems sometimes associated with sophisticated designs? The answer is a resounding yes, but there are some items you should be aware of. This awareness includes not only the bad elements of .NET applications (there really aren't many) but the positives, as well.

Designers must not only plan how to handle this influx and be prepared for the worst, but they must also understand its importance and take full advantage of what .NET has to offer in order to succeed. You must understand some of the benefits that will save money through simpler deployments, better support, and quicker update turnarounds. But you must also understand the responsibility that goes along with having a *trustworthy* and secure Web service environment for your customers and, even more importantly, for your own company. Hopefully, in the next few paragraphs I begin to answer all of these questions and provide you with the elements of .NET that you can pattern and repeat.

The .NET Framework and the World of OO

For all intents and purposes, any object-oriented pattern can be now applied to the world of .NET. This includes most of its languages (C#, VB.NET, J#, and yes, even COBOL). To obtain the benefits provided by the CLR, however, you must use one or more language compilers that target the runtime, such as VB.NET, C#, Managed C++, J#, or even one of many third-party compilers, such as an Eiffel. The .NET framework is a multilanguage execution environment; the runtime supports a wide variety of data types and language features. The language compiler you finally select will determine which features you have available. You must design your code using only those features. It's your compiler, not the runtime, that establishes the syntax your code must use and which features are drawn from the CLR. If your application must be completely usable by pieces written in other languages, your application's exported types must expose only language features that are included in the CLS. This is not to say I recommend you use only C# or VB.NET but those will be your primary choices, and you should have a relatively good reason to use other languages. That said, the CLR is one of a kind for even giving you that choice. This is something we as developers really never had, at least not at this level.

The choices have now been expanded—platform, language, and design heuristics. Regarding design heuristics, the .NET framework is a true object-oriented platform, after all. Any .NET developer now has the option of applying OO material once targeted to the likes of languages such as Java. Fortunately, there is plenty of OO material out there to give those new to .NET an opportunity for learning the basics of object orientation. In fact, I highly recommend becoming at least slightly acquainted with OO and its principles before tackling patterns. Fortunately, patterns are not a new concept, with the "gang of four" (covered later) providing us the foundation that has been built on over the last several years. You should be able to leverage much of the material out there, even if it has been targeted for another platform or even a different language, such as Java. This is one of the niceties of object orientation and of patterns—their general applicability.

That said, I'm not requiring that anyone have years of OO training before making use of the material in this book. In fact, I do not even require in-depth knowledge of .NET. This is especially true if you are an experienced programmer. For those programmers who have already worked with object-oriented languages before or even slightly object-oriented languages (some call them *component-oriented*), you should be able to grasp the content in this book. For those already comfortable with patterns and .NET, you can skip the patterns discussion in this chapter altogether. However, I would recommend reading most of Part I if you are new to any of the following:

- The .NET CLR

- The .NET Base Class Library (BCL)

- Object-oriented common practices

- XML Web services

- SOAP and WSDL

- Design, architectural, and/or implementation patterns

So if there is so much material out there on OO and patterns, why does the world need another "patterns" book? I've been asked this question countless times, so I will probably be repeating this answer throughout the following chapters, just to beat it down. With .NET and now the approaching world of XML Web services, we are on the brink of a truly unique development paradigm. Not only does .NET bring with it unique features upon which to leverage, along with its classic OO model, but it also now provides us with several new features. Primarily it now provides us with a simple XML Web services platform upon which to built standard distributed applications. As alluded to in the previous section, this power brings with it the need for design disciplines. Thus, the reason I took on this book. I want to provide those new to OO not only some .NET-friendly implementations but much more. I also want to guide those providing designs that may be taking on some of the new features of .NET; features such as Web services, XML schema generation, and custom attributes, to name a few.

Like OO, it will become very easy to abuse these new features. Most of you have already heard the horror stories of all of the badly designed object-oriented software out there—software that looked sophisticated on a whiteboard or within a class diagram but actually crawled when executed. Learning OO is much more than grasping implementation inheritance, as those who have already chipped their teeth have found out. It is the culmination of exploiting its benefits without overindulging. Implementation inheritance is not always the answer. Said in another way, not all databases are always fully normalized when they make it to production (for those who speak using an "ERD-tongue"). Many times, an object model must go through some form of "object denormalization" to perform well. For example, this includes eliminating former associations or even breaking some inheritance trees so that they instantiate faster at runtime. Another example is to employ interface inheritance instead of implementation inheritance. Using delegation and aggregation instead of encapsulation or implementation inheritance may also be an alternative. Some OO purists may be rolling over in their graves right now but the fact of the matter is that sometimes pure OO is not always the best solution. Hopefully, in this book I effectively communicate with you these tradeoffs. In the end, it is up to you to decide when it would be appropriate to apply a pattern and at what level.

The patterns and practices I provide in this book are not engraved in stone. Instead, I hope they provoke other design ideas and give you at least a starting point for creating a more robust .NET application. I tried to keep it simple so that you don't have to spend hours deciphering one pattern or idea. I want to give you the seeds of design, not provide you with absolutely all of the plumbing. You may have to support the code, after all. It seems that the more complicated, or should I say "sophisticated," the pattern is, the less it's used. I've seen some great GUI patterns that, when demoed, produced quite a few "oohs" and "aahs" but when it came to implementing them without guidance, the effort was not quite what was intended. Ideas don't have to be complicated to be effective. Those simple yet effective, tactical, and pragmatic design decisions can carry you quite a long way.

Using a pattern or a template best practice is not the panacea of all design cures. However, when applied wisely, patterns and repeatable best practices can save hours in design, even if that design will eventually be remorphed into something much different in production. The point is to begin the design process. It is much easier to begin when you have a proverbial OO tool belt at your disposal. This also applies at the implementation level. Patterns are nothing but repeatable design, architecture, and implementation practices that are given names. This book is meant to provide you with new patterns and practices unique to .NET, as well as to build on what has already been accepted as classic OO principles. Throughout the book, I will describe some of the classic design patterns that everyone should understand. I will show you which classic patterns are related to those presented and even which ones aren't. I will also provide you with a roadmap of the material in the book and a classification system to use for pulling items from your design tool belt.

How Did We Get Here?

I don't want to inundate you with yet another technical history lesson. Frankly, I think there are too many books with unnecessary "filling." The only things that should contain fillings are things you eat. Personally, many times I skip Chapter 1 in the books I read, and I hope I've saved you from having to do that here. For those who want the "Twinkie filling" right now, go to Chapter 2!

To provide you with a brief perspective so that you appreciate the "coolness" factor of .NET, let me quickly run down where we've come from. I find that understanding the motivating forces behind .NET will give you a better understanding of what it really is. This will also later frame what I'm trying to accomplish in this book.

A Distributed Introspection

When the idea of the network PC was introduced to the public, it soon received mixed reviews and was not very successful. Why? I think the right idea was there but it was a little too much too soon. Too soon in that such radical computing paradigms rarely take off quickly. Look at voice processing. By now, everyone should have a voice processor. I mean, the technology is there, it is highly effective, and it has become rather inexpensive. So why don't all of us automatically use voice processing software every day? Instead, I am still typing this book the old-fashioned way. Ideas like this take time. They take time to evolve and standardize. They take time to become commonplace enough to be the default option. The idea of a network PC may not have received enthusiasm simply because we like our computing power. For example, the majority of folks still do not use public transportation. Even though it is better for the environment and in countless other ways, most of us still would rather drive to work. The same could be said for PC computing. We still want our local PC! This includes the myriad of personal devices we own, such as palm tops, laptops, cell phones, etc. We want the power to do what we like without being online to do it because we are not always connected. This "social tendency" can be applied in facets (hold on, I'm getting somewhere).

The "too much too soon" philosophy can be found in the world of distributed computing. Distributed technologies have been around long before the Internet but until now, industry players have had decisively different opinions as to which distributed technology should be used and what infrastructure was going to get us there. It took a slower, more accepted form of technical evolution to finally provide the general public with a model upon which to build a standard distributed platform. The model I'm referring to is the Internet. Through the standard protocols of the Internet, the general public now had a standard network infrastructure upon which to build truly common distributed paradigms. Today, people expect information to be available wherever they go with whatever device they have handy. This information can come from anywhere and in any form, and the Internet is the means for delivering it.

The Internet and its bed of standard protocols (e.g., TCP/IP, NNTP, SMTP, etc.) were only the first step in organizing this distributed web of information, however. Besides the network infrastructure, you still needed several other standard protocols and formats of data interchange. Retrieving data from a Web server in the form of HTML content is one thing. Automating the organization of information flow and the interchange of information from server to server is quite another. Other standards had to emerge for us to evolve from simply sharing information on a Web server and displaying it in a browser. We needed a way to interchange information from server to server, as well as a means of intelligently accessing information from anywhere on the Internet, much like we do when calling a simple API, but in a distributed fashion.

There are many ways to distribute services across any network, including the Internet. Using remote procedure calls (RPCs), I can invoke any interface, given an infrastructure that supports either UDP or TCP. I can also use Java's remote method invocation (RMI) protocol to invoke an externalized Java class method across the Internet. For those developing applications in Visual Basic or Visual C++, COM, or more appropriately, DCOM, can be used for your "remote write protocol," as Microsoft calls it. The same goes for OMG's CORBA. Each of these protocols can be effective in distributing your application and have been for many applications. However, each has its disadvantages. Universally, each has its own proprietary wire protocol used to interchange data. This includes the actual communication protocols, as well as the data formats used for the messages passed. Individually, they each have their own shortcomings, as well. For instance, Java's RMI is simple to implement but it forces the developer to use a single language and requires enterprise additions, such as J2EE's Enterprise Java Beans, to provide any form of true scalability. Heck, even after that, scalability is still a question, sorry Sun. DCOM, on the other hand, can be implemented using different languages but falls short in its support for network firewalls. DCOM also is not object oriented and, even though VB has made building COM components simpler, it is rather complex under the hood. The same goes for CORBA. CORBA is object oriented (and component oriented), supports multiple languages, and is rather scalable if implemented correctly, but it too suffers from complexity. What is needed is a standard means of remotely invoking objects using a standard message format that can be implemented in any language. Okay, enough setup. Enter XML and XML Web services!

.NET AND XML WEB SERVICES

.NET is designed from the ground up to work with XML Web services, along with all the other Internet standards and protocols. XML Web services in .NET and Visual Studio .NET are **not** a design afterthought like they are in some languages and tools. It typically takes about 4 to 5 times more code to add XML Web services capabilities to a .NET application compared to one written in Java using tools such as JBuilder. XML is also baked into the CLR. Now streaming, parsing, and passing XML has never been easier and makes the CLR a powerful proposition, even without mentioning anything else. Using XML, you can now build standard services that can be invoked from anywhere on the Internet. As far as providing Web services in general, you don't even need .NET. Web Services can be built from scratch as long as you've provided the standard means of describing what services you offer and allow them to be invoked in standard fashion. Using .NET just makes this much easier. You can now just select the language you feel most comfortable with to implement these services.

You can also distribute any service to any device that speaks to the Internet and can read an XML stream. This idea changes how applications are viewed. Applications can now be sold as a set of services instead of an entire product. These are acute to mini-application service processors for those looking to leverage existing services within their own frameworks. No longer does each end point of a communication channel require that each support a proprietary and vendor-specific protocol. As long as you are on an Internet or other TCP/IP-based backbone and

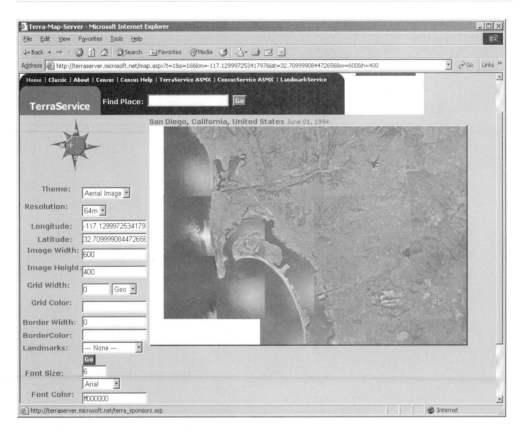

FIGURE 1.2: The TerraService main page used for interactively viewing maps and aerial shots.

interchange data using XML, you now can speak freely to one another. Clients no longer have to be tethered to wired networks and can even consist of a cell phone (as in the case of Pocket PC).

To see one of the first nontrivial public implementations of a Web service, check out http://terraserver.microsoft.net/. The Web service on this site features map and aerial photograph information from around the world utilizing the Microsoft TerraService project, along with information from the U.S. Census Bureau. To see a map or aerial photograph of any city, simply enter the city in the Find Place edit box at the top of the screen. Figure 1.2 shows an aerial photo of San Diego. On this screen, you can vary the output by using the provided ASP.NET form that will give you an update shot and clicking the Go button. This page provides the viewer with a typical Web-site-like user experience. However, this site is actually based on XML

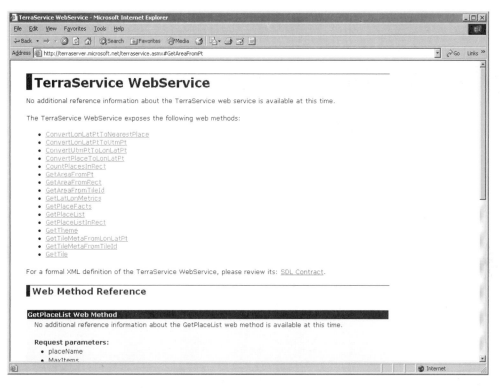

FIGURE 1.3: Web methods list from TerraService.

Web services and now can be seamlessly invoked by a process other than that of a user using a browser. Using .NET Web service methods, Terra server information can now be retrieved in a programmatic way. Here I use my browser to interact with the TerraService (http://terraserver.microsoft.net/terraservice.asmx) but this could even be done from most non-.NET development environments that support HTTP or SOAP, such as Visual Basic.

Using the following list of Web methods (Figure 1.3), other services (Figures 1.4 and 1.5) can easily incorporate TerraService information into their own sites and applications.

Other forms of public Web services already available include:

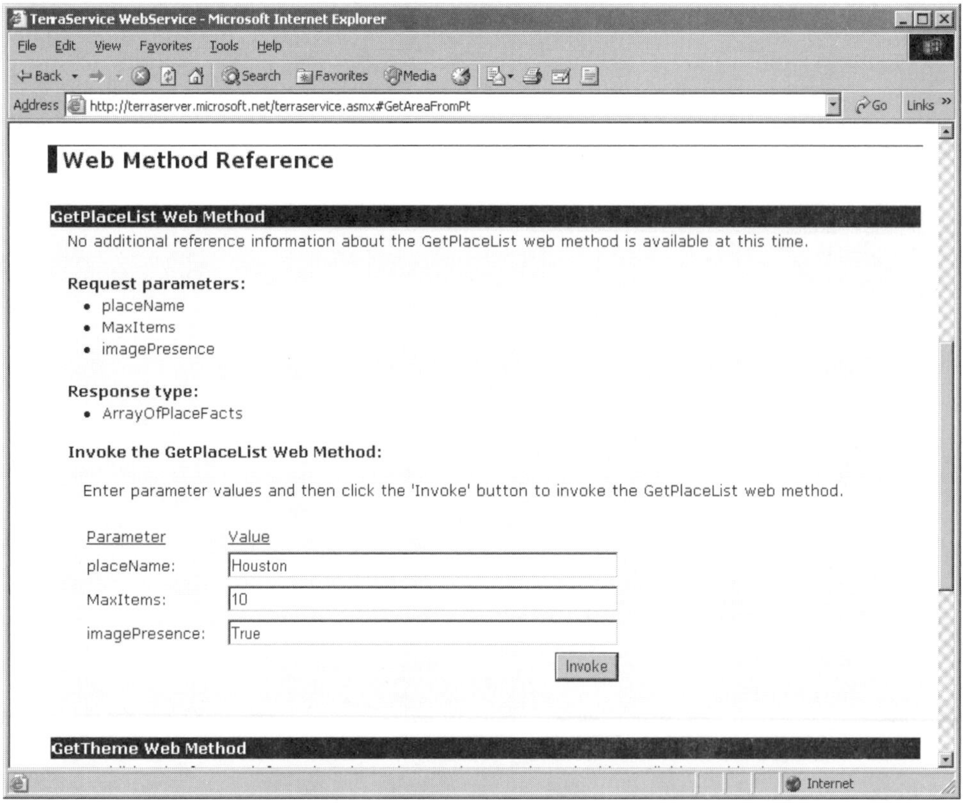

FIGURE 1.4: The GetPlaceList Web method entry page from TerraService.

- http://terraserver.microsoft.net/CensusHome.htm—U.S. Census Bureau information.

- http://www.microsoft.com/myservices/—Builds on the proven Microsoft .NET Passport and Microsoft .NET Alerts services. Allow users to store key personal information securely and control access to it.

- http://www.microsoft.com/myservices/passport/default.asp—Single Sign In and Microsoft .NET Passport Express Purchase services.

- http://www.microsoft.com/myservices/alerts/default.asp—Customers can choose to have alerts delivered to the desktop, to an email address, or to a mobile device.

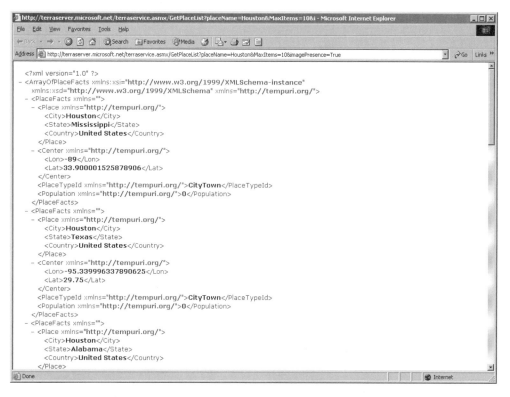

FIGURE 1.5: The GetPlaceList results after searching for Houston.

- http://xmltoday.com/examples/soap/translate.psp—Uses a SOAP/WSDL-enabled language translation service to convert any text from one foreign language to another, using the engine available at AltaVista's http://babelfish.altavista.com/.

- http://xmltoday.com/examples/soap/stock.psp—Uses a SOAP/WSDL-enabled stock quote server to convert data available from Yahoo!'s http://finance.yahoo.com/ site into XML while adding a SOAP interface.

By the time this book is published, there will be many more XML Web services publicly available, some of which will still (I hope) be free. Not all XML Web services will be implemented using .NET but as an information consumer, it usually will not matter. The point is that information can now be shared in a uniform manner using XML Web services, and it does not matter how they are implemented. This opens up many challenges to designers and architects building systems that will externally leverage these services.

Some of the issues a Web service consumer will face are:

• Reliability assurances

• Information feed recovery planning

• Application performance

• Change control

• Security

• Trustworthiness

This also presents those wishing to distribute their own services with an entirely different set of business opportunities and confrontations. The issues for a Web service provider are the same as those for a consumer (e.g., security, change control), with the following additional concerns:

• Scalability

• Fault tolerance

• Service pricing models

• Directory placement

• Categorization

When you combine the fact that several developers have never worked with a true object-oriented system or with Web service models, you should begin to appreciate the paradigm gap these folks will face. I hope you will also begin to see the need for design guidance. Microsoft itself is even beginning to provide more developer collateral in the areas of design principles and architecture guidance. The .NET framework makes it all the more simple to begin playing with objects and Web services. However, when you get past the initial "hello world" sample, you will begin to face some interesting design challenges. Now more than ever does the following OO adage apply: The better the discipline, the better the application. Rarely should developers now rely on the fact that they can throw a system together without design initiatives in hand. For those Java converts (and there will be many—I'm one), this won't even be a question; it will be a requirement.

Unfortunately, I don't have the room to exhaust all there is about XML Web services and how to build them with .NET. There will be plenty of books devoted solely to that topic. However, for those who have not had any exposure to them, I've provided the following primer in hopes that the material in this book can be better understood.

XML WEB SERVICES PRIMER

Many of the patterns and best practices presented in this book assume a certain level of knowledge in the area of Web services. It is assumed you have experience designing and developing in at least one object- or component-oriented language, as well as a basic knowledge of XML. However, I don't insist that you have any experience with designing and developing XML Web services. This section should provide you with enough information to get you started and to help you better understand those patterns that use Web services for their implementation choice. That said, I highly recommend that you acquire deeper architectural knowledge of Web services and their protocols. Understanding the protocols that surround Web services will not only aid you in better understanding the elements in this book but will also help you in your design and later debugging efforts.

This book mainly focuses on implementing Web services using the SOAP protocol over HTTP. Throughout the book, I will provide explanations in the form of technology backgrounders specifically in those areas of SOAP considered essential to grasping the implementation of the pattern presented. I have found that having material devoted strictly to SOAP at my side is not a bad idea. One good resource is *SOAP: Cross Platform Web Service Development Using XML*, by Scott Seely (Prentice Hall, 2001). The specification and tutorials on the World Wide Web Consortium (W3C) Web site at http://www.w3.org/TR/2001/WD-soap12-part0-20011217/ are another great source of information regarding SOAP.

What Is an XML Web Service?

XML Web services are somewhat loosely defined in the most general sense. I am not talking about .NET Web services because .NET provides the tools to generate both a Web services client and a server with little effort. What I'm referring to is the overall concept and technology behind it. You can construct an XML Web service without the use of any Web service-generation tool. You do not even require some of the more specific protocols, such as WSDL, to be successful. The idea of an XML Web service should be understood first before diving into each "recommended" protocol. Using its vanilla definition, XML Web services are simply distributed "invokeable" services that use XML to send data across a standard and accepted protocol. XML is also used to describe the service and the parameters that the service requires to execute remotely.

Instead of using proprietary protocols in a proprietary format, such as those employed by the likes of COM or many other now legacy distributed mechanisms, Web services simply use what is already open to the public. Not only is HTTP and XML open, but you now can actually make sense of the data packets you send to and receive from Web services because they are now self-describing and actually quite readable. Gone are the days of using proprietary binary readers to make sense of distributed data streams. Using Notepad will do just fine. Of course, for complex data structures, I'm oversimplifying it a bit, but not by much.

You can architect your own version of a Web service without the need for any specific protocols by simply using XML over HTTP. However, to distribute and comply better with the rest of the world, you must understand some of the other protocols used when building Web services. Also, to gain a true understanding of how to design Web services, you really have to understand the primary language that both describes the service and is used for all data packets. This is, once again, XML. Aside from that, you should have a general understanding of many of the protocols used to search, discover, format, transfer, and interpret the elements of a Web service. Do you have to understand each protocol in detail? No. However, the better you understand the likes of SOAP and WSDL, the more successful you will be in invoking Web services that require complex data types, such as those used for transporting relational rows of data or complex custom objects.

The exact definition of an XML Web service varies, depending on whom you ask. Some are simply exposed functionality points using standard Web protocols. In most cases, you will find SOAP being that protocol. In addition to SOAP, two other primary protocols have emerged: WSDL and Universal Discovery Description and Integration (UDDI). SOAP is the XML language for invoking a service but WSDL is how you describe to the outside world what you have to offer. WSDL allows clients to be built either by statically or dynamically accessing a service's WSDL document. For those familiar with COM, its acts as a "type library" of sorts to provide the details of the Web service, its methods, and the data types it accepts and returns. With SOAP, XML, and WSDL you provide, describe, and use fully distributable and invokeable services from anywhere on the Internet or even your own intranet. But how does one find all of the Web services on a particular server or anywhere on the Internet, for that matter? This is where UDDI comes in. Web services are registered so that users can find them wherever they may be. Once a service is found, its WSDL file can be accessed (in the case of .NET Web services, by specifying the Web service **.asmx* followed by *?WSDL*, e.g., http://www.companyxyz.com/productx.asmx?WSDL), which the client then uses to access that functionality. How the WSDL information is retrieved or how Web service consumers are built is completely vendor-dependent. Microsoft has provided a very simple means of both producing and consuming Web services using Visual Studio .NET. Figure 1.6 shows a sample WSDL file that is built in and to be used from within Visual Studio .NET using C#.

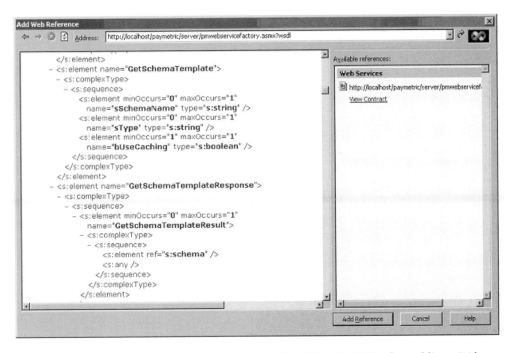

FIGURE 1.6: A sample Web service WSDL via Visual Studio .NET when adding a Web reference from Visual Studio .NET 1.0 (2001).

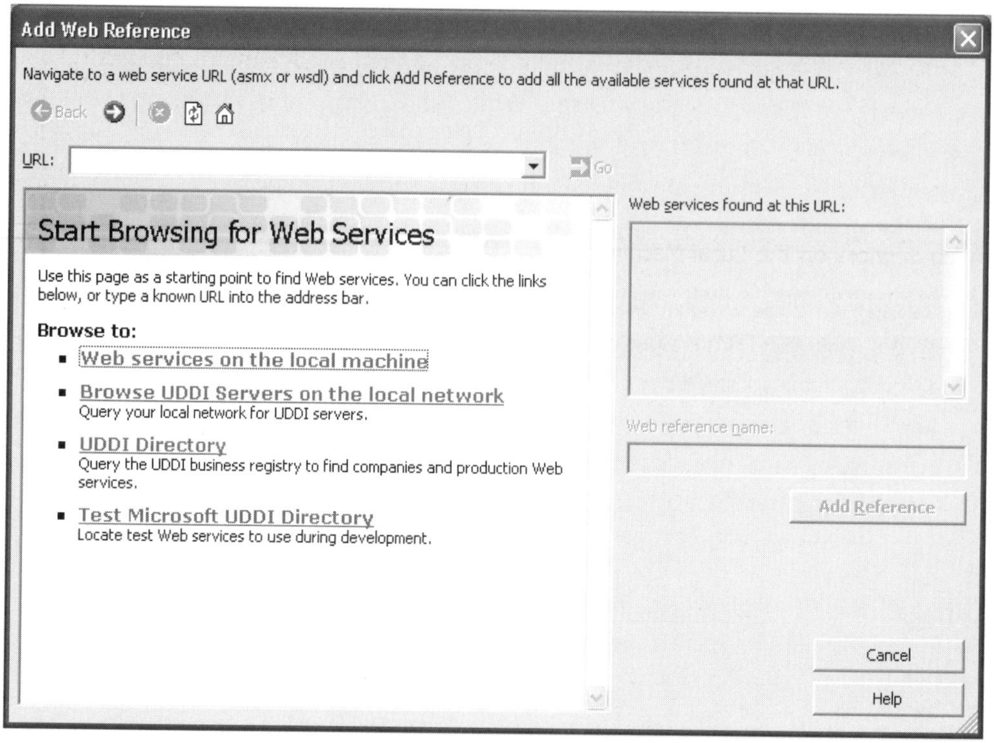

FIGURE 1.7: Using Visual Studio .NET, you can now browse for Web services locally or remotely.

If you are using Visual Studio .NET 1.0 by selecting View Contract in Figure 1.6, the appropriate Web service proxy will be generated and added to the project. From this proxy, a Web service can then be instantiated and called, just like any other .NET object (with a little help from a proxy generator or a little elbow grease). This is one way to implement this behavior. If you do not have the luxury of using Visual Studio .NET, the proxy can also be generated with command tools provided by Microsoft (such as sproxy.exe) or "manually consumed" using something like Microsoft's SOAP Toolkit. Using the SOAP toolkit, you obtain direct control over the SOAP requests sent and received against a Web service, albeit with slightly more work. If you are using Visual Studio .NET 2003 edition, you will have a slightly different Web references interface. The latest version of Visual Studio .NET has simplified this interface and included computer and even network browsing features (Figure 1.7). This radically simplifies the work required to even find a Web service, whether it exists somewhere on your machine (Figure 1.8) or

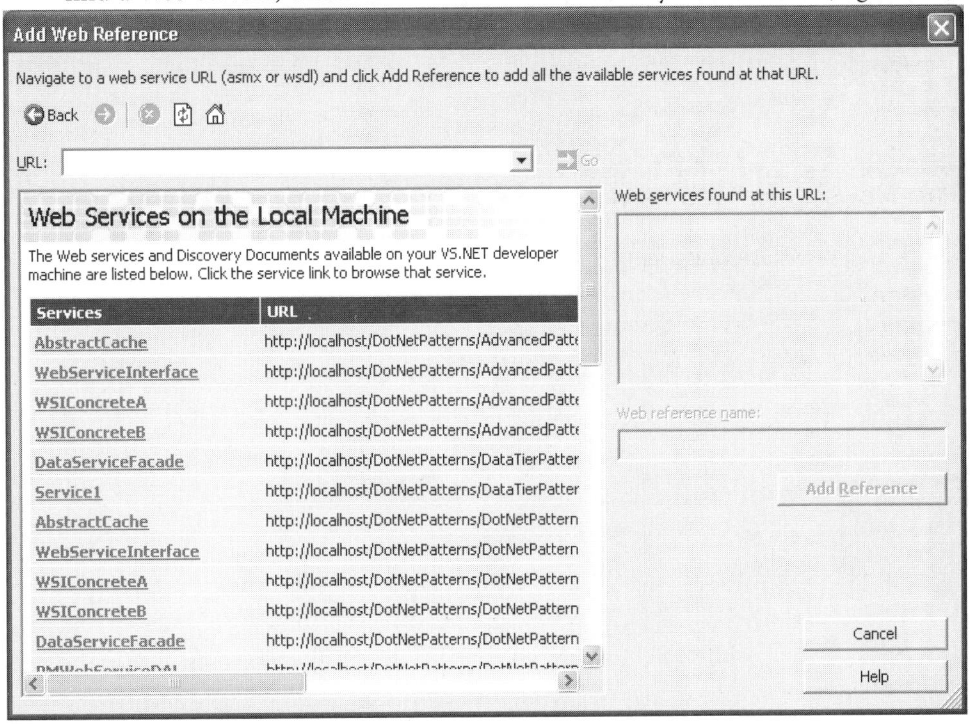

FIGURE 1.8: A sample Web service local machine listing (using 2003)—each providing WSDL to bind to.

somewhere on the Internet.

CHALLENGE 1.1

How can you abstract a Web service with a published interface without effecting bound consumers?

The solution appears in Chapter 7 – Web Service Interface.

With XML, SOAP, and WSDL, vendors can now provide their own implementations of these open standards in any way they see fit. The real benefit, however, is that the standards do exist without the traditional disputes over distributed wire protocols. Will there be vendor-specific differences in what you can or cannot do? Yes, I don't know whether we will ever get completely away from that. Just look at the differences in the J2EE space with all of the vendor implementations of EJB servers (e.g., BEA WebLogic or WebSphere). Finally a "standard bar" has been raised for what makes up a distributed service, how to access it, and how to use it. For more information on WSDL, please refer to the WSDL specification at http://www.w3.org/TR/wsdl.

Web Services and SOAP

When given any XML parser, such as a Microsoft's XML DOM component, anyone can pass a function name embedded into an XML message. Therefore, you do not need SOAP or any formal protocol around XML Web services to accomplish this. The designers of such a system could provide a specification for the outlay of the function parameters and even return XML after the function is called if they wanted. Standard XML Web services just make it easier. In fact, I helped build such a system before SOAP was a standards recommendation. SOAP simply standardizes this type of RPC mechanism. SOAP is *the* communication protocol used by XML Web services. Is SOAP required? No. Is it recommended? Yes. Only because SOAP provides a standardized means of describing the data elements that make up the messages sent to SOAP servers, including .NET servers hosting Web services. Along with WSDL and UDDI, SOAP is another element in the distributed arm of .NET and the Web services it hosts. Besides being a mechanism for invoking RPCs, it can also be used as a wrapper around entire XML documents or binary data, as is the case with the DIME protocol from Microsoft. This greatly expands what can be done with this protocol and will continue to expand as XML Web services evolve.

As mentioned, when using Web services, SOAP is not the only protocol that can be used to call Web services. For example, a simple HTTP GET request can be made as long as it is passing and receiving simple data types, such as strings. However, when you begin to work with more complex types, such as ADO DataSets (covered later in this book), it becomes necessary to use a protocol such as SOAP and more specifically, XML schemas to describe such data as referenced in the SOAP message. SOAP was designed for simplicity and elegance, and it does *not* do some of things you might expect. Some of the elements not covered (at this time) are:

- Message batching—You must create your means of batching messages/functions calls.

- Distributed garbage collection—There are no means of telling the server that the client has suddenly disappeared.

- Object references—Holding state from the client and server is an implementation-specific issue.

- Reliability protocols—This really lies at the application protocol level and can be designed into your application, especially if HTTP is being used as the communication protocol.

SOAP currently does not outline these specific elements like other remote protocols, such as DCOM and CORBA. But it does what it was intended to do—provide us with a simple, standard specification to drive the description of the data types and methods for using and producing Web services. It is important to note, however, that a SOAP "message" only specifies the XML format for the package sent across the wire. As long as you have a well-formed XML document encapsulated in the necessary SOAP tags, you have a valid SOAP message. Any compliant SOAP implementation on the server should understand the request and should service it. In fact, although the default application protocol for SOAP is HTTP, it does not require it. That's the simplicity of it. Other protocols, such as SMTP, FTP, and even asynchronous messaging protocols, will soon be supported. Because HTTP is *the* Internet protocol, it is also the default for SOAP. This is why when you hear about XML Web services, it is usually assumed that there will be a one-to-one correspondence with both SOAP and HTTP.

To truly understand SOAP, you first have to understand a few basic elements of the language that makes up a SOAP message. Once again, that language is XML. Most interaction with SOAP usually takes place through a toolkit or service of some kind. For example, the Microsoft SOAP Toolkit (Java has its own) hides the exact format of a SOAP message by providing high-level programmatic client objects to use. These clients provide the code to serialize, deserialize, send, and receive SOAP messages to and from a corresponding SOAP server, such as a .NET Web service. This simplifies developers' lives but it also shelters them from understanding the format in which their messages are bundled. Knowing such details will help your debugging *and* designing efforts in the future, and it is recommended that you become at least slightly acquainted with such details.

To do so, you first need to understand a few XML items. These "XML Basics" are included in Table 1.1.

Why will SOAP succeed in widespread fashion where others have failed? It already has. This is not to say that protocols such as COM or CORBA have

TABLE 1.1: XML tags essential for understanding SOAP-formatted messages

XML Fundamentals	Understand elements, attributes. and overall layout semantics and node facets.
Uniform Resource Identifiers (URIs)	e.g., Universal Resource Names (URNs) do not resolve to a physical location, as do URLs, but serve as resource identifiers. `urn:schemas-microsoft-com:xml-msdata`
XML Namespaces	Allow us to create elements with the same name with different type definitions. XML Nodes are named with namespace prefixes `xmlns:xsd="http://www.w3.org/2001/xmlSchema"`

XML Schemas	An option to using a document type definition (DTD), schemas provide the added benefit of not only determined document layout but repeatable type definition, as well. These are used when passing complex data types to Web services in .NET, something we will get to later in this book.
	
	`<xsd:schema id="ProductXYZ" xmlns:xsd="...">`
	` <xsd:element name="ProductData"`
	`msdata:IsDataSet="true">`
	`  <xsd:complexType>`
	`   <xsd:choice maxOccurs="unbounded">`
	`    <xsd:element name="FACTORYPACKET">`
	`     <xsd:complexType>`
	`      <xsd:sequence>`
	`       <xsd:element name="BUSINESSOBJ"`
	`type="xsd:string"/>`
	`       <xsd:element name="METHOD"`
	`type="xsd:string"/>`
	`        <xsd:element name="FILTER" type="xsd:int"/>`
	`      </xsd:sequence>`
	`     </xsd:complexType>`
	`    </xsd:element>`
	`     . . .`

failed. They will continue to be used for many years to come. There just has not been any one distributed protocol that has been adopted by so many different vendors as SOAP has. By the time this book is published, I am sure there will be even more.

So what does a SOAP message look like? Unfortunately, I don't have room to explain every element. Fortunately, SOAP's specification is rather simple, compared with other distributed protocols. To format a SOAP message and send it to a Web service requires knowledge of only a few XML tags. After all, SOAP is merely XML. Here is a sample SOAP message calling a Web service method, *GetSchemaTemplate*(). As its name implies, this Web method returns an XML schema from a database formatted as a .NET DataSet from ADO.NET.

LISTING 1.1: A sample SOAP message captured using SOAP Trace Utility.

```
<?xml version="1.0" encoding="utf-8" ?>
  <soap:Envelope
    xmlns:soap="http://schemas.xmlsoap.org/soap/envelope/"
    xmlns:xsi="http://www.w3.org/2001/xmlSchema-instance"
    xmlns:xsd="http://www.w3.org/2001/xmlSchema">
    <soap:Body>
      <GetSchemaTemplate

      xmlns="http://www.companyxyz.com/productx.net">

      <sSchemaName>FinancialPacket</sSchemaName>
          <sType>CreditCard</sType>
          <bUseCaching>false</bUseCaching>
      </GetSchemaTemplate>
    </soap:Body>
  </soap:Envelope>
```

Besides the SOAP namespace, the only two SOAP tags are Body and Envelope. In fact, just by looking at this sample you should have an idea of what most SOAP messages generally look like. This message, in particular, is used to call a Web method named *GetSchemaTemplate*, passing in the name of the schema, the type, and whether to cache the results. Each parameter is passed as in inset tag of the Web method tag. This is enclosed by the <soap:Body> tag, which contains the contents of the RPC desired. The <soap:Body> is then enclosed in a <soap:Enve-

lope> tag. The envelope is what encloses the entire SOAP message and is where you will encompass any namespaces declarations, such as:

```
xmlns:soap=http://schemas.xmlsoap.org/soap/envelope/).
```

CHALLENGE 1.2

How should exceptions be thrown and handled from Web services using SOAP?
A solution appears in Chapter 2 on page 60.

CHALLENGE 1.3

What does the return type look like in the GetSchemaTemplate sample given, and what should any complex return type be formatted as?
A solution appears in Chapter 5 on pages 205–217.

Optionally, the SOAP envelope may also contain a *SOAP header* that is not passed as part of the RPC but rather mimics behavior similar to that of HTTP headers. Unlike the *body* and *envelope* tags, *headers* are not mandatory. SOAP headers can be used to pass information such as security credentials or other message-oriented *meta* information. They are used to avoid having to add additional parameters to each RPC or in this case, each Web method called. I use SOAP headers throughout this book and will explain their use in detail in the upcoming chapter on technology backgrounders.

CHALLENGE 1.4

How can I pass security credentials using SOAP or more specifically, SOAP headers?
A solution appears in Chapter 7's Technology Backgrounder on page 327.

Security in SOAP?

Formal .NET training may not quite cover all of the areas required in designing mission-critical Web services-based systems. This is especially true of security.

Security policy dictates whether any system will be secure. Unfortunately, formal training may not provide the level of aid in developing a specific .NET security policy. I don't have nearly enough room to exhaust a topic as large as security, especially when it comes to .NET and Web services where it has been enhanced at multiple levels (authentication, authorization, configuration, and code access security). SOAP is only beginning to outline security elements, such as the *ws-security* specifications just now becoming widely known. This places some of the burden onto the developers and designers of the system. This is great for the end user but the key here is the "shift of burden" comment. Currently, that security burden rests on the developers and administrators. This means that IT must develop a level of comfort with application security that may not currently exist when deploying a Web services application.

A positive side effect to the robustness of .NET security is the fact that the CLR now relieves other areas of concern for IT. Due to its *managed* environment; the applications that run under the control of the CLR now have the advantage of granular type-safe controls. This includes protecting the system from attacks such as employing "stack walking." This protects the system not only from the immediate called operation but also from all callers of that immediate caller. In the end, this will ease some of the time spent due to attacks from outside intruders.

The depth at which security is supported in the runtime is impressive. The CLR offers granular permission-level control, even at the object level, and allows developers to react to specific permissions granted in their application code. Some of the areas you can control in .NET are:

• File I/O (isolated storage)

• Data access

• Directory services

• Event logging

• Environment

• Registry

SECURING YOUR WEB SERVICES IN .NET

Familiarity with XML-formatted system configuration files, such as *machine.config*, *web.config*, and application-specific *app.config* files is one example of how IT must integrate its infrastructure focus with that of an application. Along with controlling IIS configuration and the principles around securing traditional Web applications, these files are one of the first items used for closely controlling security. Those familiar with supporting existing COM+ applications should already have a head start on that of .NET's security paradigms but at a file level. Many elements in deploying COM+ applications, such as setting up application server security identities that run as part of a COM+ *package* (aka *application*), are conceptually similar in .NET. Like COM+, .NET supports adding security identities to processes running under Web service control. Thus it will be required that those accounts be created and managed by the IT department in charge of those application centers. It also means becoming acquainted with those configuration files and having a means by which to manage them in secure fashion. This means securing those files so that prying eyes cannot change their contents. UNIX and Apache Web server administrators are all too familiar with this process. In fact, it seems as though security administration in .NET is becoming a hybrid of UNIX, COM+, and IIS with a few new twists.

One of those twists is simplicity. Anyone who has ever configured an Apache Web server should attest to this statement; .NET security has all the power with so much more simplicity than traditional security models. This simplicity can easily be witnessed solely by opening the .NET Configuration snap-in that is installed along with the framework and soon to be a familiar part of Windows Server 2003. Figure 1.9 shows one of the screens used to control access security on any client running a .NET application, whether or not that application is Web service-based. This helps administrators control what assets on the local PC can be controlled and in what zones this policy applies.

SECURING YOUR WEB SERVICES IN .NET (CONT.)

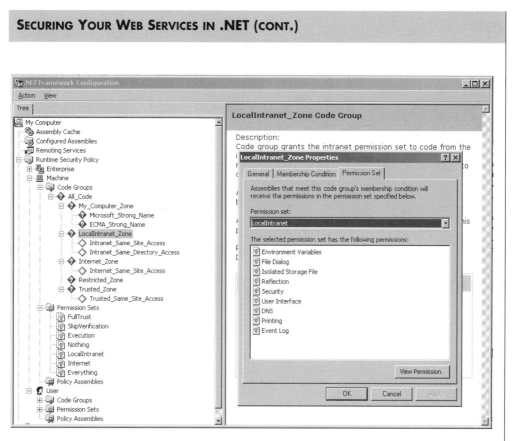

FIGURE 1.9: .NET Framework Configuration snap-in from the accessories group.

- Introspection services (reflection)

- File dialogs

Administrators can provide the overall policy and leave some responsibility to the developer to tighten further as needed. Granular security also means that applications that should easily run in production may not. During deployment, laying out security tends to be one of those overlooked items that will always bite you. Now imagine a security design at the level at which .NET has outlined. The better prepared and informed those people managing policy are, the more you are assured of deployment success.

No longer can those leading your security infrastructure be unaware of each security element at the application level. To be better prepared, developers can no longer simply learn .NET's new languages, its pure object-orientation model, or the SOAP protocol upon which complex messages will be sent to Web methods. Developers also must cooperate with IT in the permission schemes employed and the levels at which they will enforce security. This includes but is not limited to whether developers will employ role-based security, what authentication method they will use (e.g., IIS, Forms, Passport, etc.), or the code access level they require in their applications. Then they can roll their applications into the appropriate .msi file and deploy with whichever tool they see fit.

Training isn't the only area of focus here. Currently as far as SOAP is concerned, SOAP assumes that security is a transport or application issue and does not define security semantics specifically. This is changing, because there are specifications already released to add security semantics to SOAP (see ws-security). Cooperation among the infrastructure and application development teams must be better than ever. It also would be prudent to bring in an outside security consultant to help evaluate your policies and better prepare your team for this new model. Only this will help guarantee that applications will run with production when they are supposed to and not fail to load just because someone was misinformed.

WSDL

WSDL is based on the XML schema standard and uses it to describe its services. Because WSDL uses XML and is language-neutral, it is perfect for Web services that are not implemented in the same language. There is no guarantee that everyone will implement his or her Web services using .NET, although I know Microsoft would like it to be that way. WSDL uses a schema to describe where each service is and what protocols to use to access it. For example, if your Web method is like the previous example, the WSDL will inform the consumer of the service that the SOAP protocol is one protocol supported by the GetSchemaTemplate. However, because this particular method uses simple data types in the method, other protocols such as an HTTP POST or GET can also be used. If the data types of the parameters are complex, it is recommended that SOAP be used, and the WSDL will reflect that. This helps the consumer bind to the correct protocol before sending any messages to the server. This binding typically is done statically but can also be done dynamically if need be. You can build a SOAP request simply by looking at the WSDL contents, which is accessed as specified earlier in this chapter (i.e., *?WSDL*) or with a WSDL file located somewhere on the Web service server. Luckily for the developer, this usually isn't necessary because many tools exist for reading and binding to WSDL files through the proxy generated, making your life much easier. In Visual Studio .NET, you can read a WSDL file and build a proxy file based on its output. With the proxy, you can then instantiate a Web service just like any other class and call its Web methods as you would normally call a local object. Knowing the plumbing underneath this proxy-generated code may save your life at some point.

UDDI

But how do you find all of the WSDL content out there in the first place? Hopefully, that answer will be UDDI. This acts as a "Yellow Pages" for Web services. This is optional, however, because you can produce Web services for consumption without ever publishing them to the outside world. This will be the case for those services intended for specific clients. For example, there are Web servers not necessarily published in some public search engines. If you intend to be used by the general public or just want to be found, UDDI is how you do it.

Like everything else described thus far, UDDI is just an XML file. It is used to describe a business or services it offers (Web services, that is). Web services are described by using what are called *tModels* or *Type Models,* in "UDDI-speak." In most cases, the model will simply contain a WSDL file that describes the interface to the Web service. UDDI also offers means by which to search for the services you desire based on business type or physical location of that business. Once you find that business, you can search deeper for the specific Web service you are looking for by using what is called the *WS-Inspection Language*. For more information on either UDDI or the WS-Inspection Language, please refer the following links:

http://msdn.microsoft.com/library/default.asp?url=/library/en-us/dnglobspec/
　　html/ws-inspection.asp

http://www.uddi.org/about.html

HIGHLIGHTS OF .NET

If other major development releases from Microsoft could be heard as "bangs," the arrival of .NET could be heard with an atomic explosion. The last major development release was Visual Studio, when the cry for a shared integrated environment (IDE) was partially answered by Microsoft. I say partially because Visual Basic still used its own IDE in 6.0. Not only does Visual Studio .NET finally serve as the primary IDE for all .NET languages, but the .NET framework itself has complete cross-language support built into its runtime. Using cross-language inheritance, exception handling, and debugging, developers can truly choose their weapon of choice. This was a calling card of component models for years but not at the level of simplicity and single implementation support that Visual Studio .NET and the framework provide.

References to the word *new* when referring to .NET may receive a few scoffs, especially from those in the Java world. But the word *new* isn't necessarily referring to the field of computer science but to the Microsoft development community. Object-oriented languages have been around for a few decades. Managed (ergo garbage-collected) environments also have quite a track record by now. So why is .NET so different? First of all, it really isn't much different than many of the technologies already available. The problem is that those technologies are spread across several languages, vendors, and accepted platforms. The .NET framework is not any copy of one particular implementation or technology but a culmination of benefits extracted from several environments. Not only is this delivered in one framework, but it also comes to us in a form that is usable and quick to employ. To get a feel for the major components that make up the .NET framework refer to Figure 1.10 and Table 1.2. Java programmers already familiar with a Virtual Machine environment should recognize these layers.

The speed at which one will adapt and understand .NET heavily depends on that person's background. Suffice it to say, however, that once the newness hurdle is overcome, the learning rate will increase faster than any other development platform Microsoft has offered thus far—even Visual Basic. Yes, even Visual Basic. With the aid of Visual Studio .NET and Intellisense, you will soon see how quickly the learning slope slides south (say that three times fast). Hopefully before you read this book you will have jumped the initial learning hurdle of .NET. Either way, you should have a firm grasp of the following .NET building blocks. If not, then I recommend reading read one of the myriad of .NET framework books out there.

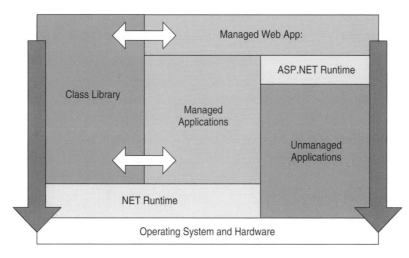

FIGURE 1.10: An overview of .NET and how it is layered into the operating system.

COMPONENTS OF .NET—A SNIPPET

I've introduced quite a few things from this point for those new to .NET: distributed technologies, the arrival of .NET, XML Web services, and even a short introduction of the protocols that get you there, such as SOAP and WSDL. Isn't this a pattern book? Patterns are only as useful as their ability to add true value. They make you look great on a whiteboard but unless technology—especially the likes of .NET—is considered and understood, your chance of success will diminish. Throughout the book, you will see a marriage of design elements with the recommended technology for implementing them. Along with the sample code, this should provide you with the enough information not only to look good in your class diagrams but also to look good in a live production. This will allow you to be strategic as well as tactical in your architecture. Now let's talk about patterns.

PATTERNS EXPLAINED

I have continually repeated in my ranting about employing sound design techniques that the use of good design transcends any technology. The use of patterns

TABLE 1.2:   An overview of .NET and its major selling features over other platforms

Interoperability support (Interop)	Migrating to .NET from existing languages and platforms has been made much easier. Especially if that environment is COM or Java. COM, Interop is built into the framework, and C# will be very familiar for those developing in Java currently. In fact, Microsoft has a migration utility to automatically migrate existing Java source code into C#.
Common language runtime (CLR)	This is the engine that is shared among all languages supported in .NET, including C#, VB.NET, Managed C++, J#, and others to come. With the help of the CLR, the developer can write base classes in VB.NET, child classes in C#, and aggregate this tree from Managed C++ (this is just one example). You choose the language during implementation.
Base class library (BCL)	What makes Java so appealing besides the managed environment and cross-platform support is its class library. The .NET framework takes the class library concept a step further by supporting it across any language and extensible for future platform variances. Now BCL-supported features such as remoting, string manipulation, exception handling, and collection management construct is the same from any language conforming to the CLI.

TABLE 1.2: An overview of .NET and its major selling features over other platforms (cont.)

Common type system (CTS)	This addresses the supported data types within the framework and how they are represented in metadata format. Each supported .NET language need only support a subset of the total data type set. Typically, it will be those types used most frequently (e.g., integer, short, long, string, char, boolean, object, interface, struct, etc.)
Simplified deployment	Say goodbye to DLL hell and the nightmare of Windows registration. Applications can now be deployed by a simple XCOPY of the assemblies, ASP.net files, and configuration files.
Full Web service and SOAP support	Complexities are optionally hidden for building Web service providers and consumers in .NET. Details of the syntax and protocol surrounding XML Web services can be fully customized if needed, however. It is truly the best of both worlds.
XML at the core	Serialization, streaming, parsing, transforming, and schema support are only some of the "baked-in" XML features of the .NET runtime.
Object-oriented ASP.NET	Use script for your clients, not your server-based code! Leverage your existing OO framework from ASP.NET and enjoy improved Web application performance due to compiled server code.

is just that kind of "transcendental experience" (apologies to Karl Rahner) you can utilize to enforce sound design principles in any technology, including .NET. Given enough time and experience, every developer, consultant, or similar professional vein has been through the gamut of providing a great solution they have known they have seen before. Maybe they've even provided the same solution but with different tools and technology. Those folks may now understand that when it comes to design, a good design is a good solution, despite the technology. No matter how good the technology may be, it is only as good as its design and specifically the implementation of it. In fact, a great design with older technology may still be good, but a bad design with good technology is usually just bad.

Many developers have used sample code or specific snippets of implementation to ease the pains of beginning development. The implementation of that code may or may not be generically repeatable but it provides you with a starting point. It provides a reference from which to remorph the existing code into something completely different. Patterns provide this aspect to an architecture or design and usually at the object level. But that does not mean they couldn't be deployed at other levels.

Patterns are repeatable and named ideas that that can be applied to a design, architecture, or implementation. This means more than just traditional design patterns of repeating a set of prearranged classes forming an object hierarchy. It can apply to any elements, some of which may be technology-specific. This doesn't mean that patterns should *not* be technology-agnostic. In fact, those that do transcend technology are considerably more useful in a designer's career. However, there may be elements of the pattern that leverage a particular technology's strong suit. As already mentioned, I will be presenting this form of technology leveraging when we get into some implementation and architecture patterns later on. Hopefully, I will provide you with all of the above—design patterns that transcend .NET, implementation patterns that predicate themselves on technology, and architectural patterns that do both.

Later, I will delve deeper into what patterns are, how they can be categorized, and how they are presented in this book. Along the way, I also give brief primers of the essential elements of object orientation so that this book can stand on its own without sifting through other references. How do you make tangible a design that is intangible yet very repeatable? How do you come up with something you've done before or even what others have done before but maybe in a new way (hint: or with a new technology)? If you are thinking to yourself, UML, you are close but not quite. UML helps but it really only contains the hieroglyphics (or language) you may need to convey your design. It is the standardized and fossilized assemblage of those UML symbols we need. Enter design patterns.

CHALLENGE 1.5

> What is the difference between an implementation pattern, an architecture pattern, and a design pattern?
>
> *Keep reading.*

HISTORY AND CATEGORIZATION

When introducing anyone to a new technology, there are always reference standards with which to begin. These reference standards usually come in the form of "defacto" standard learning materials and those who profess them. If you were learning COM, I would point you to Don Box and the book *Essential COM*. If you were learning object orientation and the Unified Modeling Language (UML), I would surely point to the "three amigos" of Rational Software and their books. The same goes for learning patterns. The founding fathers of design patterns are Gamma, Helm, Johnson, and Vlissides. These gentlemen are affectionately referred to as the "gang of four" (GoF; pronounced "gauf," as a Scot would articulate the word "golf"). The GoF have become the "three amigos" of design patterns and the pattern movement overall. No, I'm not talking about Steve Martin, Martin Short, and Chevy Chase (apologies for those who haven't seen that movie). I'm referring to Booch, Rambaugh, and Jacobsen. With the help of both the "three amigos" and the GoF, there is now a standard set of practices from which those new to object-orientation can build a foundation.

The GoF manifested the idea of *software* design patterns but the overall idea of patterns came from another source. Christopher Alexander first spoke of design patterns when referring to the actual architecture of buildings. But we are building software, not sky scrapers.

Unlike many other books, I will not be repeating the patterns in the GoF book. There is already enough material out there to provide you with an .NET implementation of preexisting GoF patterns. What is provided, however, are new twists to familiar patterns from not only the design perspective but the architecture and implementation perspective, as well. In their book, *Design Patterns: Elements of Reusable Object-Oriented Software* from Addison Wesley 1995, the GoF uses C++ and Smalltalk. However, the book is geared to the patterns themselves and not the language used to implement them. This general applicability to all languages is what makes patterns so powerful. In this book, you will be leveraging technology to a greater extent than that of the GoF. This is especially true when get into the implementation and architecture patterns. This is another reason I provide you with technology backgrounders along the way to better acquaint you with those .NET elements required to grasp the technology-specific material in this book. If you are very new to OO, please read Craig Larman's *Applying UML and Patterns: An Introduction to Object-Oriented Analysis and Design from Prentice Hall 1997.* His General Responsibility Assignment Software Patterns (GRASP) provide some of the more basic object-oriented principles as applied to design patterns, such as low coupling, high cohesion, expert, etc.

CATEGORIZING PATTERNS

The process of categorizing patterns is very subjective, to say the least. Ask two different object-oriented enthusiasts, and surely you will receive two different means of identifying patterns. This is not to say that the GoF categorization process cannot be applied. In fact, it is rather effective once you understand the patterns. The trouble is when you are just getting your feet wet with this type of material, the categories don't strike as much familiarity as they could to aid in their understanding. After all, one of the reasons for categorizing and cataloging them is to aid not only in their referencing but in their learning. You do not have to truly understand any pattern category to understand the pattern itself. You can succeed nicely by simply "thumbing" through the library of patterns and trying each one on to see whether it would benefit. However, it would still be nice for those just approaching the topic to be able immediately to recognize the category description, even if they haven't worked with patterns in the past. Besides aiding those who have read the material and may need to look up a pattern for a solution, a category should also help the discovery process. This is especially true if reading the material for the first time.

In this book, I first attempt a more familiar categorization scheme by leveraging a little of what all developers have most undoubtedly already experienced. These experiences include providing a software design, architecture, and ultimately implementation, even if it was not object oriented. This can be any design or any architecture. The point is that you should be familiar with this term and already have a concept of what makes up a *design* element and what makes up an *architecture* element. Surprisingly enough, some do not understand the difference. Part of that reason is that they tend to overlap a bit in meaning with one another. However, the act of design and the act of architecture are different, indeed. Just ask any object-oriented designer working on a detailed class diagram for a particular business service. This activity may take into account the architecture but it itself is not an architecture element. You can also approach an architect with this same question.

A sound design does not necessarily mean a sound architecture and vice versa. I know of many "sound" designs that took into account every object-oriented best practice and still suffered, due to having a poor architecture. To simplify the meaning of the differences, you can simply remember that architecture tends to closely align with technology, tools, and environmental elements and is not necessarily aligned with object-oriented concepts. On the flip side, designs should be abstracted as much as possible from these same alignments, although considerations always need to be made. Nothing is truly static, after all.

CHALLENGE 1.6

> What are some example of patterns that can be both middle-tier and/or presentation-tier patterns?
>
> *The answer appears in Chapter 3—*
> *the first example of such a pattern lies on page 108*

I also leverage off of any "common" developer experiences based on the fact that most of you have already built some form of three-tier or N-tier system in your career. This book first gives each pattern a "type" classification to mimic the types of work a developer performs. The types are implementation, design, and architecture. This book also uses well-understood principles of N-tier systems by using this other form to help classify the patterns. These broad classifications are presentation tier, middle tier, and persistence tier. These are just fancy names for user, business, and data layers or services. In fact, even these categories are rather "fungible." Patterns that are one type and one category can be easily interpreted as belonging to another type and category. So hopefully, this won't cause any heated debates over what is considered an architecture pattern at the middle tier versus one that resides on the persistence tier. What this system hopes to do is help you answer the following questions:

- How much of the pattern is abstracted from technology?

- How applicable is the pattern for a particular implementation?

- At what level is this pattern implemented?

- Is the pattern repeatable using different implementations?

- At what granularity is the pattern applied?

- Is the pattern related to a known pattern, such as a GoF pattern, and at what level?

THE PATTERN LIBRARY

This section will provide you with a brief look at the "catalog" and a short description of each pattern used for an overall reference for the rest of the book. There are also many best practices that really are isolated and technology-agnostic enough to list here but are useful nonetheless. Chapter 2 contains much more material than just the four framework patterns listed here.

General Framework Patterns

- *Remote Tracer*—Standardize and abstract a target of traced output.

- *Custom SOAP Exception Handler*—Customize SOAP Faults using exceptions.

- *System Exception Wrapper*—Adding value to system exceptions.

- *Soap Fault Builder*—Structured compliant builder for SOAP Faults.

Presentation-Tier Patterns

- *Notifying Thread Manager*—Create a thread and notify a Windows form.

- *Pollable Thread Manager*—Create a thread and periodically check status.

- *MultiSync Thread Manager*—Combine Notifying and Pollable Thread Managers.

- *Error Cross-Reference Generator*—Error ID generator used during exception handling.

- *WebForm Template*—Base template class for a quick interface layouts.

- *Stunt Driver*—Generic interface for testing a component.

- *Dynamic Assembly Loader*—Dynamic loading and caching driver.

Middle-Tier Patterns

- *Chained Service Factory*—Factory method for Web services.

- *Unchained Service Factory*—Loosely coupled Factory method for Web services.

- *Product Manager*—Abstract common business logic to handle disparate products.

- *Service Façade*—Business logic driver for Web services.

- *Abstract Packet*—Business data container to abstract incoming/outgoing data.

- *Packet Translator*—Abstract translation for different packet formats.

Persistence-Tier Patterns

- *Poly Model*—Creating a dynamic data model using XML schemas.

- *Schema Field*—Managing schemas through storage, value passing, and retrieval.

- *Schema Indexer*—Dynamic indexing for dynamic data models.

- *Abstract Schema*—Applying the abstract packet to the world of XML schemas.

Advanced Patterns

- *Abstract Cache*—Abstracting a cache container from any one implementation.

- *Web Service Interface*—Interface management for Web services consumers.

- *Loosely Coupled Transactor (LCT)*—Asynchronous model for large return sets.

- *LCT Client*—Async client model for Web services consumers.

- *LCT Server*—Async server model for Web services consumers.

HOW TO USE THE PATTERN LIBRARY

Most patterns can be taught and referenced in three ways. You can read each pattern lightly and utilize those patterns you feel will add benefit. Another option is simply to use the library list above as a reference for the future, assuming the descriptions are enough for you to get a feel for how they are implemented. However, that said, I do recommend you give each pattern a chance. That doesn't mean read this book in its entirety, although that would be great. I intended this book to act as a guide and reference. Reading even those patterns you don't immediately need will help your thought processes and may even give you different ideas. In fact, many of these patterns have been used in ways not originally intended by the commercial product featured in Chapter 6. Hopefully, they will provide you with "design food for thought," as well. I also wanted this book to stand by itself so that those new to patterns and even new to object orientation can learn the basics, as well as benefit from the book's main content.

Hopefully this chapter gave you good idea of what this book is intending to provide. The world of .NET is here to stay, and the model is quite a leap for Microsoft. With .NET, you also have at your fingertips the ease of decoupling systems across an Internet backbone. You not only have to contend with a new technology framework but you also have this new distributed power at your hands. Those new to true object-oriented concepts and their best practices may find this more of a challenge. It is also quite an opportunity to experience the best of so many technologies that Microsoft has seemingly packaged up into one "box." The remainder of this book hopes to give you a cookbook of ideas, practices, and named patterns so that you have a better opportunity to provide sound designs, sound architectures, and sound enterprise implementation using .NET.

2

Framework Patterns: Exception Handling, Logging, and Tracing

OVERVIEW

One of the primary success factors for implementing a robust framework is providing enough information at runtime so that the system can be effectively monitored. Despite how good a programmer you think you are, there will always be bugs. Hopefully, by the time your application goes to production, most of these can be discovered. However, no matter how diligent you may be, problems still arise. Eventually, you will be faced with solving the issue as quickly and as painlessly as possible. The better your framework is built to handle both preproduction and postproduction problems, the faster they will be solved.

Information is key to solving any problem. The more accurate, abundant, and accessible the errata, the better. This is especially true in postproduction, when

45

you may not have the liberty of being seated at the desktop of your users trying to solve their issues. I hope the topics in this chapter will provide you with some "best practices" that you can employ in any application, typically at the middle tier. I provide a melee of ideas, dos, and don'ts here to give you a few tips on which can be incorporated at any level. Unlike design patterns, these are not fixed to any one design but are more specific to the .NET framework. For those repeatable implementation steps, I've included a few implementation patterns that will add some benefit to any new or existing middle tier.

Like the remaining the chapters in this book, this chapter serves as a cookbook of ideas and does not have to be read in any particular order. The following topics will be covered in this chapter:

- Exception Handling

- Exception Logging

- Exception Chaining

- Building a Base Exception Class

- Tracing and Trace Listening

- Error and Call Stacks

- When, Where, and How to Log

- SOAP Exceptions and SOAP Faults

- Interop Exception Handling

    The following implementation patterns will be described in detail:

- Remote Tracer

- Custom SOAP Exception Handler

- System Exception Wrapper

- SOAP Fault Builder

EXCEPTION HANDLING

Those already familiar with Java exception handling should feel quite comfortable with the .NET implementation. In fact, if you are reading this book, you should already be throwing and catching exceptions in your code. However, I would like to go over some "advanced-basics" in the area of exception handling before we move on to creating a "base exception" class (sprinkled with a few implementation patterns). Error, or exception handling is one of those things that everyone does but unfortunately, few do it very well. With robust handling, logging, and display, your applications will better stand the test of time and should save you hours in product support. From here forward, I use the word *exception* in place of *error*, and vice versa; neither is meant to be distinctive of the other. I assume throughout this chapter that you have already had some experience working with *structured exception handling* (SEH) because this will not be a tutorial on its basics.

Figure 2.1 illustrates a typical exception-handling scenario. This should provide you generally with the proper flow of throwing and catching exceptions. You'll notice that once an exception is deemed *unrecoverable*, information is then added to provide the system with as much information as possible for determining the problem. This is where a *base exception* class becomes useful. Typically, the more you can centralize *value-added* features to this class, the easier it will be to integrate and leverage from within your framework. This is especially true of large development teams. How many times have there been framework features that were useful but unused? By centralizing important functionality such as logging in your base class and by standardizing how the exceptions should be thrown, you help guarantee its proper use. This also takes any guesswork out of proper exception handling for those developers using your framework. In an upcoming section, I will provide some of the steps for creating such a base class.

Application-Specific Exceptions

Like its C++ and Java predecessors, .NET uses a base *System.Exception* class as the parent of all thrown exceptions. Many applications can simply use this base class for throwing errors and are not required to implement their own. You may also wish to stick with using the System.SystemException-derived exceptions that come with the FCL. These include exception classes such as *System.Web.Ser-*

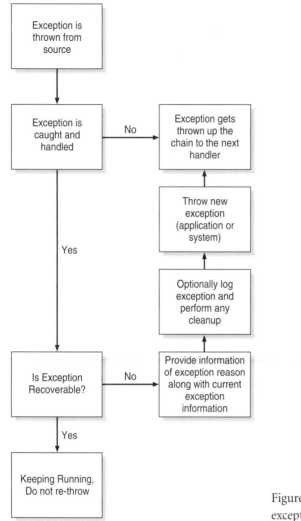

Figure 2.1: Exception flow: How most exceptions should be handled.

vices.Protocols.SoapException or *System.IO.IOException*. System exceptions of these types will also be used throughout the samples in this book. However, for special handling scenarios or to enhance your architecture, it is advisable to build your own exception base class. From there, you can begin to add functionality common to all exception handling for your framework.

From a base exception class, you can create specific error-handling classes and further centralize the process by which errors should be handled, displayed, and recorded in your architecture. This includes general framework exceptions, such as the sample *FtpException* class you will see shortly, but it also includes all those business rule-specific scenarios that warrant special handling. All custom application exceptions, including your own framework exceptions, should derive from System.ApplicationException and not System.Exception directly. Even though System.ApplicationException directly derives from System.Exception, they have identical features. However, it is important to make the distinction between the two when designing your exception classes.

Rather than using method return codes such as the HRESULTS that we have come to know and love with COM, .NET is a type-based system that relies on the exception type to help identify errors. Throwing the appropriate exception type during a given scenario is as important as specifying the correct HRESULT in the world of COM. This doesn't mean we forgo all error codes. It simply means that leveraging the exception types will initiate a more robust error-handling system.

An example of a feature-specific exception handling class can be found when providing FTP services in your architecture (as shown below). Later, I will describe how this is used when we talk about creating protocol-specific requesters in the next chapter. I am just using this as a simple example, so bear with me. Here, the exception class is expanded to facilitate FTP-specific errors and the protocol return codes that are used to describe the error. The code displayed simply delegates most of the handling to the base class *BaseException*. Our BaseException class will be described shortly. The point here is that I can now better control how FTP errors should be handled.

In this example, I am simply displaying the error in a specific format when the Message property is used. Building function-specific exception classes also eliminates the guesswork for developers having to utilize an existing framework: If a specific exception class is provided, use it. If certain rules dictate even a future possibility of special error processing, error display, or error recording, then building a custom exception class would be prudent. Once the base exception class is built for a framework, function-specific exception classes can be driven from a template, such as the following:

Listing 2.1: A sample BaseException child class.

```
public class FtpException : BaseException
{
    /// <summary>
    /// Message for the ftp error
    /// </summary>
    private string m_sMessage;

    public FtpException(){;}

    public FtpException(string sMessage, bool bLog) :
        base(sMessage, bLog){;}

    public FtpException(string sMessage, System.Exception
      oInnerException, bool bLog) : base(sMessage, oInnerException,
        bLog){;}

    public FtpException(object oSource, int nCode, string sMessage,
        bool bLog) : base(oSource, nCode, sMessage,      bLog){;}

    public PMFtpException(object oSource, int nCode, string sMessage,
        System.Exception oInnerException, bool bLog) :
        base(oSource, nCode, sMessage, oInnerException, bLog){;}

    public new string Message
    {
        get
        {
            int nCode = base.Code;
            string sMessage = GetFtpMessage(nCode);
            return new StringBuilder(
                            "FTP Server stated:[")
                            .Append(nCode)
                            .Append(" ")
                            .Append(sMessage)
                            .Append("]")
                            .ToString();
        }
        set {m_sMessage = value;}
    }
}
```

The Listing 2.1 example is not all that different from a regular exception, other than two things. We use this FtpException class to display our FTP error in a specialized way. With the following helper function, I am using the returned FTP code to look up the corresponding FTP error message from a string table called *FTP-Messages* through the System.Resources.ResourceManager. Once the code description is returned, I then build the custom FTP error message, using both the code and the description.

Listing 2.2: One example of a "value-added" operation on a base exception child.

```
/// <summary>
/// Helper to return messages from ftp message resource string table
/// </summary>
/// <param name="sCode"></param>
/// <returns></returns>
public static string GetFtpMessage(int nCode)
{
    FtpMessages = new ResourceManager("FTPMessages",
        Assembly.GetExecutingAssembly());
    FtpMessages.GetString(new StringBuilder("Code_")
                                .Append(nCode).ToString());
}
```

The other differentiator between my FtpException class and any other *System.ApplicationException* class is the constructors for this class. Notice that most of the constructors delegate to the BaseException class. This is where most of the exception handling is done. Features handled by the BaseException class include some of the following, which I will talk about in more detail in this chapter:

- Automated Exception Chaining—Handles each exception as it gets passed back up to the caller of the method containing the exception. As each exception is thrown, the cause of the exception is passed as the "inner exception" thus becoming part of the newly thrown error. This continues up the chain until the information gathered can be used for tracking the original error, logging, or handling in some other fashion.

- Automated Error Stack Formatting and Display—While exceptions are chained, they can be tracked by building an error stack containing each chained exception. Typically, this is accomplished by capturing the important elements during chaining and building a string that can be displayed or made durable.

- Automated Call Stack Formatting and Display—This is identical to that of building an error stack exception. The .NET framework automates this by providing an error stack property that can be accessed at any time. The error stack will provide details as to the method and line number causing the error. This information can also be made durable or displayed.

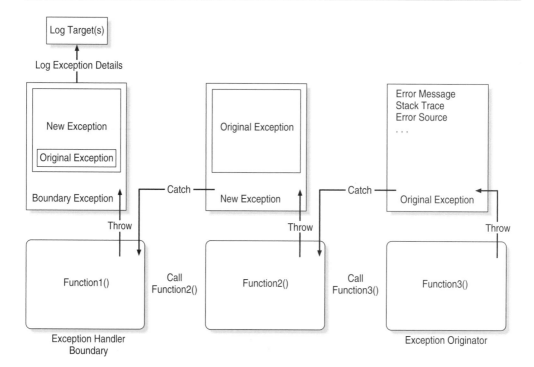

Figure 2.2: Exception chaining: How exceptions are chained using the InnerException property.

- Custom Remote Exception Handling Using SOAP—For exceptions thrown directly from Web services, this can circumvent the FCL's own default SOAP exception handling. Providing custom handling here will give you a greater level of control, especially when formatting an *SOAP Fault*, as we will see in the SOAP Fault technology backgrounder later in this chapter.

- Error Logging and Message Tracing—Provides the mechanism by which the exceptions are communicated and/or made durable during handling.

Figure 2.2 should give you a visual idea of how exception handling, chaining, and logging look from a framework perspective.

Logging is not the most important of these base exception features. Most errors in some way at some point should be made durable. The user may *not* have the luxury of viewing a message box with an error description or even understand the error message when it is displayed. It is up to you to provide a facility for recording or routing error messages so that the error either gets handled later or is read by those who can help. As a product support feature, this is a must. In the next section, I will show how you can enrich your exception handling by designing a base class to facilitate this.

CHALLENGE 2.1

Besides what has been mentioned, what other elements could be included in the base exception class?

A solution appears in the next section.

BUILDING A BASE EXCEPTION CLASS

Recording an error message does not necessarily have to be fast. I am not saying you should ignore sound design practices and provide a sloppy means of error logging. What I am saying is that your exception handling should concentrate on providing the *best* options for recording errors and not necessarily the *fastest* means of handling them. When an application fails and it begins to throw exceptions, its performance takes a back seat to that of dealing with the error itself. This is not always the case, because there are systems that require fast failing. However, the majority of the systems I have built required that the framework allow the best means of solving the problem. The first and best option for solving the problem is discovering what the problem is. Unless you are the user of the application, this may not be possible without a log and/or tracing mechanism.

Logging allows anyone to read the state of the system at any time. One of the best places to log is in the exception class itself because the exception has the necessary information to record. Logging can be done in one shot, usually in the final catch block of what could be multiple levels of exception handlers. Another option is to log in real time. Real-time logging is the recording of information while the system is running. This is also referred to as *tracing*. This helps eliminate the more difficult runtime problems that may occur and that one-time logging may not help to solve. The trick is to capture as much information as possible in the one-time log event so that tracing isn't always necessary in production. Why? Aside from slowing down performance (which you can minimize, as we will see), tracing forces the developer periodically to add tracing function throughout the code, thus cluttering it up. Before we go into how you can architect a robust and flexible tracing system, let's first show how we can build one-time logging into our exception handling.

You saw in the *FtpException* example how the user had the option of logging by passing in *true* as the last parameter (*bLog*). However, all of this functionality was passed onto the base class. Because logging usually conforms to a universal standard in your architecture, this can be implemented in your base exception handling class, as shown below:

Listing 2.3: The beginning of a real base exception class.

```
public class BaseException : System.ApplicationException
{

    private int m_nCode;

    public BaseException(){;}

    public BaseException(string sMessage, bool bLog) : this(sMessage,
        null, bLog){;}

    public BaseException(string sMessage, System.Exception
        oInnerException, bool bLog) : this(null, 0, sMessage,
        oInnerException, bLog){;}

    public BaseException(object oSource, int nCode, string sMessage,
        bool bLog) : this(oSource, nCode, sMessage, null,
bLog){;}

    public BaseException(object oSource, int nCode, string sMessage,
        System.Exception oInnerException, bool bLog) :
        base(sMessage, oInnerException)
    {

        if (oSource != null)
                base.Source = oSource.ToString();
        Code = nCode;

        // need to add logic to check what log destination we
        // should logging to e.g. file, eventlog, database, remote
        // debugger
        if (bLog)
        {
            // trace listeners should already initialized, this
            // is called to be prudent
            Utilities.InitTraceListeners();

            // log it
```

```
                    Dump(Format(oSource, nCode, sMessage,
                                        oInnerException));
        }
}


/// <summary>
/// Writes the entire message to all trace listeners including
/// the event log
/// </summary>
/// <param name="oSource"></param>
/// <param name="nCode"></param>
/// <param name="sMessage"></param>
/// <param name="oInnerException"></param>
private void Dump(string sMessage)
{
        // write to all trace listeners
        Trace.WriteLineIf(Config.TraceLevel.TraceError, sMessage);

        // see Utilities.InitTraceListeners()
        // record it to the event log if error tracing is on
        // The EventLog trace listener wasn't added to the
        // collection to prevent further traces
        // from being sent to the event log to avoid filling up the
        // eventlog
        if (Config.TraceLevel.TraceError)
            EventLog.WriteEntry("PMException", sMessage);
}

public static string Format(object oSource, int nCode, string
                    sMessage, System.Exception oInnerException)
{
        StringBuilder sNewMessage = new StringBuilder();
        string sErrorStack = null;

        // get the error stack, if InnerException is null,
        // sErrorStack will be "exception was not chained" and
        // should never be null
        sErrorStack = BuildErrorStack(oInnerException);

        // we want immediate gradification
        Trace.AutoFlush = true;

        sNewMessage.Append("Exception Summary \n")
                .Append("------------------------------\n")
            .Append(DateTime.Now.ToShortDateString())
                .Append(":")
            .Append(DateTime.Now.ToShortTimeString())
                .Append(" - ")
                .Append(sMessage)
```

```csharp
                        .Append("\n\n")
                        .Append(sErrorStack);

            return sNewMessage.ToString();
    }


    /// <summary>
    /// Takes a first nested exception object and builds a error
    /// stack from its chained contents
    /// </summary>
    /// <param name="oChainedException"></param>
    /// <returns></returns>
    private static string BuildErrorStack(System.Exception
oChainedException)
    {
            string sErrorStack = null;
            StringBuilder sbErrorStack = new StringBuilder();
            int nErrStackNum = 1;
            System.Exception oInnerException = null;

            if (oChainedException != null)
            {
                sbErrorStack.Append("Error Stack \n")
                            .Append("-----------------------\n");

                oInnerException = oChainedException;
                while (oInnerException != null)
                {
                    sbErrorStack.Append(nErrStackNum)
                                .Append(") ")
                        .Append(oInnerException.Message)
                                .Append("\n");

                    oInnerException =
                            oInnerException.InnerException;

                    nErrStackNum++;
                }

                sbErrorStack.Append("\n--------------------\n")
                            .Append("Call Stack\n")
                      .Append(oChainedException.StackTrace);

                sErrorStack = sbErrorStack.ToString();
            }
            else
            {
                sErrorStack = "exception was not chained";
            }
```

```
            return sErrorStack;
    }

    public int Code
    {
            get {return m_nCode;}
            set {m_nCode = value;}
    }
```

The logging logic in Listing 2.3 is simple. When throwing an exception, the developer has the option of logging by passing in *true* for the log flag, as shown in this FTP client code snippet:

Listing 2.4: Applying our base exception child class.

```
FtpWebResponse = FtpWebResponse.Create(ControlStreamReader);
switch(FtpWebResponse.Code)
{
    case Constants.POSITIVE_COMPLETION_REPLY_CODE:
    {
            // success  - 200
            // this reply is ok
            break;
    }
    case Constants.SERVICE_NOT_AVAILABLE_CODE:
    case Constants.PERMANENT_NEGATIVE_COMPLETION_REPLY_CODE:
    case Constants.SYNTAX_ERROR_IN_ARGUMENTS_CODE:
    case Constants.NOT_LOGGED_IN_CODE:
    {
            throw new FtpException (this, FtpWebResponse.Code,
                FtpWebResponse.GetOriginalMessage(), false);
    }
    default:
    {
            throw new FtpException (this, FtpWebResponse.Code,
                NotValidReplyCodeMessage(FtpWebResponse.Code, "PORT"),
                true); // log this error!!!!!
    }
}
```

Here I show a custom FTP exception class passing in the response code, an appropriately returned code description, and the source of the error. In the default section of the switch case statement, the developer wishes to log this exception. In the case statement directly above the default, the *FtpException* (for whatever reason) does not log. This is an imaginary scenario, but it quickly shows how to specify which exceptions are logged and which ones aren't. The logging itself is handled by the exception, as we have seen. But where does the error actually get logged?

CHALLENGE 2.2

How can you globally control where logging output is sent?
A solution appears in the next section.

Determining Where to Log (Using the Trace Object)

In the BaseException class, logging output is eventually written to one or more log targets using the statement *Trace.WriteLineIf()*. Here I use the tracing capabilities of the FCL to determine where to send the output. You can easily write to the *Windows event log*, a log file, or another target directly but I wanted to leverage what I consider one of the more elegant features of .NET—tracing.

```
// write to all trace listeners
Trace.WriteLineIf(Config.TraceLevel.TraceError, sMessage);
```

The .NET Trace class methods can be used to instrument any debug or release build of your application. Tracing can be used to monitor the health of any system during runtime but it can also act as logging mechanism. Whether you use it for logging, monitoring, or both, tracing can be great way to diagnose problems without affecting or even recompiling your application.

The *Trace.WriteLineIf* method above takes only two arguments. The first is a *boolean* parameter where I use what is called a *TraceSwitch* to determine whether I want to trace a message and at what level. Don't worry about the TraceSwitch just yet if you haven't worked with them; I will explain them in the upcoming technology backgrounder. The second parameter is simply the message I want to trace. Trace.WriteLineIf() is called from within the *Dump* method. The Dump method is, in turn, called from within the overloaded BaseException constructor.

Listing 2.5: Sample Base Exception logging routine.

```
if (bLog)
{
    // trace listeners should already initialized, this
    // is called to be prudent
    Utilities.InitTraceListeners();
```

```
            // log it
            Dump(Format(oSource, nCode, sMessage,
oInnerException));
        }
```

You'll also notice a few other goodies in the BaseException class. In Listing 2.5, you see that the *Dump* method calls the *Format* method. This method is used to prepare the output format of the error message. How you format your messages and what information is included is completely design-specific. Here my formatted message prepares a string that includes three main parts. The first part is the *source* of the error, usually passed in as *this* so that I can access the fully qualified type as well as other elements of the calling object. The second part is the error code that will be ultimately included in the recorded message. The third part is an error summary, which is the description of the error provided by the thrower. This is one set in the exception thrown that will actually be logged. The final parameter is the chained exception, which is usually the one just caught. This will be used to build our error stack because it will contain any previously caught and chained errors. The .NET framework provides the mechanism to chain and even a stack trace to use but it does not provide a formatted error stack. This is your job. Providing a full error stack each time you log is optional but it will help determine the cause of the error. This is in case the high-level error does not provide enough clues as to the cause. In fact, I'm sure you have already found that it typically doesn't.

Determining What to Log

Provide Enough Information

When building your application exception classes, especially your base exception class, you will need to determine how much information to provide. Determining this completely depends on the audience. When providing error information to users, you want to give them enough information to determine that there is a problem without inundating them with terse language or technical details that they may not understand. However, this does not mean you forgo technical information as part of your exception. This only means you do not want to display it by default. For example, when displaying an error dialog, you should show only a high-level version of the problem. Optionally, you can also add a Details button to allow the more technically savvy user get more detailed error information if he or she so chooses. You want to provide the option of information without intimidation.

Providing a high-level error description is typically the job of the last handler of the exception. This is referred to as the *exception boundary*. This could be an ASP.NET page or a GUI catching the final exception and displaying it to the user. Again, this does not in any way mean you forgo providing rich information; in fact, you should side on providing more rather than too little. Just hide the complexity from the user. One of the great things about .NET is that you don't have to provide rich information through extensive custom development. The FCL takes care of providing you with helper objects and methods that will give you as much relevant data as you can handle. The following table shows some of the informational items you can easily access using the FCL:

TABLE 2.1: Environmental information: Some examples of information providers from the FCL

Data	Source
Dates and Times	DateTime.Now
Source of Exception	Exception.Source
Type of Exception	Object.GetType
Exception Message	Exception.Message
Current Method	Reflection.MethodInfo.GetCurrentMethod
Machine Name	Environment.MachineName or Dns.GetHostName
Current IP	Dns.GetHostByName("host").AddressList[0].Address
Call Stack	Exception.StackTrace or Environment.StackTrace
OS Information	Environment.OSVersion
Application Domain	AppDomain.FriendlyName
Current Assembly	Reflection.Assembly.GetExecutingAssembly
Root Error Cause	Exception.GetBaseException
Chained Exception	Exception.InnerException

TABLE 2.1: Environmental information: Some examples of information providers from the FCL (cont.)

Assembly Version	Included in AssemblyName.FullName
Thread ID	AppDomain.GetCurrentThreadId
Thread User	Threading.Thread.CurrentPrincipal

You'll notice in Table 2.1 that a couple of the items are retrieved using .NET *Reflection*. Reflection services allow you *introspect* the public members of almost any class, including the System.Exception class. This can come in very handy when displaying detailed information during logging or display and should be explored. For more information on Reflection services, please refer to the technology backgrounder on Reflection in Chapter 4.

Building an Error Stack

One of the first things I typically provide is an *error stack*. This is not to be confused with a *call stack*; something the System.Exception class provides "out of the box." As mentioned earlier, the error stack is built around another nice feature of .NET called *exception chaining*. This is actually a well-known design pattern that the .NET System.Exception class provides for free. All you have to do is take advantage of it. This means making sure during each throw of your BaseException that you pass in the exception class initially caught, as in the following snippet:

```
catch(FtpException ftpe)
{
        throw new BaseException(this, 1234, "FTP Error: " +
                ftpe.Message, ftpe, true);
}
```

Here I am throwing a new exception, passing in a *source* object (*this*), an error code (1234), an error description, and what is now the *inner exception*. In this case, that inner exception is an *FtpException*. The last parameter (*true*) will tell this exception to log itself. This will eventually lead to the *BuildErrorStack* method being called. This is the heart of this method. The BuildErrorStack method simply loops through each chained exception, using the inner exception property of the BaseException class, as shown in Listing 2.6. The format and additional items you place here are, again, up to you. The point is that you leverage the FCL chaining facility by building a useful display medium that will hopefully help solve the issue.

Listing 2.6: Sample stack builder used in our base exception class.

```
if (oChainedException != null)
{
    sbErrorStack.Append("Error Stack \n")
                .Append("-----------------------\n");

    oInnerException = oChainedException;
    while (oInnerException != null)
    {
        sbErrorStack.Append(nErrStackNum)
                    .Append(") ")
               .Append(oInnerException.Message)
                    .Append("\n");

        oInnerException =
              oInnerException.InnerException;

        nErrStackNum++;
    }

    sbErrorStack.Append("\n---------------------\n")
                .Append("Call Stack\n")
          .Append(oChainedException.StackTrace);

    sErrorStack = sbErrorStack.ToString();

}
```

CHALLENGE 2.3

When throwing exceptions from Web services, what other steps are required? How does SOAP affect exception handling?
A solution appears in the upcoming technology backgrounder on SOAP Faults (page 65).

Throwing System Exceptions

Once you've built your base exception class and all of its helpers, you are probably going to want to leverage it as much as possible. That said, you *may* also want to take advantage of some of the *system exception classes* (e.g., System.IOException) that the FCL has to offer. How does one leverage the features of both? The answer is that you use both by employing *exception wrapping*. When you want to throw a system exception and still want to take advantage of your base exception features, you simply create a new system exception class and pass that as the inner exception of your base exception class constructor. This in effect "wraps" the system exception, allowing it to appear neatly as part of your error stack. This can all be with one (albeit long) line of code:

```
throw new BaseException(this, 120, GetMessage(120),
new System.IOException(), true);
```

Here I want to throw the system exception IOException. However, I still want to use my BaseException class features, such as error stacks, message formatting, and logging. Using exception wrapping, I get both.

MANAGING EXCEPTION BOUNDARIES

Once I've added all of my robust error handling-features to my exception classes, I am now positioned to easily determine faults, should they arise. However, there is more than just providing the error-handling mechanisms. You must also provide a model to follow for how exceptions will be handled by answering some of the questions below:

1. Where is the exception handled?

2. When should you log an error?

3. Will the exception be "remoted?"

4. Who will be the final receiver of the exception?

5. What protocols and transports is the receiver using?

This section discusses the answers to these questions and will provide you with a starting point upon which to build an *exception boundary* policy.

Throwing Exceptions from Web Services

In most Web applications, the last boundary of properly-handling exceptions is controlled by the *ASP.NET* or *Web service* code. In most cases, throwing exceptions from a Web service can be done in the same manner as throwing exceptions from anywhere else. You simply throw an exception from the Web method, and .NET takes care of the rest. If SOAP is used to call the Web method, .NET automatically wraps your exception in a corresponding *SoapException* class, nesting your original exception within it. However, in many cases the details of that wrapped exception may not suit your client application. For example, wrapping the exception in this manner may not provide the level of detail your clients require. This is especially true when the message protocol used is SOAP. Thankfully, there is a way to circumvent this automated wrapping by throwing your own SOAP exceptions in cases where custom-detailed information may be required. Figure 2.3 should give you a good visual of how exceptions are wrapped inside of a SoapException class. Notice there is no loss in the amount of detail because all information is preserved through chaining.

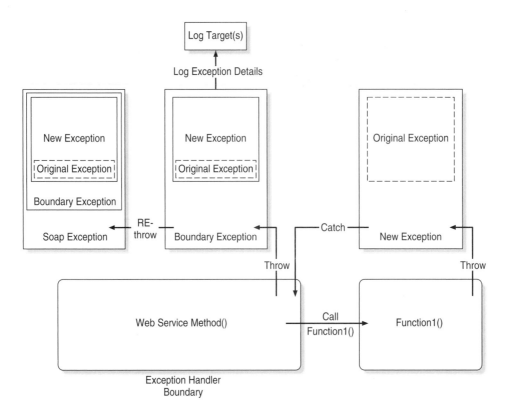

Figure 2.3: Wrapping SOAP exceptions: How base exceptions are wrapped by SoapExeptions.

This should by no means discourage the client from using SOAP—quite the contrary. Unless messages passed to Web services are rather simple and, thus, using a HTTP GET or POST is sufficient, I suggest using SOAP as your message protocol for passing data. Using SOAP will provide you with the most flexibility in passing complex types, such as *DataSet*, to your prospective Web services. With .NET, you do not have to even determine which message protocol is used. Using this wrapping technique, .NET detects the message protocol and will wrap your thrown exception in a SoapException class. However, the details provided are sparse, at best. This is especially true with SOAP Fault information. In these cases, the best practice is to throw your own SoapException. For those SOAP 2.0 clients, this means they will receive a properly formatted SOAP Fault on the client with as much detail as required. A SOAP Fault is a mechanism used to determine the details of the exception in a "SOAP-compliant" manner, such as the following technology backgrounder describes. A SOAP Fault is not simply used for low-level errors but can be the means by which all exceptions are determined, as we will see in the upcoming implementation pattern.

TECHNOLOGY BACKGROUNDER—SOAP FAULTS

As with all SOAP messages, the content of the message is included in the body and is processed on the server. In this case, the server is a Web service method. The body element contains the information necessary to invoke a Web service and will also be used to return any values upon successful completion of the business function. However, if any error were to occur, the body can also be used to return errant information in the form of SOAP Faults. The SOAP Fault element is used to carry this error and/or status information back to the calling client from within the SOAP message. If an error occurs, the SOAP Fault element should appear just like any other body element entry and should not appear more than once.

Remember that the SOAP message can be parsed like any other XML document. To determine whether an error occurs, the calling client can simply look for this fault element and read its contents to determine the exact error. Fortunately, the client from the SOAP Toolkit 2.0 provides users with a user-friendly component by which to query for this information. The SOAP client COM object simply wraps the nested contents of the fault, allowing access to the following elements:

faultcode

This element is used to determine the basic error identification and to provide an algorithmic mechanism for identifying the fault. This must be present in a SOAP Fault element, and it must be a qualified name and not the typical numbering schema used in other error determinations. The namespace identifier for these *faultcode* values is http://schemas.xmlsoap.org/soap/envelope/. The following *SOAP* faultcodes can be used:

VersionMismatch—Used for an invalid namespace in the *SOAP Envelope* element.

MustUnderstand—An element of the *SOAP Header* that was missing or invalid. See the SOAP Header technology backgrounder in Chapter 7 for more information.

Client—Used to indicate that the message was incorrectly passed and/or did not contain the right information used for the called function. This simply means it was the client's "fault" and should be retried. Retrying or repassing the information will not result in the proper processing on the server unless the contents of the passed message are changed. This is not the server's error. You set this when the caller gives the service improper information and not when something goes wrong on the server side.

Server—This is used to communicate a server failure (this can mean any failure to process the request from the server's perspective). Retrying or repassing the information may result in the successful completion of the function.

faultstring

This element is used to pass to the caller a descriptive human-readable error. It must be present in a SOAP Fault element and should provide at least some information explaining the nature of the fault. This could contain the high-level error message used to determine generally what went wrong.

faultactor

This element is used to provide information about who caused the fault and usually contains the Uniform Resource Identifier (URI) of the perpetrator. This is similar to the SOAP actor attribute in the SOAP body. Applications that do not act as the ultimate destination of the SOAP message must include this element. The final destination of a message may use this element to indicate that it alone threw the exception.

detail

This is where the most descriptive error information can be included to help determine the root cause of the problem. The detail element can be used for carrying application-specific error information related to the Web service method invoked. It should not contain SOAP header-related errors but only errors related to the message body. The absence of this element shows that the fault is not related to the Body element. This can be used to distinguish whether the Body element was even processed and is your key to show that the message was received but that an application-specific error was indeed thrown. This element is also the key to the implementation pattern: *SOAP Exception Fault Builder.* According to the SOAP specification, "other *SOAP* Fault subelements may be present, provided they are namespace-qualified."

An example of a SOAP Fault generated from the Microsoft SOAP Toolkit 2.0 *SoapServer* object is as follows (here it places an <errorInfo> element in the <detail> element to convey detailed error information to the client):

Listing 2.7: Sample Soap Fault Detail Block.

```
<soap:Fault …>
  …
<detail>
   <mserror:errorInfo
        xmlns:mserror="http://schemas.microsoft.com/soap-
           toolkit/faultdetail/error/">
   <mserror:returnCode>-2147024809</mserror:returnCode>
   <mserror:serverErrorInfo>
        <mserror:description>Failure...shutting down</
mserror:description>
        <mserror:source>error-source</mserror:source>
        <mserror:helpFile>
            help goes here
        </mserror:helpFile>
        <mserror:helpContext>-1</mserror:helpContext>
   </mserror:serverErrorInfo>
   <mserror:callStack>
        <mserror:callElement>
            <mserror:component>SomeOp</mserror:component>
            <mserror:description>
                Executing method ReturnError failed
            </mserror:description>
            <mserror:returnCode>-2147352567</mserror:returnCode>
        </mserror:callElement>
   </mserror:callStack>
  </mserror:errorInfo>
</detail>
```

This contains all of the application-specific error information as generated from the Toolkit's SoapServer object. Your own custom detail element does not necessarily need to look like this but this provides a decent example of what can be done. The more information you provide, the more robust your error handling will become, especially when this information is provided in a SOAP Fault-friendly manner.

As mentioned earlier, throwing normal exceptions using the .NET framework's SOAP exception wrapper may not always provide the details you were expecting. In fact, the main error message provides only the same generic text message: "Server was unable to process request." To provide a slightly more robust SOAP exception with a custom SOAP Fault, you need to throw your own SoapException class. By doing, so you can provide a much richer exception and still provide a SOAP-compliant fault mechanism so that all clients can better determine the error generated by the Web service. Fortunately, there is a simple way to throw SoapExceptions from your Web service without requiring much effort. In the next section, I will show you exactly how to implement this pattern by adding support to your base exception class. See the beginning of this chapter for details on building a base exception class.

Throwing Custom SOAP Exceptions

In some cases, it is difficult to find areas where Microsoft has not provided a feature desired in its framework. In fact, you have look a little closer before realizing where you could truly add benefit by adding custom behavior. Such is the case for processing exceptions from Web services when using SOAP.

As mentioned in the previous section, when you throw an exception from a Web service that is called from SOAP .NET, this automatically wraps your exception class in the *SoapException* class. For a remote client, receiving that exception will come in the form of a partially populated SOAP fault. I say *partially* because .NET does not fill in every detail. I've built a simple Web service to demonstrate this, as shown in Figure 2.4.

In Figure 2.4, you'll find a Web service called *ExceptionThrower.asmx* displayed in a browser. Here you simply specify whether you want to throw a custom SOAP exception using the following implementation pattern or using the framework wrapper. Specifying True in the edit box and selecting Invoke, you should see the output shown in Figure 2.5.

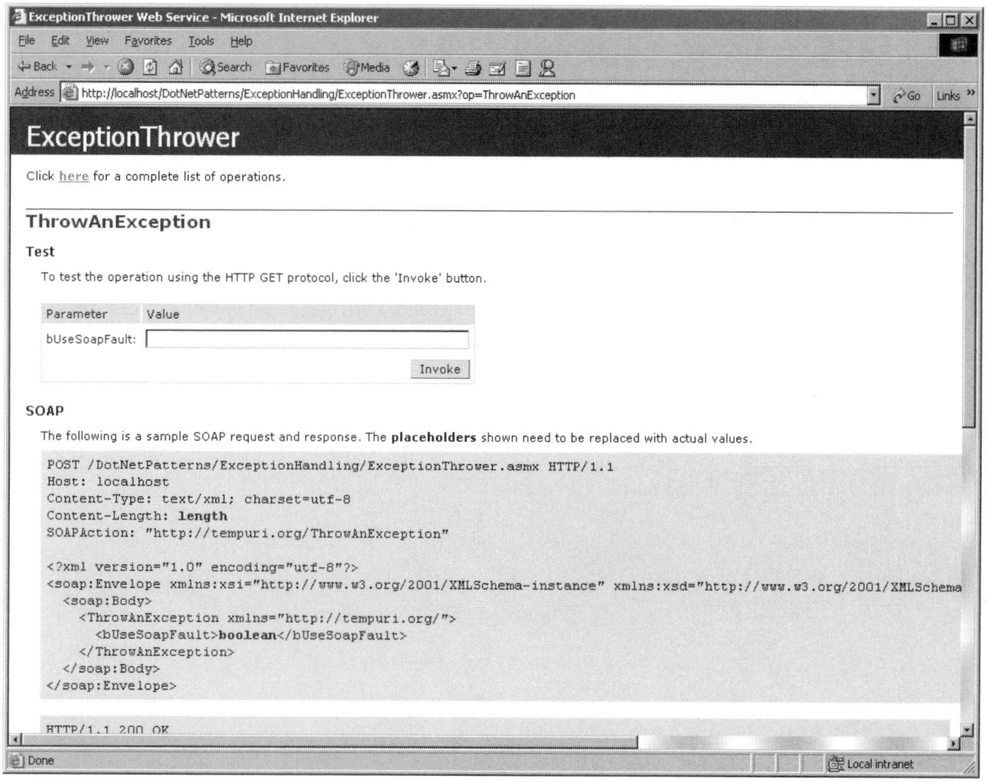

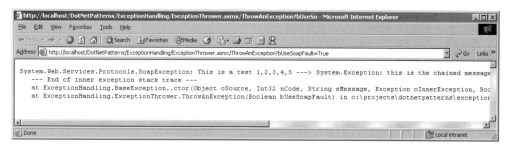

Figure 2.4: ExceptionThrower.asmx test harnesses a Web service for throwing custom SOAP exceptions.

Figure 2.5: ExceptionThrower.asmx exception output when selecting custom soap exception.

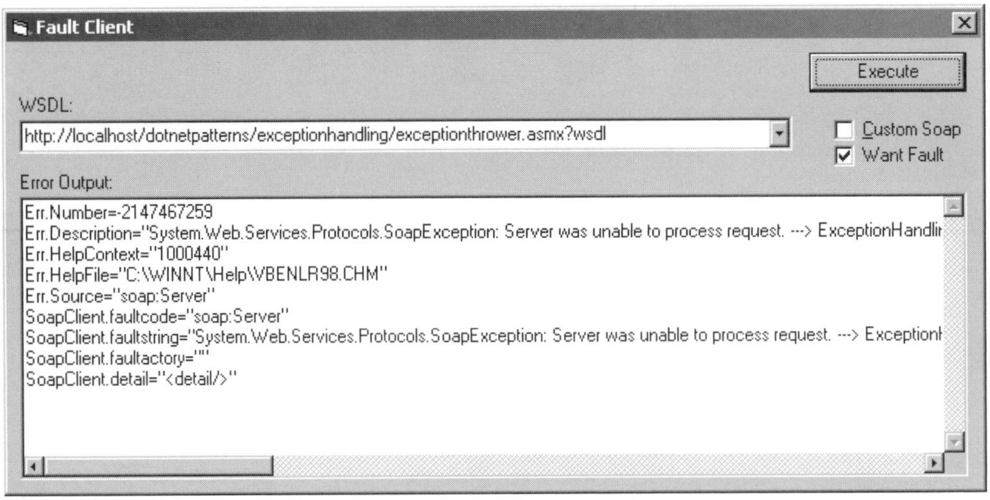

Figure 2.6: Called from a SOAP 2.0 client written in VB 6.0 (using wrapper SOAP exceptions). Does not show any SOAP Fault details.

If you run this again but select False, you should *not* be able to view the exception text. This is an apparent side effect to *not* throwing your own SOAP exceptions, at least for Beta 2. This, however, is not the real reason to throw your SOAP exceptions. To the see the real benefit of throwing your own custom SOAP exceptions, run the exceptionthrower.asmx Web service from a typical SOAP 2.0 client (Figure 2.6).

Using the test GUI, I am *not* selecting Custom Soap before I select Execute. This will call the same Web service with a parameter of False, thus using the .NET wrapper method. Notice that .NET wraps our exception in a SoapException but it provides us with a general error text before the actual error message. More critically, it does not provide us with any details (the <detail/> element is empty). Finally, it does *not* tell us where the error came from in the form of the *faultfactory* property. Now when we turn on the Custom Soap option, we should receive a much more detailed SOAP Fault (Figure 2.7).

Notice in the previous screen shot that a few things have now been provided. The faultcode property has been set to *detail*. This is optional but now we have the flexibility to set this faultcode appropriately. For more information on SOAP Fault codes, please refer to the relevant technology backgrounder in this chapter. Also notice that the general description has been replaced with our specific error message. Next, the faultfactory property has been set to the location of the exception. In this case, that location is the actual URI of the Web service. Finally and most

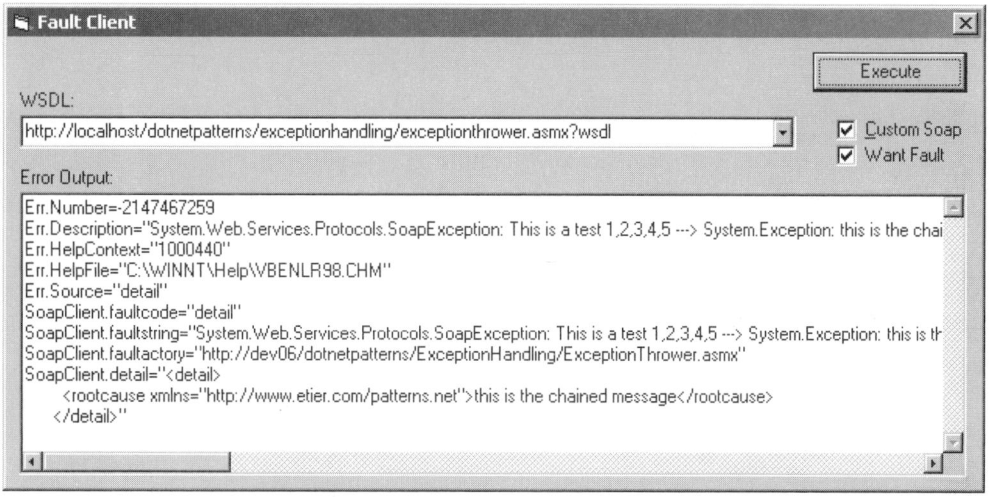

Figure 2.7: Called from a SOAP 2.0 client written in VB 6.0 (using wrapper SOAP exceptions). Shows the SOAP Fault details.

important, the *details* property has been set to the *root cause* of the error. The information provided in this property can be as detailed as you like. In fact, this would be a great place to display an error stack; as long as the details are properly formatted as SOAP-compliant, the choice is yours. Next I will show you the code behind this implementation pattern.

Adding SOAP Exception Support to BaseException

In this implementation pattern, I will place the custom SOAP exception inside of our BaseException class. This provides two benefits. First it encapsulates the details of the SoapException class from the thrower of the exception, such as a Web service method. Second, it simplifies the mechanism by which all exceptions are thrown. The easier and more standard you can make exception handling, the better. The exceptionthrower.asmx Web service, shown below, shows how to throw or *not* to throw a custom SOAP exception:

Listing 2.8: Sample Soap Fault Builder for our base exception class.

```
using System.Collections;
using System.ComponentModel;
using System.Data;
using System.Diagnostics;
using System.Web;
using System.Web.Services;
```

```
namespace ExceptionHandling
{
   . . .

   [WebMethod]
   public void ThrowAnException(bool bUseSoapFault)
   {
         if (bUseSoapFault)
               throw new BaseException(this, 1234,
                        "This is a test 1,2,3,4,5",
                        new Exception(
                        "this is the chained message",
                        null), false, true);
         else
               throw new BaseException(this, 0,
                        "This is a test 1,2,3,4,5",
                        new Exception(
                        "this is the chained message",
                        null), false);
      }
   }
}
```

The code in Listing 2.8 simply passes *true* or *false* as the last parameter of one of our BaseException class constructors. If you pass *true*, the first BaseException shown is thrown; otherwise, the same signature we used in the constructor defined in the beginning of this chapter is used.

Passing *true* will call the following constructor.

Listing 2.9: Sample BaseException ctor for allowing Soap Faults.

```
/// <summary>
/// This ctor for throwing soap exception usually from web service
/// methods
/// This will format error message in more soap fault friendly
/// manner
/// filling in fields not filled in by the default wrapper exception
/// method in .NET
/// </summary>
/// <param name="oSource"></param>
/// <param name="nCode"></param>
/// <param name="sMessage"></param>
/// <param name="oInnerException"></param>
/// <param name="bLog"></param>
/// <param name="bThrowSoap"></param>
public BaseException(object oSource,
```

```
                        int nCode,
                        string sMessage,
                        System.Exception oInnerException,
                        bool bLog,
                        bool bThrowSoap) : this(oSource,
                                              nCode,
                                     sMessage, oInnerException,
bLog)
{
    string sCause = "no root cause found";
    XmlNode oNode = null;

    if (bThrowSoap)
    {
        if (oInnerException != null)
            sCause = oInnerException.GetBaseException().Message;

        // now build the details node to use for the soap exception
        // -- use the root cause for the main text oNode =
           BuildDetailNode(sCause);

        Trace.WriteLine("Throwing Custom Soap Exception - Message "
                        + sMessage);

        // build actor or source uri to set into actor field -
        // replace .'s with /'s to make a uri from it
        // NOTE: the web service must namespace match the reqeues
        // uri if this is to be accurate
        // we can't use context without passing it so we'll build
        // one
        StringBuilder sActor = new StringBuilder("http://");
        sActor.Append(Dns.GetHostName());
        sActor.Append("/");
        sActor.Append("dotnetpatterns");
        sActor.Append("/");
        sActor.Append(oSource.ToString().Replace(".", "/"));
        sActor.Append(".asmx");

        throw new SoapException(sMessage,
                        SoapException.DetailElementName,
                            sActor.ToString(), oNode,
                            oInnerException);
    }
}
```

There are two main parts to this pattern. First, there is the building of the details property so that we can fully extract SOAP Fault details from the client. The second is the fact that I am "rethrowing" a *SoapException* back, once the properties are filled. To rethrow a SoapException, we simply call *throw new SoapException* like any other exception, and the exception should be thrown back to the calling client. Before I do that, however, I need to fill four properties that will become the SOAP Fault elements.

Each of the four properties that make up the SOAP fault will be passed to the SoapException constructor, as shown in Listing 2.9. The first parameter is any message text. Typically, as is the case here, it will be the high-level error message text we've sent when throwing our main exception. The second parameter designates the SOAP Fault code, as defined by the SOAP specification. Although this can be set to any code and your code will still work, it is considered "well formed" if you comply with standards. For this example, I've set this parameter to the detail property because I will be providing a detail explanation as part of the fourth parameter. The third parameter is the *actor* and is used to set the location of where the error occurred in the form of a URI. Here I dynamically determine the full URI path based on the *source* object provided and the machine on which this service is running. The oSource.ToString() will give me a fully qualified path string, including the namespace of the assembly under which the source object resides. This will only work if your Web service path matches this fully qualified name and is used only as an example here.

Finally, the fourth parameter provides the details section of the SOAP Fault and is a little more complicated to build so I've supplied a helper method called *Build-DetailNode*, as shown here:

Listing 2.10: Sample Soap Fault Detail Node Builder.

```
/// <summary>
/// Build the xml node used for throwing custom soap exceptions, the //
/ root cause string will be use for the main content
/// </summary>
/// <param name="sCause"></param>
/// <returns></returns>
public System.Xml.XmlNode BuildDetailNode(string sCause)
{
    XmlDocument oDoc = new XmlDocument();
    XmlNode oNode = oDoc.CreateNode(XmlNodeType.Element,
                    SoapException.DetailElementName.Name,
                SoapException.DetailElementName.Namespace);

    // Build specific details for the SoapException.
    // Add first child of detail XML element.
```

```
XmlNode oDetailsNode = oDoc.CreateNode(XmlNodeType.Element,
            "rootcause", "http://www.etier.com/patterns.net");
oDetailsNode.InnerXml = sCause;

onode.AppendChild(oDetailsNode);
return oNode;
}
```

This method uses the *System.Xml.XmlDocument* and *XmlNode* classes to build a SOAP Fault-compliant XML node. Once built, this node will be passed back and used as our detail SOAP Fault property. This can be built any way you see fit, as long as the parent detail element node exists along with its namespace; otherwise, it will not be properly displayed in your SOAP client. This SoapException.DetailElementName type is used from within our first CreateNode() call for just this purpose. After this step, you can supply your own text or custom-nested elements. In this example, I add another child node called *rootcause* and specify the text of the root cause or error, as supplied by the System.Exception class. Another variation of this pattern would be to add the full error stack as child nodes so that the SOAP fault client can see every detail of the error. Either way, the choice is yours, so have fun with it.

COM (Interop) Exception Handling

The common language runtime (CLR) seamlessly provides the ability to access COM objects, as well as allowing COM clients to access .NET code. The CLR's interoperability features also provide sophisticated exception handling when the managed layer is crossed during error scenarios. When a COM client calls a managed piece of code that throws an exception, the CLR intercepts the exception and appropriately translates it into an HRESULT. Similarly, if managed code is accessing an unmanaged COM component that returns an HRESULT, the CLR translates it into an exception. While doing so, the CLR incorporates any additional information provided by the COM *IErrorInfo* interface into the thrown managed exception class. Any unrecognized HRESULT will result in a generic *ComException* being thrown with the *ErrorCode* set to the unresolvable HRESULT.

When using COM components from managed code, this does not present many problems. However, when COM clients currently access your managed code, many of the FCL exceptions will return an HRESULT that may be unrecognizable to the calling COM client. Cases where the calling COM client must handle certain HRESULTs in an application-specific manner can cause problems.

Fortunately, the System.Exception object has an *HResult* property that can be overridden and set at any time during your error handling. To avoid problems with legacy COM clients, replace any HRESULT with that of one that is recognized by those clients to avoid such problems.

Using XML

The output format is completely up to you. A proprietary format was used in the previous examples but XML could have been used. Be forewarned, however, that this output may have multiple targets, each with its own viewers. For example, XML may not be the best display format if you are writing to the Windows 2000 Event Log. A large XML stack does not look particularly great in the Windows Event Viewer.

Another point to keep in mind is when building XML documents, be careful how you format any error strings. If the error strings contain characters interpreted as XML syntax, you may have problems formatting such errors. For example, in the previous section we built a detail XML node that made up one of the properties of our SOAP Fault. The text that was used in the detail node was the root cause of the error. If any of the text strings used for the message inside of the detail XML node happened to contain a "<" or ">" character, a format exception would have been thrown. Having errors occur in your own error handling is not something you want to have happen because it may make communicating them impossible. In fact, you may be a little embarrassed that your own error-handling code has bugs. This is not to say that you should avoid XML in your error handling. Rather, it is quite the contrary. I point this out only so that you can be extra careful when building your base exception class. The more you test your code in this case, the better.

Determining When to Log

Determining when to actually log your output can easily become one of those heated design debates. To keep things simple, however, I suggest logging at the most externally visible tier, or what I've been calling the *exception boundary*. This coincides with what .NET considers an application and where you specify your configuration files. This is also known as the *application level*. For GUI development, this is simple: Log just before you display your error. For Web service applications or for those that do not necessarily have a visible tier, I typically log just before returning from an external Web method. This refers only to error logging. Random tracing is another story and is completely dependent on how much output you want to receive and when you want to begin seeing it. For those really nasty bugs, providing a real-time, persistent tracing scheme where you trace as much as possible may be your best option. There is a way to have the best of both worlds—the ability to trace verbose information but only during times where it may be deemed necessary. We will be covering this practice in the next section.

ENABLING THE TRACE OPTION

By default, *C#* enables tracing with the help of Visual Studio.NET by adding the /d:TRACE flag to the compiler command line when you build in this environment. Building under Visual Studio.NET automatically will provide this switch for both debug and release builds. Therefore, any tracing can be viewed in either release or debug, which is something I am counting on for the following implementation pattern. Another option for adding tracing is to add *#define TRACE* to the top of your *C#* source file. The syntax and mechanism to enable tracing is compiler-specific. If you are working with VB.NET or C++, for example, your settings are slightly different. However, each .NET language should support tracing, so refer to your documentation for details.

CHALLENGE 2.4

How would you send logging output (tracing output) to a remote terminal across the Internet?
A solution appears in the upcoming section on remote tracing (page 82).

The target of the trace output is then determined by what are called *trace listeners*—the subject of the next technology backgrounder. If you are currently already familiar with trace listeners and dynamic tracing using trace switches, you can skip this section.

TECHNOLOGY BACKGROUNDER—TRACE SWITCHES AND TRACE LISTENERS

Trace Listeners

Trace listeners are thread-safe classes that derive from an abstract class called, appropriately enough, *System.Diagnostics.TraceListener*. This class contains the necessary methods to be able to control trace output. There are three out-of-the-box trace listeners included with .NET. The first is called *DefaultTraceListener* and, by default, is automatically added to a trace listener collection shared by the application. Using the *Trace.Listeners* static property, you can access this collection at any time during execution. Using the collection, you can then add or remove any trace listener. Controlling the listeners in the collection will, therefore, control your trace output. When *Trace.Write* or *Trace.WriteLine* is called, these methods will emit the message to whatever trace listeners have been added to the system. The DefaultTraceListener will receive these calls and send the output to the its designated target. For the DefaultTraceListener, that target is both the *OutputDebugString API* and the .NET log method. You should already be familiar with the OutputDebugString API; if not, please reference the Platform SDK documentation. The log method will post the message to any attached debugger in .NET.

The second trace listener is called *EventLogTraceListener*. This listeners send all output to the Windows event log. Using its *EventLog* property, you can control which event log receives the output. The third out-of-the-box listener is called *TextWriterListener*. This sends all output to any *TextWriter* or *Stream* object. This can be the *console's standard output stream* or any file.

To add or remove a listener to or from the collection, you can either use a configuration file, such as *web.config,* or do it in code. The following is an example of adding or removing a listener using a configuration file:

Listing 2.11: Adding a listener using web.config.

```
<configuration>
  <system.diagnostics>
    . . .
    <trace autoflush="true" indentsize="4">
      <listeners>
        <add name="LogFileListener"
  type="System.Diagnostics.TextWriterTraceListener,System"
          initializeData="c:\LogFileListener.log" />
        <remove
    type="System.Diagnostics.DefaultTraceListener,System"/>
      </listeners>
    </trace>
  </system.diagnostics>
</configuration>
```

You can also control the listener collection in code such as the following *Init-TraceListeners* method I use in the upcoming implementation pattern.

IMPORTANT

In the following method, I show how you can add an event log listener to the collection. However, I do not recommend you use the event log during most tracing scenarios. I typically use the event log only during error handling or more determined forms of tracing, such as message coming from Windows Services (e.g., "service starting…", "service stopping…", etc.). Otherwise, you will quickly fill it up if you're not careful.

Listing 2.12: Sample for adding an event log listener to a global collection.

```
/// <summary>
/// Adds all default trace listeners, for event log
/// tracing it first checks
/// to see if the trace level has not been set to verbose or
/// information since we
/// don't want to fill up the event viewer with verbose
/// information.
/// </summary>
public static void InitTraceListeners()
{
    FileStream oTextWriter = null;

    // We do not want to dump to the if tracing is set to
    // information or verbose
    if (!Config.TraceLevel.TraceInfo)
    {
        if (Trace.Listeners[TRACE_EVENTLOG_KEY] == null)
        {
            EventLogTraceListener oEvtLogListener = new
                EventLogTraceListener(EVENTLOG_SOURCE);
            oEvtLogListener.Name = TRACE_EVENTLOG_KEY;
            Trace.Listeners.Add(oEvtLogListener);
        }
    }
    else // travel level is set to warning or error
    {
        if (Trace.Listeners[TRACE_EVENTLOG_KEY] != null)
            Trace Listeners.Remove(TRACE_EVENTLOG_KEY);
    }
```

```
      if (Trace.Listeners[TRACE_TEXTWRITER_KEY] == null)
      {
          oTextWriter = File.Exists(TRACE_LOG_FILE)) ?
                      File.OpenWrite(TRACE_LOG_FILE) :
                      File.Create(TRACE_LOG_FILE);
          Trace.Listeners.Add(new
                  TextWriterTraceListener(oTextWriter,
                          TRACE_TEXTWRITER_KEY));
      }

      // This is a custom trace listener (see PMRemoteTrace.cs)
      // for remote tracing
      if (Trace.Listeners[TRACE_REMOTE_KEY] == null)
          Trace.Listeners.Add(new
                      RemoteTrace(TRACE_REMOTE_KEY));
}
```

First, notice that the listener collection is manipulated like any other collection in .NET. Using .NET *indexers*, I can check to see whether the listener has already been added to the collection. If you look carefully at the *InitTraceListeners* example, you'll notice a new listener class called *RemoteTrace*. This is referred to as a *custom trace listener* and is the focus of the following implementation pattern.

By adding trace listeners to a central collection, you can globally control how and where tracing output is sent. As a developer of the rest of the system, you are required to add Trace.Write or WriteLine methods only to send the appropriate information to that output for any debug or release build. This is a powerful monitoring and logging feature but how do we elegantly control whether we want to trace at all? For that matter, how to we control at what level we would like to trace? We may simply want to trace errors or we may want to provide as much information during runtime execution as possible to help determine our problems. This is where .NET *switches* come into play.

Boolean and Trace Switches

The first way to turn off any tracing is by disabling the /d:TRACE option, as mentioned above. However, doing so requires the recompilation of your code for it to become effective. What if you are in production and you do not have that option? Fortunately, you can easily control tracing dynamically and without recompilation. To do so, you use what are called *System.Diagnostics.Switch* objects. The switch objects available in the FCL are *BooleanSwitch* and *TraceSwitch*. Both derive from System.Diagnostics.Switch. All switches are configuration objects, of sorts, that read a configuration setting and provide properties with which you can check dynamically to determine whether an option has been enabled and what level. The *BooleanSwitch* is the simpler of the two and is set to off by default. To turn it on, you edit your application's *<xxx>.config* file as follows:

```
<system.diagnostics>
    <switches>
        <add name="MyBooleanSwitch" value="1" />
    </switches>
</system.diagnostics>
```

The .config file can be your web.config file if your application is a Web service, for example. With this set, you now create the BooleanSwitch object. This can be stored in a *static* variable and be accessible by any code wishing to use the switch. This BooleanSwitch data member is part of a configuration object used throughout the system to retrieve any application configuration information.

```
public static BooleanSwitch MyBooleanSwitch = new
TraceSwitch("MyBooleanSwitch",
"This is my boolean switch");
```

The first parameter of the BooleanSwitch is the name of the switch. This *must* match the name used in your configuration setting. Setting this to 1 turns on the switch; conversely, setting this to zero turns it off. Once the switch is created, the BooleanSwitch can be used to help determined things such as tracing. Instead of calling Trace.Write or Trace.WriteLine, you now call Trace.WriteLineIf. The first parameter of this method is a Boolean that when set to *true* will cause tracing to occur. Instead of simply passing *true* or *false* directly, you use the BooleanSwitch, as follows:

```
Trace.WriteLineIf(MyBooleanSwitch.Enabled, "message to trace");
```

During execution, the code will use the BooleanSwitch to dynamically check the configuration setting. If the setting is set to 1, the BooleanSwitch returns *true*, and the trace occurs. No longer do you need to recompile your code.

A TraceSwitch works in the same fashion except you also get to control the level at which tracing should be enabled. To set a TraceSwitch in the configuration file, you must specify the name of the switch (same as before) and the level at which to enable tracing. A TraceSwitch has four properties: *TraceError, TraceWarning, TraceInfo,* and *TraceVerbose.* Its configuration-level settings are:

```
0 (off), 1 (error), 2 (warning), 3 (info), OR 4 (verbose)
```

For example, to create a TraceSwitch to control all system tracing, use the following:

```
public static TraceSwitch TraceLevel = new
TraceSwitch("TraceLevel", "Tracing Level");
```

To configure this TraceSwitch to verbose, you would use the following:

```
<system.diagnostics>
      <switches>
            <add name="TraceLevel" value="4" />
      </switches>
</system.diagnostics>
```

To trace a message (only if verbose has been set), you would use the following:

```
Trace.WriteLineIf(TraceLevel.TraceVerbose, "some message");
```

This line will send a trace message only if the *verbose level* has been set in the configuration file. In fact, using any other trace level in the *WriteIf* call would trace the message because setting the configuration to verbose will send all traces. Setting this to verbose causes the TraceSwitch *trace level* to return *true* for TraceInfo, TraceWarning, or TraceError. If the configuration setting was 3 (TraceInfo), then all trace levels except TraceVerbose would return *true* and, thus, the trace would be sent. In this case, TraceInfo, TraceWarning, and TraceError would return *true* but TraceVerbose would return *false.* I will discuss the use of tracing, custom trace listeners, and trace switches in the following section.

REMOTE TRACING—BUILDING A CUSTOM TRACE LISTENER

One of the nice features of using *trace listeners* and *trace switches* is that you can centrally and dynamically control all tracing output from a central location. Taking this a step further, you now have a relatively simple means of improving product support for your applications. Such a step allows you to create your own trace listener class to completely customize the output, as well as the trace target. For

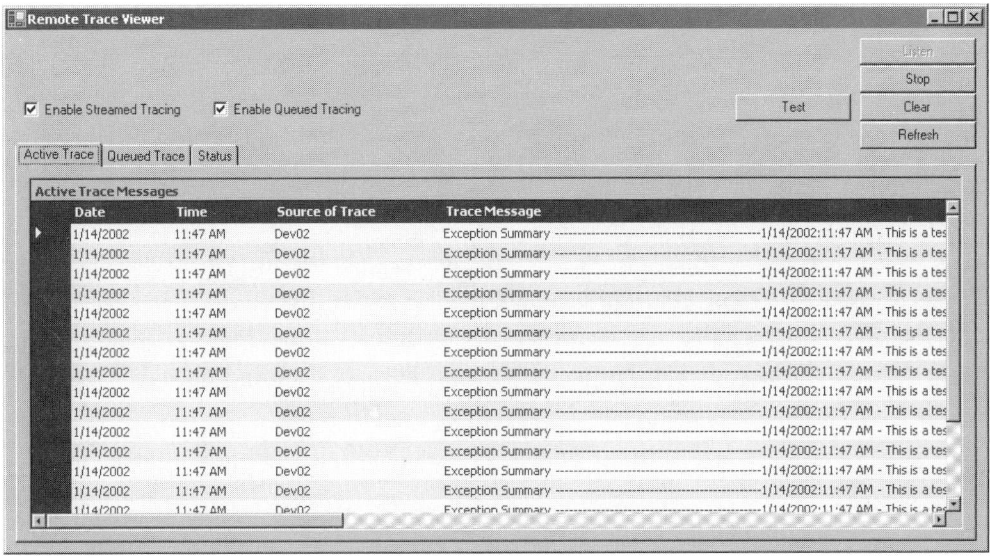

Figure 2.8: Remote Trace Viewer: Displays all remote traces coming from a message queue or TCP/IP socket.

example, you may want to remotely monitor the health of an application that was installed externally. The application you wish to monitor may not even be installed on your local network. With a custom trace listener, you now have the means of automatically tracing output from an external application to a server accessible to you. I will go through the building of such a feature using three main components:

- Custom Trace Listener/Sender—Trace listener to send trace statements remotely.

- Trace Receiver—Server that can receive trace statements from a remote source.

- Trace Viewer (optional)—Front end to view remote traces (Figure 2.8).

Building a Custom Trace Listener

Using the .NET trace listener collection, you can easily employ your own custom listeners to route and format trace output as you see fit. Custom trace listeners are manipulated like any other trace listeners. To create one, you must first derive from the *TraceListener abstract* class and create your own XXX*listener* class. The name of the class can be anything but typically it will end with the word *listener* to keep with the .NET convention. Once created, you can than add this listener to the listener collection, as we did in the previous section. You are required to implement only two methods to guarantee that your custom listener will work with .NET tracing. At a minimum, you must implement both the *Write* and *WriteLine* abstract methods. You are not required to overload them; one implementation of each is sufficient. Other elements of the TraceListener parent class may also be overridden, such as the Flush or Close methods, but only the Write and WriteLine methods are actually required for compilation. To create our custom remote trace listener, specify something like the code snippet in Listing 2.13.

Please refer to the previous technology backgrounder in this chapter for details on trace listeners and switches.

Listing 2.13: Our Remote Trace Listener template.

```
/// <summary>
/// This represents the remote tracing custom trace listener that ///
will be added during application initialization
/// and allow all tracing to be sent remotely, the tracing level is ///
determined by the trace switch which is
/// accessible via a TraceLevel static data member (Config.cs), to
/// send remote traces (if turned on), the client
/// must use the following code template:
///
///
///      Trace.WriteLineIf(Config.TraceLevel.TraceVerbose,
///             "starting packet translation...");
///
/// </summary>
///
/// <example>Trace.WriteLineIf(Config.TraceLevel.TraceVerbose, ///
starting packet translation...");</example>
/// <remarks>
/// To change the trace level you must edit the launching
/// applications configuration file as such:
/// The name attribute must match the name given to the trace
/// extension, e.g. RemoteTraceLevel
/// <system.diagnostics>
///          <switches>
///                <add name="RemoteTraceLevel" value="1" />
///          </switches>
/// </system.diagnostics>
/// 0 (off), 1 (error), 2 (warning), 3 (info), OR 4 (verbose)
/// </remarks>
public class RemoteTraceListener : System.Diagnostics.TraceListener
```

```
{
   /// <summary>
   /// Reference to the remote tracing web service
   /// </summary>
   private RemoteTracerServer oRemoteService = null;

   /// <summary>
   ///
   /// </summary>
   public RemoteTracerService RemoteService
   {
       get { return oRemoteService; }
       set { oRemoteService = value; }
   }


   /// <summary>
   ///
   /// </summary>
   public RemoteTraceListener(string sName)
   {
       // initializes the remote web service that will receive the //
remote traces
       RemoteService = new RemoteTracerService();
       base.Name = sName;
   }


   /// <summary>
   /// Writes output remotely to the remote trace web service (trace
   /// receiver
   /// </summary>
   /// <param name="sMessage"></param>
   public override void Write(string sMessage)
   {
       RemoteService.RemoteTrace(Dns.GetHostName(), sMessage);
   }

   /// <summary>
   /// same as above
   /// </summary>
   /// <param name="sMessage"></param>
   public override void WriteLine(string sMessage)
   {
       RemoteService.RemoteTrace(Dns.GetHostName(), sMessage);
   }
```

You can see that the overridden Write and WriteLine methods simply call *RemoteService.RemoteTrace*, passing the original trace message. RemoteService, in this case, happens to be a Web service running on another system. This service acts as the *trace receiver* and just so happens to be implemented as a Web service. Any receiver could have been created, as long as the RemoteTraceListener has access to it. I choose to implement the remote trace receiver as a Web service for simplicity. I could have opened a TCP/IP socket, for example, and could send the message directly to some socket server. How you implement the send or receiver is up to you.

Once your remote trace listener is constructed, you can now add it to your listener collection:

Listing 2.14: Sample routine for constructing and adding your custom listener.

```
public static void InitTraceListeners()
{
    . . .

    // for remote tracing
    if (Trace.Listeners[TRACE_REMOTE_LISTENER_KEY] == null)
        Trace.Listeners.Add(new
    RemoteTraceListener(TRACE_REMOTE_LISTENER_KEY);
}
```

Building a Remote Trace Receiver

Once added to the collection, any direct Trace.Write or Trace.WriteLine calls cause your corresponding methods to be called in RemoteTraceListener. Once called, the *RemoteTracerService.RemoteTrace* will be called. The RemoteTracerService is implemented as follows:

Listing 2.15: A sample Remote Trace Listener Web Service.

```
public class RemoteTracerService : System.Web.Services.WebService
{
    public RemoteTracerService()
    {
        InitializeComponent();
    }

    . . .

    /// <summary>
    /// Called by external clients to send all remote traces
    /// into a centrally supplied web service
    /// </summary>
    [WebMethod]
    public void RemoteTrace(string sSource, string sMessage)
```

```
        {
            EventLog oElog = new EventLog("Application",
                    Dns.GetHostName(), "RemoteTracer");

            try
            {
                // first send it to the trace queue, queue
                // should create itself if it has been deleted
                Messenger oMessenger = new Messenger();
                BusinessMessage oMessage =
                        oMessenger.MessageInfo;

                oMessage.MessageText = sMessage;

                // uri of the requesting party, this is the
                // host name
                oMessage.UserId = sSource;
                // must set the message type we are looking
                // for, this looks in the correct queue
                oMessage.MessageType = "trace";

                // send the trace to the queue
                oMessenger.Send(oMessage);

                // next send it a socket stream
                string sRemoteTraceTargetHost = "etier3";
                string sIP =
Dns.GetHostByName(sRemoteTraceTargetHost).AddressList[0].ToString();
                int nPort = 8001; // any port will do
                Utilities.SendSocketStream(sIP, nPort, sSource
                        + ":" + sMessage);

            }
            catch (Exception e)
            {
                // or socket server was not listening, either
                // way just log it and move on...
                oElog.WriteEntry(BaseException.Format(null, 0,
                        "Error Occurred During Remoting: " +
                        e.Message, e));
            }
        }
    }
}
```

Sending Traces to a Message Queue

Inside the *try/catch* block, I demonstrate the sending of the trace message to two targets. The first message target is a message queue. The second target is any TCP/

IP listening socket server. I've wrapped the message queue interaction in a class called *Messenger* to help abstract the queuing services I may be using. For this example, the following source shows the main features of the Messenger class. This implementation of the Messenger uses the .NET *System.Messaging* library to communicate with *Microsoft Message Queuing*. Sending the trace messages to a queue is completely optional but it provides a quick means of persisting messages while providing an asynchronous delivery mechanism.

Listing 2.16: Sample Business Object to be placed on a queue.

```
/// <summary>
/// This is message information send/received from a queue
/// For example, for FTP file transfers the Data property will
/// contain the actual file contents
/// </summary>
public struct BusinessMessage
{
     /// <summary>
     /// see properties for each data member
     /// </summary>
     private string sType;
     private string sUserId;
     . . .
     private string sQueueName;
     private string sMessageText;
     private string sDate;
     private string sTime;

     /// <summary>
     ///   Specifying the type sets the queue name to
     ///   send/receive to/from
     /// </summary>
     public string MessageType
     {
          get {return sType;}
          set
          {
               sType = value;
               sQueueName = ".\\private$\\patterns.net_" +
                              sType.ToLower();
          }
     }

     public string MessageText
     {
          get {return sMessageText;}
```

```csharp
            set    {sMessageText = value;}
        }

        public string Date
        {
            get {return sDate;}
            set    {sDate = value;}
        }

        public string Time
        {
            get {return sTime;}
            set    {sTime = value;}
        }

        . . .

        public string UserId
        {
            get {return sUserId;}
            set {sUserId = value;}
        }

        public string QueueName
        {
            get {return sQueueName;}
        }
}

/// <summary>
/// Used for sending asynchronous messages to a durable message
/// queue of some kind
/// This currently using MSMQ and assumes it is installed,
/// eventually this will be implemented
/// to use any queuing framework.
/// </summary>
public class Messenger
{
        /// <summary>
        /// Data member for the main message information to be sent
        /// and received.
        /// </summary>
        private BusinessMessage oMessage;

        /// <summary>
        /// Property for the message information structure, which
        /// is an inner structure
        /// </summary>
        public BusinessMessage MessageInfo
```

```csharp
{
    get {return oMessage;}
    set {oMessage = value;}
}

/// <summary>
/// Initializes an empty message information structure
/// </summary>
public Messenger()
{
    MessageInfo = new BusinessMessage();
}

/// <summary>
/// Sends the providing message info structure to a queue,
/// queuename should be set in the MessageInfo struct
/// This just set the MessageInfo property and delegates to
/// Send()
/// </summary>
/// <param name="oMessage"></param>
public void Send(BusinessMessage oMessage)
{
    MessageInfo = oMessage;
    Send();
}

/// <summary>
/// Sends the set MessageInfo data to the queue based on
/// the MessageInfo.QueueName property
/// This will be serialized as xml in the message body
/// </summary>
public void Send()
{
    try
    {
        string sQueuePath = MessageInfo.QueueName;
        if (!MessageQueue.Exists(sQueuePath))
        {
            // queue doesn't exist so create
            MessageQueue.Create(sQueuePath);
        }
        // Init the queue
        MessageQueue oQueue = new
            MessageQueue(sQueuePath);
        // send the message
        oQueue.Send(MessageInfo,
            MessageInfo.MessageType + " - " +
            MessageInfo.Uri);
    }
```

```
        catch (Exception e)
        {
                throw new BaseException(this, 0, e.Message, e,
                                        false);
        }


}


/// <summary>
/// Receives a message based on the MessageInfo.QueueName
/// of the MessageInfo struct passed in.
/// </summary>
/// <param name="oMessage"></param>
public BusinessMessage Receive(BusinessMessage oMessage,
                               int nTimeOut)
{
     MessageInfo = oMessage;
     return Receive(nTimeOut);
}


/// <summary>
/// Uses the set MessageInfo.QueueName to retrieve a
/// message from the specified queue.
/// If the queue cannot be found or a matching
/// BusinessMessage is not in the queue an exception will
/// be thrown.
/// This is a "polling" action of receiving a message from
/// the queue.
/// </summary>
/// <returns>A BusinessMessage contains body of message
/// deserialized from the message body xml</returns>
public BusinessMessage Receive(int nTimeOut)
{
     try
     {
          string sQueuePath = MessageInfo.QueueName;
          if (!MessageQueue.Exists(sQueuePath))
          {
               // queue doesn't exist so throw exception
               throw new Exception("Receive-Error"
                    + sQueuePath
                    + " queue does not
                    exist.");
          }

          // Init the queue
          MessageQueue oQueue = new
               MessageQueue(sQueuePath);
```

```
                ((XmlMessageFormatter)oQueue.Formatter)
                    .TargetTypes =
                    new Type[]{typeof(BusinessMessage)};

                // receive the message, timeout in only 5
                // seconds -- TODO: this should probably change
                System.Messaging.Message oRawMessage =
                    oQueue.Receive(new TimeSpan(0, 0,
                    nTimeOut));

                // extract the body and cast it to our
                // BusinessMessage type so we can return it
                BusinessMessage oMessageBody =
                    (BusinessMessage)oRawMessage.Body;
                MessageInfo = oMessageBody;

                return oMessageBody;
            }
            catch (Exception e)
            {
                throw new BaseException(this, 0, e.Message, e,
                        false);
            }

        }

    }
```

Sending Traces via Sockets

After creating the Messenger class, RemoteTracerService.RemoteTrace first retrieves the *MessageInfo* property to populate the message contents. The message contents are then populated and sent to the message using Send. From this point, we could return control back to the *trace originator*. However, for demo purposes, I also send the trace to a socket server on the network. I do this by setting my host, ip, and port, and calling my utility method *Utilities.SendSocketStream*. This method creates a connection with the specified host and if successful, sends the trace message as a byte stream.

Listing 2.17: Sample Socket Routine for sending any message.

```
public static string SendSocketStream(string sHost, int nPort,
string sMessage)
{
    TcpClient oTcpClient = null;
    string sAck = null;
```

```
    int nBytesRead = 0;
    NetworkStream oStream = null;

    try
    {
         oTcpClient = new TcpClient();
         Byte[] baRead = new Byte[100];

         oTcpClient.Connect(sHost, nPort);

         // Get the stream, convert to bytes
         oStream = oTcpClient.GetStream();

         // We could have optionally used a streamwriter and reader
         //oStreamWriter = new StreamWriter(oStream);
         //oStreamWriter.Write(sMessage);
         //oStreamWriter.Flush();

         // Get StreamReader to read strings instead of bytes
         //oStreamReader = new StreamReader(oStream);
         //sAck = oStreamReader.ReadToEnd();

         // send and receive the raw bytes without a stream writer
         // or reader
         Byte[] baSend = Encoding.ASCII.GetBytes(sMessage);
         // now send it
         oStream.Write(baSend, 0,  baSend.Length);

         // Read the stream and convert it to ASCII
         nBytesRead = oStream.Read(baRead, 0, baRead.Length);
         if (nBytesRead > 0)
         {
              sAck = Encoding.ASCII.GetString(baRead, 0,
nBytesRead);
         }

    }
    catch(Exception ex)
    {
         throw new BaseException(null, 0, ex.Message, ex, false);
    }
    finally
    {
         if (oStream != null)
              oStream.Close();
         if (oTcpClient != null)
              oTcpClient.Close();
    }
    return sAck;
}
```

Do not be overwhelmed by the amount of code shown here. If you haven't worked with either message queuing or the .NET network libraries, you can select another implementation. These transports are not a requirement. You could have simply written your trace message (once received by the Web service) to a file somewhere. This just shows a few options for being a little more creative and creating what could become a rather robust feature of your application's health monitoring. Keep in mind that whatever transport you use to display or store your trace messages can and will throw exceptions. Typically, exceptions should not be thrown back to the trace originator because that would defeat the purpose of tracing. *Remote trace errors should never halt a running application, and your code should take this into consideration.*

Building a Remote Trace Viewer

Now that we have a custom trace listener (to send trace messages remotely) and a trace receiver Web service (to receive trace messages remotely), how do we view them? Again, this is completely up to you. In the following code, I show a rather slimmed-down version of the production TraceViewer that is implemented in the *Product X* application we will cover in Chapter 6. In the following code, I use three System.Windows.Forms.DataGrid controls to display streamed, queued, and status messages. The controls are each bound to a grid using a System.Data.DataSet that is dynamically created in Visual Studio .NET. The DataSet was created from a corresponding XML schema file we created (see the technology backgrounder in Chapter 5 for information on XML schemas and automated DataSet creation). Two System.Threading.Timer objects are used to provide a threaded means of receiving our trace messages, both from a message queue and from a socket client. For a full listing, please download the complete source for the RemoteTraceViewer.

Listing 2.18: Sample Remote Trace Listener viewer (GUI).

```
public class frmSocketServer : System.Windows.Forms.Form
{
   . . .
   private static TcpListener oListener = null;
   private static Socket oSocket = null;


   . . .
   private System.Threading.Timer oQueuedTraceTimer = null;
   private System.Threading.Timer oActiveTraceTimer = null;
```

```
. . .
private System.Windows.Forms.DataGrid ActiveTraceGrid;
private static TraceInfo dsActiveTraceData = null;
private static TraceInfo dsActiveTraceDataCopy = null;
private static TraceInfo dsQueuedTraceData = null;
private System.Windows.Forms.DataGrid QueuedTraceGrid;
private System.Windows.Forms.DataGrid StatusGrid;
private static TraceInfo dsQueuedTraceDataCopy = null;

public frmSocketServer()
{

      //
      // Required for Windows Form Designer support
      //
      InitializeComponent();

      frmSocketServer.dsActiveTraceData = new TraceInfo();
      frmSocketServer.dsActiveTraceDataCopy = new TraceInfo();

      frmSocketServer.dsQueuedTraceData = new TraceInfo();
      frmSocketServer.dsQueuedTraceDataCopy = new TraceInfo();

}

. . .

/// <summary>
/// The main entry point for the application.
/// </summary>
[STAThread]
static void Main()
{
      Application.Run(new frmSocketServer());
}

private void cmdListen_Click(object sender, System.EventArgs e)
{
      try
      {
            cmdListen.Enabled = false;
            cmdStop.Enabled = true;
            cmdRefresh.Enabled = true;

            if (chkEnableQueued.Checked)
                  oQueuedTraceTimer = new
                        System.Threading.Timer(new
                  TimerCallback(ProcessQueuedTrace), null, 0, 40000);
```

```csharp
        if (chkEnabledStreamed.Checked)
            oActiveTraceTimer = new
                    System.Threading.Timer(new
            TimerCallback(ProcessActiveTrace),
            null, 0,
            System.Threading.Timeout.Infinite);

    }
    catch (Exception err)
    {
            EventLog.WriteEntry("…", "Trace Error: " +
                    err.StackTrace);
    }

}

private void cmdStop_Click(object sdr, System.EventArgs e)
{
        StopListening();
}

/// <summary>
/// Delegated Event Method for Timer to process Queued
/// trace messages
/// </summary>
/// <param name="state"></param>
static void ProcessQueuedTrace(Object state)
{
        EventLog oElog = new EventLog("Application",
                Dns.GetHostName(), "TraceViewMain");
        Messenger oMessenger = new Messenger();
        BusinessMessage oMessageIn = oMessenger.MessageInfo;
        BusinessMessage oMessageOut;

        try
        {
                // must set the message type we are looking
                // for, this looks in the correct queue
                oMessageIn.MessageType = "trace";

                while (true)
                {
                    // grab the message from the queue
        WriteStatus(DateTime.Now.ToShortDateString(),
DateTime.Now.ToShortTimeString(), "Listening for trace messages on the
trace queue...");

                    oMessageOut = oMessenger.Receive(
```

```
                        oMessageIn, 10);

               string sSource = oMessageOut.UserId;
               string sDate =
               DateTime.Now.ToShortDateString();
               string sTime =
               DateTime.Now.ToShortTimeString();
               string sMessage = oMessageOut.MessageText;
                     sMessage = sMessage.Replace('\n', '-');


               frmSocketServer.dsQueuedTraceData
                       .TraceMessage
                       .AddTraceMessageRow(
                              sDate, sTime,
                              sSource, sMessage);

               frmSocketServer.dsQueuedTraceData
                       .TraceMessage
                       .AcceptChanges();

          }

     }
     catch (Exception e)
     {
          // exception was probably thrown when no message
          // could be found/timeout expired
          if (e.Message.StartsWith("Timeout"))
          {
     WriteStatus(DateTime.Now.ToShortDateString(),
DateTime.Now.ToShortTimeString(), "Timeout expired listening for
messages on trace queue.");
          }
          else
          {
               oElog.WriteEntry("SocketServer - Error Occurred
                    During Message Receipt and Processing: "
                    + e.ToString());
          }
     }
}

private void StopListening()
{
     cmdListen.Enabled = true;
     cmdStop.Enabled = false;
     cmdRefresh.Enabled = false;
```

```
    if (oSocket != null)
    {
    WriteStatus(DateTime.Now.ToShortDateString(),
            DateTime.Now.ToShortTimeString(),
                    "Closing Socket ..." +
        oSocket.LocalEndPoint.ToString());
        oSocket.Close();
        oSocket = null;
    }
    if (oListener != null)
    {
    WriteStatus(DateTime.Now.ToShortDateString(),
    DateTime.Now.ToShortTimeString(),
                    "Stopping Listener ..." +
        oListener.LocalEndPoint.ToString());
        oListener.Stop();
        oListener = null;
    }

    if (oQueuedTraceTimer != null)
        oQueuedTraceTimer.Dispose();
    if (oActiveTraceTimer != null)
        oActiveTraceTimer.Dispose();
}


/// <summary>
/// Delegated event method to process socket streamed trace
/// messages
/// </summary>
/// <param name="state"></param>
static void ProcessActiveTrace(Object state)
{
    EventLog oElog = new EventLog("Application",
            Dns.GetHostName(), "TraceViewMain");
    string sSource = null;
    int nDelimPos = 0;

    try
    {
        if (oListener == null)
        {
            long lIP =
                Dns.GetHostByName(
            Dns.GetHostName()).AddressList[0]
.Address;

            IPAddress ipAd = new IPAddress(lIP);

            oListener = new TcpListener(ipAd, 8001);
```

```
                    oListener.Start();

        WriteStatus(DateTime.Now.ToShortDateString(),
                 DateTime.Now.ToShortTimeString(), "The server is
running at port 8001...");

WriteStatus(DateTime.Now.ToShortDateString(),
                 DateTime.Now.ToShortTimeString(), "The local End
                 point is  :" + oListener.LocalEndpoint);

                 while (true)
                 {  WriteStatus(DateTime.Now.ToShortDateString(),
                 DateTime.Now.ToShortTimeString(),
                 "Waiting for a connection on : "
                             + oListener.LocalEndpoint);

                 oSocket = oListener.AcceptSocket();
        WriteStatus(DateTime.Now.ToShortDateString(),
                 DateTime.Now.ToShortTimeString(),
                 "Connection accepted from " +
                 oSocket.RemoteEndPoint);

                 // prepare and receive byte array
                 byte[] baBytes = new byte[1000];
                 int k = oSocket.Receive(baBytes);
                 WriteStatus(DateTime.Now.ToShortDateString(),
                 DateTime.Now.ToShortTimeString(), "Received
                 Message...");

                 // let's do it the easy way
                 string sReceivedBuffer =
                         Encoding.ASCII.GetString(
                         baBytes, 0, baBytes.Length);
                 WriteStatus(DateTime.Now.ToShortDateString(),
                 DateTime.Now.ToShortTimeString(),
                         sReceivedBuffer);

                 ASCIIEncoding asen = new ASCIIEncoding();
                 oSocket.Send(asen.GetBytes("trace received"));

                 nDelimPos = sReceivedBuffer.IndexOf(":");
                 sSource = sReceivedBuffer.Substring(0,
                     nDelimPos);
                 string sDate =
                         DateTime.Now.ToShortDateString();
                 string sTime =
                         DateTime.Now.ToShortTimeString();
```

```
                        string sMessage =
                               sReceivedBuffer.Substring(
                               nDelimPos + 1, sReceivedBuffer.Length -
(nDelimPos + 1));

                        sMessage = sMessage.Replace('\n', '-');


                        frmSocketServer.dsActiveTraceData
                                  .TraceMessage
                               .AddTraceMessageRow(
                                    sDate, sTime,
                                    sSource, sMessage);

                        frmSocketServer.dsActiveTraceData
                                  .TraceMessage
                                  .AcceptChanges();
                    }
                }
            }
            catch (Exception e)
            {
                    if (e.Message.StartsWith("A blocking operation"))
                    {
                 WriteStatus(DateTime.Now.ToShortDateString(),
                        DateTime.Now.ToShortTimeString(), "Socket listener was
                        canceled by the system.");
                    }
                    else
                    {
                            System.Windows.Forms.MessageBox.Show(
                                   "Error During Active Trace Listening: " +
                                   e.Message);
                            oElog.WriteEntry(
                                   "Error Occurred During Message Streaming"
                                   + e.ToString());
                    }
            }
            finally
            {
                    if (oSocket != null)
                    {

                            WriteStatus(…)
                            oSocket.Close();
                            oSocket = null;
                    }
                    if (oListener != null)
                    {
```

```
                    WriteStatus(…)
                    oListener.Stop();
                    oListener = null;
             }
         }
}

private void cmdClear_Click(object sender, System.EventArgs e)
{
     frmSocketServer.dsActiveTraceDataCopy.Clear();
     frmSocketServer.dsQueuedTraceDataCopy.Clear();
}


/// <summary>
/// Adds a new message to the status tab
/// </summary>
/// <param name="sDate"></param>
/// <param name="sTime"></param>
/// <param name="sMessage"></param>
private static void WriteStatus(string sDate, string sTime,
                                string sMessage)
{
     frmSocketServer.dsActiveTraceData
                  .StatusMessage
                  .AddStatusMessageRow(
                           sDate, sTime, sMessage);
     frmSocketServer.dsActiveTraceData
                  .StatusMessage
                  .AcceptChanges();
}


private void cmdRefresh_Click(object sender, System.EventArgs e)
{
     // copy active (streamed) grid's data and bind to grid
     ActiveTraceGrid.TableStyles.Clear();
     frmSocketServer.dsActiveTraceDataCopy = (TraceInfo)
        frmSocketServer.dsActiveTraceData.Copy();
     ActiveTraceGrid.DataSource =
                 frmSocketServer.dsActiveTraceDataCopy
                        .Tables["TraceMessage"];

     // copy queued (streamed) grid's data and bind to grid
     QueuedTraceGrid.TableStyles.Clear();
     frmSocketServer.dsQueuedTraceDataCopy = (TraceInfo)
       frmSocketServer.dsQueuedTraceData.Copy();
     QueuedTraceGrid.DataSource = frmSocketServer
                 .dsQueuedTraceDataCopy
                 .Tables["TraceMessage"];
```

```
            // same for status . . .

            // refresh all grids
            ActiveTraceGrid.Refresh();
            QueuedTraceGrid.Refresh();
            StatusGrid.Refresh();

            // this is absolutely required if you want to begin using
            // the grid styles in code
            // format the active trace grid
            if (frmSocketServer.dsActiveTraceDataCopy.Tables.Count > 0)
            {
                if (ActiveTraceGrid.TableStyles.Count == 0)
                {
                    ActiveTraceGrid.TableStyles.Add(new
                        DataGridTableStyle(true));

                    ActiveTraceGrid.TableStyles[0]
                                .MappingName = "TraceMessage";
                    FormatMessageGrid(ActiveTraceGrid, true);
                }

            }

            // format the queued trace grid
            if (frmSocketServer.dsQueuedTraceDataCopy.Tables.Count > 0)
            {
                if (QueuedTraceGrid.TableStyles.Count == 0)
                {
                    QueuedTraceGrid.TableStyles.Add(new
                        DataGridTableStyle(true));

                    QueuedTraceGrid.TableStyles[0]
                                .MappingName = "TraceMessage";
                    FormatMessageGrid(QueuedTraceGrid, true);
                }
            }

            // same for status

    }

    private void FormatMessageGrid(
                    System.Windows.Forms.DataGrid oGrid,
                    bool bIncludeSourceCol)
    {
            // if column styles haven't been set, create them..
            if (oGrid.TableStyles[0].GridColumnStyles.Count == 0)
            {
                oGrid.TableStyles[0].GridColumnStyles.Add(new
```

```
                     DataGridTextBoxColumn());
          oGrid.TableStyles[0].GridColumnStyles.Add(new
                     DataGridTextBoxColumn());
          oGrid.TableStyles[0].GridColumnStyles.Add(new
                     DataGridTextBoxColumn());
          if (bIncludeSourceCol)
     oGrid.TableStyles[0].GridColumnStyles.Add(new
                     DataGridTextBoxColumn());
     }


     oGrid.TableStyles[0].GridColumnStyles[0].Width = 90;
     // you must set each columnstyle's mappingname so that
     // other properties can be set since this is bound
     oGrid.TableStyles[0].GridColumnStyles[0]
                .MappingName = "Date";
     oGrid.TableStyles[0].GridColumnStyles[0]
                .HeaderText = "Date";


     oGrid.TableStyles[0].GridColumnStyles[1].Width = 90;
     // you must set each columnstyle's mappingname so that
     // other properties can be set since this is bound
     oGrid.TableStyles[0].GridColumnStyles[1]
                .MappingName = "Time";
     oGrid.TableStyles[0].GridColumnStyles[1]
                .HeaderText = "Time";


     . . .


     // format Source and Message columns styles …


}


private void cmdTest_Click(object sender, System.EventArgs e)
{
     try
     {
          throw new BaseException(this, 0,
                     "This is a test 1,2,3,4,5",
                     new Exception(
                          "this is the chained message",
                          null), true);


     }
     catch (Exception ex)
     {
          Console.Out.WriteLine(ex.Message);
          //do nothing
     }


}
```

To run the RemoteTraceViewer, select Listen. This will start the *timer threads*, which in turn call *ProcessActiveTrace* and *ProcessQueueTrace*. Each will listen and receive messages, and will add each message to a DataSet. To test your remote tracing, select the Test button. This will throw a nested exception, which will call your remote trace Web service. Once received, both timer threads should pick up the message and display it on each grid accordingly. Several hundred pages could probably be devoted to explaining the building of a production-ready remote tracing utility but this example should get you started in right direction.

SUMMARY

Exception handling is more than just throwing and catching objects in .NET. There are many design elements in providing a robust system, and providing a sound exception handling, logging, and tracing schema are some of the first steps. In this chapter, we covered several best practices for determining when to throw, catch, and ultimately log your errors.

I went into the differences of how exceptions should be handled in a Web service application. One of the most valuable components of this chapter is how you can exploit the FCL to provide global error log control through tracing. Finally, I provided a starting point for building a remote trace utility so that, as a service provider, you can receive complete details of a production system from anywhere on the Internet. The better your exception framework design, the less time you will spend in support mode, and the more time you will actually have to code. That should be incentive enough.

Part 2

Creating the Tiers
of a Framework

3

Presentation-Tier Patterns

OVERVIEW

Tackling the content for this chapter was a challenge. The challenge wasn't due to any technical difficulties, bugs, or other problems. The challenges were in finding items not already covered by the .NET framework. No other interface framework has provided so much richness coupled with so much ease—not even Java's Swing. For that reason, most of the patterns covered in this chapter center around the "plumbing" of a presentation space typically driven by the GUI but not necessarily entailing the GUI itself. Said in another way, there are no specifics for graphic rendering, custom control creation, or other GUI-specific patterns like those covered here. Those readers who are looking for patterns detailing custom control creation or complex graphic programming will be disappointed and will be better served with a graphics book dedicated to just that purpose.

Those looking for "presentation plumbing" patterns such as those addressing the refresh rate of a business interface, improving background operation performance, driving interface threads, test harnessing, or Web form layout should find what they are looking for here. This chapter looks at how to enrich your business interfaces by leveraging some of the framework's more unique features—features either not found in other offerings such as Swing, those that have typically been difficult to implement in the past, or even those that required third-party software. Whether you are building fat, thick, or thin clients calling Web services, the following examples should provide you with a few more useful presentation tools for your toolbox.

These design patterns are included:

Notifying Thread Manager—Creates a thread and notifies a Windows form

Pollable Thread Manager—Creates a thread and periodically checks status

MultiSync Thread Manager—Combines Notifying and Pollable Thread Managers

Error Cross-Reference Generator—Error ID generator used during exception handling

WebForm Template—Base template class for quick Web-based interface layout and design

Stunt Driver—A simple yet effective service interface test harness

Dynamic Assembly Loader—Dynamic loading and caching driver

NOTIFYING THREAD MANAGER

Intent

Provide a framework for an interactive user interface to invoke a long-running operation in a more managed fashion.

Problem

Many times a user interface must initiate an operation that the developer would like to disconnect from the interface's operation. Although there are many reasons, the most common tend to be when multiple operations need to be performed at once or when an operation could potentially take longer than the user should be expected to wait for a response.

Some operations will always take time to complete. A user interface should allow a user to continue doing work while waiting for the operation, or multiple operations, to complete in background. As the use of Web services proliferate, the response times of some services will vary. The user of an interactive application (aka fat client) should not be left with just an hourglass while the operation completes.

Although the .NET framework goes a long way toward simplify initiating new threads to wrap an operation, the job of receiving the result of the operation still leaves some hurdles to be crossed. The developer of a Windows form can fairly easily fire off a thread to perform an operation and receive the result through an event but must still coordinate back with the form's thread to ensure nonoverlapping operations.

This pattern solves the problem by wrapping the logic necessary to get the operation's result, as well as any possible exceptions, back to the calling form's thread.

Forces

Use the Notifying Thread Manager pattern when:

• Working with a fat client, Windows forms implementation

• The operation is expected to take an extended or unknown amount of time

• Multiple operations could be processed at once

Structure

The structure of the Notifying Thread Manager pattern consists of two classes, the Client and the NotifyingThreadManager itself (Figure 3.1). The Client can be any class that will be the consumer of the operation provided by the NotifyingThreadManager. It must implement two additional methods to serve as the callbacks from the thread manager. The NotifyingThreadManager class implements a single method that will start the asynchronous execution. This method accepts the delegates for the two methods the client implements, as well as a reference to the actual Windows control that we will use to synchronize any callbacks.

Notifying Thread
Manager

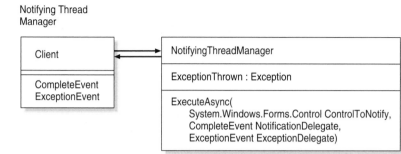

FIGURE 3.1: Notifying Thread Manager pattern.

Consequences

The Notifying Thread Manager has the following benefits and liabilities:

1. *It provides a simple calling methodology for asynchronous operations.* Because we are dealing with an asynchronous call, it is unavoidable that we need some mechanism to receive the results, but this pattern eliminates the need for the caller to know the thread management details by automatically resyncing with the calling controls thread.

2. *It can notify only one form on completion.* For simplicity of method calls and implementation, this pattern will support notifying only one target at a time. This is consistent with the intent of this pattern but should be noted.

3. *It does not address synchronization of data.* As implemented, this pattern accepts all data it needs to work on and returns the complete result set. Operations requiring any additional information from the user interface while executing will need additional synchronization techniques.

Participants

- Client—This can be any object derived from the Windows.Form.Control. It will be used to synchronize responses from the asynchronous operation back to the user interface.

- NotifyingThreadManager—This can wrap any operation that you might want to call asynchronously. It could be a long-running application, such as a lengthy calculation. It could be an operation that you cannot determine at development time how long it might take to complete, such as calling a Web service. It might even be a very short operation that you just want to initiate a number of threads to process simultaneously.

Implementation

The Notifying Thread Manager relies on the .NET concept of delegates to know what to do when the execution completes. Those familiar with C (or C++) programming will find this concept very common to function pointers. Those familiar with the "gang of four" (GoF) reference (covered in more detail in Chapter 2) will find it very similar to their Delegate pattern.

The *delegate* keyword in C# (*Delegate* in VB) allows you specify the signature of a single function type in a manner similar to how an interface allows you to specify the signature of an entire class. Once specified, you can create an instance of the delegate type to refer to a specific function and use the Invoke method of the delegate to call the original function. When calling Invoke, parameters are passed in just as though calling the original function.

The Notifying Thread Manager pattern will make use of two delegate types, one for successful completion and one for exception handling. The declarations for the delegates in this example are shown below. In our example, both delegate types take an ID and the value to be factored as the first two parameters. These values help the caller to tie the result back to the initial request when multiple requests are executing simultaneously.

LISTING 3.1: Notifying Thread Manager delegate definitions.

```
public delegate void CompleteEvent(int ID,
   ulong Factored,
   string Result);
public delegate void ExceptionEvent(int ID,
   ulong Factored,
   Exception ExceptionThrown);
```

The third parameter in both cases is the actual value we are going to act on. For a CompleteEvent, the result of the operation is passed to the caller. For an ExceptionEvent, the exception thrown is passed back to the caller.

The Notifying Thread Manager exposes only one method, ExecuteAsync, to the caller (besides the constructor). The entire purpose of this function is to store the information necessary to do the notifications and start execution of the wrapped thread. We will need to know the control that we will sync back with, as well as the two delegates to handle the result.

LISTING 3.2: Notifying Thread Manager ExecuteAsync method.

```
public void ExecuteAsync(System.Windows.Forms.Control
ControlToNotify, CompleteEvent
NotificationDelegate, ExceptionEvent
ExceptionDelegate)
{
    // Store the information we will need to notify on completion
    mControlToNotify = ControlToNotify;
    mFactoringComplete = NotificationDelegate;
    mFactoringErrored = ExceptionDelegate;

    // Start the thread
    ThreadStart startThread = new ThreadStart(DoExecution);
    mExecution = new Thread(startThread);
    mExecution.Start();
}
```

The ThreadStart instance is another example of a delegate. From the .NET documentation, you can find that the signature for any function wrapped by this delegate must take no parameters and return void. Our function, DoExecution, meets these requirements and will perform the bulk of our processing. Once the delegate is created, we pass that to the new thread we create for asynchronous processing.

In our sample application, we will be using a very slow factoring operation to act as our long-running operation. We have three ways to initiate the operation, either synchronously, using the Notifying Thread Manager, or using the Pollable Thread Manager (described next). The Notifying Thread Manager is available through any of the buttons to the right of the Notify label (Figure 3.2).

When a Notify request is added, a new DataRow is added to an internal Data-Table. This row is given a unique ID, and the start time is stored so we can calculate the execution time when complete.

The application then creates a new Notifying Thread Manager with the ID of the row added and the value to be factored. The ExecuteAsync method of the new object is called, passing the form object and delegates for both the completion and the exception cases, as shown below.

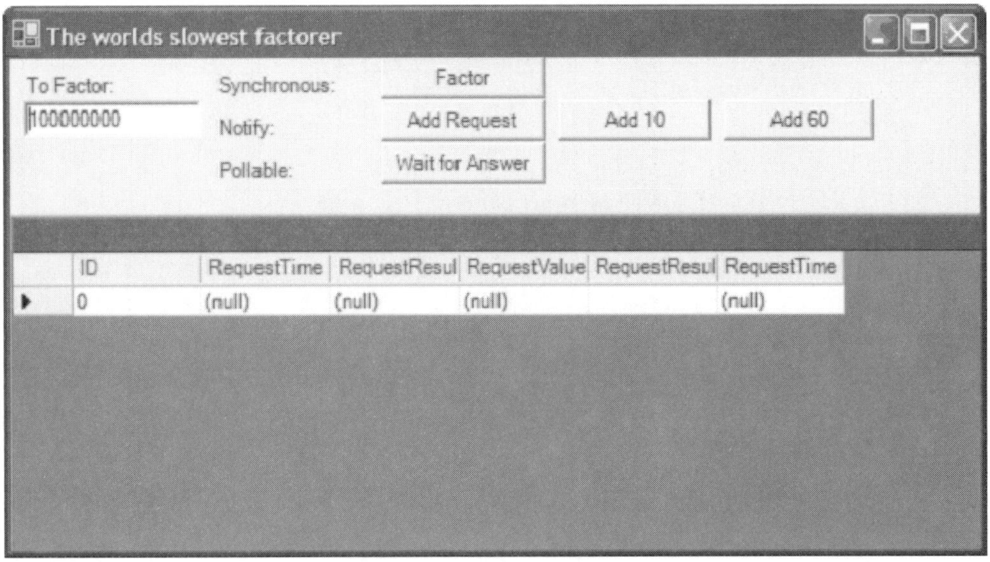

FIGURE 3.2: Sample threading application.

LISTING 3.3: Calling the Notifying Thread Manager.

```
    NotifyingThreadManager f =
new NotifyingThreadManager(rr.ID, rr.RequestValue);
    f.ExecuteAsync(this,
    new NotifyingThreadManager.CompleteEvent(FactoringComplete),
    new NotifyingThreadManager.ExceptionEvent(FactoringErrored));
```

As mentioned above, the DoExecution method does the actual work of this pattern. In our example, we use a separate class to encapsulate the actual operation to simplify readability of the example, but the actual implementation could just as easily have been included inline. Along the same lines, this function could also be a simple wrapper for a call to an external Web service.

In our example, the Notifying Thread Manager as seen in Figure 3.3 will call a static method on a Factorer class to retrieve a string containing all of the factors of an integer. This factoring algorithm was intentionally created to be as slow as possible.

As mentioned above, delegates typically call the delegate function by using the delegate's Invoke method. The only problem with this approach is that the call executes on the thread of the caller of the method. If we have multiple threads completing at the same time, we need to provide some method of synchronization to avoid overlapping calls.

FIGURE 3.3:   Notifying Thread Manager pattern.

The BeginInvoke method of the System.Windows.Forms.Control class provides the method that we will use to synchronize calls. This method executes calls on the thread that the control's underlying handle has created, taking care of the synchronization issues for us.

The drawback of this method is that the BeginInvoke method takes a parameter of the generic type delegate, which forces us to use an array of generic object values to pass values, rather than the type-safe Invoke method. This shifts type checking to runtime, rather than compile time, but the potential for problems is minimized because we are starting from a defined delegate type.

The result is a function in which the actual processing boils down to only one line. The majority of this method is in building the parameter arrays for either the success or failure of execution and initiating those methods.

LISTING 3.4: Notifying Thread Manager DoExecution method.

```
protected void DoExecution()
{
   object[] paramArray = new object[3];
   try
   {
      // Get the answer
      string strFactor = Factorer.Factor(mToFactor);

      // Build the parameter array for the completion event
      paramArray[0] = mID;
      paramArray[1] = mToFactor;
      paramArray[2] = strFactor;

      // Invoke the "Success" delegate
      mControlToNotify.BeginInvoke(mFactoringComplete,
          paramArray);
   }
   catch(Exception ex)
```

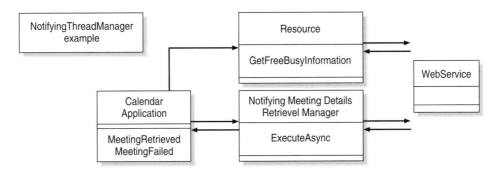

FIGURE 3.4: Notifying Thread Manager example.

```
{
    // Save the exception that occurred
    mException = ex;

    // Build the parameter array for the error event
    paramArray[0] = mID;
    paramArray[1] = mToFactor;
    paramArray[2] = ex;

    // Invoke the "Failure" delegate
    mControlToNotify.BeginInvoke(mFactoringErrored,
        paramArray);
    }
}
```

This pattern is very useful for any operation of which an application would want multiple simultaneous requests. Consider, for example, a calendar application that provides a scheduling interface (Figure 3.4). The application can retrieve all the meetings a conference room is scheduled for in one call but has to make a separate call to retrieve the details for each individual meeting.

The application can make use of the Notifying Thread Manage pattern to retrieve asynchronously the details for each of the meetings while the user looks at the current availability for the conference room. As the results from the individual calls come back, the Manager notifies the interface of the completion, and the user interface can update the details on the screen.

Related Patterns

- PollableThreadManager (Eshelman)

- MultiSyncThreadManager (Eshelman)

- Proxy (GoF)

POLLABLE THREAD MANAGER

Intent

Provide a framework for an initiating a long-running operation and periodically checking the completion status.

Problem

Although the Notifying Thread Manager provides a simple structure for calling an operation asynchronously, it assumes an event-driven application that does not have any sequential processing requirements.

In servicing a Web request, either for a service or a page, the developer does not typically have the ability to trigger notifications back to the client to indicate completion of the operation except for the actual response to the request. Once the request is complete, the operation needs to be complete.

Although it seems like extra overhead to make an operation an asynchronous fashion, there are situations were it definitely makes sense. Obviously, if there are multiple operations to be performed that are mutually independent, making the separate operations asynchronous will allow the process to take better advantage of multiple processors. This pattern will also help with situations where the user is periodically given an update of the status of the process.

Forces

Use the Pollable Thread Manager pattern when:

- Working with a request, immediate-response situation

- Operations require periodic update to users

- Multiple operations could be processed at once

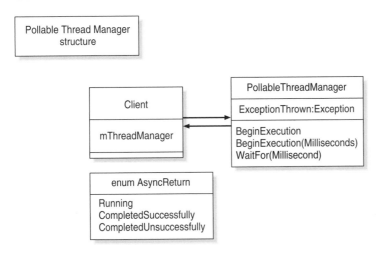

FIGURE 3.5: Pollable Thread Manager pattern.

Structure

This pattern also involves two classes, the client and the PollableThreadManager (Figure 3.5). In this pattern, the client simply holds a reference to the Thread Manager, rather than providing callbacks to the manager. The Manager provides three methods, two for initiating the execution and one to wait for the execution to complete. All three of the methods will return an AsyncReturn value, which is an enhanced Boolean value that can indicate the process is still running in addition to displaying a true or false indicator.

Consequences

The Pollable Thread Manager has the following benefits and liabilities:

1. *It provides a simple calling methodology for asynchronous operations.* As with the Notifying Thread Manager, the main object of this pattern is to simplify the calling structure for asynchronous operations. Although this seems somewhat contradictory, both patterns attempt to simplify the operation with different operational objectives.

2. *The client must periodically poll the thread manager.* If we are dealing with a Windows form, this will probably need to be done through some type of timer.

If this is being done for multiple operations for a Web request, all running threads will have to be periodically polled until all are complete.

3. *It will require tuning.* Because this pattern will provide the ability to set delays and polling frequencies, some tuning will be involved to determine the compromise that provides the best level of performance and user feedback.

Participants

- Client—In this pattern, the client can be any class that can periodically check for completion of the process execution.

- PollableThreadManager—Any operation for which you want periodically to check the processing status, especially operations that have a distinct number of steps that can indicate the progress of the operation.

- AsyncReturn—An enumeration that provides processing status, as well as completion success. In our example, we provide simply a running value, a completed successful value, or an unsuccessful completion value, but additional values can easily be added to indicate either percentage of completion or specific progress values.

CHALLENGE 3.1

When would you leverage notify versus polling in a threaded interface? Could you do both effectively?
The Multisync Thread Manager should provide you with a solution (next).

Implementation

Although the Pollable Thread Manager provides more methods to the client, the implementation is actually somewhat easier than that of the Notifying Thread Manager because delegates are not necessary for notification.

In our sample application, we use a separate form to wrap the calling of the Pollable Manager. This form creates and holds an instance of the manager as a member of the class in the form load method. The execution is also initiated at this time.

LISTING **3.5: Calling the Pollable Thread Manager.**

```
mExecute = new PollableThreadManager(mRow.ID, mRow.RequestValue);
mExecute.BeginExecution();
```

The method we use to initiate the execution, BeginExecution, is very similar to the ExecuteAsync provided by the previous pattern because the thread is initiated in the same way. The only two differences are that there are no delegates to store and that we give the caller the option of waiting for a specific amount of time before the initial call returns. For simplicity, an override is provided for Begin-Execution in our example to set the default wait to 1 second.

LISTING **3.6: Pollable Thread Manager BeginExecution method.**

```
public AsyncReturn BeginExecution(int MillisecondsToWait)
{
    // By default, we don't have an error
    mbError = false;

    // Start the thread
    ThreadStart startThread = new ThreadStart(DoExecution);
    mExecution = new Thread(startThread);
    mExecution.Start();

    // Give it a chance to complete before we go on
    return WaitForCompletion(MillisecondsToWait);
}
```

The return value of the above function allows us to return not only true or false but also the process still running value that makes this pattern possible. In a more complex implementation, this return might be expanded to include a percentage of completion in addition to a simple running value. In the event that a CompletedUnsuccessfully return code is received, the caller is expected to check the ExceptionThrown property to retrieve the actual exception that occurred.

LISTING **3.7: Pollable Thread Manager AsyncReturn enumeration.**

```
public enum AsyncReturn : int
{
    /// We have no idea how we got here.
    Unknown = -2,
    /// The transaction is not complete, yet.
    Running = -1,
    /// The transaction has completed unsuccessfully
```

```
      CompletedUnsuccessfully = 0,
      /// The transaction has completed successfully
      CompletedSuccessfully = 1
}
```

The WaitForCompletion method has the obvious potential to be called a large number of times and, although we are technically waiting anyway, we want to keep this function as small as is reasonably possible. This function will check to see whether the thread is still running and, if so, will wait for the specified time period for completion. The Join method provides our synchronization in this example by immediately returning true if the thread completes or returning false if it does not complete in the time specified.

Once we know the thread is complete, it is just a matter of returning Completed-Unsuccessfully or CompletedSuccessfully, as indicated by the mbError member.

LISTING 3.8: Pollable Thread Manager WaitForCompletion method.

```
public AsyncReturn WaitForCompletion(int MillisecondsToWait)
{
    // If the thread is either stopped or not running
    // yet, wait for it to complete
    if (0 == (mExecution.ThreadState &
             (ThreadState.Stopped | ThreadState.Unstarted)))
    {
        if (!mExecution.Join(MillisecondsToWait))
        {
            // We didn't finish yet, let the caller know
            return AsyncReturn.Running;
        }
    }

    // We have an error in execution
    if (mbError)
        return AsyncReturn.CompletedUnsuccessfully;

    // Success!!!
    return AsyncReturn.CompletedSuccessfully;
}
```

Our sample uses a timer on the form to periodically initiate our call to the Wait-ForCompletion method. If the method returns either CompletedSuccessfully or CompletedUnsuccessfully, the new status is set and the form is closed.

Again, DoExecution is our method that performs the actual work, and again, we are using a separate class to do the work, which results in a very simple function. The simple act of exiting the function terminates the thread, which allows WaitForCompletion to return Successful or Unsuccessful. In this pattern, we will store the result or the exception as a member of the class to be retrieved by the caller, once the above occurs.

LISTING 3.9: Pollable Thread Manager DoExecution method.

```
protected void DoExecution()
{
    try
    {
        // Get the answer
        mResult = Factorer.Factor(mToFactor);
    }
    catch(Exception ex)
    {
        // Store the exception
        mException = ex;
        // ...and the fact that we failed.
        mbError = true;
    }
}
```

If our calendar application example above used multiple Web services to retrieve the availability for the conference room, we might not want the user to be able to do anything to the calendar while the availability was being retrieved for the resource. The Pollable Thread Manager pattern can be used to wrap the multiple calls (Figure 3.6).

The application would begin the execution by calling BeginGetFreeBusyInfo and periodically updating the interface by using the WaitFor call to find out

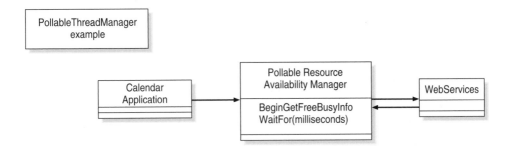

FIGURE 3.6: Pollable Thread Manager example.

whether the call is complete. The WaitFor operation can return a completion percentage, which is then used to set a progress status in the interface.

Related Patterns

- NotifyingThreadManager (Eshelman)

- MultiSyncThreadManager (Eshelman)

CHALLENGE 3.2

How would you call a Web service using the interface threading patterns shown here, and what best practices would you employ?
 The answer is in Chapter 4. By combining both the threading patterns with that of Service Factories (both Chained and Unchained), you should able to come up with a sound design for doing just this.

MULTISYNC THREAD MANAGER

Intent

Combine the Pollable and Notifying Thread Managers into one pattern that allows the client to use the best of both worlds.

Problem

Sometimes you need it all. Sometimes you not only want to be notified of completion of the operation but also want to be able periodically to check the status of the operation. In addition, sometimes you just do not know how the client will prefer to call your operation. In either situation, combining the Pollable Thread Manager and the Notifying Thread Manager gives the best of both worlds.

In processing a credit card transaction, for example, there are very distinct steps to be processed: verifying card information, contacting bank, etc. The application obviously has to know when the transaction is complete, but the ability periodically to poll the "processor" to know the status during the process helps the user to know something is going on. The application could request to be notified upon completion of the transaction but periodically update the user as to its status.

In developing a component for someone else to use, either as third-party software or even for other developers to use within the same organization, leaving the caller the option of how to call your operation greatly increases the usability of your components. The caller can choose to call your component periodically for status updates or may just fire off a call and do something else until notified of completion, based on what works best for their user interface.

Forces

Use the MultiSync Thread Manager pattern when:

- Client should have the ability to work in a Notifying mode, Pollable mode, or both.

Structure

MultiSync Thread Manager pattern (Figure 3.7) is simply a combination of the two previous patterns. The client can be any class but must be a Windows Control to use the event Notifying approach to execution. Execution can be initiated on the MultiSync Thread Manager either via the ExecuteAsync method, which requires you to provide the delegates to use for notification, or the BeginExecution method. The client can periodically poll the current execution status through the WaitFor method or just wait for notification. As in the Pollable Thread Manager, we use an enumeration to provide a more complete return code.

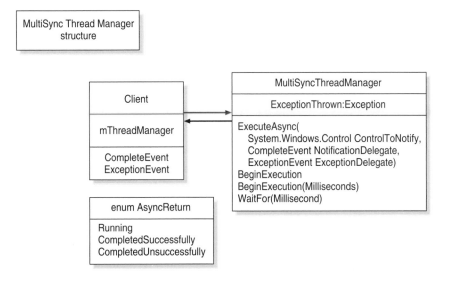

FIGURE 3.7: MultiSync Thread Manager structure.

Consequences

The MultiSync Thread Manager has the following benefits and liabilities:

1. *It provides options when calling asynchronous operations.* This pattern is intended to provide options to the client. You will probably notice the absence of the word *simple* here. Adding options will always add some level of complexity.

2. *It provides the best of both worlds* and the negative consequences that may go with them.

Participants

- Client—The client can be any class that can periodically check for completion of the process execution but must be derived from Windows.Form.Control in order to use the Notifying method of execution.

- MultiSync ThreadManager—Any operation that you want to execute asynchronously but want the flexibility to call either by polling for completion or by waiting to be notified of completion.

- AsyncReturn—An enumeration that provides processing status, as well as completion success.

Implementation

The implementation for the Notifying Thread Manager and Pollable Thread Manager intentionally allows for an easy overlap of the two patterns. The only change you must make from the previous two patterns will exist in the protected DoExecution method.

Starting from the DoExecution method of the Notifying Thread Manager, additional if statements are added to ensure that the control is not null before attempting to do the notification.

LISTING 3.10: MultiSync Thread Manager DoExecution method.

```
protected void DoExecution()
{
   object[] paramArray = new object[3];
   try
   {
      // Get the answer
```

```
    mstrFactor = Factorer.Factor(mToFactor);

    // If we have a success delegate defined, call it
    if (mControlToNotify != null)
    {
        // Build the parameter array for the completion event
        paramArray[0] = mID;
        paramArray[1] = mToFactor;
        paramArray[2] = strFactor;

        // Invoke the "Success" delegate
  mControlToNotify.BeginInvoke(mFactoringComplete,
            paramArray);
    }
}
catch(Exception ex)
{
    .
    .
    .

}
}
```

Related Patterns

- NotifyingThreadManager (Eshelman)

- PollableThreadManager (Eshelman)

ERROR CROSS-REFERENCE GENERATOR

Intent

Generate a unique ID to display to the user and store with any logged exception, which allows the user to report a specific ID to support personnel for tracking purposes.

Problem

Bad things happen to good sites. Eventually your Web site will experience an exception. The challenge is providing the users the information they need to help support personnel with the information to diagnose a problem and, ultimately, either correct the problem for the user or provide the developers with enough information to reproduce the problem.

Unfortunately, it is difficult to determine the right amount of information to provide to the user. Any technical information provided can be either overwhelming to the end user or even used against your site in a potential security exploit. If you provide too little information, either the tech support person cannot diagnose or the developer cannot track the error.

This pattern allows you to generate a unique ID for each exception that occurs. This ID should be included with every log of the exception information, as well as for the display of the exception message back to the user. In this way, the user can provide the ID to support personnel. The support personnel can use the ID to review any exception logs. If necessary, the support person can pass the information along to the developer for further investigation.

Forces

Use the Error Cross-Reference Generator when:

- You have one or more logs of error information to organize.

- Your application might have exceptions you want to identify categorically

Structure

The main class of the Error Cross-Reference Generator (Figure 3.8) provides one method, NextID, that does all of the work of the pattern. It is assumed that each ID generated will be "unique enough" in the context of the application. In other words, it will generate an ID that provides a unique ID without creating an extremely long value for a user to read back. The application must be sure to use the same ID in its response to the user as it does when logging errors.

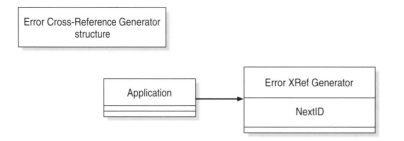

FIGURE 3.8: Error Cross-Reference Generator structure.

Consequences

The Error Cross-Reference Generator has the following benefits and liabilities:

1. *Provides a simple mechanism for correlating user errors to error logs.* By generating a unique ID that can be displayed to the user and stored in the logs, any errors stored in the logs can be tied back to the individual user.

2. *Requires an algorithm for generating the ID.* The algorithm needs to balance the need for uniqueness and ability for the user to read back the ID. An ID that is too long will make it easy for the ID to be read back incorrectly, making it next to impossible to track it back to the event logs.

Participants

- Application—self-explanatory

- Error Cross-Reference Generator—self-explanatory

Implementation

Our sample shows the Error Cross-Reference Generator pattern as used by Web-Form Template pattern described below. In this example (Figure 3.9), the Generator is used by the base class for all Web forms in the site to ensure that all exceptions provide a consistent display that includes the Error ID.

When an exception is thrown and renders the page or when one of the derived classes calls the SetError method, the TemplateBase class retrieves an ID from the Generator and stores it to make sure that only one ID will be used for all errors on the same page to be displayed to the user.

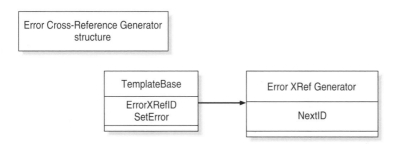

FIGURE 3.9: Error Cross-Reference Generator implementation example.

LISTING 3.11: Calling the Error Cross-Reference Generator.

```
// We only want to retrieve this once.
if (mErrorXRef.Length == 0)
   mErrorXRef = ErrorXRefGenerator.NextID();
return mErrorXRef;
```

The method we use to generate the ID in our sample is to combine a time-based value with a random number. The time value we use is the total number of seconds since the beginning of the month. Obviously, this value will repeat each month, but the application itself will display the actual date and time with the error message. The second part, the random number, is just in case we have more than one exception during a second. These are formatted as hexadecimal strings to shorten the value to be read back.

Related Patterns

- WebForm Template (Eshelman)

- Template Method (GoF)

WEBFORM TEMPLATE

Intent

Provide an automatic template framework that ensures that all pages within a site have a consistent appearance.

Problem

Many approaches exist to keep a consistent look and feel between all the pages in a site. Unfortunately, most approaches tend to require a significant level of coordination or setup to implement, either initially or on each page.

This pattern is intended to simplify creating the consistent interface, as well as integrated standard error handling.

Forces

Use the WebForm Template pattern when:

- You have a Web site for which you want to keep a consistent look across all the pages

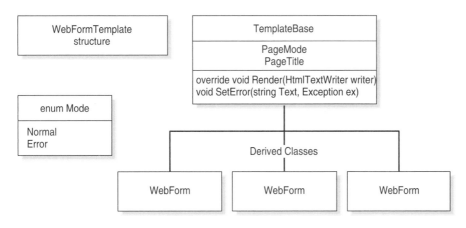

FIGURE 3.10: Rendering the WebForm Template—simple version.

Structure

The WebForm Template pattern (Figure 3.10) places most of the implementation in a base class for all Web forms in your site. This base class overrides the System.Web.UI.Control's Render method to take control of how the page is sent to the browser. Through this approach, we are able to add a consistent template to all pages.

In addition, standard error handling is provided through a SetError method that will allow all page-handling exceptions to be handled in the same way. In our sample, we set our PageMode to error when an exception is handled to indicate that a standard error message should be included in the HTML output.

Consequences

The WebForm Template has the following benefits and liabilities:

1. *All standard look and feel can be automatically included by a base class.* The developer needs only to "clean" the default implementation provided by Visual Studio and change the base class of the code behind the class.

2. *Any additional variants can be easily added.* Variations from the standard look and feel can be easily implemented by adding properties for the derived classes to set. For example, a printable page mode could be added that replaces the standard templates with the absolute minimum necessary to provide a "better" page for printing.

3. *Error handling can be easily standardized.* In our case, we use the Error Cross-Reference Generator to allow the user to help the support personnel in diagnosing the error.

4. *Visual Studio does not like you to remove the main HTML tags.* This is more of an annoyance than anything else, but because this pattern requires you to remove the HTML, HEAD, and BODY tags, an HTML error will always exist in the task list, at a minimum. At worst, I have experienced a couple of instances where this caused the design environment not to work as expected.

Participants

- WebForm Template—By serving as a replacement base class for all Web forms, this class enforces the consistent look and feel across the site.

- Derived Classes—Each Web form in our site derives from the WebForm Template base class.

- All HTML other than the content specific to the page is removed.

- Error Cross-Reference Generator—Provides the incident ID to be displayed to the user to help any issues be diagnosed and addressed.

Implementation

The TemplateBase class takes advantage of the fact that the output for all Web-Forms ultimately goes through the virtual Control.Render method. Because of this, we can override the default implementation to surround the page with a consistent page frame. In its simplest form, the code writes the top portion of the template, renders the page, and writes out the bottom portion of the template.

LISTING 3.12: Rendering the WebForm Template—simple version.

```
writer.Write(TemplateTop());
base.Render(writer);
writer.Write(TemplateBottom());
```

In our case, we add the ability to send a standard error message to the page. This can be initiated by either the derived class or an exception thrown during rendering of the page. The derived class might set the PageMode to err by calling SetError at some point in the Page Load or Web form event processing. The rendering of the page is included in a separate try/catch block to ensure that any exceptions that might occur while rendering the page are caught, and the standard error message can be included.

LISTING 3.13: Rendering the WebForm Template—more complete.

```
writer.Write(TemplateTop());
try
{
   if (PageMode == Mode.Normal)
      base.Render(writer);
}
catch(Exception ex)
{
   SetError("Error rendering page (AAB)", ex);
}

if (PageMode == Mode.Error)
   writer.Write(ShowErrorSection());

writer.Write(TemplateBottom());
```

The initial setup of the pattern requires the initial template to be designed and "coded" into the template top and template bottom functions. Both functions make use of the .NET StringBuilder class to build a stream of HTML. Any variations or options of the standard template are simply included in the appropriate function. The sample implementation shows how the Page Title is included, both in the HTML head and the header of the page.

Each new Web form to be developed is added to the project in the standard way. Once added, all code other than the first line that includes the <% Page ... %> tag is removed (Figure 3.11). The base class of the code behind the class is then changed from System.Web.UI.Page to TemplateBase. The content of the page is then designed as any other page in the Visual Studio designer.

Related Patterns

- Error Cross-Reference Generator (Eshelman)

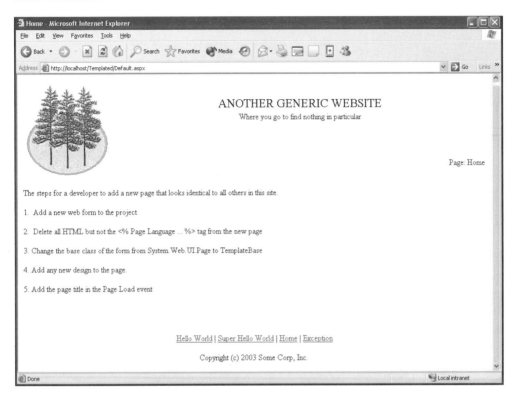

FIGURE 3.11: WebForm Template's default sample page.

DYNAMIC ASSEMBLY LOADER

Intent

Provide a pattern to simplify dynamic loading, interrogation, and caching of the types contained in an assembly.

Problem

The .NET framework provides a fairly complete set of classes to load and interrogate an assembly. This pattern enhances this functionality to simplify the retrieval of the type information from an assembly.

Once loaded, rarely will a type be used only once. This pattern will eliminate the need to return to the assembly each time the type is needed.

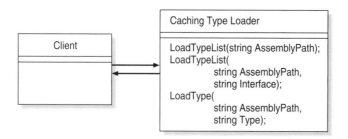

FIGURE 3.12: Dynamic Assembly Loader pattern structure.

Finally, when dynamically loading assemblies, the client application will typically be looking for a specific interface in the assembly. Because of this, a method is provided to retrieve only classes that implement a specific interface.

Forces

Use the Dynamic Assembly Loader pattern when:

- Assemblies need to be loaded at runtime without prior knowledge of the contents

Structure

The Dynamic Assembly Loader (Figure 3.12) consists of one class that does the work of loading and caching assemblies and a client that consumes the types that are loaded. The loader provides three overridden methods for retrieving types from an assembly. The first returns all types from the assembly that implements the specified interface. The second returns all types that implement a specific interface. The third returns a specific type from the assembly. Because the loader will cache what is loaded, the client is assumed to hold a reference to the loader.

Consequences

The Dynamic Assembly Loader has the following benefits and liabilities:

1. It provides a simple calling methodology for dynamically loading types from an assembly.

2. It does not simplify the construction process.

Participants

- Caching Type Loader—Provides the loading functionalities

- Client—Consumer of the types loaded

Implementation

This pattern uses .NET's reflection classes to dynamically load and interrogate an assembly. The main class used, the Assembly class, provides the ability to load an assembly from the full path.

Once loaded, each of the types is available through a collection. To create an object from a type, though, Reflection must be used to find and call the constructor to use to create an object. Anyone who ever had to use the IDispatch interface in the past will see the similarity in finding and calling the appropriate constructor (or any method). A sample of finding a constructor that takes an integer and string as parameters and calling that constructor is shown below.

LISTING 3.14: Constructing an object using Reflection.

```
using System.Reflection;


// Build the array that defines the
// parameter types that would be
// passed in to the constructor
Type[] types = new Type[2];
types[0] = typeof(int);
types[1] = typeof(string);
ConstructorInfo constructor =
myType.GetConstructor(types);


// Build the array of the actual values
// to be passed in to the constructor
Object[] objects = new Object[2];
objects[0] = 23;
objects[1] = "hello world";
object objDynamic = constructor.Invoke(objects);
```

STUNT DRIVER INTERFACE

Intent

Provide a mechanism for plugging any component into a generic black box test framework.

Problem

Testing is important, no question. Black box testing is a great way to validate a set of results against a given set of inputs. With a good test environment, black box testing can also be used to compare the speed of various implementations, do regression testing, perform stress/load testing, perform boundary value testing, etc. Typically, though, each component tends to need its own test scaffold, which makes it difficult to justify spending the time to build an environment that provides the functionality allowing for all the testing we would like to do.

This pattern is intended to allow a specific interface to be defined so that any class implementing can easily be plugged into an existing test framework, eliminating the need to rebuild each time.

Forces

The Stunt Driver interface (Figure 3.13) can be implemented for any class you want to test that:

- Has input(s) you can specify

- Has result(s) you want to review

Structure

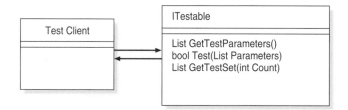

FIGURE 3.13: Stunt Driver pattern structure.

Consequences

The Stunt Driver interface has the following benefits and liabilities:

1. *It provides generic testability by implementing only two methods.* By defining the data types of the parameters needed to test the component (GetTestParameters) and a Test function that accepts the list of parameters (Test), any component can be plugged into a standard interface.

2. *It provides a place to store the default test case.* Even if the interface does not want to implement a method for storing a set of test values for testing the component, the GetTestSet provides a method for returning a number of test cases.

Participants

- ITestable component—Any component that needs to be tested

- Test Client—Client that provides the ability to load testable components, build test cases, store results, rerun for comparisons, etc.

Implementation

A number of simple implementations are included in the Calc and Factors project. I will describe the implementation of the Factors.Factor class, which adds the ITestable interface to the Factor class used for the threading patterns. This will be compared against the Calc.Add class, which takes multiple parameters.

The first method necessary is GetTestParameters. In my implementation, I am using the sorted list collection for the simplest implementation. This could easily be replaced with any collection, including a dataset or abstract packet, as appropriate. The Factor class needs only the input value to be factored so one item is added to the collection, indicating the name and type needed.

LISTING 3.15: Getting the test parameters from the Stunt Driver.

```
    public System.Collections.SortedList GetTestParameters()
    {
        System.Collections.SortedList list =
new System.Collections.SortedList();
        list.Add("Value", typeof(System.UInt64));
        return list;
    }
```

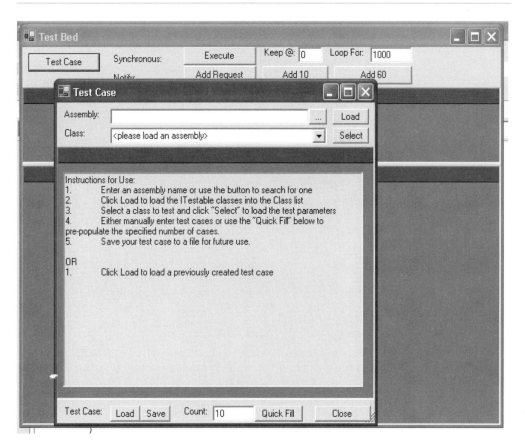

FIGURE 3.14: Configuring the Stunt Driver with the Test Bed sample interface.

It is assumed that the client will use this collection to provide an interface that allows individual test cases to be entered. The TestBed application provides a sample of one such interface behind the Test Case button (Figure 3.14) that creates a data table based on the result and allows the user to enter any number of rows, each having the values requested. In this case, each row would have one value that is a 64-bit integer.

To be honest, most of the time I don't want to have to input or remember the best test cases, so I created the GetTestSet method to speed the generation of test cases. In the case of the Factor class, the test sets generated are based on a set of random numbers to be factored. Again, this method uses the SortedList for simplicity implementation, but any appropriate collection could be used.

LISTING 3.16: Building a test set the easy way with the Stunt Driver.

```
public System.Collections.SortedList[] GetTestSet(
int Count)
   {
      System.Collections.SortedList[] alist =
new System.Collections.SortedList[Count];

      for (int i=0; i < Count; i++)
      {
         alist[i] = new System.Collections.SortedList();
         alist[i].Add("Value", r.Next());
      }
      return alist;
   }
```

Finally, to perform the actual test, the class must simply pull the value from the input parameter list and pass this to the method that does the actual work. Here, the class has the ability to pass back any result information desired by simply adding it to the parameter list.

LISTING 3.17: Testing with the Stunt Driver.

```
public bool Test(
ref System.Collections.SortedList Parameters)
   {
      System.UInt64 val =
UInt64.Parse(Parameters["Value"].ToString());
      Parameters.Add("Result", Factorer.Factor(val));
      return true;
   }
```

When dealing with more than one parameter as the input, it is just a matter of adding additional items to the test parameter list returned by the first method. For example, the Calc.Add class takes two values, so the GetTestParameters function would look like Listing 3.18:

LISTING 3.18: Adding items to the test parameters.

```
public System.Collections.SortedList GetTestParameters()
    {
        System.Collections.SortedList list =
new System.Collections.SortedList();
        list.Add("Value1", typeof(int));
        list.Add("Value2", typeof(int));
        return list;
    }
```

Each of the other methods needs only to retrieve or set the additional value.

Related Patterns

- Dynamic Assembly Loader (Eshelman)

4

Middle-Tier Patterns

OVERVIEW

Earlier in the book we explained how middle-tier patterns don't necessarily dictate a physical deployment designation. In reality, any of the following patterns, whether they are considered design-oriented, architectural-oriented, or the like, can be implemented and physically deployed anywhere in an application. The middle-tier "category" does not necessarily predicate that these patterns belong on a server somewhere physically separated from a user client. When considering the location transparency of Web services, what makes up a middle tier can mean any logical combination of pattern, structure, or logic. The only really identifying characteristic among these patterns is the fact that they typically help implement components that:

- Do not provide any graphical or console interface characteristics (aside from debugging, e.g., using trace output to a debugger)

- House business rules

- Do not directly interact with persistent storage

That does not mean these cannot be applied to some graphical interface or even be part of a sophisticated data persistence design. These patterns simply belong to the category most likely to house the nonvisual business rules of the application.

Because middle-tier patterns cannot simply be considered strictly "design" patterns, they are more difficult to classify. Depending on how you implement them, they may have the ability to be part of several more traditional categories (see *Design Patterns—Elements of Reusable Object-Oriented Software*[1]—GoF). For example, the *Product Manager* pattern can be considered both *creational* and *behavioral*. The middle-tier classification only helps group a broadened combination of "middleware-friendly" patterns without having to give them a more traditional classification that you would find in these other sources of information. That is the point. We wouldn't have even organized them at all except that they become difficult to reference once there are several patterns to select from. For these reasons, the following patterns can be classified as middle-tier patterns.

Most of the following examples keep with the general solution "theme" and use our credit card processing application to drive the example code. We cover the following patterns in this chapter:

Chained Service Factory—Creating a single entry point for Web services

Unchained Service Factory—A late-bound single entry point for the Web services

Product Manager—Handling unmanaged code in a managed way

Service Façade—Delegating complex logic from Web services

Abstract Packet—Passing complex parameter sets into Web services

Packet Translator—Translating those complex parameters sets

---

1. Erich Gamma, Richard Helm, Ralph Johnson, John Vlissades. Addison-Wesley, 1995. ISBN 0-201-63361-2.

With important (and related) mention to the following design patterns:

- Factory Method (GoF)

- Abstract Factory (GoF)

- Façade (GoF)

- Builder (GoF)

- Value Object (Sun)

- Proxy (GoF)

- Adapter (GoF)

CHAINED SERVICE FACTORY

Intent

Provide a single Web service method to allow the provider the flexibility of invoking different business functionality without directly affecting Web service clients. Provide a single entry point into a complex business framework.

Problem

Web service providers will eventually begin to provide Web services that go beyond accepting simple requests or providing simple responses. Not that Web services themselves need to complicated, but if they intend to be truly useful, the data sent to and from these services can become sophisticated. This pattern addresses the need for providing a Web service that not only performs a useful business function but also provides these services in a very flexible manner for invoking *any* business function. The single entry point is one of the first steps in defining what Microsoft has coined as a *service-oriented architecture.*

As providers begin to deploy these services, there will also be a need to change the logic behind those services. There needs to be a way to isolate the Web services client from these changes due to new features or altered implementations. Although no Web client can always be fully protected from future Web service functionality, the interfaces that they bind to should remain somewhat steady. The same goal of providing a standard interface "contract" to bind to (used in a more traditional implementation) can also be applied to the design of Web service methods. The Web service method can be thought of as just another interface contract to adhere to and, thus, should be generic enough to facilitate those inevitable implementation changes. This is the distinct difference between services and APIs. Services, or more specifically, serviced-oriented architectures, should be based on messages, not remote procedure calls (RPCs). The trick to designing this type of architecture is to focus on being service-oriented and not object-oriented at this service entry point. You'll have plenty of opportunity to apply OO heuristics to the inner plumbing of your service architecture later.

We solve this problem the same way we solve the problem in a typical OO application—by fashioning a Web service method interface "contract." The interface contract will then maintain its definition by accepting the same set of parameters (including the return values) for each Web client. The Web client just needs the interface definition of the Web method to invoke any business function within the framework supported by this Web method. Each Web client would then be protected from future changes while still allowing the Web service provider flexibility in changing its function implementations.

The challenge in providing this generic interface-based Web service contract is that the parameters passed in the Web method also must either be generic or their type representations must be dynamic. They must be flexible and instructive enough to be able to describe the functionality that a Web client wants to call. In essence, the Web service method must become both a "factory" and a "delegator" for locating and calling the requested business functionality. The requested functionality must be described not by the Web method but by the contents of the generic parameters passed.

We implement this as a single Web service method with a single signature— *Execute()*. The parameters passed to Execute() provide the routing information or "factory inputs." By using a generic data type such as an ArrayList or a string containing XML, the Web service method can use those parameters to determine which business function needs to be created and called. The Web service method then becomes the "factory" for generating all requested business objects and becomes the single point of contact for all Web clients. In our example, all automated check processing or credit card authorizations function through the same Web service interface. The FinancialServiceFactory.Execute() is then called, whether it is a credit card customer requesting an authorization or a client requesting a credit report. Each request is funneled through the same interface and the same Web method. FinancialServiceFactory's job is to read the contents of the

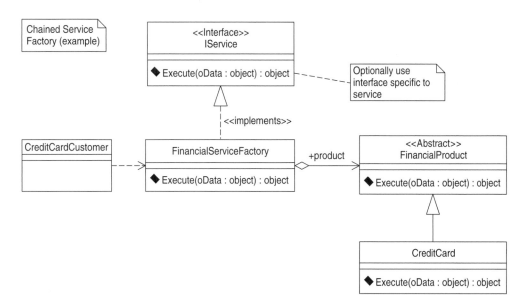

FIGURE 4.1: Service Factory implementation class diagram.

passed oData object, instantiate the appropriate FinancialProduct, and call the requested service. Figure 4.1 shows one possible implementation diagram of this pattern. To view the generic structure please reference Figure 4.2.

This presents another problem, however. What type is generic and dynamic enough to describe any functionality that each Web client may require of the Web service? If you are thinking XML, you are close. If you are thinking of XML schema definitions, you are even closer. The answer is the .NET DataSet. How did we arrive at that type? Well, DataSets are the perfect complement to a generic, type-safe data packager that not only understands an XML schema definition but also provides the developer with the facilities to manipulate them easily. See the Abstract Packet section later in this chapter; for an even deeper understanding, reference Chapter 5 for the technology backgrounder on XML schemas.

Forces

Use the Chained Service Factory pattern when:

- Business function interfaces may change in the future.

- Multiple Web service methods are provided on the server.

- Web service clients cannot be controlled.

- Changing client code would be difficult.

Structure

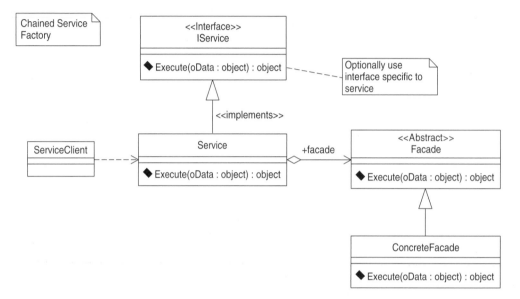

FIGURE 4.2: Service Factory generic class diagram.

Consequences

The Chained Service Factory has the following benefits and liabilities:

1. *It provides a single entry point into the system.* Due to the fact that only one method acts as the entrance into the framework, this allows greater control over who is calling into the system and more control over interface standards. It also provides a simple way of announcing services to the provider. Frameworks and services (especially within a large organization) are constructed all of the time. The key to selling them is providing a simple yet generic approach to calling the functionality.

2. *Eases system monitoring.* Because all traffic is routed through this single point of contact, monitoring the system becomes simpler. Using HTTP monitoring

applications (such as IIS Loader) simplifies the developer's profiling efforts because system load can primarily be determined through this one entry point.

3. *It isolates any Web client from Web method signature changes.* As stated in the above section, it gives a single entry point into the system and a generic signature that allows future services to be provided without affecting the external interface. This eliminates unnecessary Web service client proxy generations from occurring.

4. *It provides the ability to add future framework objects into the system.* Related to item 3, this also allows future subframeworks to be added easily into the system. For example, if all back-end business logic could be controlled by a primary controller object (see the Service Façade section in this chapter), that controller would be the instantiated target of the Chained Service Factory object. The Chained Service Factory would only need to be passed the service (from the client), at which time it would instantiate and delegate the business logic to that "controller." This places another level of abstraction and delegation into the model but it allows future "controllers" to be "plugged" into the system. This would allow not only changes to business functions but also additions to completely different sets of services. In our example, the primary set of business services involves credit card authorizations. For example, a scheduling system could then be built in the future. It could schedule any number of generic events, such as administration activities, batch reporting, etc. Adding another "free standing" scheduling façade into the system would now be much simpler. The Web client can then still activate this new set of functionality, using the same primary interface or entry point that was used for credit card authorizations.

5. *Calling* simple *Web service-based business functions requires more setup.* Although this design promotes the above benefits, it also introduces a bit of complexity when exposing "simple" functionality. Calling any Web services in this fashion involves preparing the parameters using a generic scheme. In our example, the data type I use happens to be a DataSet. This DataSet can be then populated with a least one row of information providing the metadata that can then be used to determine which business service and specifically which methods should be called. The metadata can be of any schema. That is the point. You now have the freedom to come up with any configuration of parameter data that you see fit.

Datasets do not have to be used but for our example, this seems to be the best and most flexible approach. The DataSet would be a single, generic, self-describing package that the Web client uses to request a specific back-end business function, using the Chained Service Factory as its entry point. The problem with designing such a sophisticated self-describing parameter is that now you are forcing the Web client to package its parameters for each and every call. This packaging occurs even for simple service requests unless you provide an entirely different Web method. For some cases, building a complex set of metadata commands and packaging them up just to call a simple business function via Web service may seem like overkill at times. It may be prudent to design a Web service method and separate interface for those cases. The designer must also take into consideration that passing complex types to Web service methods using a data type such as a .NET DataSet requires SOAP as the calling protocol. This means that the designer will not be able to test the Web service from a standard browser utilizing a simple HTTP GET or POST action and, thus, must create a custom test harness to test the Web service.

Participants

- ServiceClient (CreditCard Customer)—A Web service client for the credit card customer. This becomes the Web service proxy.

- Service (Financial Service Factory)—Contains a Web method that acts as a single point of entry into the system. This entry point unpackages the service request, instantiates the correct service (e.g., Service Façade), and calls a standard method on that service.

- Façade (Financial Product)—Defines a factory method to route the business request to the appropriate product. This is the entry point for each set of business functionality. It may contain all the business rules for a particular business category or may further delegate business behavior. This is usually an abstract or implementation parent that can contain logic such as data object construction or data preparation code (see the *Packet Translator* section in this chapter).

- ConcreteFaçade (Credit Card)—Implements the factory method for the business request. This entity optionally acts as a "controller" or Service Façade to other subordinate downstream business objects.

Implementation

The word *chained* in the pattern name comes from the fact that the instantiated service, which is created by the Web method, is early bound to that Web service. In other words, the Web method knows at design time what types it will be creating. When a credit card client calls Execute() on the FinancialServiceFactory, this method acts as a factory to any FinancialProduct derived class. The oData parameter passed can be of any generic data type, as long as it holds descriptive parameter data. Descriptive data refers to a form of "metadata" that can be used to describe what business functions the client wishes to invoke. The client's responsibility is to provide the metadata and package it is using with the rules defined by the Web method on the server. The metadata can take any form and be held using several generic types, as long as that type is flexible enough to contain this metadata and can be easily marshaled across the established invocation boundary.

In Listing 4.1, once the metadata is packaged and passed to the Web service, it is then used by the FinancialServiceFactory to instantiate the appropriate financial product—the CreditCard object in our example. The following code displays the signature of the Web method within the FinancialServiceFactory object. Notice the single parameter used to pass the data to the Web service. A .NET DataSet was chosen here due to its flexibility. A DataSet can then be used not only to contain this metadata but also to contain all of the actual data passed to the requested business function. The metadata can then be contained within a separate DataTable type as part of the DataSet. Other DataTables containing the actual data to be processed by the business function can also be passed without requiring the Web service to hold state between method invocations. All metadata and instance data is passed with one call to the Web method. The metadata is interrogated, the appropriate service is instantiated (see switch/case statement), and a standard method is called on that service. From that point on, it is up to the service (or FinancialProduct in our example) to disseminate it from there.

LISTING 4.1: Service Factory method sample implementation.

```
[WebMethod]
public DataSet Execute(DataSet dsPacket)
{
DataSet ds = new DataSet();
    FinancialProduct oProduct = null;
    string sService;
```

```
// call static translator method to extract the service
// name for this packet
    sService = PacketTranslator.GetService(dsPacket);
    switch (sService)
    {
        case Constants.PAYMENT_SVC:
            oProduct = (FinancialProduct) new CreditCard();
            break;
        case Constants.REPORT_SVC:
            oProduct = (FinancialProduct) new CreditReport();
            break;
        default:
            return ds;
    }
    // invoke the DoOp factory method on the facade
    ds = oProduct.Execute(dsPacket);
return ds;
}
```

Like any factory, a switch case statement is used to instantiate and early bind the CreditCard product to the FinancialServiceFactory. The financial product is determined in this example by a string value passed in the oData parameter. More specifically, the string is passed as part of a metadata DataTable as part of the passed-in DataSet (oData). The string is extracted from the Dataset's DataTable, as shown. A DAL (Data Access Layer) object is used to ease our work with the database (to see how the DAL is implemented, please reference Chapter 5. The data access specifics can be ignored for now; simply pay attention to the how the metadata column is accessed to extract the value of the service type. The returned *string* is then used by the *switch* statement above to determine which FinancialProduct to instantiate. Because both the CreditReport object and the CreditCard object inherit from the abstract type FinancialProduct, the lvalue in our case can be typed as the abstract type and its factory method called. Once Execute is then called on our instantiated FinancialProduct, that specific product can then disseminate the passed data as it sees fit. Listing 4.2 shows the helper method used to extract the service type from the incoming metadata.

LISTING 4.2: Service Factory metadata helper method.

```
public static string GetService(DataSet ds)
{
DAL oDAL = new DAL();
    string sValue = null;
```

```
// grab first and only row of the meta table passed as part of
// the dataset
    oDAL.Data = ds;
object oTemp = oDAL[Constants.META_TABLE, "SERVICE_COLUMN"];
    if (oTemp != null)
         sValue = (string)oTemp;
    else
         throw new Exception("…");

    return sValue.TrimEnd();
}
```

For example, if the Credit Card customer passes CreditCard as the service, it is used to instantiate the CreditCard class from the FinancialServiceFactory. Where this pattern differs from a typical factory method (GoF) is that it uses a Web service method to invoke the factory. It also differs in that it uses a generic data type to hold any of the parameters passed from any Web service client (a credit card customer, in this case). The DataSet is that generic type. A DataSet was chosen due to the fact that it is SOAP-friendly and very dynamic in that it can hold just about any structured data. Using DataSets provides the architecture with the most flexible alternative. Another option would be to use an ArrayList or even a generic custom object.

A Service Façade pattern can be used to add yet another level of abstraction between the Financial Service Factory and the FinancialProduct objects. Instead of using the metadata to instantiate a FinancialProduct, a Service Façade instead could then be instantiated and called. The mechanism is the same as it is in this example, just with an added level of abstraction. This would provide the ability to plug any service into the framework at any time without affecting bound Web service clients. For example, a schedule system façade could be implemented and added to the framework. This would then allow any Web client the ability to call this new "broad-based" service using the same calling semantics as calling for CreditCard services. The client simply has to package the metadata as before except that now it will be requesting a different service. The only code that would be required to change is the switch case statement setup in the Web service method. This change is required due to the fact that .NET is inherently early bound. The class type must be known ahead of time (the Service Façade object, in this case) and must be instantiated specifically based on the metadata passed in by the Web client. In the next section, I show you another pattern, the Unchained Service Factory, that eliminates this early bound requirement. This is possible using .NET Reflection capabilities and will be explained in the upcoming technology backgrounder.

As you can see, this can be implemented with several levels of abstraction. The point and benefit to this is minimizing the impact on all of your current Web service clients while still providing your services the flexibility of adding new, more broadly based services to the framework at will.

Related Patterns

- Factory Method (GoF)

- Abstract Factory (GoF)

- Unchained Service Factory (Thilmany)

- Strategy (GoF)

UNCHAINED SERVICE FACTORY

Intent

Provide a single Web service method to allow the Web service provider the flexibility of easily interchanging the services without directly affecting bound Web service clients. Unlike the Chained Service Factory, however, this pattern uses .NET Reflection to implement late binding. Late binding allows the Web service the ability to instantiate any back-end business object without requiring code changes at the Service Factory level. Combining a factory object with the services of Reflection provides the design with a truly loosely coupled architecture on which to build.

Problem

This pattern solves the same problems as does the Chained Service Factory. The difference lies in the problem of forcing the developer to make changes to the switch/case code in the Service Factory class if any new business objects were to be added to the framework. Using Figure 4.3, if additional FinancialProduct derived objects were to be added to the system, the switch/case statement code in FinancialServiceFactory would have to change. The change would reflect the instantiation of the new class, based on that new service being requested by a complying Web client. As mentioned in the Chained Service Factory, business objects instan-

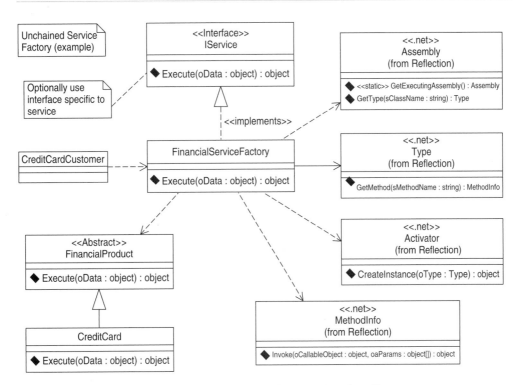

FIGURE 4.3: Unchained Service Factory implementation class diagram.

tiated by the "factory" in this manner are early bound to the service (thus the word *chained* in the pattern name).

Early binding means naming a type at compile time or design time (e.g., using the new keyword against a class)—in essence, building the vtable before execution. Late binding, on the other hand, refers to the technique of resolving a given type at runtime, as opposed to compile time. Late binding eliminates the need to know or name a type during design. It allows you to resolve and later reference a type and its members at runtime. This solution is then implemented in a much more dynamic and loosely coupled fashion. Although early binding will perform slightly faster in most respects, it does require recompilation of the code if any new features were to be added. Late binding protects the code from future deliberate recompilations. However, it does so at the penalty of slightly slower code performance. This is due to the fact that runtime type resolution generally will take longer than a vtable lookup. The tradeoff between slightly slower performing code versus increased flexibility must be weighed by you.

In the case of the Chained Service Factory, the added flexibility that is received by implementing late binding outweighs the slight decrease in performance. Using this pattern, however, only the initial instantiation and execution of the factory method is actually late bound. From the point of instantiation and initial execution onward, the remaining business object will be known and, thus, early bound. Also, the fact that there are only a few types needing to be resolved increases the benefit received from using late binding.

The Unchained Service Factory shows how using Reflection can aid you in eliminating code changes to the Service Factory. No longer does there need to be a fixed switch/case statement where each class must be predetermined and instantiated with the new keyword. The Web client requests the service as before by bundling the service request in some generic type, such as our DataSet. Instead of building of a switch/case statement, the developer can now extract the service name from the metadata and using that string, dynamically instantiate the target business object by name. Besides using .NET's Reflection classes (explained below), the designer also must name the targeted business objects using, at least in part, the same string that is requested by the Web client. Naming data types (classes, in our case) allows the developer to use text strings passed into the Web service method as our identifier of the class. This identifier is then used by the Reflection libraries to perform the runtime lookup and creation.

Anyone who has developed in Visual Basic, especially those who have built a similar factory using programmatic identifiers for this very purpose, should be already familiar with this technique. Using Visual Basic, a client could pass in a string of the programmatic identifier of the COM component they wished to create, and the receiving factory could then create that component on that value. Now that .NET no longer requires the use of programmatic identifiers (everything is based on name types), the type name itself must be used to provide this same feature. The difference here is that .NET is inherently early bound, and the developer must use Reflection to implement late binding.

Forces

Use the Unchained Service Factory pattern when:

- Business function interfaces may change in the future.

- Multiple Web service methods are provided on the server.

- Web service clients cannot be controlled.

- Changing client code would be difficult.

- Changes to a "chained" or early bound implementation of a factory would be inconvenient (to avoid having to edit code on a regular basis for all directly callable business functions).

- Late binding a publicly executable business function will not significantly impede performance.

Structure

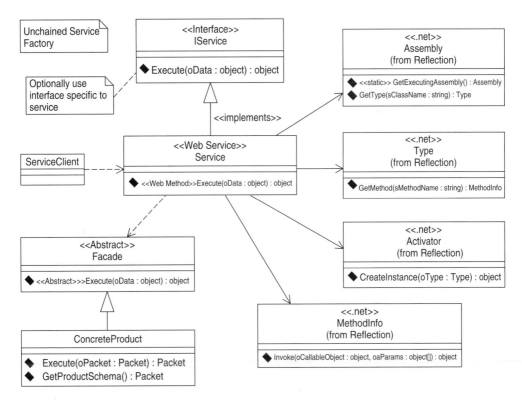

FIGURE 4.4: Unchained Service Factory generic class diagram.

Consequences

1. *Provides a true late-bound loosely coupled Web service.* Unlike the Chained Service Factory, the developer no longer must edit any code when business objects are added to the system. Using .NET Reflection services to invoke all initial

business objects, you can now easily add business objects into the system without forcing code compilations due to the factory having to early bind to any of the new business objects. This also isolates the Web clients from having to make any code changes on the client, even when calling significantly enhanced areas of the system, as long as the business objects added on the server conform to a standard contract and can be instantiated from the factory.

2. *Adds a small performance hit to the factory interface.* Using .NET Reflection services to instantiate the business object at that factory interface will slightly decrease performance. This is due to the fact that a business service must be "discovered" at runtime and, therefore, cannot be early bound. The impact should be minimal because all business services from the initially instantiated business object inward should be early bound. Only the initially instantiated business objects (FinancialProduct) or façades require reflection.

3. *Provides a single entry point into the system.* As stated in the above pattern, only one method acts as the entrance into the framework. This allows greater control over who is calling into the system and more control over interface standards. It also provides a simple way of announcing services to the provider. Frameworks and services (especially within a large organization) are constructed all of the time, but the key to selling them is providing a simple yet generic approach to calling them. With Reflection, any business function can be represented.

4. *Eases system monitoring.* As stated in the above pattern, because all traffic is routed through this single point of contact, monitoring the system becomes simpler. Using HTTP monitoring applications (such as IIS Loader) simplifies the developer's profiling efforts because system load can primarily be determined through this one entry point.

5. *It isolates any Web client from Web method signature changes.* As stated in the above section, it provides a single entry point into the system and a generic signature that allows future services to be added without affecting the external interface.

6. *It provides the ability to add future framework objects into the system.* Related to item 3, this also allows future subframeworks to be added easily into the system. See the Chained Service Factory section for details.

7. Calling *simple* Web service-based business functions requires more setup. See the Chained Service Factory section for details.

Participants

- ServiceClient (CreditCard Customer)—A Web service client for the credit card customer. This becomes the Web service proxy.

- Service (Financial Service Factory)—Contains a Web method that acts as a single point of entry into the system. This entry point unpackages the service request, instantiates the correct service (e.g., Service Façade), and calls a standard method on that service.

- Façade (Financial Product)—Defines a standard method to route the business request to the appropriate product. See the Chained Service Factory section for details.

- ConcreteFaçade (Credit Card)—Implements the standard method for the business request optionally acting as a "controller" or façade to other subordinate downstream business objects.

- Assembly—.NET framework class. This represents the currently running assembly from which to load the requested objects.

- Type—.NET framework class. This represents the type of the requested object.

- MethodInfo—.NET framework class. This represents the method of the requested service.

- Activator—.NET framework class. The object that creates the requested object once all reflection types are identified and created.

Implementation

Implementing this pattern is identical to that of the Chained Service Factory with one exception. Instead of building of what could eventually become a large switch/case statement (depending on how many business object types will be created), the developer must now use Reflection. Using the data types from the System.Reflection namespace, we now dynamically instantiate our FinancialProduct object or any other requested object by name. In the first step of the Execute() method, the service string is extracted as before in the Chained Service Factory. A reference to the current running assembly is then retrieved (explained below), and the business object type we are looking to create is returned. Retrieving this type requires the string we packaged in the DataSet (returned in the PacketTranslator.GetService()).

Once retrieved from the helper method, the string is concatenated to a fully qualified path that tells the reflection method GetType() which object we are looking for. Once the type is returned, we can create the object in memory by calling CreateInstance() using a Reflection "Activator." Don't worry, all of the Reflection material will be explained shortly. From that point on, we retrieve a method to call, bind our parameters, and invoke the method. The trick to calling any method in our newly created business object is guaranteeing that the method signature of that business object will always be consistent. Not providing a standard method signature on a creatable and callable business object in this design would significantly complicate the code. In fact, all business objects in this example implement a factory method themselves, which is called, you guessed it, *Execute()*. This is not a hard requirement, but it will make plugging in future business objects (that will be "launchable" from this Service Factory) much simpler and much cleaner.

Listing 4.3 shows this in action.

LISTING 4.3: Unchained Service Factory implementation using Reflection.

```
[WebMethod]
public DataSet ExecuteLateBound(DataSet dsPacket)
{
    DataSet ds = new DataSet();
    Assembly oPMAssembly = null;
Type oFacadeType = null;
    object oFacade = null;
    MethodInfo oFactoryMethod = null;
    object[] oaParams = null;
    string sService;

    // GetService code listed in ChainedServiceFactory section
sService = PacketTranslator.GetService(dsPacket);

// load the assembly containing the facades
    oPMAssembly = Assembly.GetExecutingAssembly();

// return the type and instantiate the facade class based
// on the service name passed
oFacadeType = oPMAssembly.GetType("CompanyA.Server" + "." +
    sService + "Facade");
oServiceFacade = Activator.CreateInstance(oFacadeType);

// Return the factory method for the chosen facade
// class/type
    oFactoryMethod = oFacadeType.GetMethod("Execute");
```

```
// bind the parameters for the factory method - single param
// in this case - dsPacket (DataSet)
    oaParams = new object[1];
    oaParams[0] = dsPacket;

    // invoke the Execute factory method of the chosen facade
    ds = (DataSet) oFactoryMethod.Invoke(oFacade, oaParams);
    return ds;
}
```

To understand the code completely, however, we need to dive a little into the .NET Reflection services.

Technology Backgrounder—.NET Reflection Services

For those who've been developing Java applications for some time, Reflection should be very familiar. In fact, .NET's implementation of its Reflection services matches that of Java's, almost feature for feature. For the rest of the folks who have not worked with any form of Reflection services before, this may seem a bit new. For COM developers, introspecting services through a set of standard interfaces is nothing new. Utilizing the basics of COM development and the QueryInterface() method, a developer can dynamically inspect the interface makeup of most COM components. Along those lines, using facilities such as type library information also provides a means for introspecting the types and services of binary entities. Reflection services provide exactly what the Java runtime intended—to provide a runtime programmatic facility to introspect and manipulate objects without knowing their exact type makeups at compile time.

Using types defined in the System.Reflection namespace in .NET, the developer can programmatically obtain metadata information about all data types within .NET. This can be used for building tools along the line of ILDasm.exe, where assemblies can be examined for their underlying makeup. Also, Reflection provides the ability to utilize late binding in an application that requires it (e.g., implementing our pattern). For those developing .NET/COM interoperability applications that implement late binding through IDispatch, this can also come in very handy. Using data types in the reflection namespace, one is able dynamically to load an assembly at runtime; instantiate any type; and call its methods, passing any of the required parameters. Instead of declaring those types at design time, the developer uses the abstracted data types included in Reflection. There are data types that represent objects, methods, interfaces, events, parameters, and so forth. To bind the generic types of Reflection with those that the developer actually wants to work with, normal strings are used to name them at runtime. This may seem a little strange until you begin working with Reflection types, so the best suggestion is just to start writing a few examples. Some of the more useful members of the System.Reflection namespace are included in Table 4.1.

The first data type in the reflection namespace you need to familiarize yourself with is the Type data type. This isn't a misprint; the actual name of the data type is *Type*. Type is a class that provides methods that can be used to discover the details

TABLE 4.1: Some Members of the System.Reflection Namespace

Assembly	Define and load assemblies, load modules that are listed in the assembly manifest, and locate a type from this assembly and create an instance of it at runtime.
Module	Discover information such as the assembly that contains the module and the classes in the module. You can also get all global methods or other specific, nonglobal methods defined on the module.
ParameterInfo	Information discovery of things such as a parameter's name, data types, whether a parameter is an input or output parameter, and the position of the parameter in a method signature.
PropertyInfo	Discover information such as the name, data type, declaring type, reflected type, and read-only or writeable status of a property, as well as getting/setting property values.
EventInfo	Discover information such as the name, custom attributes, data type, and reflected type of an event. Also allows you to add/remove event handlers.
FieldInfo	Discover information such as the name, access modifiers (e.g., public), and the implementation details of a field, as well as getting/setting field values.
MethodInfo	Discover information such as the name, return type, parameters, access modifiers, and implementation details (e.g., abstract) of a method. Use the GetMethods or GetMethod method of a Type object to invoke a specific method, as we do in this example.

behind other data types. However you cannot directly call "new" on the Type class. It must be obtained through another "type-strong" data type, such as our Product object below:

```
Product oProduct = new Product();
Type t = oProduct.GetType();
```

Another technique is to do something like this:

```
Type t = null;
t = Type.GetType("Product");
```

Something you will see quite often when using attributes or any other method that requires a System.Type data type—getting a Type object using the typeof() keyword:

```
Type t = typeof(Product);
```

Once we have a Type object, we can get to the objects methods, fields, events, etc. For example, to get the methods (once we have the Type object), we call t.GetMethods() or t.GetFields(). The return values of these calls return other data types from the Reflection namespace, such as MethodInfo and FieldInfo, respectively. Hopefully, you're starting to get the picture.

Finally, to get our pattern working, we first retrieve the current assembly by calling GetExecutingAssembly(). This retrieves an Assembly object so that we can later return a Type object representing a data type requested by the Service Factory:

```
    Assembly oPMAssembly = null;

/ load the assembly containing the facades
oPMAssembly = Assembly.GetExecutingAssembly();
oFacadeType = oPMAssembly.GetType("NamespaceA.ProductFacade");
```

Once we have the assembly, we can retrieve the business object using a normal string, such as the one passed to us in the Service Factory method Execute(). Once we have a returned Type object, we can now actually instantiate the object. This requires using what is called the *Activator class* in Reflection. The Activator is the key to implementing late binding in .NET. This class contains only a few methods, one of which is called CreateInstance(). Here we pass our newly returned Type object, which results in the runtime creation of our desired business object. Once our object is created, the next step is to bind parameters and retrieve a MethodInfo object to call. This is accomplished by first binding the method parameters as an object array, retrieving a MethodInfo type by calling GetMethod("<method to call>"), and finally calling Invoke on that newly returned MethodInfo type, as shown:

```
oFactoryMethod = oFacadeType.GetMethod("Execute");

oaParams = new object[1];
oaParams[0] = dsPacket;

// invoke the Execute factory method of the chosen facade
ds = (DataSet) oFactoryMethod.Invoke(oFacade, oaParams);
```

That's it. Now the developer can pass any data type string into the Service Factory, and as long the requested business object implements a standard interface, any object can be created. This is just the tip of the iceberg for the Reflection services, and I strongly urge you to explore other features of this powerful namespace for yourself. Be forewarned, however, that because there will be some performance penalty when using Reflection, it should be used sparingly.

Related Patterns

- Factory Method (GoF)

- Chained Service Factory (Thilmany)

- Proxy (GoF)

- Abstract Factory (GoF)

- Strategy (GoF)

CHALLENGE 4.1

When would you implement both Chained and Unchained Service Factory patterns as part of the same architecture?
See Chapter 6 on Product X to see why they did it (pages 303–309).

PRODUCT MANAGER

Intent

Provide a framework to which to migrate unmanaged code. Help isolate clients from semantically different technologies. Control "unmanaged" code in a more managed fashion.

Problem

When building a business services framework in .NET, unless you are lucky, you will have to support some form of legacy services (e.g., DLLs, COM components, or any unmanaged code). It is strange having to refer to existing COM components as legacy. This is especially true because COM+ is still used with .NET. However, when dealing with unmanaged pieces of code, more care should be given. Whether it is an existing framework that you are migrating from or some other third-party application that you must integrate, this issue will be there. The trick is not figuring out the bridging technology upon which to call these legacy services but how to still provide a clean design. How does one design a set of managed .NET code when some of those services will be using unmanaged services? How does one isolate the client from knowing or caring that the services it requests are actually being handled by unmanaged code?

For starters, abstracting a calling client from the back-end business services will help. This will isolate the technical differences apparent only in the object bridging those services. Those who have used the Abstract Factory (GoF) or Strategy Pattern (GoF) should be very comfortable with this design approach. The Product Manager takes a step further by combining these patterns (so to speak) to form a design that will not only provide a standard contract upon which to call any back-end business service but also a level at which to isolate any code that will act as the "bridge" between managed and unmanaged code. The main controller of any services exposed by either managed or unmanaged code is the client of the Product Manager. This client takes the form of a façade object in our example. Here, in the PaymentFacade, we control which product to instantiate and, using contracted methods on each product, ask the Product Manager to execute the requested service (Figure 4.5). The PaymentFacade object acts as the controller to the Product-Manager. It interacts only with the "contracted" interface provided by this abstract base class. All of the common business implementation code for this design is

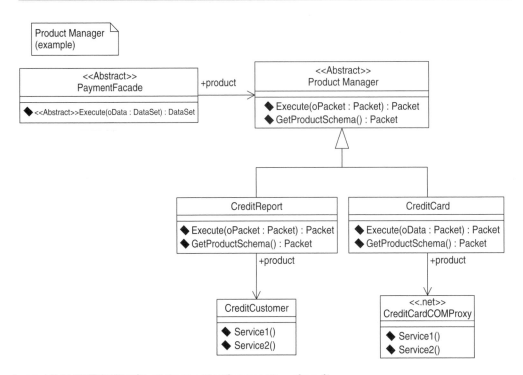

FIGURE 4.5: Product Manager implementation class diagram.

located in the ProductManager base class. Any of the product-specific implementation code resides in the child classes of the Product Manager. Specifically, code to handle unmanaged versus managed semantics will be located in these child classes.

For example, let's say you wish to use XML schemas to describe each underlying packet that is passed from object to object. Each packet can also be passed into each product class. To provide such a feature, the designer may wish to store that schema in a database and load a packet from that schema. This is something you will see in Chapters 5 and 6. Retrieving that schema from the database will be done in the same exact way, no matter which product child class the controller is talking to. Hence, this is some of the common code we are referencing. All the controller needs to know is that a schema must be retrieved to hydrate a packet. The common code for retrieving this schema can be easily placed in an abstract parent ProductManager class. This is part of the code common to both unmanaged and managed code.

Each product child object merely has to override methods that provide the base ProductManager class with the key to use to retrieve these schemas. All the database logic code still resides in the base class of the abstract ProductManager parent. Code specific to each product resides in the child product classes. This is object orientation 101. The difference is that all product-specific code to call unmanaged or unmanaged code remains in the child classes. The unmanaged product child class still benefits from any of this common code while still isolating the controller from any the differences through the use of the abstract parent.

For a product that must bridge older technologies such as a COM component, a product child class simply acts as the calling proxy to the underlying COM code. Using the model below, a CreditCard product acts as a normal client to the COM proxy code generated with the .NET/COM interoperability tools. Any COM-specific package or unpackaging occurs in this CreditCard product object. The CreditReport object is a standard common language runtime (CLR)-managed object. It can call other .NET help objects or be self-contained; it doesn't matter. The point is, neither the client nor even the controller class know or care that the back-end business functions running may be unmanaged code. This design also provides the unmanaged code access to common managed services. All in all, this pattern allows common .NET-friendly code to be shared in an abstract base class while isolating product-specific code in the derived product child classes.

Forces

Use the Product Manager Pattern when:

- Migrating old business services into a new technology platform.

- Bridging COM services from a .NET framework.

- Calling semantically different business services from a single interface, such as when using some form of "factory" pattern (e.g., Abstract Factory, Chained Service Factory, etc.).

- You want to leverage common code yet isolate technology-specific code from a common caller.

Structure

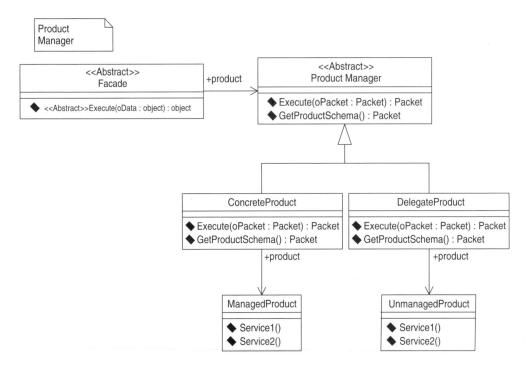

FIGURE 4.6: Product Manager generic class diagram.

Consequences

1. *Isolate technology-specific implementation details.* When building a framework that will employ calling unmanaged code, most likely there will be technology-specific nuances that will be included, for example, if the unmanaged code provides business services that would initially take too long to migrate fully over to the unmanaged world. The best solution would be to leverage off those services from the managed code. Typically, this is done with a bridge or proxy. Doing so may incorporate technology-specific details. However, that should not affect the "managed" architecture. If these unmanaged services were to be COM+ components, there may be some technology-specific attributes. These could include those that control transaction semantics or other COM+-specific attributes. Abstracting these details will help isolate calling clients and help decouple technology semantics within a framework aimed at creating managed-friendly semantics. The abstraction can be easily implemented using an interface imple-

mentation contract defined by the managed framework. Taking it a step further, an abstract class (ProductManager) can then be created to house common code that both managed and unmanaged products can share. All technology-specific code can then reside in the derived product classes, isolating the Controller Class (Façade, in our example) from implementation details.

2. *Provide a migration path to the new .NET framework.* Fully reengineering legacy business services is a luxury most development teams do not have. Leveraging those business services as much as possible usually is the best answer. Providing a migration path to the "new managed world" then seems to be the best architectural solution. By isolating technology details as mentioned in the previous consequence, the Product Manager provides a migration path to this managed world. External legacy services can then be incorporated into the architecture by deriving themselves by an abstract parent class that may contain managed code common to all services. The derived product class can then simply act as a client to the external services, as any other client would act if it were not implemented using managed code. The designer can then slowly migrate functionality to this derived product class without affecting common code.

3. *Leverages common managed code for managed calling proxies to unmanaged code (that's a mouthful).* Building a proxy to unmanaged code should also provide access to the common architecture code to which Product Manager objects have access. By implementing an abstract base class and placing all common managed code here (the ProductManager), the managed proxy to the unmanaged code will, through inheritance, still have access to it. This will promote leveraging as much of the new architecture as possible, even when calling legacy services such as COM components.

Participants

- Façade (PaymentFacade)—"Controller" class that acts as a client to the Product Manager. The façade, in this case, speaks only "Product Manager language." This simply means only public interfaces exposed by the Product Manager and implemented by the specific products will be callable from the façade.

- ProductManager (Same name as implementation)—The abstract base class for each product object in the design. There can be a Product Manager for each category of product. This contains the standard interface "contract" (abstract functions) that must be implemented by each derived product class. It also contains all code common to all products in the class tree.

- ConcreteProduct (CreditReport)—Contains all code for the business logic on the managed code side. This can be self-contained or it may aggregate other downstream business objects. It must implement all abstract members of the ProductManager to conform to the Product Manager's contract.

- ConcreteDelegate (CreditCard)—Contains all code for the business logic on the unmanaged code side. This usually acts as the gateway to the external service or unmanaged code. It must also implement all abstract members of the ProductManager to conform to the Product Manager's contract.

- ManagedProduct (CreditCustomer)—Optional helper class used to implement the managed business code fully.

- UnmanagedProduct (CreditCardCOMProxy)—This represents either the proxy code or the third-party services. In the case of calling COM components, this is the generated proxy code (using tblimp.exe utility or VS.NET). Whether a generated proxy or third-party library, this is any unmanaged code that the architecture wishes to leverage.

Implementation

One of the benefits of implementing the Product Manager pattern is its general applicability. Like similar patterns, such as Abstract Factory and Factory Method, this pattern can be applied to many scenarios through the architecture. There can be several difference Product Manager abstract classes. If the designer so chooses, there can be a single common Product Manager class from which to derive all product classes. The ProductManager class can be driven directly from a GUI-based client or from another business object, such as a controller or façade. In our example, we use a Façade object to manage the ProductManager abstract class. The PaymentFacade participates in the creation of the appropriate Product class (CreditCard and CreditReport, both derived from ProductManager). Because each Product class derives and implements the "contract" for the Product Manager, the façade calls only those interfaces exposed by the ProductManager abstract class (e.g., Execute()), as shown in Listing 4.4.

LISTING 4.4: Product Manager Factory Method implementation.

```
public Packet Execute(Packet oPacket)
{
      ProductManager oProdMan;

   switch (oPacket.Type)
     {
         case CREDIT_CARD_TYPE:
             oProdMan = (ProductManager) new CreditCard(oPacket);
             break;
         case PMConstants.CHECK_TYPE:
             oProdMan = (ProductManager) new CreditReport(oPacket);
             break;
         default:
             oProdMan = null;
             break;
     }
   return oProdMan.Execute();
   }
```

In essence, this code is acting as another factory on each product. In addition, it is calling the established "strategy" style interface to invoke the action on the product (see the Strategy Pattern section from the GoF). Once invoked, the product is able to disseminate the action by either further delegating the call or by handling the invoked business function immediately. In the "eyes" of the Execute() statement above, only the signature of the Product Manager is known. The fact that CreditCard is delegating to the proxy COM wrapper is unknown. Both CreditCard (forwards to unmanaged code) and CreditReport (forwards to managed code) look the same to the façade in this scenario. When Execute() is finally called on the CreditReport object, it looks something like as shown in Listing 4.5.

LISTING 4.5: Product Manager delegation implementation.

```
public override Packet Execute()
   {
        Packet oPacketOut;

        switch (Packet.Action)
        {
            case AUTHORIZE_ACTION:
                oPacketOut = Authorize();
                break;
            case CAPTURE_ACTION:
                oPacketOut = Capture();
```

```
                        break;
                case GET_PRODUCT_SCHEMA_ACTION:
                        oPacketOut = GetProductSchema();
                        break;
                default:
                        oPacketOut = null;
                        break;
        }
        return oPacketOut;
}
```

Here you see that, like the Façade object, the Execute method of the CreditCard product simply determines (by using another property of the packet) which business function this should delegate to. If the packet requests an "authorization," this will call a local method, Authorize(). Authorize() will delegate to a proxy object that was generated via tblimp.exe. The authorization will actually occur in unmanaged code, and the CreditCard product object is simply acting as a client to that code. This not only provides a migration path from COM services already written, but it also isolates the controller or Façade object from knowing when this is handled in unmanaged or managed code. The Authorize() method looks something like this (Listing 4.6):

LISTING 4.6: Sample Product Manager worker implementation.

```
public Packet Authorize()
    {
        Packet oPacketOut = new Packet();
        // COM Proxy object

        COMAuthorizer oAuthorizer = new COMAuthorizer();
        // .. build COMPacket from Packet
        oAuthorizer.DoOp(COMPacket, null);
        // .. build Packet from returned COMPacket
        return oPacketOut;
    }
```

Implementing the other product object, CreditReport in our example, is exactly the same. The difference is that CreditReport contains all managed code. CreditReport and CreditCard can each leverage common code contained in the abstract ProductManager. However, both can still contain technology-specific implementation details hidden from the outside world.

Related Patterns

- Factory Method (GoF)

- Chained Service Factory (Thilmany)

- Unchained Service Factory (Thilmany)

- Virtual Proxy (Grand)

- Abstract Factory (GoF)

- Strategy (GoF)

CHALLENGE 4.2

What other kind of products could utilize the Product Manager besides what is shown here?

See Chapter 6 on Product X to see (pages 296–303).

SERVICE FAÇADE

Intent

Encapsulate business logic using a "controller" class to become the primary entry point from which all business logic (usually of a specific business category) will be contained and/or driven. Provide Web services with single entities to call directly.

Problem

For this pattern, probably the simplest of all mentioned patterns in this book, the problem solved is also simple. When developing Web services in .NET, developers may immediately get the tendency to begin placing business logic within the code directly behind the Web service class provided by VS.NET. This includes any Web methods added to a Web service. The problem here is that, as you may already surmise, "cluttering up" this section with business rules and complex logic can soon become very difficult to manage. Another problem with this sort of "develop before design" approach is that if you desire to reuse those services elsewhere, it will always force the calling client to go through the Web service to do it. The architecture actually may "require" that all back-end business functions be called from a single entry point, such as a Web service. This is probably due to security and control. However, this may not be the most efficient means of invoking business services. Those who have already been developing Web services realize that there is a performance penalty when invoking a business function through a Web service if called as a standard Web service client.

To provide the "best of both worlds," that is, to provide an optional means to force all traffic through a Web service while also allowing other means of invoking controlled business functions, a Service Façade should be used. The Service Façade, like a traditional façade, simply provides a "controller" object to expose all public "callable" business functions to any external clients. The Service Façade becomes the server to the actual code directly behind that of the Web service and its Web methods (Figure 4.7). Instead of cluttering the implementation directly behind the Web method, this simply delegates calls to the appropriate Service Façade object. This also provides another means of invoking the business functions without forcing the client to go through the Web service or act as a Web service client. The Service Façade could be called from a standard ASP.NET implementation or another server component.

The difference between a traditional façade pattern and a Service Façade is "architectural," meaning that the Service Façade must take into account the possibility of both Web methods acting as a client to the façade and other non–Web-service clients. This is implementation-specific. For example, exceptions thrown from the Service Façade should take multiple clients into account, as well as provide a Web service-friendly error-handling mechanism. In some cases, you should avoid throw-

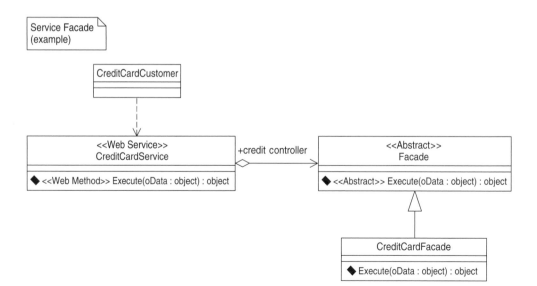

FIGURE 4.7: Service Façade implementation class diagram.

ing exceptions altogether or in some designs do so when transactions are logged. The point is that Web service clients may need to be taken into account at this level.

Forces

Use the Service Façade Pattern when:

- Implementing complex business logic that may be called externally.

- Servicing multiple clients from a Web service.

- Code becomes too complex to place directly into a Web service class.

- The design calls for categorizing business functionality that may contain different means of handing architectural features, such as exception handling, logging, security, etc.

- Web service class inherits from System.Web.Services.WebService and must also inherit from another base class in order to receive additional functionality, such as when needing to derive from System.EnterpriseServices.ServicedComponent. (This is the case when the controllers become COM+ components, because multiple-implementation inheritance is not supported in .NET.)

Structure

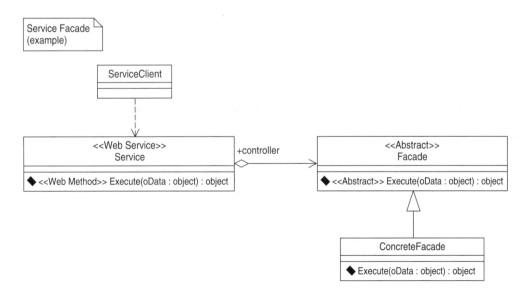

FIGURE 4.8: Service Façade generic class diagram.

Consequences

1. *Eliminates having to place complex logic within the language implementation of a Web service or ASP.NET file directly* (aspx or asmx source). Instead of "cluttering up" the source code directly within a Web method, the developer should utilize a Service Façade class. A Service Façade is strictly a façade that coordinates and houses complex business logic for a specific business category.

2. *Provides manager for specific business areas.* A Service Façade also acts like a traditional Façade pattern in that it manages specific business areas, providing high-level business functions typically exposed to the public. The exposed business functions in this case will be accessible to the Web service. A Web method can be defined for each publicly exposed façade function, or functions can be grouped into single Web method. Using a single Web method was explained in the Service Factory sections in this chapter.

3. *Provides an entity in which to house Web service-specific exception handling.* When throwing exceptions to external calling clients, the architecture must take into the account the tier that will be directly callable. In the case of the Service Façade, any Web service clients will be indirectly calling the Service Façade because the Web service stands between the client and the Façade class. In order for some clients to receive rich error-handling adjustments, there may need to be adjustments made to the architecture, depending on where the client is located.

4. *Provides an entity in which to house Web service-specific parameter passing.* Along the same lines as the above point, passing data between tiers physically located on the same machine could be quite different. There may be architectural scenarios, such as when the calling protocol uses SOAP, where changes to the parameter passing scheme need to be made. These architectural adjustments could be housed within the logic of the Service Façade. Neither the callable business object within the system nor the Web service class itself should be cluttered with this type of logic. Doing so will provide a more reusable design.

Participants

- Service (CreditCardService)—This is any Web service containing Web methods. Each Web method calls a requested exposed business method on the façade. This can be specific methods or simply (as in our case) a single interface method (e.g., Execute()). The Web service simply becomes the direct interface to the Web client. The Web method does not contain any business-specific functionality. The business rules are all delegated to the ConcreteFacade class or any of its optional parent entities.

- Façade (Same name as implementation)—Base class for any façade classes that act as a controller to any service. The façade, in this case, speaks only the "language" of the business as it publicly exposes high-level business functionality. This simply means that only public interfaces are exposed to its Web method clients. Web service client requests are delegated from a Web method to the Service Façade.

- ConcreteFacade (CreditCardFacade)—The main implementer of the publicly available business interface. This class could be self-contained or could delegate to other specialized business objects. Most business rules are contained or driven from here, especially those related to packaging data that must be sent back to the Web service client.

Implementation

The beauty of the Service Façade pattern is that is it simple. It requires more forethought only when it begins to provide the facilities to take into account its Web service clients (as mentioned earlier). Such facilities include handling exceptions or parameters in special ways. However, features such as these are implementation-specific. How to design exception handling or data passing is really another topic and is covered in Chapter 2. The Service Façade, however, provides the construct within which to build these features so that once again, the code directly "behind" the Web methods remains clean, and the business services housed by the Service Façade remain reusable. Implementing the Service Façade is very similar to any of the controller or manager classes that I'm sure you have designed in the past.

Keep in mind that the Service Façade, like a traditional façade (GoF), is the driver of publicly available business logic. It should require more forethought if you are designing a more complicated system (no kidding, right?). The point is, if there will be several categories of business functionality, different approaches should be considered. One implementation approach would be to use an abstract class or interface from which to derive each façade. In fact, this is what our example uses. This is certainly not a requirement and shows only one implementation. Another approach is to create a full implementation-inheritable base class for all façades.

The choice is yours and depends more on how the Service Façade itself will be implemented. For example, if you building a mission-critical system that must support multiple clients, shared resources, and possible transaction management, then implementing your Service Façade classes as COM+ components may be a wise choice. If this is the case, you should use either a simple interface or a full base class as the parent to your Service Façade. The reason is that .NET does not support multiple inheritance. Deriving from more than one base class is not permitted unless the class you are also deriving from is an interface. If you are a Java programmer, you are already familiar with this rule. Because adding COM+ features requires inheriting from the System.EnterpriseServices.ServicedComponent, you could make the parent Façade class inherit from it, thus gaining this functionality for each Service Façade child class. You could if your parent Façade class was an abstract class and you still wanted to derive from another base class, but it would seem odd and would not (considered by some) be the cleanest of designs. For our example, I use an abstract base class with the option of knowing that this could be relatively easy to change to an implementation base class if I so desired. We could then incorporate COM+ features by using ServicedComponent as its base class. For now, let's just stick with an abstract parent class to the Service Façade (Listing 4.7).

LISTING 4.7: Service Façade sample implementation.

```
public class PaymentFacade : Façade  // Façade is abstract
{
private ProductManager m_oProduct = null;

    public PaymentFacade(){;}
public PaymentFacade(DataSet RawPacket) : base (RawPacket){;}
    public PaymentFacade(Packet oPacket) : base (oPacket){;}

    public override DataSet Execute(DataSet dsPacket, bool bCache)
    {
        Packet oPacket;

        // builds the packet from the raw dataset
        PreparePacket(dsPacket);

        if (Product == null)
{
            Product = CreateProduct(GetPacket());if (bCache)
            {
                Product.PrepareCache();
            }
```

```
            }
            else{
                Product.Packet = GetPacket();}
            oPacket = Product.DoOp();

            // return raw packet back to caller
return PreparePacket(oPacket);  // this returns a DataSet
    // from a Packet using the
    // PacketTranslator
            }

            public ProductManager Product
            {
                get { return m_oProduct; }
                set
                {
                    m_oProduct = value;
                }
            }

            public ProductManager CreateProduct(Packet oPacket)
            {
                ProductManager oProdMan;

    // packet type should have been set during PreparePacket()
    // in calling DoOp...
                switch (oPacket.Type)
                {
                    case Constants.CREDIT_CARD_AUTH:
oProdMan = (ProductManager) new Product1(oPacket);
                        break;
                    case Constants.CREDIT_CARD_SETTLE:
                        oProdMan = (ProductManager) new Product2(oPacket);
                        break;
                    default:
                        oProdMan = null;
                        break;
                }
                return oProdMan;
    }

    // for testing only..
    public object SomeOtherBusinessFunction()
    {
            //…
    }
}
```

The Service Façade, once you take away some of the mentioned design options, is really a container with publicly accessible business methods. This example uses a single point of entry into the façade, as was demonstrated in the Service Factory sections earlier in this chapter. This was done to allow the Service Façade not only to be called from within a Web method but also to be used in the factory. This implementation, once plugged into a factory, delegates all specific business details to a Product Manager class (also described in this chapter). The PaymentFacade below is a ServiceFacade in charge of all credit card payment transactions. It can be called by several different Web methods (e.g., CreditCardAuthorize, Credit-CardSettlement). Although most of the specific business rules are delegated to other classes, this façade understands one service type—payments. In essence, it is the kernel of the payment system. Using the data from the passed DataSet (e.g., Packet.Type), it will determine which Product class (e.g., CreateProduct()) should handle the incoming transaction. In our example, this is also where the packet is "prepared" and transformed into a more malleable data format, one that the business components of this type can easily work with. As you can probably surmise, this is only the tip of the iceberg. Much more functionality can now be place within the Service Façade. For the PaymentFacade, it would obviously be those features specific to payment processing. The point is that the ServiceFacade is the place to focus any high-level business design. For prototyping reasons, this may also be the place where you begin your conceptual work. It can become the best place to begin "sketching out" a high-level design.

Related Patterns

• Façade (GoF)

• Proxy (GoF)

ABSTRACT PACKET PATTERN

Intent

Provide an abstract container used to pass parameters to any objects within a framework. This will also serve to package discrete parameters into a single and more efficient data-marshaling package.

Problem

Whether you are working with Web services or any publicly available business function, eliminating unnecessary data traffic is important. Most server-based services will take a variety of parameters to perform any one business function. Variables anywhere from strings to bytes to arrays will need to be passed to these business services, and they should be passed in the most efficient manner. Most object-oriented designs call for some form of encapsulation. This may be data objects providing "accessors" (getters) and "mutators" (setters) used to interact with the business data. Interaction with these objects occurs through "hydration" using mutators or through "extraction" using accessors. This type of multiple round trip get/set interaction is fine when an object is local or when the interaction is simple. Multiple gets and sets across the network would not be good. In general, where this scenario falls short is when the objects involved are separated by some form of boundary.

Boundaries come in many forms. There are network boundaries, process boundaries, domain boundaries (.NET), and storage boundaries (I/O), etc. The problem is that as a developer, interacting with objects using several round trips to set and get data can become a problem—a performance problem. This is especially apparent when calling business objects across network boundaries where each get or set call adds a significant performance hit to the overall transaction. Aside from being wasteful in network usage, it also forces the server object to maintain state in between accessor/mutator invocations. In some cases, holding state may be necessary but this should be used carefully.

An option in avoiding multiple round trips during object interaction is to pass all parameters into the method at once. For some designs, this is perfectly fine. In those cases, the parameter list may include only one or two data elements that you must pass to an object. Most of time, however, this is not sufficient. One or two parameters can quickly become three, four, five, and many more. Maintaining business methods with long parameter lists (although done) is not recommended. This is where the Abstract Packet comes into play. It is simply a container for those parameters. It is a generic container with the ability to hold as many parameters as are necessary to facilitate any business object, as long as that business can receive that packet's data type (Figure 4.9). This also simplifies the signature of most business methods because now a business method can be typed with a single parameter. This also applies to return values. The return value can be of the same

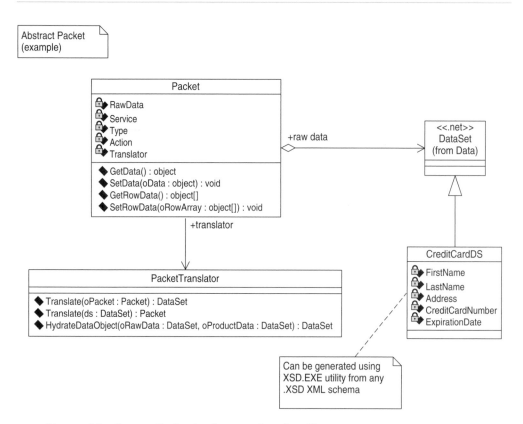

FIGURE 4.9: Abstract Packet implementation class diagram.

type, as long as that type is generic enough to contain data that will be returned from any business function.

Forces

Use the Abstract Packet pattern when:

- Web services will be used that contain more than two or three parameters.

- Business functions need to contain a standard signature contract to isolate future changes.

- Parameter types change frequently for business methods.

- Working with services crossing expensive boundaries (process, network, etc.).

Structure

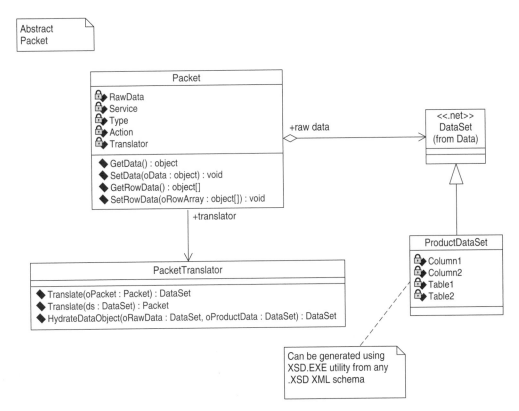

FIGURE 4.10: Abstract Packet generic class diagram.

Consequences

1. *Improves the parameter-passing efficiency.* When all parameters are bundled into one object, the developer will have more control on how to marshal those parameters. This includes any serialization that may take place. This also provides a controlled means of retrieving or unpackaging those parameters within the containing object.

2. *Provides a container in which to build dynamic parameter sets.* For those scenarios where the set of parameters can vary frequently, the Abstract Packet provides the container in which to build such a facility. In our example, the Packet class simply aggregates an already dynamic data type in the form of an

ADO.NET DataSet object. Using the DataSet data member, the Packet can take any shape and contain any data. As long as the business method that receives this packet knows how to interact with it, the packet can be used throughout the framework. The packet then can contain any data and be passed to each tier of the framework without implementing specific behavior for each representation of the packet. Only the business method that must directly interact with the packet's data must know what data elements it requires. For example, at this stage, the business method would call the packet's GetData() and request specific fields from the packet. The packet, in turn, delegates the lookup to the aggregated DataSet. To the rest of the system, this is just a generic packet.

LOOK AHEAD

Another option to this pattern is to bind a "type-strong" Data Service object that will be a child of a DataSet and, thus, can also be bound to the packet when the packet is built or translated. This new option provides a type-strong DataSet that any business method wishing to interact with the packet can use instead of using the packet's delegation methods. Using a type-strong DataSet is one way to avoid boxing/unboxing and can improve performance. Not to mention that it provides a much friendlier development environment for Visual Studio .NET users, especially those who love Intellisense. Using a type-strong DataSet will be fully discussed in the Chapter 5.

3. *Eliminates the binding of business methods to technology-specific data types, such as those in ADO.NET (DataSet).* This simply avoids forcing business methods from including ADO.NET types in their signatures and provides another level of abstraction.

4. *Hides the implementation details of the aggregated inner type (a DataSet, in this case).* Business methods, even those directly interacting with the data, do not require any of the details for manipulating types such as a DataSet. Those services directly interacting with the packet can simply use the methods provided by the packet. Methods such as GetData() require only parameters such as a field name to retrieve the underlying information. Keep in mind that a DataSet does not have to be bound to an actual database; a field name can be just a name of a column from the DataSet that could have been generated dynami-

cally. As mentioned earlier in the *Look Ahead* sidebar, there is also another means of interaction (see Chapter 5).

Participants

- Packet (Same name as implementation)—This is the Abstract Packet itself. This class acts as a form of "flyweight" in that its job is to contain data that can be shared efficiently with the rest of the system. It will act as a container of both extrinsic (passed-in) and intrinsic (static) data used by the rest of the system to route a request and perform an action.

- Packet Translator (same)—This includes any packet translation that constructs a packet using an overloaded method called *Translate()*. The Translator constructs the destination object and maps the appropriate values into the new data object. This construction and translation logic is business-specific. The goal is to simplify and abstract this logic. The client does not know or care how the construction or translation takes place or which Translate method to call. The client simply invokes Translate(), and the overloaded method takes care of invoking the appropriate method based on the type passed. Refer to the Packet Translator section later in this chapter for details.

- DataSet (same)—This is a standard ADO.NET DataSet object. This can represent any data schema, whether it is based on a persistent data model or not. This becomes the actual data container with a callable wrapper. This wrapper is the Packet class. The packet holds descriptive data elements to identify the packet, which can then be used for routing or other logic. Any other generic container such as an ArrayList, object[], etc., can be used as well.

- ProductDataSet (CreditCardDS)—This is the business-specific data services class (data access object). This is a classic data services object that directly represents a view on a database or other persistent set. This class is strongly typed to the specific data elements of a particular business service or database. It inherits from a DataSet to gain any ADO.NET features, such as serialization and XML support, to allow it initialize or extract the data once it is hydrated.

Implementation

The Abstract Packet was implemented primarily to aggregate a DataSet. In fact, the DataSet type in .NET can be used as an Abstract Packet with and of itself. For a technology backgrounder on ADO.NET and DataSets in particular, please refer to Chapter 5. Those already familiar with DataSets will understand that a DataSet is a generic object that can hold just about any data representation in memory. A DataSet can be dynamically built and hydrated from a database or, as is the case in this example, be hydrated from an XSD schema. The beauty of our Abstract Packet example is the fact that it does not "reinvent the wheel." The Packet class does not try to duplicate functionality that a DataSet already provides. It simply delegates to it and acts as an aggregator of an existing Dataset. The other data members of the Packet class are simply used to identify the packet for use by the architecture as this packet gets passed from service to service.

To build a packet, one must first have a DataSet object. In our example, a Web service receives and returns the DataSet type. When a DataSet is passed into our Web service, it instantiates and builds an appropriate Packet object. The building step can become complex and, therefore, should be farmed out to another service, such as a Packet Translator (covered later in this book). The primary step in building a packet is simply to set the DataSet as a data member of the packet. This is done using the Data property of the packet. The remaining properties of the packet are optional. More properties can be added to the packet as needed by the business requirements. The point is that the DataSet, now a member of the packet, still contains most of the data. When data needs to be extracted from a packet, its GetData methods or indexers can then be called, which delegates to the DataSet. The Packet class can now become the primary parameter passed to all business methods. This is similar to the functionality of an Adapter Pattern (GoF).

A DataSet could have been passed instead, but using a Packet class provides another level of abstraction. This abstraction will safeguard those methods from change and provide a high-level interface to those services that may not need to know how to manipulate a DataSet directly. The DataSet can be as simple as representing a single table or as complex as representing an entire database with constraints and all. By using a DataSet, all data can be treated as though directly contained within an actual database. This is true even if the DataSet is strictly represented in memory. Within the Packet class, methods can be designed to manipulate the DataSet in any way it sees fit. One caveat to this particular implementation, however, is the fact that the Packet class does not contain any type-specific methods. For example, each overloaded SetData() method takes an object as one of its parameters. Although this facilitates setting any data type of any field in the DataSet, this also introduces what .NET refers to as *boxing*. It is recommended that for performance-intensive implementations, type-specific methods should be created to avoid this side effect.

Technology Backgrounder—Boxing/Unboxing

Those already familiar with details behind value types, reference types, and the process of boxing/unboxing can skip this section. For those wanting more information, read on.

In the .NET CLR, you have two general types: value types and reference types. Value and reference are similar in that they both are objects. In fact, everything in the CLR is an object. Even value types are objects in that they have the System.ValueType as a parent class, which has System.Object as its parent. Each primitive type is represented by an equivalent class. For example, the primitive types of int and long in C# both alias the System.Int32 and System.Int64 classes, respectively, both of which have System.ValueType as parent. Other value types include structs and enumerations (enums). If it inherits from System.ValueType, it is treated as a value type in the CLR.

Value types are handled a bit differently than reference types in that they are passed by value. Passing by value means that a copy of the value is made prior to calling the function. For most value types, the cost of making this copy is small and usually outweighs the performance issues that arise when dealing with reference types. Value types represent a value that is allocated on the stack. They are never *null* and must contain data. Any custom value type can be created simply by deriving from System.ValueType. When creating your own value types, however, keep in mind that a value type is *sealed*, meaning that no one else can derive from your new type.

Reference types are based on the heap and can contain null values. They include types such as classes, interfaces, and pointers. These types are passed by reference, meaning that when passed, the address of the object (or pointer) is passed into the function. No copy is made. Unlike value types, when you make a change, the original value is changed, as well, because you are now dealing with a pointer. Reference types can be used when output parameters are required or when a type consumes a significant chunk of memory (remember that structs are value types, and they can grow quite large). However, they also must be managed by the CLR. This means that they must be kept track of and garbage collected. This also will add a performance penalty. Value types should be used wherever possible to improve performance and to conserve memory. If your object consumes a lot of memory, a reference type should be used, bearing in mind that any destruction or finalization of your type is going to be nondeterministic.

Once you understand the technical differences of how value types and reference types are treated, you will understand how *unboxing* and *boxing* work. Values types can become reference types, and the opposite is true as well. This can be forced or this can be automatic. The CLR will automatically convert a value type into a reference type whenever needed. This is called *boxing*. Boxing refers to converting a stack-allocated value into a heap-based reference type. An example of this would the following:

```
int nFoo = 1;// nFoo is a value type
object oBar = nFoo;     // oBar is a reference type of type
// System.Object
```

Here, a box is created and the value of nFoo is copied into it. To translate, heap space is allocated, and the value of nFoo is copied into that memory space and now must be temporarily managed. When a value is boxed, you receive an object upon which methods can be called, just like any other System.Object type (e.g., ToString(), Equals(), etc.). The reverse of this process is called *unboxing*, which is the just the opposite. A heap-based object is converted into its equivalent stack-based value type, such as:

```
int nFoo = (int)oBar;// oBar is a reference type
```

Unboxing and boxing, although convenient, can also become a small performance bottleneck and should be used with care. For methods that will be called extremely often, as will our Packet data object, using a System.Object type as a parameter where value types will be expected should anticipate a low performance. This is due to boxing. Methods such as these can be changed to support a System.ValueType but you must also create methods to except other types, including strings (which, by the way, are not value types).

Most of the methods and indexers defined in this class delegate to the Data property. The Data property simply returns the m_dsRawData member variable of this class (which is the DataSet we are wrapping). The Packet class uses this property to delegate most of the calls to the wrapped DataSet to return data, set data, and so on. This uses the DataSet for the heavy lifting. Wrapping the DataSet in this aspect gives the Abstract Packet its "Adapter" qualities, allowing it to be passed to all business services that accept a Packet data type. Listing 4.8 contains code for a typical Abstract Packet implementation.

LISTING 4.8: Typical Abstract Packet implementation.

```
public class Packet : IDisposable
{
        private DataTableCollection m_oData = null;
        private DataTable m_dtMeta = null;

        private DataSet m_dsRawData = null;

        private string m_sType;
        private string m_sService;
        private string m_sAction;

        private PacketTranslator m_oTranslator = null;

        public Packet()
        {
           RawData = new DataSet();
           Translator = new PacketTranslator();
        }

        public Packet(PacketTranslator oTranslator) : this()
        {
           m_oTranslator = oTranslator;
        }

        public static bool operator == (Packet p1, Packet p2)
        {
           if ((object)p1 == null && (object)p2 == null)
              return true;
           if ((object)p1 != null && (object)p2 == null)
              return false;
           else
              return p1.Equals((Packet)p2);
        }

        public static bool operator != (Packet p1, Packet p2)
        {
           if ((object)p1 == null && (object)p2 == null)
              return false;
           if ((object)p1 != null && (object)p2 == null)
              return true;
           else
              return !p1.Equals((Packet)p2);
        }
```

```csharp
public DataSet RawData
{
   get { return m_dsRawData; }
   set { m_dsRawData = value; }
}

public DataTableCollection Data
{
   get { return m_oData; }
   set { m_oData = value; }
}

public DataTable Meta
{
   get { return m_dtMeta; }
   set { m_dtMeta = value; }
}

public string Type
{
   get { return m_sType; }
   set { m_sType = value; }
}

public string Action
{
   get { return m_sAction; }
   set { m_sAction = value; }
}

public string Service
{
   get { return m_sService; }
   set { m_sService = value; }
}

public PMPacketTranslator Translator
{
   get { return m_oTranslator; }
   set { m_oTranslator = value; }
}

public string TransId
{
   get { return m_sTransId; }
   set { m_sTransId = value; }
}

// assume first table in collection
public object GetData(string sColumn)
```

```
        {
           DataRow dr = null;
           object oReturn = null;

           if (Data[0].Rows.Count > 0)
           {
              dr = Data[0].Rows[0];
              oReturn = dr[sColumn];
              if (oReturn == System.DBNull.Value)
                 oReturn = null;
           }
           return oReturn;
        }

        public object GetData(string sTable, string sCol)
        {
           return GetData(sTable, sCol, 0);
        }

        public object GetData(string sTable, string sCol, int nRow)
        {
           DataRow dr = null;
           object oReturn = null;

           if (Data[sTable].Rows.Count > 0)
           {
              dr = Data[sTable].Rows[nRow];
              oReturn = dr[sCol];

              if (oReturn == System.DBNull.Value)
                 oReturn = null;
           }
           return oReturn;
        }

        public object[] GetRowData(string sTable, int nRow)
        {
           object[] oRowArray = null;

           if (Data[sTable].Rows.Count > 0)
           {
           oRowArray = Data[sTable].Rows[nRow].ItemArray;
           }

           return oRowArray;
        }

public void SetRow(string sTable, int nRow, object[] oaRow)
        {
            Data[sTable].Rows[nRow].ItemArray = oaRow;
```

```
        }

        public void SetData(string sCol, object oVal)
        {
           DataRow dr = null;

           if (Data[0].Rows.Count > 0)
           {
           dr = Data[0].Rows[0];
           dr[sCol] = oVal;
           }
        }

public void SetData(string sTable, string sCol,
     object oVal)
        {
           SetData(sTable, sCol, 0, oVal);
        }

public void SetData(string sTable, string sCol, int nRow,
     object oValue)
        {
           DataRow dr = null;

           if (Data[sTable].Rows.Count > 0)
           {
              dr = Data[sTable].Rows[nRow];
              dr[sColumn] = oValue;
           }
        }

        public string this[string sColumn]
        {
           get
           {
              return Convert.ToString(GetData(sColumn));
           }
           set
           {
              SetData(sColumn, value);
           }
        }

        public string this[string sTable, string sColumn]
        {
           get
           {
return Convert.ToString(GetData(sTable, sColumn));
           }
           set
```

```
            {
               SetData(sTable, sColumn, value);
            }
         }

         public string this[string sTable, string sColumn, int nRow]
         {
            get
            {
               return Convert.ToString(GetData(sTable, sColumn, nRow));
            }
            set
            {
               SetData(sTable, sColumn, nRow, value);
            }
         }

         public static string SafeCastString(object oValue)
         {
            string sReturn;

            if (oValue != null)
               sReturn = (string)oValue;
            else
               sReturn = "";

            return sReturn;
         }

         public static decimal SafeCastDecimal(object oValue)
         {
            decimal dReturn;

            if (oValue != null)
               dReturn = (decimal)oValue;
            else
               dReturn = (decimal)0.0;

            return dReturn;
         }

         ...

         public void Dispose()
         {
            RawData.Dispose();
         }

      }
   }
```

Related Patterns

- Value Object (Alur, Crupi, Malks)

- Adapter (GoF)

- Composite (GoF)

PACKET TRANSLATOR

Intent

Facilitate the construction or mutation of complex data elements or objects into separate forms without knowing the details of the objects being translated. Translate Abstract Packets from one representation to another.

Problem

Similar to that of the "gang of four" Builder pattern, the Packet Translator separates the construction of a complex object from its representation. However, in addition to the Builder, this also facilitates a method to translate the complex object from one type to another and back again. The point of this translation service is to provide a means upon which to place the logic necessary to receive data packets of one format and convert them into another format. This is extremely typical when implementing an Abstract Packet pattern or any general object containing data parameters that must pass into another section of code that may understand a different set of values. For example, the Abstract Packet object a designer uses to pass data into the system may be quite different than the object used to pass from business service to business service. Different layers of the system or even different tiers sometimes require different parameter "packaging" rules. The data elements necessary for parameter passing at a business tier may be completely different for what is required at the persistence or data tier.

What this pattern solves is a fixed method of translation such that the implementation of the translation is generic and separated from its representation. Like an Adapter Pattern (GoF), this pattern provides an object different in interface yet containing similar internal data. The Packet Translator not only centralizes the translation implementation of turning one packet format into another but also provides a standard set of methods to do so. The calling of a Packet

Translator will typically occur in a base class hidden from any concrete client, such as a Service Façade.

Forces

Use the Packet Translator Pattern when:

- Using an Abstract Packet in your framework.

- The format of received data does not match that used within the framework.

- You want to isolate complex construction logic for an Abstract Packet.

- You want to standardize the packet-building process within a framework.

Structure

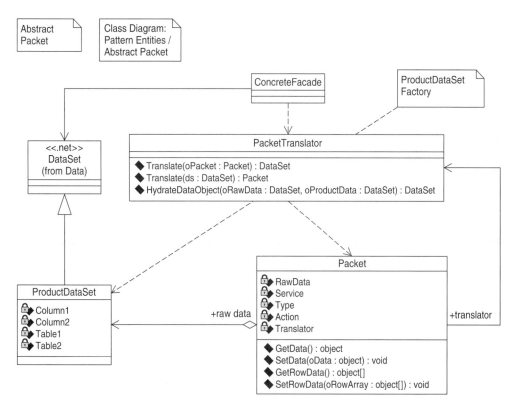

FIGURE 4.11: Packet Translator generic class diagram.

Consequences

1. *Encapsulates complex construction details of an Abstract Packet or any complex object.* Typically when working with more than one set of data parameters, the logic used to map those parameters can become complex. This is especially true when incoming parameters do not directly match that of outgoing parameters. In our example, a DataSet is the external object format that must be translated into another Abstract Packet format called *Packet*. The construction of the Packet class can become complex and should be delegated to another entity. Complex construction such as this should also be abstracted in the likelihood that other translations may occur using different object formats.

2. *Provides a standard means of translating two object formats into one another.* Translating packets can soon become a systemwide process. If there is more than one public entry point into an existing framework, this pattern will provide a standard means by which to translate packets of any format.

3. *Centralizes the construction and binding of type-strong objects into an Abstract Packet.* Although this could be considered an optional feature of the Packet Translator, creating type-strong data objects is a preferred approach when binding the data that will either reside on or be aggregated by the Abstract Packet. HydrateDataObject() in the Packet Translator can also be used from a factory to create the appropriate type-strong data object that must be bound to an Abstract Packet. Please refer to the Abstract Packet Pattern section earlier in this chapter for more information. The implementation section below will explain how our example utilizes a type-strong data object and binds it to an Abstract Packet, using the Packet Translator.

Participants

- ConcreteFacade (CreditCardFacade)—This is simply the driver object of the pattern. This entity can be any client that directly interacts with the Packet Translator. In our example, this is a CreditCardFacade object that during construction receives an external packet and translates it into a Packet object. Actually, in the CreditCard production application, the logic for packet translation lies in the parent class of all façades, alleviating the need to duplicate this process in each ConcreteFacade implementation. This is not a requirement, however.

- PacketTranslator (Same name as implementation)—This is the heart of the pattern. All pattern logic is implemented here. This includes translation that constructs both object formats using an overloaded method called *Translate()*. The ConcreteFacade simply has to call Translate() on the Packet Translator, passing in the appropriate data object. In our example, if a business service is called, passing an external data object such as a DataSet, Translate () is then called, passing the DataSet to the Translator. The Translator constructs the destination object and maps the appropriate values into the new data object. This construction and translation logic is business-specific. The goal is to simplify and abstract this logic. The client does not know or care how the construction or translation takes place or which Translate method to call. The ConcreteFacade just invokes Translate(), and the overloaded method takes care of invoking the appropriate method, based on the type passed. Keep in mind that if you are using data objects of the same data type, an overloaded Translate method will not work because the signature will be the same. For those cases, a different Translate method should be created, such as TranslateA() and TranslateB(). The remaining piece of translation is the optional use of a type-strong data object in the translator. This is not a requirement but when using an Abstract Packet that does not include typed methods, this can improve performance of your application. The first step to implementing either Translate() method is to construct the destination data object. For those cases where a type-strong version of that data object can be used, a factory method should then be implemented to perform this construction. The factory method will construct a type-strong class based on some information in the received data object. For example, when receiving a DataSet type data object, HydrateDataObject() is called from the initial Translate method. In fact, this Translate method becomes our factory (see below). Here, the correct type-strong class is instantiated, hydrated with the incoming data from the DataSet, and returned to the calling Translate() method to complete the translation. Naming this method *HydrateDataObject()* seemed appropriate because an XML schema with instance data was used to "hydrate" our type-strong data object once it was constructed. How the data is actually "sucked" into in the newly constructed data object is up to the developer, and again, this is optional for the pattern. For more information on type-strong data objects, please refer to Chapter 5.

- Packet (same)—This is the destination data object. This is typically an Abstract Packet that will act as a container to all business data passed to each method in the framework. The business methods in the framework "speak" the Packet language while the external world speaks the "DataSet" language. DataSets are mentioned next.

- DataSet (same)—This represents the external data object. This type is passed into our business framework from the outside world. A DataSet is a great choice for this data object, due to its dynamic nature, flexible representation, and the fact that many .NET tools down the line will be supporting it. This type is optional. Other types could have been chosen for the PacketTranslator pattern, and for smaller applications, a DataSet could be considered overkill. For simpler cases, an ArrayList could have been used or even a custom data object. Keep in mind, however, that choosing a custom data object brings with it unique challenges to the data-marshaling world, and it is recommended that you stick with a "standard" .NET data type. This is especially true when using SOAP as your transport protocol.

- ProductDataSet (CreditCardDS)—This represents the type-strong data object. This inherits from the DataSet and again is optional. Type-strong data objects are discussed in Chapter 5.

Implementation

Figure 4.12 looks much more complicated than it really is. The base of the pattern lies in the encapsulation of the packet construction. All construction and translation take place in one location—PacketTranslator. Where the class model becomes more complex is when a type-strong data object is used. In our case, that type-strong data object is a child class of a DataSet called *CreditCardDS*, and using it (as mentioned many times in this section) will be one of the focuses of Chapter 5.

The code in Listing 4.9 is implemented in the client of the translator. In our example, this is the CreditCardFacade class. It simply takes an external DataSet object, instantiates the PacketTranslator class, and calls Translate. It, like the Translator, uses an overloaded method called *PreparePacket* to alleviate its client from having to know which method to call. The return value of each Prepare-Packet is the appropriately formatted data object.

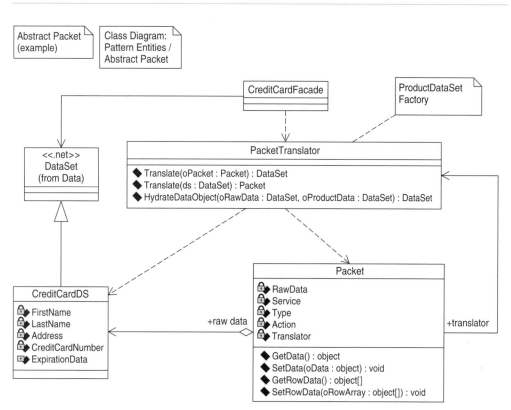

FIGURE 4.12: Packet Translator implementation class diagram.

LISTING 4.9: Abstract Packet sample implementation—preparing packets.

```
public Packet PreparePacket(DataSet dsRawPacket)
{
try
    {
        SetRawPacket(dsRawPacket);
PacketTranslator oPacketTranslator = new
PacketTranslator();

SetPacket(oPacketTranslator.Translate(
GetRawPacket()));
    }
catch(Exception e)
    {
    ...
    }
    return GetPacket();
```

```
}

public DataSet PreparePacket(Packet oPacket)
{
    try
    {
        SetPacket(oPacket);
        PacketTranslator oPacketTranslator = new
    PacketTranslator();

        SetRawPacket(oPacketTranslator.Translate(
        GetPacket()));
        ...
        return GetRawPacket();
}
```

The code in Listing 4.10 shows the implementation of each Translate method in the PacketTranslator object, along with our HydrateDataObject(). In this example, a DataSet is received, and in the above PreparePacket, the Translate(dsRawPacket) is called. Here the Translate method acts as factory and instantiates the appropriate type-strong data object. Because each type-strong data object inherits from DataSet, the returned type from HydrateDataObject is of type DataSet. In fact, as was mentioned earlier, the Packet type simply contains our DataSet. For those cases that use type-strong data types, this type can actually be downcast to the appropriate type-strong DataSet and later accessed by those methods wishing to interact with type-specific behavior. This is great for Visual Studio's Intellisense! To construct our destination Packet, HydrateDataObject() is called, passing into it both the incoming DataSet via dsRawPacket and the newly instantiated type-strong DataSet called *CreditCardDS*. Here in HydrateDataObject(), we use the XML serialization services of .NET to perform the data hydration of the destination object (see the technology backgrounder in Chapter 5). Once hydrated, it is returned to Translate(), which in turn returns the entire packet back to Prepare-Packet(). You should also notice that before HydrateDataObject() is called, members of the Packet are filled with high-level data that will be used to route this packet. This is optional but points out that this is the place to implement such construction behavior. Finally, the other Translate method that is called with a packet must be turned into a DataSet. This is much simpler, at least in our example, because the DataSet is already contained in our Packet class on the way out and simply needs to be returned as is.

LISTING 4.10: Packet Translator sample implementation—translating packets.

```
private DataSet HydrateDataObject(DataSet dsRawPacket,
                                        DataSet oDataObject)
    {
    System.IO.MemoryStream stream = new
    System.IO.MemoryStream();
        dsRawPacket.WriteXml(new XmlTextWriter(stream, null));
        stream.Position = 0;
        oDataObject.ReadXml(new
    XmlTextReader(stream),XmlReadMode.IgnoreSchema);
        return oDataObject;
    }

    public Packet Translate(DataSet dsRawPacket)
    {
        Packet oPacket = new Packet(this);

        // fill in packet values from DataSet (rawPacket)
        oPacket.Type = GetType(dsRawPacket);
        oPacket.Service = GetService(dsRawPacket);
        oPacket.Action = GetAction(dsRawPacket);

        switch (oPacket.Type)
        {
            case (Constants.CREDIT_CARD_TYPE):
            {
    oPacket.RawData =
    HydrateDataObject(dsRawPacket, new
    CreditCardDS());
                break;
            }
            case (Constants.TYPEB):
            {
                ...
                break;
            }
            default:
            {
                oPacket.RawData = dsRawPacket;
                break;
            }
        }

        return oPacket;
}

public DataSet Translate(Packet oPacket)
```

```
{
    return oPacket.RawData;
}
```

Related Patterns

- Value Object (Alur, Crupi, Malks)

- Builder (GoF)

- Abstract Packet (Thilmany)

5

Persistence-Tier Patterns

OVERVIEW

In the previous chapter, we covered some patterns with what you could call "fungible" applicability, compared with the others in this book. This simply means that business-tier patterns can really be applied anywhere in your code. These patterns can reside on the client or on a server, or they can be interspersed among different distributed layers throughout your enterprise. However, they usually find themselves at the core of the business or middle layer, as presented in the implementation examples. In this chapter, data tier patterns derive from their use of stored data and are usually of commercial data stores such as SQL Server, Oracle, or even DB2.

Many times, the following patterns will be strictly found at a true data tier and can even be used to design an entire data management system or framework. They can be the "design" tools employed to develop a self-contained data management system or even a third-party product whose job is to provide data services in a generic way. The principles covered in this chapter really stand on their own and are offered only as an option for developing data layers. They can be used with more traditional data architectures in part or in their entirety. As you will see, this form of data access is a slight departure from the usual.

Many of the patterns in this chapter have a particular synergy with one another—they feed off of each other. Each idea in this chapter is an island, but as a group, they also work cohesively as a single unit, or *macropattern,* if you will (not to be confused with the scriptlike code baked into old versions of Excel). In fact, many of these patterns have been implemented in the commercial application featured in Chapter 6 and should be running in a product at many of the Fortune 500 companies that bought the product by the time this book is published.

It doesn't matter whether an application is broken up into physical layers or not; the patterns covered here are focused on one common thing—data management. It should be noted, however, that most of these patterns do not directly tie themselves with any one particular persistent data store. Whether data is stored at the file level or an enterprise database system is used, these patterns should help any developer design the routines to "get at" that data and present it in the most robust and reusable fashion. In fact, even though most of the patterns here have been implemented in C#, many of them can be considered technology-agnostic and can easily be implemented in other languages. This even applies to non-.NET languages such as Java (gasp!). That said, the implementation approach here does lean heavily on the some of the "XML magic" included in the .NET framework and on ADO.NET, in particular.

Some of this technology "magic," such as the use of XML schemas, will be covered in backgrounders throughout the chapter. I hope to show you why it is so powerful that Microsoft incorporated XML into its framework. Through these examples I hope to show XML in a whole new light and deliver on all of the capabilities alluded to over the past several years.

As before, each implementation example will keep with the general solution "theme" and use a financial processing application to drive the example code. We cover the following patterns and practices in this chapter:

• Poly Model (a "composite" pattern)

• Schema Indexer

- Schema Field

- Abstract Schema (using Abstract Packet)

- Poly Model Factory (*using Factory Method*)

  With important (and related) mention to the following design patterns:

  Factory Method (GoF)

  Abstract Factory (GoF)

  Façade (GoF)

  Abstract Packet (Thilmany)

  Interface (GoF)

I hope you will find this chapter rather unique. Instead of diving into the typical "data best practices" you always seem to get, I've take a slightly different approach by relating each pattern as whole and giving you an entire data framework to work with. Although this approach is atypical, its benefits have already been noticed, and it is in production at my company as I write this. Take heed, it may take some patience to get the whole picture but once you complete this chapter, I hope you will understand what I'm talking about. Along the way, I will contrast the presented Poly Model with more traditional data practices. Even if you don't apply Poly Models directly in your code, you will still get a good idea of what XML power I've been speaking of through this book. It may even help you build a more traditional data access layer with a new outlook, allowing you to "think outside the box," even if that box is the same old data access layer.

Before I delve into each pattern, I first need to introduce the idea of XML schemas and their relationship to ADO.NET DataSets. Most of the patterns deal in some way or another with XML schemas, so unless you have extensive experience building type-strong DataSets in .NET, I suggest reviewing the following technology backgrounder. For those who haven't used XML schemas or even for those who are unfamiliar with how ADO.NET leverages off of XML schemas, the following section should help at least give you an overview of one of the most significant additions to ADO.NET.

TECHNOLOGY BACKGROUNDER—SCHEMAS AND DATASETS

XML Schema

An XML schema is simply a data-friendly or, more specifically, a database-friendly meta-language built around XML. The XML schema definition language, usually encompassed in an .XSD file, enables you to define the structure and data types for XML documents that you would find when designing a database. Until now, there have been a few formats floating around, including a more proprietary version from Microsoft supported by ADO 2.6 and earlier and Biztalk 2000, supported in the XDR format. Fortunately, we've arrived at a World Wide Web Consortium (W3C) standard that is completely supported by Microsoft .NET and ADO.NET. The XSD supported by ADO.NET adds custom elements (in the true Microsoft fashion) but it does so in a compliant way, and they should not affect parsers not using .NET. For those building interoperable applications, this is indeed good news.

Creating an XML schema is just like creating any other XML document but with a few standards and rules. An XML schema document (XSD) is based on the W3C 2001 recommendation specifications for data types and data structures. You create an XML schema by defining elements and attributes that make up types, such as complex types, that conform to the W3C XML schema Part 1 structures recommendation for the XML schema definition language. You also define and reference data types using the W3C XML schema Part 2 specification. There are built-in types, such as *string* and *integer*, but you may also create your own custom data types such as you would find in the Microsoft implementations.

To create an XML schema, you must first begin with a schema element such as the following in Listing 5.1.

LISTING 5.1: XML schema snippet random example for the Poly Model pattern.

```
<xs:schema
id="PolyModel"
targetNamespace="http://www.etier.com/PolyModel.xsd"
. . .
xmlns:xs=http://www.w3.org/2001/xmlschema
xmlns:msdata="urn:schemas-microsoft-com:xml-msdata">
```

You should notice that the XML schema is first composed of a top-level *schema* element. The *schema* element definition must include the namespace above. After this element, the document may contain any number of complex and simple type definitions, using the *simpleType* and *complexType* element tags:

- SimpleType—Represents the type definition for values that are used as text of an element or attribute. This data type cannot contain nested components, such as elements, or have any attributes.

- ComplexType—When defining types such as those that describe a database table, you use this type. This is for elements that contain any attributes and/or other elements, such as the columns that make up a database table.

These tags are used to create your custom types. These types include those that represent the tables, fields, and any keys your schema may define, such as the following schema:

LISTING 5.2: The Customer schema to be used throughout this chapter.

```xml
<?xml version="1.0" encoding="utf-8" ?>

  <xs:schema
        id="Customers"
        targetNamespace="http://www.etier.com/Customers.xsd"
    . . .
    xmlns:xs="http://www.w3.org/2001/xmlschema"
    xmlns:msdata="urn:schemas-microsoft-com:xml-msdata">

     <xs:element name="Customers" msdata:IsDataSet="true">
          <xs:complexType>
            <xs:choice maxOccurs="unbounded">
              <xs:element name="Customer">
                <xs:complexType>

             <xs:sequence>
                 <xs:element name="CustomerID"
                    type="xs:string" />
                 <xs:element name="CompanyName"
                    type="xs:string" />
                 <xs:element name="ContactName"
                    type="xs:string"
                    minOccurs="0" />
                   <xs:element name="ContactTitle"
                    type="xs:string"
                    minOccurs="0" />
                 . . .
                 </xs:sequence>
```

```
                    </xs:complexType>
                    </xs:element>
                       . . .
                  </xs:choice>
            </xs:complexType>
            <xs:unique name="CustomersKey1"
               msdata:PrimaryKey="true">
                  <xs:selector xpath=".//Customer" />
                  <xs:field xpath="mstns:CustomerID" />
            </xs:unique>
      </xs:element>
</xs:schema>
```

One of the nice aspects of XML schemas is that you need to know only a few schema semantics to use them effectively in your application. For this reason, I will cover only what you minimally need to understand in order to implement the patterns in this chapter.

Schemas and DataSets

What is an XML schema in the .NET world really?

- It describes any data model, whether that model stays in memory or is persisted.

- When using constraints, it can be used to validate any data being inserted into a DataSet at runtime.

- It establishes the relational structure of the DataSet's tables and columns. It can specify the key columns, constraints, and relationships between tables.

- It specifies whether its "shape" will be hierarchical or key-based.

- It serves as an accepted standard for describing any complex data using XML.

The patterns throughout this chapter continually refer to a DataSet as being of two types: typed and untyped. You will see the terms *typed* and *strongly typed* used interchangeably, even though they are subtly different in their context. So what are they? An untyped DataSet is just any instantiated DataSet with no direct relationship to any given XML schema. A typed DataSet is a class that has been generated from a schema, something you will see in the Schema Field pattern below. There really isn't any difference between a typed DataSet and the actual schema itself because the DataSet, in essence, becomes the schema in "class form." This means that you can work with a schema "through" the DataSet class, using its typed members to access elements of the schema and the typed instance data it may contain. The schema represents a possible persistence target that would represent a DataSet if it were saved as XML. A schema is the skeleton of a DataSet object and for most purposes, they can be seen as one and the same in .NET.

When working with the Visual Studio XML Designer, you have the option of creating a schema from scratch or from the existing data model through Server Explorer, which you can use in your code to bind to a DataSet. Schemas and DataSets can also be created programmatically from any data source that you have access to at runtime. Taken a step further, Visual Studio will even automatically generate a working DataSet class from the created schema. The DataSet Visual Studio creates what is considered the strongly typed DataSet I referred to above. It is strongly typed in that the DataSet it creates inherits from the DataSet class and provides strongly typed methods and data members so that you can access members of the schema by name. This means you can access tables and columns by name, instead of iterating through collections or using indexers.

For example, to access a column in code from a strongly typed DataSet, it would look something like the following:

LISTING 5.3: Code snippet showing the manipulation of the strongly typed DataSet.

```
Customers dsCustomers = new Customers();
//Customers is a dataset

Customers.CustomerRow oRow = dsCustomers.Customer.NewCustomerRow();

    oRow.CompanyName = "The eTier Group";
    oRow.ContactName = "Christian Thilmany";
    oRow.Phone = "713-555-2343";
    . . .
```

The *Customers* class is simply a DataSet-derived class that is autogenerated from Visual Studio. Instead of instantiating a DataSet, you instantiate the strongly typed DataSet as such and manipulate the data in a schema-specific manner by referencing its members by name. This is much cleaner and easier to read than the default means of using indexers in ADO.NET. No more keeping track of index values for columns or tables or having to assign numbers to constants that represent those index numbers. However, there are few things to watch out for that we'll cover shortly in this chapter.

When changes are made to a schema file, the definition of the DataSet class actually changes at design time. They are both essentially schema files in the XML Designer, with the difference being that typed DataSets have an associated class file as a DataSet child. At design time, untyped DataSets do not contain any structure or instance data; therefore, XML schemas cannot be generated from untyped DataSets. This doesn't mean you cannot serialize this object to XML, but that is another topic altogether. However, during runtime, once the DataSet has been populated with instance data through its normal untyped DataSet routines, a schema based on that instance data can be generated in code. If you've ever worked with SQLXML (version 3.0 at the time of writing this book) for SQL Server and/or the ADO XML support, you have already had a taste of this sort of behavior (albeit not as streamlined). This is one of the most powerful features of .NET and ADO.NET, specifically. With typed DataSets, you now have an in-memory data model that, at one point, COM+ promised to support with the "In Memory Database" (IMDB), which was unfortunately never delivered.

An ancillary benefit to using strongly typed DataSets from the Studio Designer is that the DataSet also incorporates table and column names into the statement completion feature (see *Intellisense*). The code is not only easier to read but with *Intellisense* it is much easier to write, with type mismatch errors being caught at compile time or even composition time, rather than runtime. In Studio, any pre-existing data table can be dragged into the designer window or even loaded by file. The designer also displays both the XML version and a more readable Access-style layout of the data structure. This provides you with the best of both design worlds. Once created, an .XSD file will appear in your current project, which you will see in the tree. Hidden from your defaulted view is the generated DataSet class I just spoke of unless you have chosen to view all files in the Solution Explorer. The generated file should be right off of the .XSD file just created. Like the Web service proxy code that is generated by the compiler, Visual Studio also includes a file behind the scenes during a save in Studio. To see the file generated, simply go to File Explorer and look for a source file with the name of the DataSet schema you gave upon creation. You can then see what exactly is generated to get a better feel for the strongly typed code if you don't want to use Intellisense for browsing.

Creating Typed DataSets

As mentioned, the XML Designer in Visual Studio can automatically generate a typed DataSet for you from your schema (.XSD). Follow these steps:

1. From the Project menu, select Add New Item, highlighting the project you want this added to.

2. In the New Existing Item dialog box, select DataSet from the Data folder and click OK.

3. Double-click the newly created schema (.XSD) in the Solution Explorer if the XML View is not currently open.

4. From here you can drag an existing table from the Server Explorer or create a schema from scratch.

5. From the context menu in the XML Designer, select Generate DataSet if it isn't already selected.

6. Each time you save the schema in the project, the typed DataSet will be recreated to match the new structure. You should also have this class available in *Intellisense* and be able to use it in code.

NOTE

All XML schemas created in Visual Studio conform to the W3C specification for schemas. There are some features of ADO.NET that could not be described with the default schema syntax. In those cases, custom attributes were used to define ADO.NET-specific items. You can find these custom features when viewing the schema in the Studio XML View mode. They can be identified with the "msdata:" qualifier. This does *not* make these schemas noncompliant because the specification allows for custom attributes (they will be ignored by parsers that do not support that attribute).

So what does the generated typed DataSet code look like? Here is a brief sample of the Customer typed DataSet generated from the XML Designer. This is generated from Visual Studio, so you should rarely, if ever, have to manipulate this code. In fact, I discourage you from doing just that unless you will not be changing it (highly unlikely because schemas change constantly as data requirements change, thus the reason behind this chapter).

Much of the autogenerated code has been omitted from the following because it is quite long. This is shown only to get a feel for some of the type-strong code behavior automatically built for you by Visual Studio. Who needs a "magical black box" for data handling like you get with Contained Manager Persistence (J2EE/

EJB) when you can have complete control with generated data object code such as the following?

LISTING 5.4: The Customers "typed" DataSet shown as code—as generated by Visual Studio .NET.

```
//-------------------------------------------------------------
// <autogenerated>
//     This code was generated by a tool.
//     Runtime Version: 1.0.3705.209
//
//     Changes to this file may cause incorrect behavior and will
//     be lost if
//     the code is regenerated.
// </autogenerated>
//-------------------------------------------------------------

namespace DataTierPatterns.Data {
    using System;
    using System.Data;
    using System.Xml;
    using System.Runtime.Serialization;


    [Serializable()]
    . . .
    public class Customers : DataSet
        {

        private CustomerDataTable tableCustomer;
        private JOBDataTable tableJOB;
        private OrderDataTable tableOrder;

        public Customers()
            {
            this.InitClass();
. . .
        }


        . . .


public CustomerDataTable Customer
{
        get
        {
            return this.tableCustomer;
        }
}
```

```
          .  .  .

[System.Diagnostics.DebuggerStepThrough()]
      public class CustomerDataTable :
  DataTable, System.Collections.IEnumerable
            {

          private DataColumn columnCustomerID;
          private DataColumn columnCompanyName;
          private DataColumn columnContactName;
          private DataColumn columnContactTitle;
          private DataColumn columnAddress;
          private DataColumn columnCity;
          private DataColumn columnRegion;
      .  .  .

    internal CustomerDataTable() :
              base("Customer")
        {
            this.InitClass();
        }


        .  .  .

        internal DataColumn CustomerIDColumn
        {
            get
        {
                return this.columnCustomerID;
            }
        }

        internal DataColumn CompanyNameColumn
        {
            get
            {
                return this.columnCompanyName;
            }
        }

        public void AddCustomerRow(CustomerRow row)
        {
            this.Rows.Add(row);
        }

        public CustomerRow AddCustomerRow(
string CustomerID,
string CompanyName,
```

```
string ContactName,
string ContactTitle,
string Address,
string City,
string Region,
string PostalCode,
string Country,
string Phone,
string Fax)
        {
            CustomerRow rowCustomerRow u61 ?
            ((CustomerRow)(this.NewRow()));
            rowCustomerRow.ItemArray = cf2 new object[]
        {
                CustomerID,
                CompanyName,
                ContactName,
                ContactTitle,
                Address,
                City,
                Region,
                PostalCode,
                Country,
                Phone,
                Fax};
            this.Rows.Add(rowCustomerRow);
            return rowCustomerRow;
        }

        public CustomerRow FindByCustomerID(
string CustomerID)
```

. . .

Schema Types

When you create your XML schema from scratch, you have to choose between two primary types of schema in reference to the relational data you may hold. When creating schemas in any tool, you have two approaches for representing relational data, and the structure used to create the schema will reflect that.

Nested Relationships

This uses a hierarchical relationship between tables that reside within elements and the children of those elements. Before databases were modeled using XML, this was my preferred way to represent data. The problem with this representation is that it isn't as efficient in layout as the relationship type below unless only a few tables are represented.

Nested relationships involve creating tables with columns just like a one-to-many scenario (next), except single-column definitions may also contain the complete definitions of any related tables. Nested elements may be easier to read and understand immediately, but structures may have to repeated throughout the XML file. This repetition can be avoided using the following type.

One-to-Many Relationships

This is the preferred option when directly modeling database entities. The relationships are represented as separate tables of rows that are using common columns to relate to one another. The common columns are defined as primary keys and as references for those tables, using a referenced key as a foreign key. The Edit Key and Edit Relation dialog boxes can be used for creating keys and creating relationships as needed. This takes a bit more thought to create but is much more efficient and "ERD-like" than using hierarchical links.

One-to-many relationships involve creating individual tables with columns just like the hierarchical option. However, creating your XML schema also involves designating the common columns as keys (e.g., primary keys) and/or as keyrefs (e.g., foreign keys). Once defined, you then create the relationships between them and finally apply the constraints. There is more thought that must go into this but the design is much cleaner and more efficient.

Tables, Columns, and Keys

Next I will briefly go over the main elements of an XML schema. I will explain how database entities such as tables, columns, and keys are represented in an XML schema.

Tables

Using XML, tables are represented as "complex" elements. The columns are then represented as subelements and attributes of that complex element. The name of the table is equal to the name of the element. The names of the columns in the schema are equal to the names of the subelements and attributes that make up the complex element. The following XML schema represents a table named *Customers* with several columns. Each column is an element with the attributes used to provide the name and type of the column. Notice that each column makes up the

> **NOTE**
>
> Although I explain the process here, you do *not* have to enforce any relationships between your tables. In fact, depending on your design, you may not even need to assign columns as having primary keys. Relating your tables in the schema will only grant you the option of enforcing referential integrity in your code at runtime and will mimic what happens during a typical database operation. However, in this book and in the commercial application featured, I do not create relationships in many cases. I avoid as many relationship definitions as I can for flexibility. Personally, I'd rather use code to police my relationships because most rules are too complicated to represent the rather simple relationship constraints a schema would provide. Most of the data in both the application and patterns featured are custom validated *before* all of it is inserted into the typed DataSet. This provides me with the flexibility of using the tables as temporary storage without having to worry about integrity violations (see the Abstract Packet pattern in chapter 4). The choice is yours but keep in mind that defining hard relationships also may involve a loss of some flexibility when using typed DataSets. I prefer to have this flexibility and prefer making my schema easier to read in the process. This is not to say this is a bad practice; it is only my preference for schema definition. Your use of these schema constraint constructs should be a design decision and will vary on your implementation.

sequence of the complex type with the minOccurs attribute used to denote what fields can or cannot be null.

LISTING 5.5: Complex Customers element from the Customers schema.

```
<xs:element name="Customers" msdata:IsDataSet="true">
        <xs:complexType>
      <xs:choice maxOccurs="unbounded">
        <xs:element name="Customer">
          <xs:complexType>
            <xs:sequence>
        <xs:element name="CustomerID"
                                  type="xs:string" />
   <xs:element name="CompanyName"
                            type="xs:string" />
   <xs:element name="ContactName" type="xs:string"
minOccurs="0" />
<xs:element name="ContactTitle" type="xs:string"
minOccurs="0" />
```

. . .

Columns

As mentioned, columns are elements within a complex table element. Any elements without a minOccurs attribute are considered required columns, whereas the elements with the minOccurs='0' attribute are considered optional columns. The type attribute shown below and the types in this example are defined as simple types (types that are built into all XML schemas). Listing 5.5 shows how to define a table and its columns.

Primary Keys

To constrain columns to contain unique values, you can create a key. In the XML Designer, adding a key that does not have the DataSet Primary Key option selected will create a unique key instead of an xs:key as below. Unique constraints simply ensure that columns do not contain duplicate values, and the difference (as you'll see) between the two is subtle. The following example shows how to define the CustomerID column from the Customers table as a DataSet primary key in the schema:

LISTING 5.6: Sample primary key shown in the Customers schema.

```
<xs:key name="CustomersKey1" msdata:PrimaryKey="true">
<xs:selector xpath=".//mstns:Customer" />
<xs:field xpath="mstns:CustomerID" />
  </xs:key>
```

You can use the toolbox in the XML Designer to drag a key over to the table (element) to which you want to assign a key. You may also select the Add menu by right-clicking on the table. This will create a key and can be viewed in the XML view, such as the example shown above (Listing 5.6).

Unique Keys

Unique constraints can allow null values, whereas primary key constraints do not allow null values: This is the primary difference I alluded to above. There is another consideration to make when deciding whether to use a primary or unique key. Tables can have multiple unique constraints but only one primary key. My schema requires that the CustomerID column must be unique, so a primary key or a simple unique key could have been used. Listing 5.7 shows how to define a unique key and reference an element in the schema:

LISTING 5.7: Sample generic unique key shown in the Customers schema.

```
<xs:unique name="CustomersKey1" msdata:PrimaryKey="true">
        <xs:selector xpath=".//Customer" />
        <xs:field xpath="mstns:CustomerID" />
    </xs:unique>
```

Unique keys are created with the XML Designer the same way primary keys are. The only difference is one option on the dialog.

Keyrefs

To enforce referential integrity within your typed DataSet, you optionally set up keyrefs. A keyref creates the "many-side" definition of a one-to-many relationship. This is just like setting up a foreign key during database design. A keyref must reference either a primary key or a unique key, as is the case with Listing 5.8.

LISTING 5.8: Overall flow of activity of the Poly Model "composite" pattern.

```
<xs:keyref name="CustomersOrders" refer=".//CustomersKey1">
        <xs:selector xpath=".//Orders" />
        <xs:field xpath="CustomerID" />
    </xs:keyref>
```

This can also be created using the toolbox in the XML Designer. Using the Edit Relation dialog box, you can select the rules that affect what happens to related data. These rules enforce the *referential integrity* of the schema. When updating or deleting a record in a primary key column, there can be many records in another table that reference the primary key. Table 5.1 briefly describes each constraint managed from this dialog box.

TABLE 5.1: Constraints Available in the Edit Relation Dialog Box

Rule	Description
Cascade	Update or delete all related rows.
SetNull	Set related rows to null.
SetDefault	Set related rows to the specified DefaultValue.
None	No action taken.

I think it's time to begin talking about Poly Models. You should have been provided enough XML schema background to get your foot in the design door at this point. As mentioned, Poly Models are a little different than what you're probably accustomed to. These next patterns really need to be read in their entirety to get a true perspective of their application scenarios but I hope you will find them a refreshing option to data access that provides you with another tool to use in your application.

POLY MODEL PATTERN

Intent

To be able to provide a dynamic data model that can be edited without affecting a physical data model and with minimal to no impact on an existing data services framework.

Problem

The core patterns of this chapter lie in the assembly units of the Poly Model pattern. For this reason, this particular pattern can be considered a "composite" pattern of sorts. No, it isn't a pattern implemented in a strange new language, so you can continue reading. A composite pattern is simply an ensemble of highly related design and architecture patterns that, as a whole, make up a pattern itself, sort of like a miniature framework. This idea gets into some of the subtle nuances of pattern naming and classification, so consider this somewhat subjective of the author. Also I think a different pattern classification is necessary here because, unlike design patterns, a composite pattern does not limit itself to one primary object model and relates more to architecture and implementation than design. However, unlike both architecture patterns and implementation patterns, it is not tied to any one technology. This is important to remember because XML and schemas in particular benefit from the fact they are *not* implementation-specific. It is only a matter of topic that the Poly Model pattern presented here happens to be implemented using .NET and more specifically, XML schemas. Also, like design, architecture, and implementation patterns, a composite pattern is still repeatable and, thus, can be named and reused in many scenarios.

One of the scenarios the Poly Model pattern fits into is one that involves an application that has an ever-changing data model. Have you ever tried to design a framework that could never sit still because the data model behind changed so often? Those of you who have implemented N-tier frameworks should all be familiar with how data modeling changes impact a system and the effect it has on each and every layer above the data layer. If one field is changed, it can have a radiating effect with each layer by forcing the design to be altered in many places instead of just one. A data model has always been one of those "design" pieces that need to be solidified before production. This issue came up for me in the commercial product featured here, and it is exactly where the Poly Model pattern idea was spawned.

What if you could build into a data tier design the ability for the data tier to retrofit itself into any ERD—dynamically? Take that a step further: How would you like to be able to alter the ERD with little to no impact on the rest of the system? Does this *sound too good to be true*? Creating such a model does present its drawbacks, as we will uncover. However, if implemented strategically, the Poly Model pattern can save many man hours and, more important, eliminate some of the down time of any production applications that have continually changing databases.

Unfortunately, implementing the Poly Model pattern will take a little patience. It is recommended that the following patterns be understood and implemented before completely assembling the Poly Model pattern. In fact, as mentioned earlier, this pattern differs in that it is a sum of the parts (or patterns, in this case) that make up this chapter. It is presented first only to "frame" the rest of the contents. If you want to skip ahead and read how each of the following patterns are presented, you may skip this for now and come back. However, to get a feel for the following patterns, such as Schema Field, I suggest you keep reading.

Forces

Use the Poly Model pattern when:

- Specific parts of a physical model may change regularly.

- You want to simplify the complexity of managing a data object for each table in a database.

- You want to eliminate the job of mapping data objects of the data layer to one or more tables in the database.

- Certain sections of an existing database do not have to be normalized and can benefit from not having to be physically remodeled due to logic design changes in the future.

- Dynamic aspects of a model will not affect overall performance.

- A mechanism is required to pass large DataSets.

- DataSets need to be self-describing in nature ("in-memory database support").

Structure

Unlike most of the structure sections in this book, the Poly Model does not contain the typical class diagram. That is because the Poly Model is a composite of other patterns and practices described in this chapter. To begin the Poly Model, you first need a data schema. Fortunately for you, Visual Studio .NET could not have made it any simpler to create XML schemas. In fact, if you prefer to model your schema in a database such as SQL Server, you also have this option. Visual Studio .NET will allow you to drag and drop a table from any compliant database into the schema design workspace using the Server Explorer. For those more comfortable with designing tables in enterprise databases such as SQL Server or for those new to Visual Studio .NET, this presents a very convenient option. You may also create a data schema from scratch inside of Visual Studio. The choice is yours. The following schema (Figure 5.1) will be used for the implementation examples in this chapter. I've presented both the Visual Studio view and the XML output (to get a feel for what our XML schema will resemble) for three tables, two of which will be manipulated in the patterns that follow.

As you can see on the left of Figure 5.1, the Server Explorer can be used to drag a preexisting table into Visual Studio (layout only) and thus avoid having to create the schema from scratch. Keep in mind that the actual table will *not* be used to store the actual data in this example; this is the main premise of the pattern. The database shown here is used only to create our XML schema. So where will the instance data go? In Figure 5.2, you will see the actual physical model that will hold not only our instance data but the XML schema itself.

CHALLENGE 5.1

How complex should a single schema be? How many tables should exist in one schema?

The upcoming "Poly Schemas" note will address this question.

As you can see in Figure 5.2, the schema used is nothing more than an XSD XML schema generated in Visual Studio. The only main difference between this

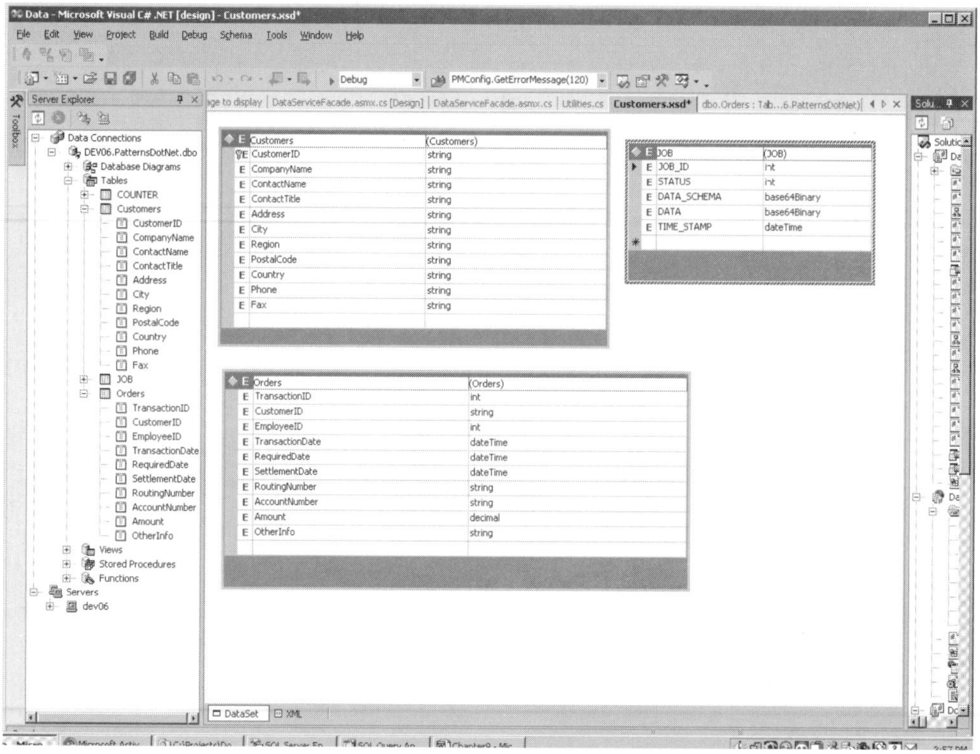

FIGURE 5.1: DataSet view of the XML schema design used in this chapter.

schema and a typical XML schema is the msdata:IsDataSet="true" attribute in the first element tag. This basically tells us that this is meant to be used in an ADO.NET DataSet, which is something we will get to shortly. To get a better understanding of what this pattern accomplishes and what elements you need, you should be aware of the activities that occur in a framework that supports dynamic modeling. Applying the Poly Model pattern comes down to the following six main runtime activities that are covered, in part, in every helper pattern contained within this composite:

• Storing XML schemas

• Retrieving XML schemas

• Hydrating XML schemas with XML instance data

• Storing XML instance data along with their XML schema references

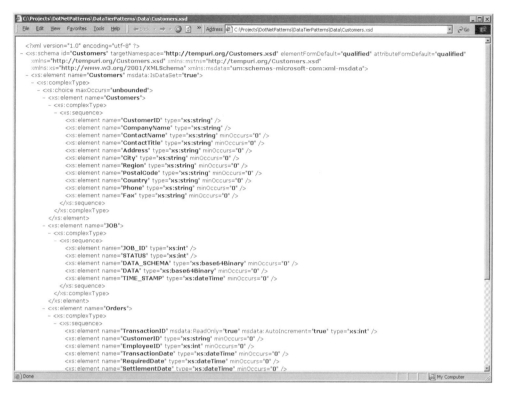

```
  C:\Projects\DotNetPatterns\DataTierPatterns\Data\Customers.xsd
 File  Edit  View  Favorites  Tools  Help      Back         »   Address     C:\Projects\DotNetPatterns\DataTierPatterns\Data\Customers.xsd              Go

   <?xml version="1.0" encoding="utf-8" ?>
 - <xs:schema id="Customers" targetNamespace="http://tempuri.org/Customers.xsd" elementFormDefault="qualified" attributeFormDefault="qualified"
     xmlns="http://tempuri.org/Customers.xsd" xmlns:mstns="http://tempuri.org/Customers.xsd"
     xmlns:xs="http://www.w3.org/2001/XMLSchema" xmlns:msdata="urn:schemas-microsoft-com:xml-msdata">
   - <xs:element name="Customers" msdata:IsDataSet="true">
     - <xs:complexType>
       - <xs:choice maxOccurs="unbounded">
         - <xs:element name="Customers">
           - <xs:complexType>
             - <xs:sequence>
                 <xs:element name="CustomerID" type="xs:string" />
                 <xs:element name="CompanyName" type="xs:string" />
                 <xs:element name="ContactName" type="xs:string" minOccurs="0" />
                 <xs:element name="ContactTitle" type="xs:string" minOccurs="0" />
                 <xs:element name="Address" type="xs:string" minOccurs="0" />
                 <xs:element name="City" type="xs:string" minOccurs="0" />
                 <xs:element name="Region" type="xs:string" minOccurs="0" />
                 <xs:element name="PostalCode" type="xs:string" minOccurs="0" />
                 <xs:element name="Country" type="xs:string" minOccurs="0" />
                 <xs:element name="Phone" type="xs:string" minOccurs="0" />
                 <xs:element name="Fax" type="xs:string" minOccurs="0" />
               </xs:sequence>
             </xs:complexType>
           </xs:element>
         - <xs:element name="JOB">
           - <xs:complexType>
             - <xs:sequence>
                 <xs:element name="JOB_ID" type="xs:int" />
                 <xs:element name="STATUS" type="xs:int" />
                 <xs:element name="DATA_SCHEMA" type="xs:base64Binary" minOccurs="0" />
                 <xs:element name="DATA" type="xs:base64Binary" minOccurs="0" />
                 <xs:element name="TIME_STAMP" type="xs:dateTime" minOccurs="0" />
               </xs:sequence>
             </xs:complexType>
           </xs:element>
         - <xs:element name="Orders">
           - <xs:complexType>
             - <xs:sequence>
                 <xs:element name="TransactionID" msdata:ReadOnly="true" msdata:AutoIncrement="true" type="xs:int" />
                 <xs:element name="CustomerID" type="xs:string" minOccurs="0" />
                 <xs:element name="EmployeeID" type="xs:int" minOccurs="0" />
                 <xs:element name="TransactionDate" type="xs:dateTime" minOccurs="0" />
                 <xs:element name="RequiredDate" type="xs:dateTime" minOccurs="0" />
                 <xs:element name="SettlementDate" type="xs:dateTime" minOccurs="0" />
 Done                                                                                    My Computer
```

FIGURE 5.2: XML view of the XML schema design used in this chapter.

- Storing index field names and field values for later lookups

- Looking up XML instances using stored index field names and values (Poly Model queries)

These activities combined make up the Poly Model pattern as outlined here but each can be useful in its own right and, thus, have been divided into the child patterns that follow. Many more elements must go into a product-ready system, some of which I talk about in this book. The featured commercial application in Chapter 6 uses each of these patterns to implement this dynamic data model, using these patterns and many more not covered in this book.

For example, to be able to throw a large amount of data at something like a dynamic model requires a little more thought in the areas of caching and other optimizations that should be implemented in order for the system to perform well. That is not to say that using the Poly Model will guarantee a slow system, but be forewarned that *it will be slightly slower than a more traditional physical model.* For the "batch-oriented" type product featured in Chapter 6, the primary goal was flexibility, with performance coming in at a close second. This was not as much of an issue as it would be in a more transactional system. Also, the Poly Model does not have to be utilized in its entirety. For example, columns can be added to any normalized physical model for those parts of that model that may change often. That way, you get the best of both worlds. Performance-sensitive data can be normalized, indexed, and queried as you've always done. Those parts of the model that you feel may change can then be added to a schema-based dynamic model (as shown in this chapter) to continue to provide you with some flexibility.

The following diagram will help explain some of these activities and show the main components of the Poly Model pattern. As you'll notice, the child patterns of the composite drive the implementation of it as a whole. Besides the activities, the components involved are a mix of business classes, actual XML schemas, and the physical tables. These components include the following:

- Client "driver"

- Business schema(s) (e.g., a sample customer schema)

- Business instance data and schema(s) (e.g., the customer DataSet)

- Schema table "schema storage"

- Data table "instance data storage"

- Index table "lookup fields"

As you can see from Figure 5.3, a driver initiates a Poly Model conversation by first requesting a schema. This has to be done only once and can be done during application startup or even installation; caching the schema will obviously improve performance and, thus, avoid unnecessary repetitive requests. Once the schema is retrieved, it can then be used to initialize the DataSet. At this point, the DataSet becomes a strongly typed DataSet (see the schema technology backgrounder section earlier in this chapter). This allows specific tables and columns to be directly accessible from the client or driver using method names specific to the schema. Any data that then flows from the client to the actual data store will

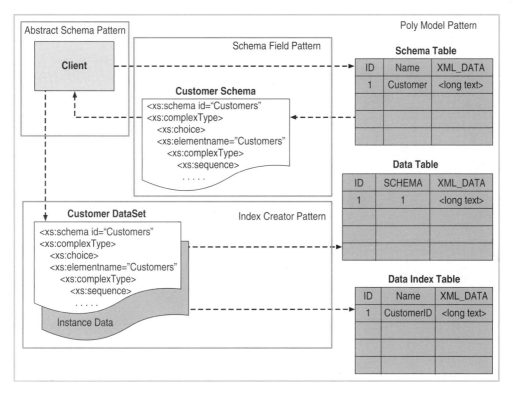

FIGURE 5.3: Overall flow of activity of the Poly Model "composite" pattern.

utilize this DataSet containing the originally requested schema, along with any instance data. The instance data comes from two sources. The first source comes from those scenarios where the client needs to save transaction data to the database, in which case the instance data will come from the client. The second source comes from scenarios where data is simply retrieved from the database. Here the schema and instance data should be returned in an already strongly typed DataSet to be consumed from the client as needed. To make use of a schema, you have to generate, store, and eventually retrieve one. That is where the Schema Field pattern comes in and is the next featured pattern.

Consequences

- *Isolates a framework from the ramifications of a changing data model.* Data models do and will always change, even after production. For those systems where

POLY SCHEMAS

One technique worth mentioning here in regard to working with custom schemas is the size of the schema—more specifically, the number of tables and complexity of the schema required. Although this is a design-specific decision, there are some best practices you may use going forward. All of the examples in this book and all of the schemas used during development have been what I term *Poly Schemas*. Poly Schemas are simply the inclusion of multiple tables in one schema (.XSD). If you are thinking "no kidding," let me clarify. I am talking about placing most, if not all, of your tables in one schema! This is especially true during the early stages of development because working with one initial schema will save you time and headaches moving forward. "Versioning" a schema is difficult enough with the same type of schema, but managing multiple schema versions of the same type can become extremely daunting if you are not careful.

Will using 20 tables versus 3 tables in a schema increase the size of your DataSet? Yes, but only at the schema level. The instance data itself will reside only when there is actual data in the DataSet. In other words, unused tables from the schema will appear only in the definition, and that typically will not cost you much in size and even less in performance. If anything else, I'd advise using a single schema for every major type of activity you are performing. For example, I use one schema for each major transactional area (Customers schema), one for the decision support and routing (see the Chained Service Factory of Chapter 4, and one for administration activities (see the Schema Indexer section later in this chapter). Again, the choice is yours but employing this Poly Schema implementation technique may save you from future hair pulling.

The only things to be truly worried about are specific memory limitations of passing large XML instance DataSets to Web services and the deserialization of those large sets. As of the time of writing this book, this limitation appeared to be around 2 MB. The rule of thumb I use for passing data to Web services that are using XML schemas is to limit my packet to under this threshold. For large packets, I recommend using Microsoft's DIME protocol typically used for SOAP attachments. The other option is to break up your packet logically, although this requires a little forethought.

change is common (and often), this pattern will provide the necessary insulation from those changes affecting the system. It will also minimize and may even eliminate the amount of resultant implementation changes that typically follow. Through the use of XML schemas to dynamically represent the schema used for each stored transaction, the data model is dynamically read into memory at runtime and can be altered on a transaction-by-transaction basis.

- *Provides an in-memory representation of the data model for data passing.* This provides the ability to pass any data from object to object. Schemas can be used to pass self-describing data, thus abstracting any business operation from any specific data representation. This pattern provides a stepping stone for implementing the Abstract Packet pattern for passing such data (see Chapter 4).

- *Complicates data query mechanisms.* When using Poly Model, a system must be designed (unless data never needs to be queried) to provide searchable lookup columns because all XML instance data will be stored in one column. One of the simplest means of building such a lookup column feature is to implement a solution using the Schema Indexer pattern in this chapter. Using an XML Schema Indexer customizable column, its corresponding value is dynamically stored in a separate table from that of the instance data but is typically stored at the same time in a two-phase operation. Later, that column can be used for instance data lookups using a cross-reference foreign key from the Index table.

- *Slows down transactional storage and data retrieval.* Despite the great advantages of providing a system with a dynamic data model system, there are some performance disadvantages. However, for those systems that can compensate for this disadvantage and/or be classified as nontransactional, this disadvantage can be addressed. The performance hit comes in two forms. Mainly due to the fact that two tables must be accessed, both for storage and retrieval, the operation will be slowed down to some extent. The other performance issues may arise at the repetitive storage of duplicate XML instance data. How much this slows down your performance is completely due to the complexity and the size of the instance data. Some normalization is warranted. It is recommended that those parts of the data architecture that require fast transactional throughput still utilize a normalized physical model.

- *Eliminates building an entire set of data access classes using SQL.* One of the biggest benefits of the Poly Model pattern is the ability to centralize the SQL for the entire business framework. Business objects or the specific data access objects no longer have to contain specific SQL for every table they access. In traditional data access layers, it is customary to have one or more tables represented by individual classes incorporating the SQL used to access those entities right in the classes themselves. As you will find out, using the Poly Model eliminates much of this SQL code. In fact, most of the data access objects can be eliminated altogether because the SQL is no longer specific to multiple tables. The only SQL used here will be contained in the Poly Model entity and the few child classes that inherit its functionality. I will touch on this point again later when I get into the mechanics and the child patterns of the Poly Model.

Participants

- Client (Data Service Façade)—This can be any client, not necessarily a front end. In fact, the client usually consists of your business-tier code directly accessing the data architecture. To simplify things in this implementation, the client is actually both a front end and the Web service that drives the data architecture.

- Data Access Object (Same name as implementation)—The generic data access object(s) of the data architecture.

Implementation

What if your business object could use the same method to store a transaction, no matter what table you write or what fields you populate? What if the same applied for retrieving instance data or any query, for that matter? Most application architectures would call for the business object to aggregate a specific data object that is tied directly to one or more tables and contains the SQL for those entities. The Poly Model completely abstracts this need, providing a generic data access framework, no matter what physical model is used. The beauty of the Poly Model is that it is rather simple, compared with some of the more complicated dynamic modeling out there using XML.

So what does the Poly Model look like in code? Storing a transaction, for example, looks like the simplified code snippet in Listing 5.9. Keep in mind that a Packet object is simply a wrapped DataSet object.

LISTING 5.9: StoreTransaction method that drives the Poly Model persistence engine.

```
public virtual bool StoreTransaction(Packet oTrans)
{
      try
      {
            . . .
// Delegates to provider-specific call
bResult = DBStoreTransactionRecord(oTrans);
            if(bResult)
```

```
        {
            // Schema Indexer - used for storing lookups
            // see schema Indexer Pattern later in this
            // chapter
        return StoreKeys(oTrans);
        }


        . . .


        return false;
    }
```

The code in Listing 5.9 delegates to a provider-specific implementation of the same function. After that, it calls StoreKeys. StoreKeys implements the Schema Indexer pattern, which is another child pattern I'll cover in this chapter. Until then, I will focus only on the actual data and data log storage. The following code takes the packet, stores the data in the data log, and finally stores the entire DataSet as XML in the instance data table, using the displayed stored procedures:

LISTING 5.10: Called by StoreTransaction to store data in the DATA table and DATA_LOG table.

```
public override bool DBStoreTransactionRecord(Packet oTrans)
    {
        try
        {
        . . .
            if(oTrans == null)
                return false;

            int iNumTries = 0;
            bool bResult = false;
            StringBuilder sb = null;

            while(iNumTries < DTPConstants.MAX_DB_ATTEMPTS)
            {
                // Write the database log record to the
                // DATA_LOG table
                bResult = DBStoreTransactionRecord(
                oTrans, "sp_DNPaternsUpdateDataLog");
                if(bResult)
                {
                    . . .
                    // Write the database record to
                    // the DATA table
                    return DBStoreTransactionRecord(
                    oTrans, "sp_DNPatternsUpdateData");
```

```
            }
            . . .
            iNumTries++;
        }
    . . .
return false;
}
    . . .
return false;
}
```

LISTING 5.11: Storing the actual instance data passed, using a DataSet and passed-in stored procedure.

```
public override bool DBStoreTransactionRecord(Packet oTrans,
string sStoredProcedureName)
    {
        try
        {
            if(oTrans == null)
                return false;
            if(sStoredProcedureName.Length == 0)
                return false;

            PolyModelData oDB = null;
            oDB =
            ModelFactory.CreatePolyModelData(
            sStoredProcedureName,
            CommandType.StoredProcedure);
            if(oDB == null)
                return false;

        v// Bind input stored procedure parameter
        vSqlParameter oInParm1 = null;
            oInParm1 = (SqlParameter)
            oDB.AddDataParameter("@TransID",
            SqlDbType.BigInt, ParameterDirection.Input);
            if(oInParm1 == null)
                return false;
            oInParm1.Value = oTrans.TransactionID;

            // Bind input stored procedure parameter
            SqlParameter oInParm2 = null;
            oInParm2 = (SqlParameter)
            oDB.AddDataParameter("@schemaID",
            SqlDbType.BigInt, ParameterDirection.Input);
            if(oInParm2 == null)
                return false;
            oInParm2.Value = oTrans.ProductschemaID;
```

```
        // Bind input stored procedure parameter
        SqlParameter oInParm3 = null;
        oInParm3 = (SqlParameter)
        oDB.AddDataParameter("@xmlData",
        SqlDbType.Image, ParameterDirection.Input);
        if(oInParm3 == null)
           return false;
        string sxml = string.Empty;
        sxml = oDB.WriteXml(oTrans.RawData,
        XmlWriteMode.Ignoreschema);
        oInParm3.Value = Encoding.ASCII.GetBytes(sxml);

        SqlParameter oOutParm = null;
        oOutParm = (SqlParameter)
        oDB.AddDataParameter("@RowCount",
        SqlDbType.Int, ParameterDirection.ReturnValue);
        if(oOutParm == null)
           return false;

        // Execute the stored procedure
        int iRowCount = 0;
        iRowCount = oDB.ExecuteNonQuery();

        // Get the result of the stored procedure
        int iCount = 0;
        iCount =
        Convert.ToInt32(oDB.GetDataParameterValue("@RowCount"));
        if(iCount == 1)
           return true;
   }
   . . .
   return false;
}
```

Both stored procedures are straightforward but are worth showing. The following is the stored procedure used for updating the data log:

LISTING 5.12: Stored procedure used for saving to the DATA_LOG table.

```
CREATE PROCEDURE dbo.sp_DNUpdateDataLog @TransID BIGINT, @schemaID
BIGINT,
@xmlData IMAGE AS


. . .


INSERT INTO dbo.[DATA_LOG] (TRANS_ID, SCHEMA_ID, xml_DATA, TIME_STAMP)
VALUES (@TransID, @schemaID, @xmlData, GETDATE())
```

```
. . .
GO
```

The next stored procedure is not much different. It will save data to the main instance data table that will be used for queries later:

LISTING 5.13: Stored procedure used for saving XML instance data to the main DATA table.

```
CREATE PROCEDURE dbo.sp_DNUpdateData @TransID BIGINT, @schemaID BIGINT,
@xmlData IMAGE AS

. . .

IF EXISTS (SELECT * FROM dbo.[DATA] WHERE TRANS_ID = @TransID)
    BEGIN

UPDATE dbo.[DATA] WITH (HOLDLOCK)
SET TRANS_ID = @TransID, SCHEMA_ID =
@schemaID, xml_DATA = @xmlData, TIME_STAMP = GETDATE()
WHERE TRANS_ID = @TransID
    END
ELSE
    BEGIN
        INSERT INTO dbo.[DATA] (TRANS_ID, SCHEMA_ID, xml_DATA,
TIME_STAMP) VALUES (@TransID, @schemaID, @xmlData,
GETDATE())
    END

. . .
GO
```

Much like the remaining code in this chapter, the above snippets are straight-forward. They do not rely heavily on any specific technology other than using XML and its schema from a generated DataSet. For every transaction that is stored, a reference to its schema will also get stored, along with the instance data, as XML. The fields that make up the physical model are used solely for storing the XML content, indexing the schema, and providing a transaction ID for later lookup (see the Schema Indexer section later in this chapter). Gone is the need to map each individual field of an object to individual fields of the database through a more traditional "data services" layer. Other than generating the appropriate keys for lookup, we now have given the developer a great deal of flexibility. This frees you from the daunting tasks of maintaining such a data services layer and all of the data objects that go along with it. For those systems that can put up with slightly slower transaction throughout and slightly larger DataSets, the Poly Model can really begin to shine. Once the framework is in place, the Poly Model allows much faster time to market and the elimination of hours of tedious data class development and maintenance.

Creating the Poly Model can have some great value propositions but data isn't very useful if you can't look up what you've now stored. Your data isn't much good to you if you cannot easily query for it. This is especially true during your development and debugging efforts because you will not be able to simply view the data in SQL Server—the instance data itself is now an "image" field stored in one column of the DATA table. This does present a slight problem in that tools have to be built to view this data. Tools specifically designed to view Poly Model data, such as the SQL tools, have been built to construct a complex filter so that you can get to specific rows of data while developing your business applications. But rest assured, those tools are *not* difficult to implement. The foundation for building these tools lies in designing a facility so that queries can be made against this denormalized physical model. This will be covered in detail when we discuss the Schema Indexer pattern later in this chapter.

Related Patterns

- Factory Method (GoF)

- Abstract Packet (Thilmany)

- Schema Field (Thilmany)

- Delegate (GoF)

- Schema Indexer (Thilmany)

SCHEMA FIELD PATTERN

Intent

To be able to store, retrieve, and manipulate data schemas dynamically. The means for passing descriptive metadata in an abstracted N-tier architecture.

Problem

Data schemas can be one of the most effective means by which data can be manipulated, stored, passed, or retrieved. They provide the structure and the backbone to what would otherwise be just another data abstraction layer manifested in ADO.NET. But what is the best way to create a schema? Once created, where does the schema go? How do you determine what schema to use? Where are the schemas kept, if anywhere? These are some of the questions I hope to answer in this chapter. However, the .NET framework has given you many means by which to manipulate schemas and DataSets. You can create from scratch at runtime any structure you want. You can also import any preexisting schema into a DataSet at runtime. You can use one schema containing many tables like a "floating" ERD or you can have one schema for each area of a database used for one particular purpose. You don't even have to know that a schema exists behind the scenes by strictly using ADO.NET against any supported database. The choices are many. So which one is the best? Well, that depends on what you need but here I try and provide the best of all worlds.

To support the Poly Model pattern, you must first have some structure to hold data. The basis of the pattern does not use a physical model for this purpose but the structure must come from somewhere. The only physical structure that will store instance data is the data table I mentioned in the previous section. This table does not contain any business structure, however, and that is where the schemas come in. To store business data, you must first have a schema, its instance data, and a key or two for lookup. To begin with, however, you must first have the schema defined. Once you have your schema or schemas, you need a place to put them. That is where the schema table comes in. As mentioned earlier, the only fields required of this physical table are an ID and the column that will hold the actual schema.

I do recommend a few more fields to add a little more flexibility to your solution, so I've created the schema table shown in Figure 5.4 in SQL Server.

Schemas do not have to be stored in a database but when you begin to work with several schema versions and types, creating a database table is usually the best option. This even goes for using strongly typed DataSets. You can use strongly typed DataSets to manage each schema at runtime. However, when using multiple versions, you must then manage different code sets, one for each DataSet/schema. Using a database table will simplify your life by providing a place to store your streamed schemas in one place.

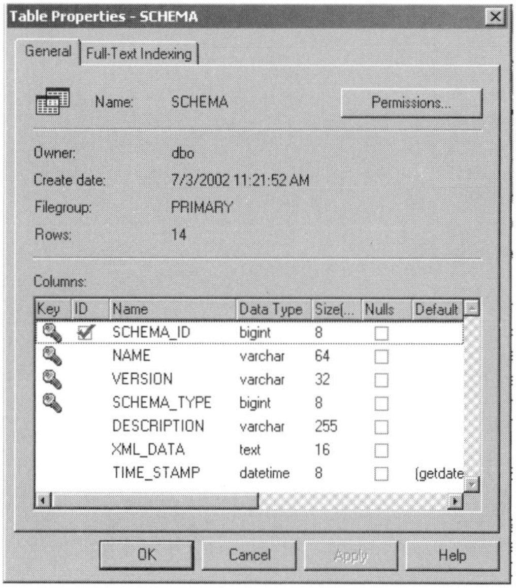

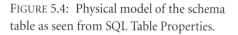

FIGURE 5.4: Physical model of the schema table as seen from SQL Table Properties.

Once you have your schema table, you can readily store your schemas, retrieve them at runtime using any version, instantiate your DataSet with the schema structure, and manipulate your data in memory as though you were working with any normal data services layer. Once you have your schema table, you then need to store at least one schema so that it can be retrieved and used within your architecture at runtime. Storing and retrieving schemas is the basis for this pattern and will give you the structure required to create your "floating" ERD in memory. To begin to get a feel for the structure of the Schema Field pattern reference Figure 5.5.

Forces

Use the Schema Field pattern when:

- Complex XML must be stored and organized by structure and/or type.

- Using the Poly Model pattern.

- Multiple schemas are used and categorized.

- Unmanaged clients need to pass DataSets into a .NET backbone.

- Using strongly typed DataSets that may contain multiple versions.

Structure

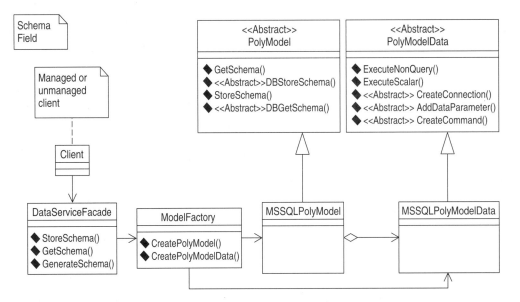

FIGURE 5.5: The Schema Field pattern class diagram.

The number of entities in the structure of this pattern is deceiving. The simplicity of the Schema Field pattern lies in the association between the DataServiceFacade, the ModelFactory, and the Poly Model object itself. The PolyModelData class represents generic data access functionality and does not have to be represented exactly as shown. Any data access methods could have been used. However, I believe it is important to abstract those lower level services with that of the PolyModel class. As you proceed deeper into the Poly Model pattern, you will see exactly what I'm referring to.

The Poly Model pattern is more generic than any "typical" data access layer. The Poly Model child class MSSQLPolyModel contains the specific SQL commands used to carry out each request. Only generic ADO wrapper implementations have been placed in the PolyModelData entity. Other than the PolyModel and the MSSQLPolyModel class, there is little reason to have any other business-specific entities that contain SQL as you typically see in most other data access layers. You have just eliminated hours of SQL design and encapsulation that you would normally have at this layer in the architecture. In fact, because most data access layers access numerous physical tables instead of only a few, as the Poly Model does, you typically have SQL spread throughout your classes. Most data access layers may even have one class for every table that it must access with the corresponding SQL command. This is *not* the case when employing the Poly Model pattern. Most of the SQL can now be centralized in one or two entities. In this case, those entities are the PolyModel class and the MSSQLPolyModel class. This is another advantage of using Poly Models. As far as the Schema Field pattern is concerned, the only SQL used is that SQL needed to carry out the retrieval and storage of the schemas themselves. Later I will show you how this is very similar to the handling of the actual instance data. During normal query and save operations, I will save and retrieve customer information using very generic SQL and utilizing the services of the Schema Field pattern as a starting point.

Consequences

- *Eliminates the need to manage multiple versions of strongly typed DataSet classes as part of the code tree.* Schemas do not have to be stored or retrieved. Using a factory, a strongly typed DataSet could be dynamically instantiated and used within the architecture without ever having to go to the database. This presents a problem, however. Future versions may be created after an application has gone to production, and supporting older versions may be necessary. In cases such as these, storing and retrieval schemas with the Schema Field pattern are strongly recommended.

- *Provides a means by which to retrieve structured XML in any capacity, including support for unmanaged clients.* For unmanaged clients, storing schemas in the database will provide direct access for those clients. The .NET DataSet does not have to be instantiated in this case, and the unmanaged client can treat the schema as any other well-formed XML document. This provides an interop layer for bridging technologies other than .NET. Remember that XML is universal.

- *Provides a schema version management framework.* As mentioned above, to support client access, older schemas will require some version management. Versioning the schemas while storing them and providing the code to dynamically access them will give the developer a starting point at which to build version management at the schema level.

Implementation

In the implementation that follows, you should notice quite a bit of code to do something as simple as storing and retrieving what amounts to a single field in the database. Do *not* be disheartened from this. I show most of the code used to perform such an operation so that the remaining patterns of this chapter can be better understood. It is the storing and retrieval of schemas that drives the rest of the PolyModel pattern, and it is crucial to its understanding. That said, the code below is rather self-explanatory and shows how a simple string value can hold the entire structure of your "floating" ERD or database in memory.

Once you have your structure, creating a DataSet from it is rather simple from .NET. The following code snippet (Listing 5.14) shows how to take your schema from memory and generate, or "hydrate" a DataSet from that point:

LISTING 5.14: Helper method to create a structure DataSet from an XML schema.

```
virtual public void ReadXmlschema(DataSet oDS, string sschema)
  {
     if(oDS == null)
        return;

     System.IO.StringReader oReader = null;
     oReader = new System.IO.StringReader(sschema);
     if(oReader != null)
        oDS.ReadXmlschema(oReader);
  }
```

If you are using other tools besides .NET to send and receive DataSets, you will have to build your own DataSet, using something such as Microsoft's XML DOM to manipulate a schema manually and duplicate what .NET has conveniently placed into the DataSet class for you. In fact, in the application featured in Chapter 6, we've done just that; virtually creating the DataSet class in an unmanaged world. This is one way to appreciate what Microsoft has done with ADO.NET and XML!

The following code will kick-start your ability to apply the Poly Model by first allowing you to generate a schema and save it. For this implementation, I am using only one schema I created in Visual Studio, called *Customers*. It is the same schema I introduced in the previous section and will be the schema I use throughout this chapter. In the Generate Schema Web method, I simply construct the Customers object (as you will remember from the previous section, this will be generated by Visual Studio) and once the schema is created, I called StoreSchema(). Before calling the StoreSchema function, I insert a dummy blank row so that the returned schema will show the instance data to give you a feel for the structure in the browser. Once in the StoreSchema function, I immediately instantiate a class called PolyModel that acts as a factory for my data provider.

Once I have the PolyModel class, I call StoreSchema(), and I pass the product name, version, description, type, and, of course, the actual DataSet. These are optional but are recommended to give you the most flexibility when adding other schemas to your framework. The product name is the friendly name for the schema and will be used for lookups other than the key. The version can be used to distinguish multiple versions of the same schema. For example, if you anticipate the schema changing slightly and you want to support older schemas, versioning is your friend. Versioning can be tricky. Versioning Schema Field additions will be much simpler than trying to manage schemas whose fields have been deleted. Deleted fields can cause problems for pieces of code expecting them to exist, so be careful. Besides the other obvious parameters of description and DataSet, the type parameter categorizes the schema and again is optional. For example, in the production application featured in Chapter 6, we use three primary types of schemas:

1. Decision schemas—used for dynamic routing of logic.

2. Lookup schemas—used in the Schema Indexer pattern explained in this chapter.

3. Product schemas—used to hold typical instance data, such as the Customers data generated from the schema featured here.

LISTING 5.15: Used to generate and optionally save a schema to the database SCHEMA table.

```
[WebMethod]
   public DataSet Generateschema(
        string sProduct, string sVersion,
        string sDescription, bool bStore)
   {
      Customers dsCustomers = null;
      try
      {
         dsCustomers = new Customers();

         Customers.CustomerRow oRow =
      dsCustomers.Customer.NewCustomerRow();

 // solely for testingoRow.CustomerID = "123";
         oRow.CompanyName = "The eTier Group";
         oRow.ContactName = "Christian Thilmany";
         oRow.Phone = "713-555-2343";
      dsCustomers.Customer.AddCustomerRow(oRow);
         dsCustomers.Customer.AcceptChanges();
```

```
        if (bStore)
            Storeschema(sProduct, sVersion,
    sDescription, dsCustomers);
        }
    catch(Exception ex)
    {
        throw new
    BaseException(
    Utilities.BuildErrorMessage(
    "Exception thrown",
    ex.Message), true);
        }
        return dsCustomers;
    }
```

LISTING 5.16: Helper method to save the passed-in schema to the database using the Poly Model object.

```
[WebMethod]
public DataSet Storeschema(string sProduct,
string sVersion, string sDescription, DataSet ds)
{
    try
    {

    ModelFactory.CreatePolyModel().Storeschema(
    sProduct, sVersion,
    DTPConstants.SCHEMA_TYPE.PRODUCT, sDescription, ds);
    }
    catch (Exception ex)
    {
        throw new
    BaseException(
    Utilities.BuildErrorMessage(
    "Exception thrown",
    ex.Message), true);
    }

    return null;
}
```

The following StoreSchema method is called from the previous Web method, and it simply delegates to my specific provider's DBStoreSchema method. This only provides another level of abstraction for my implementation.

LISTING 5.17: Generic StoreSchema method from the PolyModel class.

```
public virtual bool Storeschema(string sName,
string sVersion,
DTPConstants.SCHEMA_TYPE eType,
string sDescription,
DataSet oschema)
   {
      bool bResult = false;

      try
      {
         Profiler.BeginInstrumentation();

         //Check argument
         . . .

         int iNumTries = 0;

         StringBuilder sb = null;

         while(iNumTries < DTPConstants.MAX_DB_ATTEMPTS)
         {
            //Write the schema to the database
            bResult = DBStoreschema(sName,
      sVersion, eType, sDescription, oschema);
            if(bResult)
            {
               //See if we are in a retry loop
               if(iNumTries > 0)
               {
                     . . .
               }
               return true;}

   . . .

   iNumTries++;
      }

      . . .
      return false;
   }
   . . .
   return false;
}
```

The heart of the implementation lies within the DBStoreSchema method below. Looking through the code, you should immediate recognize that this is like any other ordinary ADO save routine, however. The only difference is I am using a stored procedure called *sp_DNPatternsUpdateschema* to update the schema table with my schema. Up to this point, many of the original parameters have been passed inward, and now it's time to extract the schema itself and update the database with it. Two things should be pointed out here. The following snippet uses another factory to create a provider specific to SQL Server. This "Data Factory" is a very clean way to support multiple providers on the back end in case you are using Oracle. The following code is used to actually create the SQL Server provider and connect to the database. How you implement this piece is up to you.

LISTING 5.18: Using a provider factory to create the appropriate Model object.

```
PolyModelData oDB = null;
   oDB =
      ModelFactory.CreatePolyModelData(
      "sp_DNPatternsUpdateschema",
      CommandType.StoredProcedure);
   if(oDB == null)
      return false;
```

The second snippet worth pointing out is how to extract the schema from the DataSet. Fortunately for you, .NET makes it easy. Here I call WriteXml(), which is shown in Listing 5.19. WriteXml() uses a StringWriter class to pass into the DataSet's overloaded version of WriteXml and simply tell it to write the schema only. That's it for generating and saving schemas!

LISTING 5.19: Extracts the schema from PolyModelData object.

```
string sxml = string.Empty;
   sxml = oDB.WriteXml(oschema,
      XmlWriteMode.Writeschema);
   if(sxml.Length == 0)
      return false;
   oInParm5.Value = sxml;
```

Below is the DBStoreschema method from the MSSQLPolyModel class:

LISTING 5.20: Shows the use of a store procedure to store the schema field.

```
   public override bool DBStoreschema(string sschemaName,
string sVersion,
```

```
DTPConstants.SCHEMA_TYPE eType,
string sDescription, DataSet oschema)
    {
      try
      {
          Profiler.BeginInstrumentation();

          //Check inputs
          if(sschemaName.Length == 0)
             return false;

          //Check argument
          if(eType == DTPConstants.SCHEMA_TYPE.UNKNOWN)
             return false;

          //Check argument
          if(sVersion.Length == 0)
             return false;

          //Check argument
          if(oschema == null)
             return false;

          //Check argument
          string sDescription2 = sDescription;
          if(sDescription.Length == 0)
             sDescription2 = "Default Description";

          PolyModelData oDB = null;
          oDB =
      ModelFactory.CreatePolyModelData(
      "sp_DNPatternsUpdateschema",
      CommandType.StoredProcedure);
          if(oDB == null)
             return false;

          //Bind input stored procedure parameter
          SqlParameter oInParm1 = null;

          oInParm1 = (SqlParameter)
      oDB.AddDataParameter("@Name",
      SqlDbType.VarChar, 64,
      ParameterDirection.Input);
          if(oInParm1 == null)
             return false;
          oInParm1.Value = sschemaName;

          SqlParameter oInParm2 = null;
          oInParm2 = (SqlParameter)
```

```
oDB.AddDataParameter("@Version",
SqlDbType.VarChar, 64,
ParameterDirection.Input);
   if(oInParm2 == null)
      return false;
   oInParm2.Value = sVersion;

   SqlParameter oInParm3 = null;
   oInParm3 = (SqlParameter)
oDB.AddDataParameter("@schemaType",
SqlDbType.BigInt,
ParameterDirection.Input);
   if(oInParm3 == null)
      return false;
   oInParm3.Value = (long) eType;

   //Bind input stored procedure parameter
   SqlParameter oInParm4 = null;
   oInParm4 = (SqlParameter)
oDB.AddDataParameter("@Description",
SqlDbType.VarChar, 255,
ParameterDirection.Input);
   if(oInParm4 == null)
      return false;
   oInParm4.Value = sDescription2;
   //Bind input stored procedure parameter
   SqlParameter oInParm5 = null;
   oInParm5 = (SqlParameter)
oDB.AddDataParameter("@xmlData",
SqlDbType.Text, ParameterDirection.Input);
   if(oInParm5 == null)
      return false;
   string sxml = string.Empty;

   sxml = oDB.WriteXml(oschema,
XmlWriteMode.Writeschema);
   if(sxml.Length == 0)
      return false;
   oInParm5.Value = sxml;

   SqlParameter oOutParm = null;
   oOutParm = (SqlParameter)
oDB.AddDataParameter("@RowCount",
SqlDbType.Int, ParameterDirection.ReturnValue);
   if(oOutParm == null)
      return false;

   //Execute the stored procedure
   int iRowCount = 0;
```

```
      iRowCount = oDB.ExecuteNonQuery();

      //Get the result of the stored procedure
      int iCount = 0;
      iCount =
   Convert.ToInt32(
   oDB.GetDataParameterValue(
   "@RowCount"));
      if(iCount == 1)
         return true;
   }
   catch(SqlException e)
   {
      LogSQLException(e);
   }
   catch(Exception e)
   {
      Trace.WriteLineIf(
   Config.TraceError, e.Message);
   }
   finally
   {
      . . .
   }

   return false;
}
```

LISTING 5.21: Serializes, in memory, a string representation of the schema stored in the DataSet passed.

```
virtual public string WriteXml(
     DataSet oDS, XmlWriteMode eMode)
{
   if(oDS == null)
      return string.Empty;

   System.IO.StringWriter oSW = null;
   oSW = new System.IO.StringWriter();
   if(oSW == null)
      return string.Empty;

   oDS.WriteXml(oSW, eMode);

   return oSW.ToString();
}
```

Now you should have a Customers schema saved. So how do you retrieve and populate a DataSet? Like storing schemas, retrievals are self-explanatory and start with a driver method called *GetSchema()*. This method creates a Poly Model object as before, calls StoreSchema() from the Poly Model object, and uses a simple SQL command to retrieve the schema from the database. Once the schema has been returned as a string, it can be traversed manually from any unmanaged client or simply used to construct a DataSet.

LISTING 5.22: Web service driver for retrieving schemas from the database.

```
[WebMethod]
    public DataSet Getschema(string sschemaName,
    string sVersion, DTPConstants.SCHEMA_TYPE eType)
    {
        PolyModelData oDB =
    ModelFactory.CreatePolyModelData();

oDB.ReadXmlschema(ModelFactory.CreatePolyModel()
    .DBGetschema(sschemaName,
    sVersion, eType));
        return oDB.Data;
    }
```

LISTING 5.23: Poly Model method for retrieving schemas from the database using straight SQL.

```
public override string DBGetschema(
string sschemaName, string sVersion,
DTPConstants.SCHEMA_TYPE eType)
    {
        try
        {
            Profiler.BeginInstrumentation();

            //Check inputs
            if(sschemaName.Length == 0)
                return string.Empty;
            if(sVersion.Length == 0)
                return string.Empty;
    if(eType == DTPConstants.SCHEMA_TYPE.UNKNOWN)
                return string.Empty;

            StringBuilder sbSQL = new StringBuilder();

            //Define the query to execute
                sbSQL.Append("execute
            //sp_executesql ");
```

```
sbSQL.Append("N'SELECT xml_DATA FROM" +
"dbo.[SCHEMA] WHERE NAME = @schemaName" +
"AND VERSION = @schemaVersion AND" + "SCHEMA_TYPE = @schemaType', ");

        sbSQL.Append("N'@schemaName VARCHAR(65), " +
"@schemaVersion VARCHAR(32), " + "@schemaType BIGINT', ");

sbSQL.AppendFormat("@schemaName ='{0}', " +
"@schemaVersion = '{1}', @schemaType = "
+ "{2} ", sschemaName,
sVersion, Convert.ToInt32(eType));

    return GetschemaBySQL(sbSQL.ToString());
}
. . .
return string.Empty;
}
```

This section contained quite bit of code but that is exactly the heart of this pattern, which borders more on implementation than design. The Schema Field pattern is an implementation solution but also the process pattern for saving and retrieving the actual bits and bytes of the schema to a persistent store.

Related Patterns

- Schema Indexer (Thilmany)

- Poly Model (Thilmany)

- Delegate (GoF)

- Abstract Schema (Thilmany)

- Factory Method (GoF)

- Abstract Packet (Thilmany)

SCHEMA INDEXER

Intent

To be able to index, create a set of lookup keys, and provide a means of data retrieval for Schema Fields (above) and the Poly Model composite pattern.

Problem

When using the Poly Model pattern, unless you know the transaction ID key of the stored record, you will have a difficult time retrieving that data. Traversing each record, reading its XML instance data, then performing an XPath query on the returned XML would take a prohibitive amount of time. The Schema Indexer, a child pattern to the Poly Model, performs this task by adding an additional step to each transaction's save operation.

If you recalled during the StoreTransaction operation in the first section, there was a call to StoreKeys(). (StoreKeys() will be shown in the implementation section below). The Schema Indexer solves the Poly Model lookup problem by storing, in a separate table, all required key field values from the XML instance data, then referencing the original transaction ID. It references the transaction ID from the DATA table such that it can be the basis for lookup later, utilizing predefined meta-information for determining which fields to use. With both the field value used for lookup and the transaction ID from the XML instance data, the data can be retrieved using an INDEX table. The transaction ID of the INDEX table acts as a foreign key to the DATA table. The fields and the values used are dynamically configurable, and I provide a means to save this information at runtime.

The Schema Indexer is undoubtedly coupled to the Poly Model and the schema using the implementation provided. However, this pattern can be applied in other scenarios, such as caching, and thus stands on its own as well. There are several ways to solve the problem of allowing field queries on Poly Models, and this is only one solution to that problem. You will find, however, that this can quickly become a very complicated feature. However, simplicity is the key here, and the Schema Indexer should fit the mold of each pattern in the chapter by remaining simple to implement and I hope simple to understand, as well.

The reason transaction retrievals were not immediately displayed in the Poly Model pattern is that I felt this pattern must first be understood as a composite. This is also due to the fact that during most query operations, unique values such as transaction IDs may not be known. This pattern rounds out the Poly Model by building a dynamic index during each save operation. Once built, the index can then be used to look up the appropriate transaction key that points to the XML instance data stored in the DATA table. If you've ever built your own database or worked with indexes in the past, this should be second nature, and you may even want to develop your own means of field lookup. For those who have not, the

Schema Indexer provides a simple means for providing lookup functionality for your Poly Model implementation.

Forces

Use the Schema Indexer pattern when:

- Using the Poly Model pattern.

- Multiple schemas are used and categorized.

- Queries are required on fields other than the primary key of any instance data table.

- The fields used for lookup need to be dynamic and configurable.

- Two-phase save operations do not prohibit usability or affect performance.

Structure

The structure simply consists of three methods and one schema element. DeleteKeys(), StoreKeys(), and StoreKey() are the methods used to store the actual lookup key information. LOOKUP (Listing 5.24) is the XML element used as the structure by which its instance data will contain what actual tables and columns will be used to look up information from other tables (in your data store) or from other XML elements.

These methods are typically provided as part of the Poly Model classes, such as those shown in the Schema Indexer class diagram (Figure 5.6).

Once you understand the premise and examine the code behind the StoreKey methods, the Schema Indexer pattern is rather self-explanatory. The only other structural element in this pattern is the XML entity used to hold the lookup or reference meta-information. Next you must define what fields will be stored in the INDEX table. This is where the LOOKUP schema element comes into play. This XML item can be added to the Customer's schema (shown in the Poly Model section) or it may reside in its own schema. Its instance can be stored separately or as part of the main schema itself.

The structure is rather simple, as you can see:

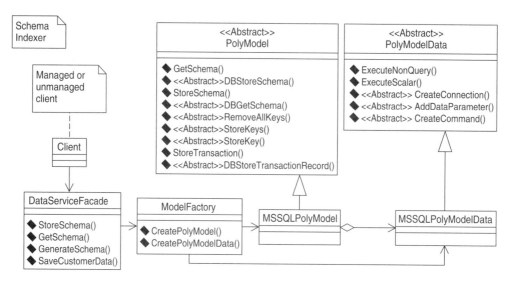

FIGURE 5.6:   Schema Indexer pattern class diagram.

LISTING 5.24: Sample LOOKUP element structure to be used for lookup column instance data.

```
<xs:element name="LOOKUP">
   <xs:complexType>
      <xs:sequence>
         <xs:element name="TABLE" type="xs:string" minOccurs="0" />
         <xs:element name="COLUMN" type="xs:string" minOccurs="0" />
      </xs:sequence>
   </xs:complexType>
</xs:element>
```

The important thing is that somehow the LOOKUP element and its associated instance data must be accessible during transaction save operations. In the implementation of this pattern, the lookup instance data is stored along with the entire schema used for saving Customer information. In this case, the instance data of the LOOKUP element will look something like Listing 5.25 (notice that both the LOOKUP structure and its diffgram data are part of the same XML document):

LISTING 5.25: Sample Data schema with LOOKUP element and sample LOOKUP instance data.

```
<?xml version="1.0" encoding="utf-8" ?>
<DataSet xmlns="http://tempuri.org/">
```

```xml
<xs:schema id="Customers" targetNamespace="http://tempuri.org/Customers.xsd"
xmlns:mstns="http://tempuri.org/Customers.xsd" xmlns="http://tempuri.org/
Customers.xsd" xmlns:xs="http://www.w3.org/2001/xmlschema"
xmlns:msdata="urn:schemas-microsoft-com:xml-msdata"
attributeFormDefault="qualified" elementFormDefault="qualified">
 <xs:element name="Customers" msdata:IsDataSet="true">
<xs:complexType>
<xs:choice maxOccurs="unbounded">
<xs:element name="Customer">
<xs:complexType>
<xs:sequence>
    <xs:element name="CustomerID" type="xs:string" />
    <xs:element name="CompanyName" type="xs:string" />
    <xs:element name="ContactName" type="xs:string" minOccurs="0" />
    <xs:element name="ContactTitle" type="xs:string" minOccurs="0" />
    <xs:element name="Address" type="xs:string" minOccurs="0" />
    <xs:element name="City" type="xs:string" minOccurs="0" />
    <xs:element name="Region" type="xs:string" minOccurs="0" />
    <xs:element name="PostalCode" type="xs:string" minOccurs="0" />
    <xs:element name="Country" type="xs:string" minOccurs="0" />
    <xs:element name="Phone" type="xs:string" minOccurs="0" />
    <xs:element name="Fax" type="xs:string" minOccurs="0" />
    </xs:sequence>
    </xs:complexType>
    </xs:element>


.   .   .

<xs:element name="LOOKUP">
<xs:complexType>
<xs:sequence>
    <xs:element name="TABLE" type="xs:string" minOccurs="0" />
    <xs:element name="COLUMN" type="xs:string" minOccurs="0" />
    </xs:sequence>
    </xs:complexType>
    </xs:element>
    </xs:choice>
    </xs:complexType>
<xs:unique name="CustomersKey1" msdata:PrimaryKey="true">
    <xs:selector xpath=".//mstns:Customer" />
    <xs:field xpath="mstns:CustomerID" />
    </xs:unique>
    </xs:element>
    </xs:schema>
<diffgr:diffgram xmlns:msdata="urn:schemas-microsoft-com:xml-msdata"
xmlns:diffgr="urn:schemas-microsoft-com:xml-diffgram-v1">
<Customers xmlns="http://tempuri.org/Customers.xsd">
<LOOKUP diffgr:id="LOOKUP1" msdata:rowOrder="0">
    <TABLE>Customer</TABLE>
```

```
    <COLUMN>CompanyName</COLUMN>
    </LOOKUP>
<LOOKUP diffgr:id="LOOKUP2" msdata:rowOrder="1">
    <TABLE>Customer</TABLE>
    <COLUMN>ContactName</COLUMN>
    </LOOKUP>
    </Customers>
    </diffgr:diffgram>
    </DataSet>
```

During a call to StoreTransaction() in the PolyModel child class, StoreKeys() will be called to get the lookup information (above) and store its referenced fields as part of the INDEX table. This is a two-phase operation, and it will slightly impact performance because of that fact, compared with the single table insert you would get with traditional database I/O. The other methods, StoreKey() and RemoveKeys(), are helper methods used by StoreKeys() to delete the keys initially and store each key, respectively.

Using this schema element and instance data to pass to the StoreKeys method, you can dynamically build your own cross-reference index table. Any future data retrieval can query the INDEX table, find the queried fields, and look up the reference transaction ID. Again, this will be a two-step operation. Once the transaction ID is found on the queried INDEX record, the actual XML instance from the DATA table can then be queried. It must be accomplished in that order. All of these steps seem like a lot of work. However, the benefits you receive by implementing such a model will pay huge dividends. Each time you need fields, tables, or any other data element, you avoid having to consistently maintain your data access layer once the framework is built. The flexibility of this solution makes up for the fact that you will have two operations instead of one for storage and retrieval. Everything is a tradeoff but the benefits to systems such as the one featured in Chapter 6 make this pattern a viable choice.

Consequences

- *Provides a dynamic means of adding an index to transactional data.* Through the use of a two-phase operation storing transactional information using a Poly Model, an index can be built and later used for queries. This adds the benefit of being able to query on multiple fields other than the transaction ID column of the original transaction.

- *Provides a means by which to retrieve structured XML content in any capacity, including support for unmanaged clients.* For unmanaged clients, storing schemas in the database will provide direct access for those clients. The .NET DataSet does not have to be instantiated in this case, and the unmanaged client can treat the schema as any other well-formed XML document.

- *Adds complexity to the schema and additional steps during transactional operations.* Although the benefits of being able to perform complex queries can outweigh its consequences, there are added steps to consider. This complexity is minimal but the architecture must be understood and well designed through solid index handling; otherwise, debugging may become more difficult.

- *Adds a second phase to all of the transactional save operations and will slightly decrease performance.* This consequence goes without saying because there is an extra step to be performed. In most cases, a managed two-phase commit may be necessary unless database cleanup operations can be added to ensure data integrity.

Implementation

In the Poly Model pattern implementation above, one call is made for each corresponding call to the StoreTransaction method. After the XML instance data is stored, we must store the lookup keys for fields we will be looking up in the future. These fields must be defined at some point. Typically, they are defined during some configuration ceremony, such as application setup. They can even be set up dynamically, based on an implementation-specific algorithm. For my purposes, I use a separate schema definition called a *Lookup schema* to define the structure of what makes up the Lookup fields referenced below. The Lookup schema should be set up and persisted so that at runtime it can be passed along with the instance data each time a transaction must be stored. A convenient way to transport the Lookup schema reference along with any other form of metadata for the packet is to use the Abstract Packet pattern, as mentioned in Chapter 4 The Schema Indexer code does just that!

In Listing 5.26, the StoreKeys method receives a packet containing the following items that will be used to save the index information. This method then stores the

CHALLENGE 5.2

> What about data retrievals? How should they be designed using the Poly Model and the Schema Indexer?
>> *The end of the chapter will discuss options for Poly Model data retrievals.*

following information to be later referenced by your retrieve methods or as part of an ad hoc query facility defined by you:

- Original XML Instance Data—used for finding the field value to be referenced for future queries and stored in the INDEX table.

- Lookup Schema—provides the structure of the lookup field data.

- Lookup Schema Instance Data—the actual lookup fields.

- Transaction ID—used for the foreign key of the INDEX table.

LISTING 5.26: Method called to save lookup column when saving all transactions in the Poly Model.

```
public override bool StoreKeys(Packet oTrans)
{
    try
    {
        if(oTrans == null)
            return false;

        //Delete all existing keys
        bool bRemoveKeys = false;
        bRemoveKeys = RemoveAllKeys(oTrans);

        string sxmlschema = null;
        sxmlschema =
    GetschemaAsString(
    oTrans.ProductLookupschemaID);
        if(sxmlschema.Length == 0)
            return false;

        PolyModelData oDB =
    ModelFactory.CreatePolyModelData();
        oDB.ReadXml(sxmlschema, XmlReadMode.Readschema);

        if(oDB.Contains("LOOKUP") == false)
            return false;
```

```
   int iRowCount = 0;
   iRowCount =
oDB.Data.
Tables[LOOKUP_DATATABLENAME].Rows.Count;

   for(int i = 0; i < iRowCount; i++)
   {
      string sTable = string.Empty;
      sTable =
Convert.ToString(oDB[LOOKUP_DATATABLENAME,
LOOKUP_DATACOLUMN_TABLE, i]);
      if(sTable.Length == 0)
         continue;

      string sColumn = string.Empty;
      sColumn =
Convert.ToString(
oDB[LOOKUP_DATATABLENAME,
LOOKUP_DATACOLUMN_COLUMN, i]);
      if(sColumn.Length == 0)
         continue;

      string sValue = string.Empty;
      sValue =
oTrans.RawData.Tables[sTable]
.Rows[0][sColumn].ToString();
      if(sValue.Length == 0)
         continue;

      bool bResult = false;
      bResult = StoreKey(
   oTrans.TransactionID, sColumn, sValue);
   }

   return true;
}
. . .
```

The RemoveAllKeys method (Listing 5.27) is the cleanup method called during each StoreKeys() invocation. This ensures that we are refreshing the lookup information and keeps us from duplicating index data.

LISTING 5.27: Cleans up all lookup keys from the INDEX table—typically right before the StoreKey operation.

```
public override bool RemoveAllKeys(Packet oTrans)
   {
      try
```

```
{
    Profiler.BeginInstrumentation();

    // Check argument
    if(oTrans == null)
       return false;

    // There must be a Transaction ID to use to lookup
    // all corresponding keys
    if(oTrans.TransactionID == 0)
       return false;

    StringBuilder sbSQL = new StringBuilder();
    //Define the query to execute
    sbSQL.Append("execute sp_executesql N'DELETE FROM " +
"dbo.DATA_IDX WHERE TRANS_ID = " +
"@TransID', ");

    sbSQL.AppendFormat(
"N'@TransID BIGINT', @TransID = {0}",
oTrans.TransactionID);

    PolyModelData oDB = null;
    oDB = ModelFactory.CreatePolyModelData();
    if(oDB == null)
       return false;

    // Execute the query
    int iRowCount = 0;
    iRowCount =
Convert.ToInt32(oDB.ExecuteNonQuery(sbSQL));

    return true;
}
. . .
```

Finally, StoreKey() is called by StoreKeys() for each key to store, and the information is stored in the index using the stored procedure DNUpdateDataIdx (Listing 5.28). This method takes the transaction ID and saves it to the index table. The transaction ID will later be treated as a foreign key to look up the original DATA record stored. The other two columns stored in the INDEX table are the column name and the column value from the actual instance data.

LISTING 5.28: Helper method to store the lookup key—rarely called publicly.

```
    public override bool StoreKey(long lTransID, string sKeyName,
string sValue)
```

```
{
  try
  {
    if(lTransID == 0)
       return false;

    if(sKeyName.Length == 0)
       return false;

    if(sValue.Length == 0)
       return false;

    PolyModelData oDB = null;
    oDB =
ModelFactory.CreatePolyModelData(
"sp_DNUpdateDataIdx",
CommandType.StoredProcedure);
    if(oDB == null)
       return false;

    // Bind input stored procedure parameter
    SqlParameter oInParm1 = null;
    oInParm1 = (SqlParameter)
oDB.AddDataParameter("@TransID",
SqlDbType.BigInt,
ParameterDirection.Input);
    if(oInParm1 == null)
       return false;
    oInParm1.Value = lTransID;

    //Bind input stored procedure parameter
    SqlParameter oInParm2 = null;
    oInParm2 = (SqlParameter)
oDB.AddDataParameter("@Name",
SqlDbType.VarChar, 64,
ParameterDirection.Input);
    if(oInParm2 == null)
       return false;
    oInParm2.Value = sKeyName;

    //Bind input stored procedure parameter
    SqlParameter oInParm3 = null;
    oInParm3 = (SqlParameter)
oDB.AddDataParameter("@Value",
SqlDbType.VarChar, 255,
ParameterDirection.Input);
    if(oInParm3 == null)
       return false;
    oInParm3.Value = sValue;
```

```
        // Bind output stored procedure parameter (holds T-
        // SQL RETURN(x) value)
        SqlParameter oOutParm = null;
        oOutParm = (SqlParameter)
   oDB.AddDataParameter("@RowCount",
   SqlDbType.Int,
   ParameterDirection.ReturnValue);
        if(oOutParm == null)
           return false;

        //Execute the stored procedure
        int iRowCount = 0;
        iRowCount = oDB.ExecuteNonQuery();

        //Get the result of the stored procedure
        int iCount = 0;
        iCount =
   Convert.ToInt32(
   oDB.GetDataParameterValue("@RowCount"));
        if(iCount == 1)
           return true;
    }
. . .
```

The stored procedure to update the INDEX table is as follows in Listing 5.29 (some of the nonapplicable implementation is not shown).

LISTING 5.29: Stored procedure source for storing lookup values to the INDEX table.

```
CREATE PROCEDURE dbo.sp_DNUpdateDataIdx @TransID BIGINT, @Name
VARCHAR(64),
@Value VARCHAR(255) AS

. . .

IF EXISTS (SELECT * FROM dbo.[DATA_IDX] WHERE TRANS_ID = @TransID AND
NAME = @Name)
    BEGIN
       UPDATE dbo.[DATA_IDX] WITH (HOLDLOCK) SET TRANS_ID = @TransID,
NAME = @Name, VALUE = @Value, TIME_STAMP = GETDATE() WHERE TRANS_ID =
@TransID AND NAME = @Name
    END
ELSE
    BEGIN
       INSERT INTO dbo.[DATA_IDX] (TRANS_ID, NAME, VALUE, TIME_STAMP)
VALUES (@TransID, @Name, @Value, GETDATE())
```

```
    END

.   .   .

GO
```

Once the XML instance data has been stored its index information should also be stored and you are now ready to query the data using a "Poly query," if you will. The method of querying depends a lot on how the Schema Index was created and is very implementation-specific. For example, queries can be built dynamically or they can be canned. The queries can return a single table or all corresponding tables in the instance data. The return rows can be packaged as individual packets in a sort of "packet collection" or all records can be contained in one XML stream. The choices are many and probably would warrant a book of their own.

One implementation of a Poly Model query is shown in the Listing 5.30 code snippet. Here, only the table in question is returned in its own XML instance data as part of a packet. This is only one solution option, so I'll leave it up to you how to decide to implement yours. In fact, the Abstract Packet pattern was used as part of the means to contain the DataSet to keep metadata such as transaction ID separated in each packet for each row returned. These routines are implemented as part of a Web method used to return any row based on query logic as part of a where clause, using a corresponding Where object to build the query.

The following Web method simply gets the ball rolling by generating a new schema to be stored (for details, see the Schema Field pattern section in this chapter). In addition to the schema, lookup instance data using the LOOKUP entity shown earlier is added to a schema diffgram. This allows you to find the lookup tables and columns while storing transactions using StoreKeys by incorporating the referenced schema with the instance data for the lookup. There are other ways you can design this but the following is one of the easiest ways to get up and running:

LISTING 5.30: Sample schema generator coupled with sample LOOKUP instance data for convenience.

```
[WebMethod]
    public DataSet GenerateCustomerschema(string sProduct,
        string sVersion, string sDescription,
        bool bStore)
    {
        Customers dsCustomers = null;
        try
```

```
    {
        dsCustomers = new Customers();

        // add lookup instance data at this time...
        Customers.LOOKUPRow oRow =
    dsCustomers.LOOKUP.NewLOOKUPRow();

        // solely for testing and showing instance data....
        oRow.COLUMN = "CompanyName";
        oRow.TABLE = "Customer";
        dsCustomers.LOOKUP.AddLOOKUPRow(oRow);
        dsCustomers.LOOKUP.AcceptChanges();

        oRow = dsCustomers.LOOKUP.NewLOOKUPRow();
        oRow.COLUMN = "ContactName";
        oRow.TABLE = "Customer";
        dsCustomers.LOOKUP.AddLOOKUPRow(oRow);
        dsCustomers.LOOKUP.AcceptChanges();

        if (bStore)
            Storeschema(sProduct, sVersion,
        sDescription, dsCustomers);
        }
        catch(Exception ex)
        {
            throw new
    BaseException(Utilities.BuildErrorMessage(
    "Exception thrown", ex.Message), true);
        }
        return dsCustomers;
    }
```

The following Web method was used only for testing and shows how a Where-Collection object can used to build a query using the Poly Model and Schema Indexer as a prerequisite. This an ad hoc query-testing method used to build a query and send it to the Poly Model for data retrieval. If the lookup columns have been set up and data has been saved, data can be retrieved using something like the code in Listing 5.31.

LISTING 5.31: Sample ad hoc query method used for testing Poly Model queries.

```
    [WebMethod]
    public DataSet GetTransactionByWhereCollectionEx(string sColumn1,
string sValue1, string sColumn2,
string sValue2, string sColumn3,
string sValue3)
    {
```

```
      PolyModelWhereCollection colWhere =
ModelFactory.CreatePolyModelWhereCollection();

if (sColumn1 != string.Empty)
        colWhere.Add(sColumn1, sValue1);
     if (sColumn2 != string.Empty)
        colWhere.Add(sColumn2, sValue2);
     if (sColumn3 != string.Empty)
        colWhere.Add(sColumn3, sValue3);

     return ModelFactory.CreatePolyModel()
     .GetTransaction(colWhere).RawData;
   }
```

The following is called from the above test method and immediately passed to DBGetTransactionBySQL(), extracting a custom SQL command built using the WhereCollection object:

LISTING 5.32: Sample transaction retrieval method using a WhereCollection SQL builder.

```
public virtual Packet GetTransaction(
PolyModelWhereCollection colWhere)
   {
     StringBuilder sb = null;

     try
     {
        //Check argument
        if(colWhere == null)
           return null;
        Packet oOut = null;
        int iNumTries = 0;

        while(iNumTries < DTPConstants.MAX_DB_ATTEMPTS)
        {
           oOut =
     DBGetTransactionBySQL(colWhere.GetSQL());
           if(oOut != null)
           {
              if(iNumTries > 0)
              {
        . . .
              }
           return oOut;
        }

           . . .
           iNumTries++;
```

```
}
.  .  .
```

The following is one of the primary Poly Model helper methods used to retrieve the schema and its instance data, and to fill the Abstract Packet with meta-information, such as the lookup ID, for later reference.

LISTING 5.33: Helper method used by most calls to GetTransaction() in the Poly Model.

```
public override Packet DBGetTransactionBySQL(string sSQL)
    {
    try
    {
        Profiler.BeginInstrumentation();

        if(sSQL.Length == 0)
            return null;

        PolyModelData oDB = null;
        oDB = ModelFactory.CreatePolyModelData();
        if(oDB == null)
            return null;

        int iResult = 0;
        iResult = oDB.ExecuteFillQuery(sSQL);
        if(iResult == 0)
            return null;

        //See if the DataTable table exists
        if(oDB.Contains(DEFAULT_TABLENAME) == false)
            return null;

        long lschemaID = 0;
        lschemaID = (long) oDB[DEFAULT_TABLENAME,
    DEFAULT_SCHEMA_ID_COLUMN_NAME];
        string sxmlschema = string.Empty;
        sxmlschema = GetSchemaAsString(lschemaID);
        if(sxmlschema.Length == 0)
            return null;

        PolyModelData oDB2 =
    ModelFactory.CreatePolyModelData();
        if(oDB2 == null)
        vreturn null;

        oDB2.ReadXmlschema(sxmlschema);
```

```
    // Extract xml for transaction from the DataTable
    string sxml = string.Empty;
    byte[] baxml = null;
    baxml = (byte[]) oDB[DEFAULT_TABLENAME,
    DEFAULT_XML_COLUMN_NAME];
    if(baxml != null)
    sxml = Encoding.ASCII.GetString(baxml);
    if(sxml.Length == 0)
        return null;

    oDB2.ReadXml(sxml);

    Packet oPacket = new Packet();
    oPacket.RawData = oDB2.Data;

    // Extract transaction id and the schema id
    oPacket.TransactionID = (long) oDB[DEFAULT_TABLENAME,
    DEFAULT_TRANS_ID_NAME];
    oPacket.ProductschemaID = lschemaID;

    // Set the schema lookup id
    oPacket.ProductLookupSchemaID = (long)
GetCurrentLookupSchemaID(
oPacket.ProductSchemaID);

        return oPacket;
    }
    . . .
```

If you already have the transaction ID of the original transaction, there is no need to build a query. You simply call the following:

LISTING 5.34: Simple GetTransaction method uses the transaction ID directly (rarely used).

```
public virtual Packet GetTransaction(Packet oPacket)
    {
        try
        {
            Profiler.BeginInstrumentation();

            if(oPacket != null)
                return GetTransaction(oPacket.TransactionID);

            return null;
        }
        finally
        {
```

```
    . . .
    }
```

GetTransaction() drives the lower level database I/O method. The signature of this Poly Model operation should remain consistent from design to design. The retry logic implemented here is optional.

LISTING 5.35: Method used for all calls using a transaction ID directly.

```
public virtual Packet GetTransaction(long lTransID)
{
    StringBuilder sb = null;

    try
    {
        // Check argument
        if(lTransID == 0)
            return null;

        Packet oOut = null;
        int iNumTries = 0;

        while(iNumTries < DTPConstants.MAX_DB_ATTEMPTS)
        {
// Read the transaction from the database
            oOut = DBGetTransactionRecord(lTransID);
            if(oOut != null)
            {
                if(iNumTries > 0)
                {
                    sb = new StringBuilder();
                        sb.AppendFormat(
    "Retries have reached maximum",
    iNumTries, lTransID);
                }
            }

            . . .

            iNumTries++;
```

```
    . . .
```

This low-level database I/O operation can have many forms (e.g., stored procedure, transactional, etc.). This is shown only to frame and complete the implementation.

LISTING 5.36: Database-specific helper method for GetTransaction (transaction ID).

```
public override Packet DBGetTransactionRecord(long lTransID)
    {
      try
      {
         if(lTransID == 0)
            return null;

// load it from the database.
         if(DoesTransactionExist(lTransID) == false)
            return null;

         StringBuilder sb = new StringBuilder();

         //Define query to execute
         sb.Append("execute sp_executesql N'SELECT " +
"* FROM dbo.DATA WHERE TRANS_ID" +
" = @TransID', ");
         sb.AppendFormat("N'@TransID BIGINT',
@TransID = {0}", lTransID);

         return DBGetTransactionBySQL(sb.ToString());
    }
```

. . .

That is it for the Schema Indexer and Poly Models. This pattern contains a lot of code. Much of this is due to the fact that many of the practices for this pattern are very implementation-specific and I wanted to show how one version of a Schema Indexer was implemented. I believe the code is the best means of giving you the quickest way to visualize the implementation. The Schema Indexer belongs as a rather tightly coupled child pattern to the overall composite, Poly Model. The idea of using dynamic, "hand-rolled" indexing is of necessity and can have several implementations. Through many years of data access development, database developers have taken for granted the automatic indexing power of the database back end and most likely have never had to write one themselves. They aren't difficult to write; they just require a little design and a lot of creativity for their implementation. I hope you got a taste of that here.

Related Patterns

- Schema Field (Thilmany)

- Delegate (GoF)

- Packet Translator (Thilmany)

- Poly Model (Thilmany)

- Abstract Schema (Thilmany)

- Abstract Packet (Thilmany)

- Factory Method (GoF)

6

Process Patterns: Applying .NET Patterns to a Commercial Product

OVERVIEW

The motivation behind this book began with the frustration of rarely finding material that is both theoretical and practical. There are just too few resources available that present sound theory as well as the practical examples to demonstrate it. As .NET matures, that case is slowly changing,. Through MSDN and its own patterns and practices articles, Microsoft is committed to providing .NET developers with as much architecture guidance as possible. However, besides having a .NET case study to resource, there are still too few step-by-step enterprise stories that document the use of patterned practices. This was the motivation behind this chapter.

In the book, I not only want to present the patterns but show them practically implemented in a real product. That also was how this chapter originated. I have read a lot of material that presents wonderful theory but unfortunately does not have the practical code to showcase it. Either the sample code is missing or it contains implementations so simple they are either useless or are exemplified in such a way as to cloud their meaning. I asked, Why can't there be more books that actually show you how their practices were applied to real applications sold to real individuals? This chapter and the product I will introduce provide me with the opportunity of presenting the material and a staging ground for my patterns and practices.

The examples used in this chapter refer to an actual commercial software company. For the sake of protecting their intellectual property all examples I will refer to the company as Company ABC. One of their primary financial services products will be featured here and will be referred to as Product X.

Company ABC, Inc. brought me on as a consultant to immediately begin converting its framework code base for a "cash cow" product to the .NET world. This chapter is devoted to the process of not only creating a commercial application using .NET and Web services but also applying the theories illustrated in this book to that product. It is this "story telling" that I hope will serve the purpose of solidifying an understanding of how the book's principles may be applied to a real-world application. All of the patterns in Chapter 4 and Chapter 5 and most of the others from other chapters are currently running in production and shipping as this commercial product is being sold. Doing this not only allowed me to showcase the patterns and their theories but also provided a real-world template upon which to tweak them as needed. This made the framework more design-conscious and the design more product-focused. From another perspective, this effort has also allowed me to eliminate patterns I believe do not serve some practical purpose. Those eliminated patterns may look great within a Rose diagram but I hesitated to cover them in this book because they do not carry much commercial weight and could be applied only in extreme cases. I did this to keep from doing what I see in many design books—throwing "cool" but strictly theoretical and academic content at the reader.

Before I move into the implementation process and the "plugging-in" of each pattern into the final product, I first must give a little bit of a background. To explain how each pattern was applied, I will first provide you with a brief summary of the product itself and the business case behind it. I will also provide you with a little bit of the technology and business elements within ProductX so you will better understand its features.

PRODUCTX AND THE COMMERCIAL FRAMEWORK

To understand a little about the actual product and how I applied each pattern, you must first understand a little about what ProductX does. ProductX and the framework on which the product runs (referred to as the *Commercial Framework* from this point forward) were the first introduction in 2001 for Company ABC, Inc. to this .NET effort. The framework was first developed to help bridge an existing product suite from Company ABC and to develop from the ground up the "plumbing" components for all future .NET products to use and eventually migrate to. The architecture was to house all .NET products in enterprise fashion. After all, these applications were installed on an application server in a Web form. The architecture would need to include all of the typical requested elements of a mission-critical application: scalability, reliability, failover, high transactional throughput, expandability, etc. Using a Web form, load balancing, session state caching, server clustering, and asynchronous Web services features, to name a few, we were able to achieve these aforementioned critical elements.

But where did we start? We first exercised a risk matrix and applied a high-risk mitigation plan to a set of proof-of-concept (POC) delivery vehicles. The first POC would involve a bridge to the existing COM architecture. A path was needed so that a smooth migration from the older products housed in COM to the new would be possible. A bridge was developed so that the existing products, which were all C++/COM-based, could easily be executed through .NET with minimal migration complexities. The second piece to the mitigation plan was to build all aspects of a framework so that pure .NET products could use a solely .NET platform without using the bridge. These are the typical plumbing pieces that I'm sure you are familiar with (e.g., exception handling, data access, caching, logging, business managers, etc.).

The framework itself was a major undertaking because all existing core COM framework functionality was to be eventually rewritten in C#. This would give Company ABC a framework that would be 100% managed code, all written in C# with a "back-door" option of running seamlessly through a bridge for any functionality not yet ported to .NET. This strategy not only gave the company some insurance that the .NET product could be delivered sooner rather than later but it also provided a smoother migration path for production because so much code had already been written and continued to be written in C++ and COM. Although the new framework would be a complete redesign and reimplementation, the older framework had to be leveraged. There was just too much COM/C++ code to be migrated in a short period of time (6 months to a year). This bridging effort was how the Product Manager idea was created and what drove our generic Service Façades from the get-go.

As you have probably experienced, migrating an entire company to one technology, especially to something as new as .NET, is a major undertaking. The only safe path to success in this scenario is to provide as many smaller victories as possible along the way. Migrating to the platform for every product at once is risky and unnecessary. The Microsoft .NET framework and Visual Studio .NET make this transition much smoother than migrations I have experienced in past (the 16-bit to 32-bit jump comes to mind). Whether the code needing to be migrated was C++, Visual Basic, or even Java, the "interop path" is well paved in .NET.

- Through managed C++ extensions, we were able to move certain pieces of existing C++ (compiled in VC++ 6.0) to .NET.

- Through COM Interop, we were able to bridge all COM functionality, leveraging XML as the meta-language.

- Through SOAP, we were able to connect to older, "hand-rolled" XML Web services used in the older framework.

- Through the ease of using J#, we were able to migrate existing Java source code to the final C# destination, allowing us to leverage hundreds of lines of code and to do it in small "chunks." A full FTP client written in C# and migrated from Java is included with this book and demonstrates the ease at which thousands of existing Java samples (with code) can be leveraged using J# and C#.

To summarize, the three major goals we had in providing a .NET framework were:

1. *Provide a smooth migration path for existing COM products using a "product bridge."* For example, this is where the *Product Manager* pattern came into play, and its implementation is shown here.

2. *Build the foundational features required for native .NET products to run under.* This included components and services used for data access, error handling, custom logging, presentation, template coding, containment, aggregation, decision making, reporting, scheduling, business rules inference, etc.—basically all of the goodies required to build a true enterprise system. Some of this, such as data access and decision making, are featured here.

3. *Exploit some of new features of C# and the .NET Framework.* This included the goal of not only duplicating framework functionality but also leveraging some of the "cool stuff" .NET has to offer, such as Web services, dynamic invocations (reflection), XML-based configuration, XML-based data access using ADO.NET, etc.

Item 3 above was important for several reasons. Not only was current framework functionality rewritten but new services were also added that exploit what .NET has to offer; otherwise, why do it? Plenty can be said about the fact that C# solutions can be delivered much quicker than traditional C++ or even Visual Basic applications. But this engineering rhetoric is harder to sell to a customer.

For management, the time to market for a C# application is a tremendous value. Of course, this assumes that your development skills are up to speed. Getting everyone on board takes time, and that first leap is never quite as smooth as anticipated, so you had better have business reasons for migrating or you can forget it. Also (and more practically), it would have been quite silly simply to replicate features without taking full advantage of things such as Web services, XML configuration, disconnected data sets, SOAP integration, and all of the other niceties of running in a managed environment. Such undertakings, especially for companies the size of Company ABC, are rare. Framework projects typically do not generate revenue, so this particular effort was definitely considered "R&D." For us, the quicker Company ABC had an actual sellable product "out of the door" that ran in the new Commercial Framework, the better. Besides developing the framework and the bridge, a product had to be selected that would run on it and be written completely in .NET. An electronic check-processing application called *ProductX* was just that product.

As mentioned, R&D for a small company is an expensive undertaking. Company ABC took on some risk by devoting several resources to a non–revenue-generating project. It also took on the risk of moving an entire framework from C++ to C# and Managed C++. Companies experiencing the jump from the 16-bit to the 32-bit world had similar issues. Fortunately, today many of those migration nightmares have been overcome through better practices and especially better tools. In a nutshell, it is much easier today to migrate to a new world such as .NET than it ever was in the world of Windows from DOS. That said, it was still a primary goal to get a minimal framework up, get it to talk to the existing COM framework, and develop a simple yet sellable product to run natively within it.

It would not be until the product could run in the new framework that the business benefits of this effort would be seen. ProductX was the first 100% .NET product for Company ABC and was not simply designed as a Web service wrapper around another technology core. Like the new framework itself, all of ProductX is written in C# and ASP.NET and is designed to exploit fully all of what .NET has to offer, including Web services. How these .NET features were leveraged and what patterns were used is the subject of this chapter. ProductX was chosen because Company ABC did not have a product for processing electronic check transfers (it had solely focused on payment cards to this point); this was a new market, and this product could be developed rather quickly. This was the perfect product benefit combination for an already relatively expensive R&D undertaking.

What is ProductX?

If you've ever paid using your credit card over the Internet or had your paycheck automatically deposited, there is good likelihood that it may have been handled by one of Company X's products. Using one of the many financial services backbones (e.g., FDMS), Company ABC's products may, one day, be responsible for ensuring your paycheck electronically appears each pay period. ProductX uses what is called an *Automated Clearing House* (ACH). This provides the format and rules used to handle "electronic checklike" capabilities using a regulated and standard means of transferring money between two parties. ProductX is regulated by an organization called NACHA (the National Automated Clearing House Association). A visit to NACHA's Web site at http://www.nacha.org will tell you more about the association:

> *NACHA represents more than 12,000 financial institutions through*
> *direct memberships and a network of regional payments associations,*
> *and 650 organizations through its industry councils. NACHA develops*

operating rules and business practices for the Automated Clearing House Network and for electronic payments in the areas of Internet commerce, electronic bill and invoice presentment and payment (EBPP, EIPP), e-checks, financial electronic data interchange (EDI), international payments, and electronic benefits transfer (EBT).

CHALLENGE 6.1

Why would any company commit to converting its existing commercial application and framework to .NET and C#?

See the Competitive Advantage section later in this chapter to see why Company ABC did.

Why Should Consumers or Businesses Use this Type of Product?

Taking more than one form of payment increases the value of a vendor, whether in retail or commercial business. At the other end of that offering lies the cost of transacting a payment, and the businesses that offer any format must take into account that cost. For the consumer it's choice; for the retailer it's cost. Imagine a world without any form of payment other than cash. Aside from the savings you might have in all of the interest you pay, your options would be extremely limited. Taken in another direction, imagine a world without personal or commercial checks. This simply points out the need for variety of options in the payment-collecting process. By offering your customers the ability to pay directly from their checking or savings accounts, you are extending the flexibility of their buying power. By using this product, companies can remove the financial limitations of accepting payment from only a few available sources.

Consumers need options, and businesses need a cost-effective and consumer-friendly means of providing that option. Credit cards (or payment cards, if you like) are only one means of a fund transfer conduit. The other major choice is the check. ProductX's electronic check provides the adjunct to the payment card world. Soon with ProductX, electronic fund transfers will be commonplace, and you will not be able to imagine a world without it. For those who perform most of their financial transactions on the Internet, this has already become an indispensable option. I don't want to think about not having my paychecks automatically deposited or not having the flexibility of paying my mortgage by phone or Internet. I don't like using credit cards, so for me this is an incredible option. For others it should be too, because it is a proven fact that more people have checking accounts than have credit cards. Many more people have savings accounts or are simply trying not to use credit cards, due to the high interest rates.

The Federal Reserve Board's automated check mechanism has been around for years, but until recently only the largest companies and banks had access to it. Company ABC, Inc. brings this option to businesses that accept checks and those who pay by check. In turn, the benefits of this option are passed on to those consumers who use it as their primary financial vehicle. It does not matter whether your business is a small "mom-and-pop shop" or a Fortune 500 enterprise; automated checking can save thousands of dollars on both ends. With Company ABC's products, electronic checks provide more options for businesses customers and will save money through cheaper transaction costs over both payment cards and manual exchanges.

To summarize what this product can provide:

• Reduced returns for invalid accounts

• Lowered transaction costs versus other forms of payment

• Substantially lower product-return fees

• Quicker availability of funds using direct deposit

• Transactions from savings as well as checking accounts (you currently can't deduct from a savings account using NACHA-formatted transactions)

• Reporting options and the ability to optimize cash flow projections

• Elimination of debiting and payment guesswork and the payment synchronization that must occur

• Travel time cost reduction (unnecessary trips to the bank, etc.)

• More efficient receivables management

A .NET Product in the Financial World

These days, if a business offers a new convenience-oriented service to consumers, take a closer look! Chances are that electronic checking may somehow be involved in the company's operational support mechanisms. For example, consumers who elect to pay monthly for things such as subscriptions typically must agree to pay using Electronic Funds Transfer (EFT). In this case, EFT is simply a fancy name for the use of automated check debit transactions.

Checks Superior to Credit Cards

The discount rates and labor costs associated with credit card transactions effectively reduce the profitability ratios of the business, especially when contrasted with automated check payments. Further, once customers have exceeded their annual credit allowances, the company must manually generate additional monthly credit card transactions. As a result, many companies prefer that members utilize the monthly automated check payment option. To encourage signups, these companies are now providing training to customer support staff in the features and benefits of using the automated check payment option. Clearly, when contrasted with other payment methodologies, automated check-based payment processing can offer a company greater amounts of information to monitor the cash flows of its business more effectively. For most companies, the automated check is truly an accounts receivable "savior" that is more than just an efficient mechanism for payment collections.

In 1996, securities dealers moved from a 5-day to a 3-day settlement period for securities purchases (called *T+3*). Some firms began to view the automated check as an attractive alternative to "a check in the mail" for receiving timely payments. In contrast, the mutual fund industry embraced the automated check system long ago, because it has always essentially had a "T+1" settlement period. In other words, payments and/or instructions for mutual fund purchases received on one day usually means the money must be in the mutual fund on the following business day. The automated check can be a perfect vehicle for accomplishing this. Shareholder instructions for purchases received during the day are converted into an automated check debit file and sent that evening for transmission to the firm's originating bank; settlement the next day provides the money for the mutual fund.

Automated Check Payments Reduce Operating Expenses

By utilizing the automated check system for every appropriate payment transaction, many companies have been able to reduce operating expenses.

The Technology and Rules Behind Automated Check

This checking network is a highly reliable and efficient nationwide batch-oriented electronic funds transfer system governed by the NACHA operating rules, which

provide for the clearing of electronic payments for participating depository financial institutions. The American Clearing House Association, Federal Reserve, Electronic Payments Network, and Visa act as operators. These are the central clearing
facilities through which financial institutions transmit or receive automated check
entries. The financial institutions are the banks or processors that receive and send
the payments for those parties participating in an automated check transaction.
Figure 6.1 illustrates an overview of the roles taken in electronic checking.

An automated check transaction can include the following:

- Direct deposit of payroll, Social Security, and other government benefits, and
  tax refunds

- Direct payment of consumer bills such as mortgages, loans, utility bills, and
  insurance premiums

- Payments between corporations

- Electronic checks as part of accounts receivable or accounts payable departments

- E-commerce payments (Internet-related payment options)

- Federal, state, and local tax payments

- International transactions

- Interdepartmental deposit consolidations

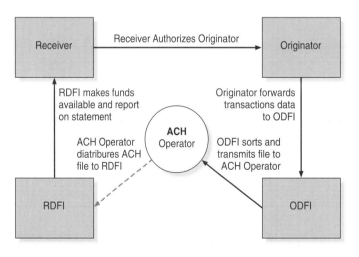

FIGURE 6.1: A brief overview of the roles involved in an electronic check transaction.

Figure 6.1 depicts the roles for the following parties:

Originator. Any individual, corporation, or other entity that initiates entries into the ACH Network.

Originating Depository Financial Institution (ODFI). A participating financial institution that originates check entries at the request of and by (ODFI) agreement with its customers. ODFIs must abide by the provisions of the NACHA Operating Rules and Guidelines.

Receiving Depository Financial Institution (RDFI). Any financial institution qualified to receive check entries that agrees to abide by the NACHA Operating Rules and Guidelines.

Receiver. An individual, corporation, or other entity who has authorized an Originator to initiate a credit or debit entry to a transaction account held at an RDFI.

CHALLENGE 6.2

What were some of the first patterns used, and why this application? What patterns are typically the first to be utilized when designing a framework from scratch?

See the Competitive Advantage section later in this chapter for the answer to both of these questions. HINT: Chapters 2 and 4.

Electronic Check Web Servicing

Our electronic check product, ProductX, is one of many .NET products from Company ABC, Inc. that provides payment processing. What makes ProductX special, aside from the fact that most of it is written and designed using .NET, is that it fully leverages a custom framework that leverages the patterns presented in this book. As mentioned earlier, the Commercial Framework was designed to provide the plumbing for all .NET payment products going forward. This is the .NET framework upon which all of Company ABC's products, even those written in C++, will eventually run, once migrated fully or through a provided bridge. As of writing this book, many Company ABC products still exist in C++ and COM.

To leverage those "legacy" applications fully, I designed a bridge from the .NET framework to the older framework using the COM Interop services from .NET. By the time this book is published, many of those products will have already been fully migrated over to .NET with much of the code modified using managed C++

extensions or rewritten completely in C#. For all new product development moving forward, C# will be the language of choice. Company ABC is committed to making C# the language that is used, not only for high-level pieces such as the code used at the presentation, business, and data tiers of an application but for low-level pieces, as well. For example, the FTP server and client components were all written using C#. As an added bonus, I've included the full source code for this FTP component with the book. This piece is currently running in production and can easily be used to create a full-fledged FTP client in C# (currently it does not have a graphical interface and is Web services-driven).

As stated earlier, ProductX for electronic check processing is only one piece of the total product suite puzzle available from Company ABC, Inc. Others include payment card processing, reporting, and other financially related services provided by integrating electronic payment capabilities with features of accounting packages such as SAP, Microsoft Great Plains, or Microsoft CRM (Customer Relationship Management), to name a few. The ProductX product (or any of the payment products) constitutes more than just the handling of financial transactions on the back end. The competitive advantage of each of the financial products mentioned here lies in how well they integrate with accounting packages (written from other parties). Such an example is shown in Figure 6.2, depicting the user interface integration of ProductX with Microsoft CRM.

Microsoft CRM is a new sales force automation tool from Microsoft's Business Solutions Division, which is part of the recent Great Plains acquisition. By integrating the front end of this product into CRM, ProductX gains the front-end vehicle for driving electronic check transactions for customer service or sales representatives using that particular product to complete a money transfer. With CRM, users can manage customers and products, and when the time comes, they can pay for product using their financial information and ProductX to the drive the money transfer. For the thousands of companies using SAP, Company ABC has built a company around being one of few payment processing vendors for SAP. You can't have a back end without a front end to drive it. Company ABC is in the business of providing that back end with just enough GUI integration pieces to complement preexisting accounting packages.

Figure 6.2 shows what this product looks like from Microsoft CRM's Orders screen. With Microsoft CRM, ProductX provides a simple means of accepting payments for sales orders using electronic checking instead of credit cards. The following screen is automatically populated from the Orders screen from within

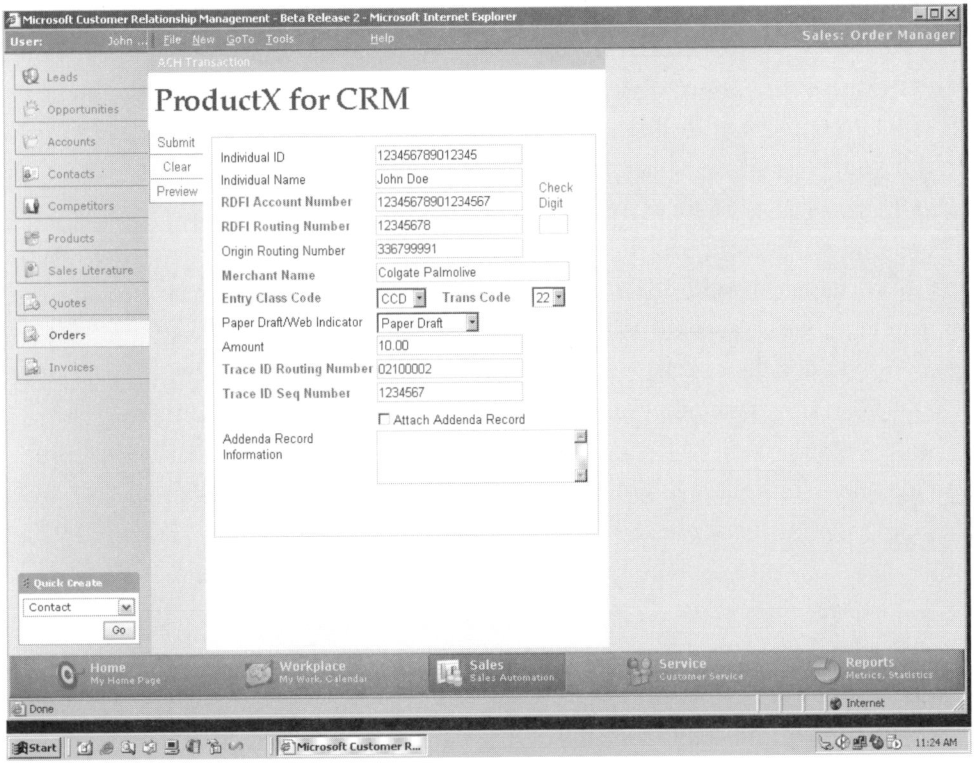

FIGURE 6.2: Electronic check entry screen as seen integrated into the Microsoft CRM Sales Force Automation Tool. This is a Web form screen using server-side controls in ASP.NET.

CRM, using the current ID, Customer Name, Amount, and for some customers; the account numbers. Once populated with the required fields, the user simply selects Submit, and the checking transaction will be saved using the Commercial Framework on the back end. Then each night via customized schedule, all unprocessed checking transactions will be retrieved from the database, and an electronic check data file will be prepared and sent to one of many configured NACHA-compliant processors.

Once prepared, the transaction file is sent (typically FTP) to one or more financial processors associated with this particular customer (or merchant). Settlement of funds typically takes three days, and a confirmation report is then sent back to the originating merchant. Both client-side and server-side validations will occur to guarantee that each information field is correctly received. This product currently integrates with SAP and CRM. CRM is completely Web-based, and all integration typically uses an ASP.NET front end to gather any information. For SAP's integration, the user interface design is created using the development environment of SAP and is slightly different in appearance than the interface shown in Figure 6.2, although it is still Web-based.

The power of ProductX and of most of the Company ABC's product suite is on the server. Once integrated into an existing financial front end, all payment processing happens behind the scenes using the server plumbing provided to each merchant by Company ABC. Here, transactions are managed, sent, received, and reported on so that in the end, the merchant saves money transaction by transaction and receives the other many benefits awarded by each product in the payment suite. For example, if a company uses Microsoft Great Plains to manage customer receivables, ProductX can help automate the receipt and transfer of all necessary funds by providing a means to transfer cash electronically. If that same accounting package is used to manage employee payroll, ProductX can automate the transaction of depositing those funds each pay period.

ProductX can handle electronically and seamlessly anything that can occur with a check, saving the customer money. For credit cards or any payment card option, Company ABC offers other product options, as well.

Now that you have a brief overview of the ProductX product, let's discuss its architecture. To do this, however, you first have to understand a little about the Commercial Framework.

Each product running on the .NET framework handles different aspects of a "payment processing" scenario, with each product playing a specific role. Each provides different options, benefits, and technological scenarios. Each is governed by different rules, and those rules are constantly changing, as must the products that manifest their features. The payment card and ProductX product provided by Company ABC will be an ever-changing and dynamic product suite. Microsoft's .NET and the framework I've built using it has simplified the process of keeping those products up to date. This robustness and ease of maintenance is the entire reason for going through the trouble of using some of the patterns I'm about to discuss.

You should now have a very high level understanding of the ProductX product featured here, and now I can discuss how it was built. Now it's time to look at the architecture behind the framework and how the patterns in this book were applied to its backbone. I would also like to talk a little about how ProductX was integrated into one of the accounting packages Company ABC supports and show what patterns were used during process. It's time to apply design theory to implementation practice.

.NET TECHNOLOGY: A COMPETITIVE ADVANTAGE

So what makes .NET and this new framework different from its competitors and warrants its use for this project? Why was .NET even selected by Company ABC over C++, aside from the obvious "time-to-market" advantages? How did the patterns presented in this book help with that? Why are design principles more important now with .NET than they ever have been in the past with traditional Microsoft languages? Finally, all of the questions accumulated from the previous chapters will be answered here. That is why I even went through the trouble of telling you about this product in the first place. Showing a real commercial application's architecture is the best the way to hammer this stuff home from theory to reality. No more simple e-commerce storefront examples, no more "Adventure Works" demos, and no more Microsoft "Northwind" examples. Major apologies to Microsoft because these well-known demo applications are great, but I thought presenting an application that was generating revenue would be even better. So let me begin to answer these questions.

Why is .NET a Competitive Advantage?

When I was contracted by Company ABC to look into converting its existing framework to .NET, my first response was to ask why. I knew several reasons but I wanted to know why *they* wanted to do this. Company ABC's lead architect's response was "time to market" and "flexibility." It takes only a few demonstrations to realize why this is true. Time to market is important for all vendors, so I'm not going to rehash the obvious. But what makes .NET and its design potential so flexible is exactly what I will be talking about. With C++, you have the means of creating truly sophisticated and robust applications but unfortunately, the investment in time, resources, and money is also great. With Visual Basic, you can decrease this investment with the added risk of possibly poorly designed applications or one that is inflexible to customization. For those Visual Basic programmers who are laughing at this statement, try on .NET for one year, then go back Visual Basic 6.0; enough said.

Microsoft .NET bridged those worlds for Company ABC by providing the technological means for designing a truly robust, flexible, and sophisticated backbone using resources that already exist and without throwing manpower and money at the effort. The flexibility I'm talking about rests in more than the features and Web service creation capabilities that the .NET framework provides. It's about the run-time environment and the languages themselves. Microsoft finally has a purely object-oriented environment to call its own. I think the market misses this with .NET in all of the Web services media it generates. The framework is much more than Web services.

The framework provides a truly object-oriented development environment with XML at the core. However, this also presents a challenge to the existing developers out there, especially those mired in technology without any care for sound design. To borrow a corny phrase from the movie *Spiderman*, "with great power comes great responsibility." With .NET, Web Services, and simplified distributed and object-oriented computing with XML, it has never been true more than it is today. The design is now more than ever the key.

Everyone talks about design flexibility but I see very few designs that actually feature it. How many frameworks have you seen that were truly simple to maintain? For the customers of Company ABC, this type of flexibility is what they were referring to when answering my earlier "why" question. As mentioned in the product backgrounder, electronic check processing and all of the payment products must easily integrate with existing accounting packages. They must be integrated quickly, and they must be flexible enough to withstand constant change because these accounting packages change almost annually in version, in rules, and in feature set. This does not refer to flexibility only on the front end. For Company ABC, it is even more important that flexibility be seen on the back end or middle tier, as well.

The system that was delivered provided this flexibility, and it did so without sacrificing simplicity. For example, the time I spent transferring the code to those who now had to support it couldn't have been any easier. In fact, I spent only about three days doing code walkthroughs. The rest of the system was picked up through documented designs (using Rose), a simple yet effective architecture, and the documentation generated from comments all throughout the code. The autodocumentation features of Visual Studio .NET alone saved me countless hours. I guess this is a cautionary tale for those who are looking for unethical job security.

Payment processing rules change monthly, and with the myriad of financial processors out there, the change is neverending. For example, NACHA submits rules updates every few months. This means that the financial processors (the people behind the banks) must change how they interpret a checking transaction. These constant rule changes mean the companies running the financial transactions through must also be aware of those changes. The companies that purchase ProductX want to be able to adapt to those new rules, so that software must be flexible enough to withstand this change in all areas of the system. This is primarily one of the reasons you see so many financial institutions adopting .NET. For more proof, go the http://msdn.microsoft.com/vstudio/productinfo/casestudies/ and see the myriad of financial case studies out there featuring .NET.

The payment processing software must be flexible enough on both the front end and the back end to anticipate these changes without requiring a software update from Company ABC. This has presented a challenge to Company ABC and led to the importance of leveraging some of the flexibility and robustness built into the .NET framework (e.g., Web services, Reflection, XML schemas, etc.). In fact, you probably have noticed that most of the patterns presented in this book center around achieving this flexibility. From the data tier and the Poly Model to the Unchained Web Service Factory, building a fungible architecture is the key to success in this business, as it is in most.

Some of new architecture features of the Commercial Framework *not* supported in the existing COM framework that was to be bridged included the following:

- Dynamic data tier and data model

- Full SOAP 1.1 support

- Multiplatform support through standardized integration

- Full XML schema support

- Asynchronous entry point for .NET AND *non-*.NET clients

- Remote tracing

- Asynchronous network operations

- Dynamic error-logging control

- Dynamic remote configuration

- Dynamic deployment

- Web services support

COMMERCIAL FRAMEWORK VISION STATEMENT

The original vision statement used before risk mitigation for ProductX and the Commercial Framework was something like the following:

This application is a step-by-step migration of the existing credit card product using the .NET set of technologies. It will eventually include all features from that original product with the addition of several new .NET features. These new features will come from a business feature level as well as an architecture level and will provide Company ABC with a flexible and simple architecture to build all financial products going forward. (See Figure 6.3.)

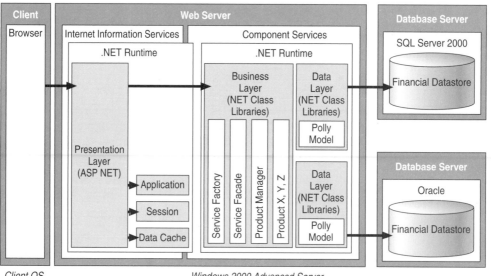

FIGURE 6.3: Commercial Framework conceptual model (major components).

• "Pluggable" business products design

• Simplified financial processor (bank) control

Initially, this product will include a full bridge to the legacy system for those not yet installing .NET on their server systems or on their workstations. This new product will support the existing legacy product using a bridgelike COM Interop layer to communicate with all back-end COM components. This Interop layer will utilize the .NET COM/API Interop layer as part of the new .NET framework in the first release. A full migration of all original features will constitute the second release of the Commercial Product and include full credit card features.

Without using .NET, many of these things would be rather complicated to design and write. Now I just assume their existence in every major framework I build. It's very easy to get spoiled and forget how much effort had to be put forth in order to receive these niceties. Things such as dynamic data tiering are provided by using Poly Models and must be designed. However, leveraging items such as XML schemas and SOAP support make your job all that much easier. Dynamic error logging, dynamic configuration, and remote tracing are all covered in Chapter 2 and all leverage many built-in implementation patterns that the Commercial Framework offers.

Hopefully, you appreciate by now that the .NET base class libraries are not simple "api wrapper" libraries. They have been designed with patterns "baked in," mostly at the implementation level. Base class library features such as asynchronous networking and Web services are all built on the Observer pattern. Delegate patterns are used everywhere, as you saw in Chapters 3 and 4. Loose coupling, adaptors, and factories are all baked into the .NET framework—some design- and some implementation-focused. Take a look at how some of the libraries were delivered, and you'll see a plethora of best practices that you get to leverage in your code every day.

So let's dive a little deeper into the technology advantages of .NET and what specifically helped Company ABC achieve its robust "poly architecture," if you will. First I need to describe briefly the main modules or features from this product's architecture. These modules are areas of the architecture that were either migrated to .NET or created from scratch.

Table 6.1 shows necessary plumbing for most frameworks that were applied in this case.

CHALLENGE 6.3

> Why were Web services so important? What server-to-server protocol was used? Why was .NET remoting not leveraged?
>
> .NET remoting will be a part of the next Commercial Framework release for Company ABC but scalability was more important for electronic check and payment card products, due to the number of transactions versus the performance per transaction.

TABLE 6.1: Major architectural features of the commercial framework

Service name	Description	Subfeatures	Purpose
Loosely Coupled Web Services	Web services for driving any function within the Commercial Framework. Uses both early bound and late-bound operations.	*Interface-based Web Services*—We can abstract all Web Service implementations using traditional interfaces. *Unchained Service Factory* – Chapter 4 pattern implementation using .NET Reflection services. *Chained Service Factory*—Another Chapter 4 implementation using a more traditional factory implementation.	Abstracts client from Web service implementations using framework features such as traditional interface-based programming and late binding using Reflection.
Service Façades	Used for driving all business objects and driving packet translation.	*Service-Based Façades*—Using more general framework encapsulation tailored for Web Services, Product Manager Classes, and Abstract Packets and their translation.	Provides a means of invoking all framework features without having to call the Web service interfaces.
Managed Client Framework	C# implemented helper methods for calling into the Commercial Product architecture from any .NET client, including ASP.NET. Same library can be used for *WinForm* and *WebForm* applications. For example, the same client routines were used for both the CRM client and the managed administration client tools for the Commercial Product using WinForms.	*Web Service Proxies*—Repetitive Web Service calls made helper methods here a must. *Packet Preparation and Poly Model Tools*—Abstract Packet preparation was made universal no matter what type of client was calling into the framework.	Provides the driver for packet preparation and result set operations to and from the product Web services

TABLE 6.1: (cont.)Major architectural features of the commercial framework (cont.)

Service name	Description	Subfeatures	Purpose
Unmanaged Client Framework	Same as the managed client services (row above) except for unmanaged clients.	*Unmanaged Poly Model Tools*—Proxy and DataSet tools used for sending product service requests from any unmanaged code, including C++ 6.0 and Visual Basic 6.0. Remember you do not need .NET to call a .NET Web service. *Custom C++ Unmanaged DataSet*—Representing the DataSet to the unmanaged world *Web Service Proxy*—Used for packaging unmanaged requests and sending to the product Web services. This was a SOAP 2.0 client proxy calling into the Commercial Product architecture.	Most financial packages (SAP at the time, etc.) did *not* support .NET or any form of Web client integration at the front end (except Microsoft CRM).[a]
Poly Model	All classes that make up the data service tier for the product. All implemented using the Poly Model pattern, as outlined in Chapter 5.	*Data Access Interface*—Contains all callable data operations that mimic those of ADO.NET. *Filter Builder*—Builds the filter used for Poly Model queries. *Common Data Operations*—Operations and helper methods used for Poly Model-specific behaviors such as schema retrieval, storage, and dynamic indexing, as shown in Chapter 5. *Data Source Implementations*—These are data source-specific implementations of the Poly Model Interface as defined in main Data Access Interface.	Provides a flexible data model, which was needed because payment rules processing and customer data requirement changes were frequently encountered.

TABLE 6.1: (cont.)Major architectural features of the commercial framework (cont.)

Service name	Description	Subfeatures	Purpose
Messaging and Message Listening Windows 2000 Service	Wraps MSMQ for sending and receiving messages from a queue. Can be swamped with other durable queues.	*Asynchronous Web Services*—Provides an asynchronous Web service for unmanaged clients without an asynchronous proxy, as in Chapter 7. *Message Routing Service*—Windows 2000 service used for picking up messages and routing them appropriately through the framework. *Messaging Manager*—MSMQ helper operations for sending and receiving messages.	Provides loosely coupled services, especially for unmanaged clients.
Network Services	General networking helper methods used to communicate to payment processors.	*General Network Libraries*—This includes queue-based messaging, FTP, sockets, and other network I/O facilities.	Used to send or post FTP files, send streamed strings to any socket server, etc.
FTP Client and FTP Web Services	Fully functional FTP services used for sending ProductX transactions and receiving ProductX confirmations from participating payment processors. Full source code is included with the book.	*FTPWebRequest*—Used by the Network Services component for FTP sends and receives. This is a fully implemented FTP client written in C#. It can also run in a Web service–driven environment on the server. *FTPWebResponse*—Used by the *FTPWebRequest* object for processing FTP control codes and socket responses.	Used because some processors that accept ProductX transactions will accept only FTP streams.

Service name	Description	Subfeatures	Purpose
Remote Tracing	Exception handling and logging tracing mechanism used for remotely communicating real-time production and debug information to product support. Featured in Chapter 2.	*Trace Viewer*—Graphical viewer used for receiving remote traces from a system on a customer's server. This is used by support to dynamically turn "on" tracing and view a real-time status of a customer's remotely installed Commercial Product system. *Web Service*—Centrally receives all remote tracing from a remote system. Used for customers using firewalls. *Trace Switching and Custom Trace Listener*—Dynamically controlling all system tracing functionality in code using .NET custom trace listener interfaces.	Provides simplified product support, especially for users not directly controlling the production server where the software is installed.
Scheduling Service	Windows 2000 Service that "fires off" scheduled events. All events are run directly from the framework with a service acting like any other framework client.	*Schedule Viewer*—Reads scheduled events from the data using the Poly Model. Reads in XML instance data as a packet and uses the router to send it. *Schedule Action Router*—Web service client proxy that uses schedule information packets to send to the framework.	Used because most payment card settlements and ProductX nightly processing is done in a background and scheduled event.

TABLE 6.1: (cont.)Major architectural features of the commercial framework (cont.)

Service name	Description	Subfeatures	Purpose
Exception Handling and Tracing Framework	Driver for logging and remote tracing during errors, base class for all custom exceptions and exception formatting. Also custom trace extensions make up this set of services.	*Base Exception Class*—Self-explanatory and covered in Chapter 2. *SOAP Exception Handling*—Self-explanatory and covered in Chapter 2. *Custom SOAP Trace Extension*—A programmatic means for capturing SOAP data packets from our Web services for debugging and production support.	Designing the base class was the impetus for driving our remote tracing.
Instrumentation	Simple means of handling custom profiling and instrumentation without the need for any third-party software.	*Inline Instrumentation Operations*— Self-explanatory.	We did not have many product-ready third-party options for .NET, so we wrote our own.
Abstract Data Packet	Packet container for any product data packet passed from tier to tier in the framework.	*Abstract Packet*—Encapsulates all data passed in the framework and provides the means to serialize, extract, and manipulate that data based on XML schemas.	Implements the Abstract Packet pattern from Chapter 4 and provides a single parameters type for all data passing.
Product Manager	Used for abstracting differences between managed and unmanaged products (e.g., ProductX, ProductY)— the framework for all products.	*Abstract Base Class*—Abstract parent class for the Product Manager hierarchy. Simplifies packet packaging and unpackaging of product-specific data packets and facilitates their routing.	See Chapter 4 for details.

TABLE 6.1: (cont.)Major architectural features of the commercial framework (cont.)

Service name	Description	Subfeatures	Purpose
Packet Translator	Used for converting packets to/from DataSets.	*Translator*—Standard "contract" to translate packets between an XML schema-driven DataSet to an Abstract Packet and reverse.	Provides a universal means of translating input and output packets.
ProductY	Driver class that drives all payment card processing within the framework.	*Product Manager*—Plugs into Product Manager hierarchy and drives all payment card processing. This is the driver object for the Translator and Mapper objects. *Translator*—Maps packets to ProductY components using same pattern and interface as Packet Translator *Mapper*—Maps the XML schema and Poly Model object to a COM model for the existing ProductY payment card product. This is part of the legacy product bridge, as outline earlier.	Drives payment card processing.
ProductX	Driver class that drives all electronic check processing within the framework.	*Product Manager*—Plugs into Product Manager hierarchy and drives all ProductX processing. This is the driver object for the ProductX Merchant, Processor, File, Batch, Record, and Field objects.	Drives ProductX processing.

a. Currently, SAP has a .NET Web services toolkit.

Many of the architecture components described in Table 6.1 are discussed here. From a logic flow perspective, the call originates from the left side of the diagram from a *managed* or *unmanaged* test client. This is a *placeholder* class to show that any managed client can be used to call into the framework using one of the Web Service Factory patterns. A Web Service Factory is implemented by the Chained and Unchained Service Factory (Chapter 4) and is the entry point into the framework. Any of the payment products can be executed from this point, using standardized methods to invoke the business component (more on this in the next section). From the Web Service Factory, a call is made to instantiate the correct Service Façade (e.g., PaymentFacade) that in turn uses the Product Manager to instantiate the correct product.

Once the product (e.g., ProductX) is created, it further delegates its logic to the more specific objects. These child or aggregated objects from the Product Manager are business-specific and contain the rules that drive the originally requested action. Any action can be requested, as long as the request is encapsulated using the appropriate XML schemas. For every requested business function, there is an XML schema specific to that area. The only schema that is used for all business components is a schema called the *decision* schema. The decision schema simply contains the "verbs" (to borrow an old but effective COM vernacular) that are used by the framework to instantiate the correct Service Façade, instantiate the correct product, and invoke the correct method.

A decision schema looks like the following (Listing 6.1):

LISTING 6.1: Example metadata-oriented decision schema for routing messages and invoking downstream business objects in the service factories of the framework.

```
<xs:element name="DECISION">
    <xs:complexType>
        <xs:sequence>
            <xs:element name="TYPE" type="xs:string" minOccurs="0" />
                <xs:element name="ACTION" type="xs:string" minOccurs="0" />
                <xs:element name="SERV" type="xs:string" minOccurs="0" />
                <xs:element name="SERVER" type="xs:string" minOccurs="0" />
                <xs:element name="SUBTX" type="xs:string" minOccurs="0" />
        </xs:sequence>
    </xs:complexType>
</xs:element>
```

The instance data for the decision schema informs the Web Service Factory what the client wants the framework to do. Creating this meta-language for our framework allows me to use one or two entry methods into the system and prevents future Web service signature changes from affecting its clients. The Web Service Factory's job is to read the decision schema's instance data and instantiate the appropriate Service Façade. From there, the packet is translated into something the framework will recognize, and the drum beats on.

When the packet reaches the Product Manager, the framework begins to delegate from the generic to the specific. From this point, the framework elements are used only in support of the specific business objects that drive products residing on top the framework. ProductX is an example of one of those products. ProductX resides within the Product Manager hierarchy, and from its ProductX class it drives the rules that give ProductX its life. The components that support the reusable features of ProductX, such as exception handling, are those for which these patterns are presented. This "plumbing" and the patterns used are what I will cover in the next section. Many of the architecture services covered should be very familiar.

In fact, most of the Commercial Framework consists of roles you typically see in most frameworks:

- Managers (Web Service Façades and Product Manager)

- Factories (Unchained and Chained Service Factories)

- Delegates (Product Manager and Unmanaged Proxy)

- Exception handling and logging (Remote Trace, etc., from Chapter 2).

- Data access (Poly Model)

- Parameter packaging (Abstract Packet and Packet Translator)

- Caching and other optimizations (Caching, Web Service Interface, etc., from Chapter 7)

- And many more…

APPLYING .NET PATTERNS

Up to this point, I've provided background on what Company ABC does and the products it produces, and I have given you an overview of the architecture. Now I will turn my attention to the patterns I used to create the architecture. Not all of the patterns covered in this book will be discussed here but I will talk about the most important ones. I'll even try to go over the order in which the patterns were created and how they were implemented in code. I will give an overview of the process patterns we used to come up with the design and architecture patterns themselves, as well as some of the implementation options we employed.

Applying the Service Façade Pattern

One of the challenges of creating a framework, or any application for that matter, is trying to figure out where to start. Designing a generic framework without a specific product to reside on it presents even a larger challenge. Fortunately, I had a product to target and even a legacy framework (the C++/COM framework) to model the new one on. Given that I probably could have started designing any piece first, like most designers, I begin with the most obvious—the point of entry into the architecture. The Service Façade was the pattern I designed and implemented first. The Service Façade, as discussed in Chapter 4, is what Microsoft calls a *service interface*. It provides the contract with the outside world. Other than the Web Service Factory (which I will cover in the next section), it represents the initial entry point into the framework, and its logic drives all other services. In fact, because I knew that Web services would be used, I wanted to create an entity that would be friendly to Web service clients, memory-managed clients, and even unmanaged clients in some aspects. Before creating the Web service, I also needed an object to instantiate with the first Service Façade designed providing me this. For more background on Service Façade, Service Interface, and Service Agents, please review Chapter 4 or visit Microsoft's own patterns and practices Web site at: www.microsoft.com/practices/.

The way the Service Façade was created was based on the fact that it would be called from a Web service (thus the word *service*) and the fact that it drives one area of the framework. This area is also considered a service, so the pattern name plays a dual role. The first area or service of the framework I was to accommodate was payment processing. This is the core of the Commercial Framework and will support the transaction activity of the system (e.g., credit card authorization, electronic check entries, etc.). Other services include things such as reporting, batching, workflow, or other main business activities. Each service would have a predefined name and eventually be made up of one of the parameters used in the decision schema described earlier. Using the service name and predefined naming standard allowed me to instantiate any Service Façade in a late-bound fashion using Reflection.

Coupled with a standard entry point method signature, the Service Façade could be created by a client using a simple string or, in this case, an XML schema. Listing 6.2 is a snippet from the Web Service Factory (see the section on implementing the Unchained Service Factory later in this chapter for details). It shows how the service name is read from an incoming packet (DataSet dsPacket, in this case) and used to instantiate the appropriate Service Façade. The Service Façade instantiated below is called *PaymentFacade*, and the method invoked is called *Execute*. The parameter passed to Execute is simply the raw DataSet passed in this method from the client. That way, this acts simply as a generic factory and does not care which business schema or parameter list was used, other than what service was required.

LISTING 6.2: Reflection code snippet used in the Service Factory for late-bound action.

```
. . .

DataSet ds = new DataSet();
   string sService = PacketTranslator.GetService(dsPacket);
   Assembly oAssembly = Assembly.GetExecutingAssembly();

   string sTypeName = . . . // build object string

   Type oServiceFacadeType = oAssembly.GetType(sTypeName);
   object oServiceFacade =
   Activator.CreateInstance(oServiceFacadeType);
   MethodInfo oFactoryMethod =
   oServiceFacadeType.GetMethod("Execute");

   object[] oaParams = new object[2];
   oaParams[0] = dsPacket;
   oaParams[1] = false;

   ds = (DataSet) oFactoryMethod.Invoke(oServiceFacade, oaParams);

. . .
```

From this point, it is the Service Façade's job to decipher further how to route the request and what business product should be created deeper into the framework. Listing 6.3 is a stripped-down version of the PaymentFacade's constructor and Execute method. Much of reusable servicing of this class is in the parent Façade.

Here you can see how the Execute is called with the original DataSet and delegated to the Product Manager (CreateProduct method). Before CreateProduct() is called, however, an *Abstract Packet* is prepared from the raw DataSet in the PreparePacket method because the Product Manager understands only Abstract Packets. It is here that the packet is translated (see Packet Translator from Chapter 4), and its driver code is shown in Listing 6.3.

LISTING 6.3: A sample Service Façade called *PaymentFacade* for handling all payments.

```
public class PaymentFacade : Facade
    {
        . . .
        public override DataSet Execute(
        DataSet dsPacket, bool bCache)
        {
            Packet oPacket;
            PreparePacket(dsPacket);
            . . .
    if (Product == null){
            Product = CreateProduct(GetPacket());}
    if (bCache)
            {
                Product.PrepareCache();
            }
            else
            {
        Product.Packet = GetPacket();
    }
            oPacket = Product.Execute();
            . . .
// return raw packet back to caller
            return PreparePacket(oPacket);
    }
. . .
```

The following factory method CreateProduct() instantiates the proper Product Manager for the requested service in the Service Façade. Using a switch case construct and a "type" string to identify the correct Product Manager, the Service Façade can then delegate the call and its packet to the appropriate business object. The type string is set during packet preparation in the Service Façade, which is originally passed in the decision schema by the client. From here, the Product Manager takes over and further delegates responsibility to its own child objects as needed. In short, the decision schema elements determine how the request is routed using a service string to create the Server Façade, the packet type to create the Product Manager, and finally the Action string to invoke the correct method within the Product Manager (see the Product Manager section below and in Chapter 4).

The parameters, passed by the client, are prepared and sent through to the recipient business object as needed. Usually the parameters are untouched by the rest of the framework, and only the decision schema is read so that the request can be routed. This is crucial to the architecture and abstracts the Service Façade from having any business-specific behavior coupled within it. The specific parameters can be contained in a unique schema designed specifically for that one business object or objects. For electronic checking (ProductX), there is a product schema and for credit card payments (ProductY), there is a schema designed to house its own specific parameters. The Service Façade is simply a vanilla conduit to facilitate this creation and routing between a client and product itself.

LISTING 6.4: The Product Manager factory method for creating the correct product object.

```
public ProductManager CreateProduct( Packet oPacket)
    {
       . . .
ProductManager oProductManager;

    switch (oPacket.Type)
    {
       . . .
      case Constants.PRODUCTY_TYPE:
         oProductManager = ( ProductManager) new
    ProductY(oPacket);
         break;
      case Constants.PRODUCTX_TYPE:
         oProductManager = ( ProductManager) new
    ProductX(oPacket);
         break;
. . .
      default:
         oProductManager = null;
         break;
    }
    return oProductManager;
  }
  . . .
```

One thing that should be noted is that the code snippet in Listing 6.4 shows the Product Manager being instantiated as an early bound object. The next version of this architecture will facilitate a late-bound one in the Product Manager itself (recall only the Unchained Service Factory piece is late bound using Reflection). This mode will work similarly to the Unchained Service Factory and will allow the Product Manager to be late bound using .NET Reflection, as shown in this section.

Applying the Product Manager Pattern

Now that I've provided the perfect segue to the Product Manager pattern, let me discuss how we went about implementing it for ProductX. The following abstract class, appropriately named *ProductManager*, contains the generic methods used by all child classes of Product Manager. For ProductX, things such as packet preparation, schema retrieval, instrumentation, etc., can be abstracted from the child class and placed in the parent class.

The following shows only a few of the methods used by ProductX and the child class used for electronic check processing. The other element of the following code snippet defines the "contracted" method that all child Product Managers must implement. The Execute method must be implemented so that the Service Façade can generically delegate all action to the business object. Other standardized method signatures can also be added so that all products adhere to the framework. The other standardized methods added to this product manager were GetProductSchema(), PrepareCache(), and PreparePacket(). All must be implemented by each Product Manager child class so the Service Façade or any external client can retrieve the specific XML schema associated with the particular product and can do so in a "contracted" standard fashion. Because different products implement different schemas and their means of access may vary, this method should be handled by the product whose schema is requested. PrepareCache() does what it sounds like and performs whatever expensive operations that are common and at the same time can be held in memory for the next invocation/round trip. For more on caching, please refer to the Abstract Cache pattern featured in Advanced Patterns section of Chapter 7. The PreparePacket method is meant to allow the product to manipulate the packet so that it has a chance to retrieve itself from cache if that is an option. This is a very generic "contract" and will vary greatly, depending on the business implementation. The PreparePacket method is used to determine whether a primary key has been generated for the transaction during a single save operation.

For this architecture, I use a database counter to control primary key values from either Oracle or SQL Server. It is in this method that a primary key can be generated, provided to the packet, and eventually saved if that is the requested operation. This is typically database access 101 and only frames the implementation discussion here. How you determine uniqueness in your packet (using something such as database counters) is up to you. The point is first to define all contract methods that all children of Product Manager must implement to avoid refactoring headaches down the line.

LISTING 6.5: The contract interface for one Product Manager implementation.

```
public abstract class ProductManager
{
    . . .
    protected Packet PrepareSchema(string sType)
    {
        CommonData oData = null;
        Packet oPacket = null;
        . . .
if(Packet != null)
        {
            oData = DataFactory.CreatePolyData();
            if(oData != null)
            {
                . . .
oPacket = oData.GetProductSchema(sType);
                . . .
            }
        }
        return oPacket;
    }

    public abstract Packet Execute();
    public abstract Packet GetProductSchema();
    public abstract void PrepareCache();
    public abstract bool PreparePacket( Packet oPacket);
    . . .
    public bool PreparePacket()
    {
        . . .
```

There are two things worth pointing out in the code snippet for Listing 6.6. Here is an example of only one product in the Product Manager hierarchy that could be implemented. This happens to be our product, ProductX. The constructor, among other initialization activity, reads the passed-in Abstract Packet and provides the DataSet that the packet wraps for convenience. How the packet is passed to the product is product-specific, and this is only one interpretation. The only other item I should point out is the call to GetProductSchema() in the PrepareCache().

For a schema-based system such as the Product Manager, it would be wise to cache all schemas. XML Product Schemas should change infrequently enough to justify them sitting in memory for a few hours, thus speeding up repetitive calls. Remember that those schemas are usually going to be stored in a database somewhere. If you can cache that activity, you will obviously save a database round trip later on. If caching is used in a Web form, then I highly recommend using something outlined in "Use Data Caching Techniques to Boost Performance and Ensure Synchronization" by David Burgett, published in *MSDN Magazine*, December 2002. Burgett clearly explains some best practices for data caching in a Web form environment and goes into the means of updating your cache from server to server to ensure data consistency. All back issues of *MSDN Magazine* can be viewed online at http://msdn.microsoft.com/msdnmag/default.aspx.

LISTING 6.6: Code snippet from a sample Product object (ProductX).

```
public class ProductX : ProductManager
   {
      public ProductX(Packet oPacket)
      {
         . . .
   Packet = oPacket;
         Data = (ProductSchema) Packet.RawData;
         . . .
      }

      public override void PrepareCache()
      {
         . . .
   if (CachedSchema == null)
            CachedSchema = GetProductSchema();
         . . .
      }
```

The heart of the Product Manager derived product is the Execute function. Here you can see that this is where further ProductX routing takes place for this business object. The Packet.Action property, which was set during packet translation, is used to call the appropriate ProductX method. All arguments will be passed in the Product Schema's instance data and will be read by the routed business operation if necessary. The Execute method can very easily grow too large and may require the use of a Strategy, Façade, or Chain of Responsibility (GoF) pattern to decouple some of this functionality among different "experts."

LISTING 6.7: Factory method implementation of the Product object.

```
    public override Packet Execute()
    {
       Packet oPacketOut = null;
       Operation = Packet.Action;
       . . .
switch (Packet.Action)
{
          case GET_PRODUCT_SCHEMA_ACTION:
          {
             . . .
             oPacketOut = GetProductSchema();
    . . .
             break;
          }
          . . .
          case ProductX_SAVESCHEDULE_ACTION:
    {
                . . .
                oPacketOut = SaveTransaction(false);
                . . .
                break;
          }
          case ProductX_VALIDATEPACKET_ACTION:
          {
             . . .
             ValidatePacket(Packet);
             . . .
             oPacketOut = Packet;
             break;
          . . .
          return oPacketOut;
  . . .
```

The snippet in Listing 6.8 from the ProductX class shows the use of Prepare-Schema from the parent Product Manager. It checks the cache to determine whether one already exists in memory and, if so, uses it.

LISTING 6.8: A code snippet for retrieving Product Schema from ProductX.

```
public override Packet GetProductSchema()
{
   Packet oPacketOut = null;

   if (CachedSchema == null)
{
      . . .
oPacketOut = PrepareSchema(PRODUCT_SCHEMA);
   }
   else
   {
      . . .
oPacketOut = CachedSchema;
   }
   return oPacketOut;
}
. . .
```

The following functions are product-specific yet generic enough to be implemented in the main ProductX product class. Implementing any code in the main Product Manager child is optional because this object can be used solely for routing. These methods can represent any business service; these are just specific to ProductX. Keep the Service Façade premise (or Service Interface premise) in mind when designing your product business object. ProductX is only a driver of functionality. How much code is placed in this class depends on the complexity of your business service.

For most complex business operations, especially those that must be coordinated as part of a lengthy workflow, it would be wise to keep the main product object as lean and abstract as possible. The driver of a Product Manager inherited child class should never know what is going on beneath the scene and should have only one or two driver methods that it's coupled against. All business details should be implemented and handled as abstractly as possible so that, if need be, the product object itself could be called directly without much knowledge of its inner workings. This provides the best head start in the more complicated design world of workflow orchestration driven by EAI products such as Microsoft Biztalk.

```
public Packet ReceiveFile(){. . .}

public Packet CleanupFiles(){. . .}

   public Packet DeleteIndex(){. . .}
```

The next method is the most commonly used ProductX operation because it is used to save the ProductX entry into the database. This action occurs when the user gathers the user's checking account information and other transaction information so that it can be saved to the database for later scheduling. Once scheduled, the transaction will be processed in batch mode to whatever financial processor has been configured for that installation. The Packet property is sent to other helper functions to validate, prepare, and eventually save the packet contents to the Poly Model-driven database. This is a good example of the typical packet in and packet out operations using the Product Manager.

LISTING 6.9: One sample Product object driver implementation of a database save routine.

```
public Packet SaveTransaction(bool bValidate)
{
   Packet oOutPacket = Packet;

   try
   {
      if(Data == null)
         throw new Exception(. . .)

if (bValidate)
      ValidatePacket(Packet);

. . .

  PreparePacket(Packet);
       . . .

if (!PolyModel.StoreTransaction(Packet))
      throw new Exception(. . .)
      oOutPacket = Packet;
   }
   . . .
   return oOutPacket;
}
```

The ValidatePacket() called from SaveTransaction() delegates its responsibility to aggregated child objects called *Merchant* and *Processor*. The merchant aggregated object is also used during a "collect or aggregation" type operation, which is used to format the final ProductX output before sending it to the processor (Listing 6.10). The Processor object is created using the ProcessorFactory, and the Validator interface is then use to validate the packet's contents. This serves as server-side validation, with exceptions being thrown for invalid parameters such as an invalid account number.

LISTING 6.10: Sample code snippet for server-side validation using the Product object.

```
public bool ValidatePacket( Packet oProdPacket)
{
    bool bValid = false;

    try
    {
        . . .
        Packet oMerchantPacket = GetMerchant();
        . . .
Validator = (IValidate)
ProcessorFactory.CreateProcessor(
oMerchantPacket, oProdPacket);

if (Validator == null)
        throw new Exception(. . .)

return Validator.ValidatePacket(oProdPacket);
    }
    . . .
}
```

PreparePacket(), previously referenced, checks to see whether the packet has a transaction ID already assigned to the incoming ProductX entry. If it does not, the transaction ID is generated, and the packet is assumed to be a new record. If a transaction ID were to be read, the packet operation can typically be assumed to be an update. Again, this behavior is specific to this product. Other implemented product classes may "prepare packet" using a different set of business rules.

LISTING 6.11: A brief look at preparing packets and driving the financial output from ProductX.

```
public override bool PreparePacket( Packet oPacket)
{
    try
    {
        if(Packet != null)
        {
            string sTransID = GetCurrentTransID();
            . . .
            if (sTransID == string.Empty)
```

```
        {
            . . .
        vsTransID = GenerateTransID()
        }
        oPacket.TransID = Convert.ToInt64(sTransID);
        . . .
        return true;
    }
    else
        return false;

    }
    . . .
    }

}

public Packet Collect(bool bSend)
{
    . . .
    // build the packet here…
    return oOutPacket;
}
```

I've included a visual workflow of the ProductX object involved in producing a ProductX file (Figure 6.4). The ProductX file is the content sent to the processor and is used to complete an end user's financial transaction. Each object in the ProductX product (e.g., File, Batch, Record, etc.) plays a part in the final file preparation. The entity details are abstracted from the Product Manager but as you can see, they are coordinated by the main ProductX product object.

As you can see, the Product Manager can be designed in slightly different ways, depending on the requirements. The focus of this pattern is to handle XML schema packets so as to route, describe, and control all business operations within the framework. It defines the operation skeleton for all products in the framework so that they better conform to the framework standards and place as much of the business logic where it belongs—in the product class.

Applying the Unchained Service Factory Pattern

When originally embarking on the migration from COM to .NET, one of the first conceptual solutions involved using Web services. After all, it is the Web services technology that initially demands your attention and not all of the goodies you receive with the framework. Also, once the Product Manager was complete, the next

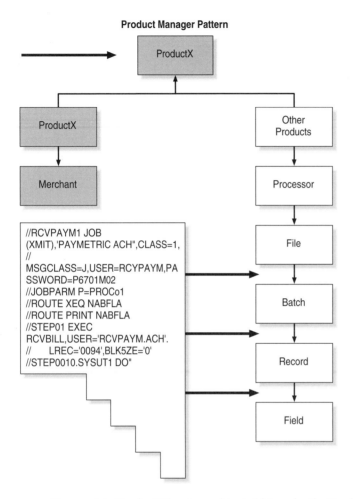

Product Manager Pattern

FIGURE 6.4: ProductX business objects (driven by the Product Manager) for transaction output preparation.

design and implement task was to create a more robust entry point into the Commercial Framework. Fortunately, wrapping my initial framework in Web services was rather simple, thanks to Visual Studio .NET. With attributes, it was rather easy to provide this type of interface quickly. However, once the technology was proven, what was still needed was a more flexible and robust service interface to make the Commercial Framework more invokeable from a greater number of clients.

After all, I wanted a single entry point into the system for several reasons. First, there were security concerns with publishing every callable business method as a Web service and the difficulty of managing multiple public interfaces. Second, scalability issues were a factor. Throttles had to be placed on methods that could be invoked across the Internet and where bottlenecks could lie. Third, I wanted the Commercial Framework to be used as it was intended, meaning that no one should be able to invoke a low-level business service without going through one or two entry points into the system. This insures that all aspects of the framework are obeyed and that other hidden pieces of the architecture are still being executed correctly. Finally, I wanted the public interfaces into the framework to be flexible.

Once these Web services were published, I didn't want Web service clients to have to alter their own bindings once any public Web method's signature was altered. This included the addition of brand-new service coverage. I wanted a framework that could withstand these types of back-end changes. Through the use of self-describing parameters, I wanted the business methods to be invoked so that the same signature could be used for any callable service within the framework. Using a meta-language; flexible, self-describing data types such as the DataSet; and XML schemas, the Unchained Service Factory became a viable design.

As mentioned, everything or nearly everything should flow through one or two entry points into the framework. However, there are instances where exceptions need to be made. Exceptions to the rule are made on a case-by-case basis and are judged mostly by both the frequency of the requested service and the odds of its signature ever changing. As you'll see in the example code below, most business activity must flow through one entry point, Execute(...). This serves as the initial public call into the Commercial Framework but means that any back-end business method can be invoked through it. Because of its flexibility, making this call does require some parameter preparation so that the parameters passed can be routed to the appropriate product manager and the framework can respond accordingly. One of these preparations is that of using an XML schema to describe and house the instance data that will be passed into the Web service Execute method. This schema must come from someplace, whether it's persistently stored or retrieved dynamically. For those clients who do not yet have a recent copy of a viable business schema, another publicly callable method is provided to give them just that. Enter the GetSchemaTemplate() method.

This public Web method provides the clients with a callable interface so that any product schema can be retrieved and used to prepare the business method invocation that would ensue. Does this mean this has to be called every time a business method needs to be invoked? Absolutely not! It does mean that those clients may want to cache the schema or be relatively assured that the schema will not change often. If caching is not available and the product schemas change very frequently, this will have to be called each time. Hopefully, neither of the latter situations will be common because one network round trip is obviously better then two.

The GetSchemaTemplate method can be called using any one of four public entry points into the Commercial Framework. It can be called directly using GetSchemaTemplate(). This method then calls EBInvoke(). EBInvoke() calls into the Company ABC framework using an early-bound means of invoking a business service. This is a departure from the "late-bound" access offered by the Unchained Service Factory in this section. EBInvoke() is early bound to the business object it instantiates and will be slightly faster yet less flexible than its late-bound counterpart. LBInvoke() could also be called externally because it directly invokes the Company ABC framework in a flexible late-bound fashion and is the driver method for the Unchained Service Factory. The final external method is just the Execute method itself that simply delegates to LBInvoke(). The GetSchemaTemplate method is provided as a convenience for the caller. If the client so chooses, only Execute() could be called for all services. Here, GetSchemaTemplate() delegates to EBInvoke() for performance reasons only.

As alluded to in Chapter 4 and introduced as part of the Company ABC framework here, the Execute call serves as that single entry point into the system. In the following code snippet (Listing 6.12) you can see some of the implementation behind Execute(), GetSchemaTemplate(), and the two other entry points into the Company ABC framework.

LISTING 6.12: A typical Web method that can be called outside the service factory yet still leveraging it in its implementation.

```
[WebService(. . .)]
public class WebServiceFactory : WebService
{
   . . .
   [WebMethod]
public DataSet GetSchemaTemplate(string sType, bool bUseCaching)
   {
      . . .
      try
      {
         SetMetaInfo(dsDec, sType, GET_SCHEMA_ACTION);
         . . .
if (bUseCaching)
            ds = EBInvoke(dsDec, true);
         else
```

```
                ds = EBInvoke(dsDec, false);
        }
        . . .
        return ds;
    }
. . .
    [WebMethod]
    public DataSet Execute(DataSet dsPacket)
        {
            DataSet ds = new DataSet();
            ds = LBInvoke(dsPacket);
            return ds;
        }
```

The major difference between the helper methods EBInvoke and LBInvoke are
how the façades are constructed and called. EBInvoke uses a traditional static "factory method" style, using a switch/case statement to route and create the requested
business service by creating the appropriate Service Façade class. Once created, a
standard method called *Execute* (once again) is called on the Service Façade, and
the framework delegates the call to the Service Façade. From there, the Service
Façade can control where the request should be further routed, if at all. Typically,
the Service Façade will route the request to an appropriate Product Manager class,
as mentioned earlier in this chapter.

**LISTING 6.13: From the Chained Service Factory, this code snippet shows the static
form of a factory.**

```
[WebMethod]
[TraceExtension()]
public DataSet EBInvoke(DataSet dsPacket,
    bool bCacheObject)
{
. . .
    try
    {
        sService = GetService(dsPacket);
        switch (sService)
        {
            case PAYMENT_SVC:
                . . .
    oFacade = ( Facade) new
    PaymentFacade();
                . . .
                break;
            case Constants.REPORT_SVC:
                . . .
```

```
    oFacade = ( Facade) new
  ReportFacade();
          . . .
          break;
        default:
          return ds;
    }
  . . .
  ds = oFacade.Execute(dsPacket, bCacheObject); return ds;
}
```

The LBInvoke entry point method, on the other hand, is the default means of calling into the framework. This method is delegated by the main Execute method and uses Reflection in a late-bound fashion (thus the *LB* notation) to instantiate and call a factory method on any Service Façade. This is a completely generic function that allows any Service Façade to be called, as long as it follows the naming convention. The naming standard used for the Service Façade is up to you.

The decision schema passed into this method will help determine where to route the request. Although this form of entry into the system is late bound and therefore slower, it provides a great deal of flexibility. This flexibility allows any Service Façade to be added to the system at any time without affecting the public Web method interface, thus not affecting any bound clients. How much slower is this method, compared with the early bound version (EBInvoke)? The performance difference is only a few milliseconds slower, and I believe the benefits outweigh the disadvantages in this case. That is why the late-bound version is the only one defaulted and delegated by the call to Execute().

LISTING 6.14: This is the late-bound version of Listing 6.13 using Reflection.

```
[WebMethod]
  [TraceExtension()]
  public DataSet LBInvoke(DataSet dsPacket)
  {
    . . .
  // see UnChained Service Factory for locals

    try
    {
       sService = GetService(dsPacket);

       oAssembly = Assembly.GetExecutingAssembly();

       string sTypeName = . . . // build object string
```

```
    oServiceFacadeType =
oAssembly.GetType(sTypeName);
    oServiceFacade =
Activator.CreateInstance(
oServiceFacadeType);
    oFactoryMethod =
oServiceFacadeType.GetMethod(
FACTORY_METHODNAME);
    . . .
    ds = (DataSet)
oFactoryMethod.Invoke(oServiceFacade,
oaParams);
    }
    return ds;
}
```

In Chapter 4 we covered in great detail the design and implementation of this pattern. With the Commercial Framework, I did not stray much from the template code cover in that chapter, and it follows the template code included with this book to the letter. Providing a generic entry point for any framework is crucial, and this pattern provides only one implementation example of how this was made flexible yet effective.

Applying the Poly Model Pattern

Showing all of the means by which the Commercial Framework employs the Poly Model could take up a chapter of its own. In this section, I would like to show you the main drivers of the Poly Model and some of its key elements because Chapter 5 goes into enough detail on the structure not to be repeated here. Some of the key elements include the four main pieces of the Poly Model, the data factory, the database I/O layer, the generic Poly Model (storing/retrieving schemas), and a little about the indexing used for queries. So let's dive right in.

I use the storage of a ProductX transaction as an example and perfect segue into the Poly Model. In Listing 6.15, I have presented a code snippet from the ProductX Product Manager that drives the Poly Model. You should recognize this method because it was covered earlier. Only the critical calls that relate to the Poly Model are shown. Here the Data Factory is used to create the correct Poly Model object and its StoreTransaction method invoked to store a ProductX transaction. Let's first follow the call to the Data Factory.

LISTING 6.15: A typical save operation driver.

```
public Packet SaveTransaction(bool bValidate)
    {
        Packet oOutPacket = Packet;

        try
        {
            . . .
        PreparePacket(Packet);
        if(!DataFactory.CreatePolyData().StoreTransaction(Packet))
            return oOutPacket;
    }
```

As mentioned earlier, the Data Factory uses a Factory method to instantiate the correct Poly Model object based on both configuration settings and any defaults that may be set. The Data Factory in this case will create the correct Poly Data object such as in Listing 6.16.

LISTING 6.16: The factory method of the Data Factory.

```
static public PolyData CreatePolyData()
    {
        if(GetDBType() == DataConstants.DBTYPE.SQL)
            return new PolyDataSQLServer();
        else if(GetDBType() ==
        DataConstants.DBTYPE.ORACLE)
            return new PolyDataOracle();

        return null;
    }
```

The PolyData object returned is determined by calling GetDBType(), which uses a configuration setting to determine whether Oracle or SQL Server Poly Data object should be used. Only one installation can be assigned one Poly Data for this particular scenario. For scenarios where a mix of data stores are used, an alternate means of determining the Poly Data object would need to be created.

The PolyData class is the parent class for any database-specific Poly Model class. This parent class acts as the client interface for any Poly Model interaction. The Poly Data then uses other components from the Poly Model to access the database or to build Poly Model queries. The database-specific SQL commands are controlled by the child classes of the PolyData. For this example, StoreTransaction() is called on the returned Poly Data object to store any ProductX transaction. When doing so, all components from the Poly Model objects are used in this scenario. Going further into the StoreTransaction call, you will see the Oracle version of StoreTransaction() (Listing 6.17).

LISTING 6.17: A typical nested save operation used against Oracle.

```
public virtual bool StoreTransaction( Packet oTrans)
    {
       try
       {
         . . .
       bResult = StoreTransactionRecord(oTrans);
          if(bResult)
          {
             . . .
             return StoreKeys(oTrans);
          }
}
       return false;
    }
```

StoreTransaction() calls StoreTransactionRecord (Listing 6.18) from the database-specific Poly Data object returned in the initial call. In StoreTransaction-Record(), an SQL command-specific version of StoreTransactionRecord() is called twice. The first call inserts a record into the DATA_LOG table, and the second actually inserts the record into the DATA table. This is part of the Poly Model pattern and is covered in detail in Chapter 5.

Once the record is stored in both the DATA_LOG and DATA tables, the indexes are stored using the Field Indexer pattern. The StoreKeys method drives the Field Indexer in this case. Each implementation is different, and the Poly Model Field Indexer for ProductX is no exception. To design your own, please review Chapter 5. It is the work that was put into the Field Indexer that will make your query breathe easier and your Poly Model perform as you intended. The Field Indexer pattern should give you a head start in the right direction.

LISTING 6.18: The nested save operation using two phases—one for the index and one for data.

```
public override bool StoreTransactionRecord( Packet oTrans)
    {
       try
       {
          bResult = StoreTransactionRecord(oTrans, . . .));
```

```
    if(bResult)
    {
        if (DBGetTransactionRecord(lTransID) == null)
        {
            . . .
// insert command
        }
    else
        {
            . . .
// update command
    }
        return StoreTransactionRecord(
    oTrans, sUpdateOrInsertCommand);
    }
```

The code snippet in Listing 6.19 shows the Oracle-specific version of Store-TransactionRecord(). Here, Oracle parameters are used (some are not shown) to bind to an embedded PL/SQL command. This is one means of storing XML schemas using the BLOB data type. Oracle streams and stored procedures could also be used and, in fact, are used in the architecture as well. This particular example uses Microsoft's version of the native Oracle provider located in System.Data.OracleClient. (This can be downloaded from Microsoft for free.) The code for creating the sequence number used for the primary key is also shown for clarity.

LISTING 6.19: A full nested Poly Model save operation using ADO.NET against Oracle.

```
public override bool StoreTransactionRecord(Packet oTrans, string sSQL)
    {
        PolyData oPolyData = null;

        try
        {
            . . .

            oPolyData = DataFactory.CreateDB(sSQL, CommandType.Text);
            OracleParameter oInParm0 = (OracleParameter)
        oPolyData.AddDataParameter(. . .);
            . . .
    long lNextCounterValue = GetNextCounterValue(. . .);
            oInParm0.Value = lNextCounterValue;
            . . .
            OracleParameter oInParm2 = (OracleParameter)
        oPolyData.AddDataParameter(. . .);
            . . .
```

```
        oInParm2.Value = oTrans.ProductSchemaID;
        OracleParameter oInParm3 = (OracleParameter)
oPolyData.AddDataParameter(. . .,
OracleType.Blob,
ParameterDirection.Input);

string sXML = oPolyData.WriteXml(oTrans.RawData,
XmlWriteMode.IgnoreSchema);
        oInParm3.Value = Encoding.ASCII.GetBytes(sXML);

    int iRowCount = oPolyData.ExecuteNonQuery();if(iRowCount == 1)
        return true;
    }
    . . .
finally
    {
        if (oPolyData != null)
            oPolyData.Close();
    . . .
```

Unfortunately I cannot show all of the code I would like to, although I believe I show enough to provide you with the essential details to see how one implements the Poly Model patterns in Chapter 5 in a real-world application. Hopefully, this will be only a starting point for you and will give you firm lift toward building an industrial-strength Poly Model in your application. Good luck and happy Poly Modeling.

INVOKING OUR FRAMEWORK FROM THE PRODUCTX WEB CLIENT

The implementation examples for the server components I just went through would not be complete without the sample code that drives them. The code snippet in Listing 6.20 shows how you can generically prepare and call into the Commercial Framework using the helper methods shown. Here you begin by preparing a Packet object (DataSet with XML schema) on the client, fill the Packet with instance data from any external interface, and send it to the server with an entry-point method (Execute method) to invoke one of the business methods provided by ProductX. The ServerExecute method takes any "action" and relays it to the server for a response. Several helper methods have been provided, such as Prepare-Packet(). PreparePacket() simply calls GetSchemaTemplate() to retrieve a product schema (in this case, the ProductX XML schema), fills the DataSet with instance data as input from a Windows interface, and finally calls the Execute method with an action of SaveTransaction.

LISTING 6.20: The client-side driver code for the running transaction against our framework.

```
    private DataSet ServerExecute(string sType, string sAction,
string sTransactionTableName,
bool bDisableOutput,
out StringBuilder sbOutput,
out StringBuilder sbLog,
out long lTransTime)
    {
. . .
    try
    {
        localhost.WebServiceFactory sf = new
        localhost.WebServiceFactory();
        . . .
ds = PreparePacket(false, sType);
        sf.SetMetaInfo(ref ds, sType, sAction, "1");
        . . .
    sf.Credentials = new NetworkCredential(. . .);
    dsReturn = sf.Execute(ds);

    if (dsReturn != null && !bDisableOutput)
    {
    . . .
    /* process response */
        }
    }
. . .
    return dsReturn;
    }
```

The following shows one of the child screens used for setting up and testing the ProductX server and Commercial Framework. Figure 6.5 shows the input for all required ProductX fields to provide the user a means for saving a ProductX transaction. The ProductX data is entered, the packet prepared, and the ProductX transaction is saved using the steps briefly summarized in this chapter. Once the ProductX transaction is saved, it can be reviewed and edited or a final ProductX document can be created. An example of this ProductX output is also shown in Figure 6.5. Here you can see an example of the type of financial output a bank (processor) would receive from a merchant when ProductX transactions are pro-

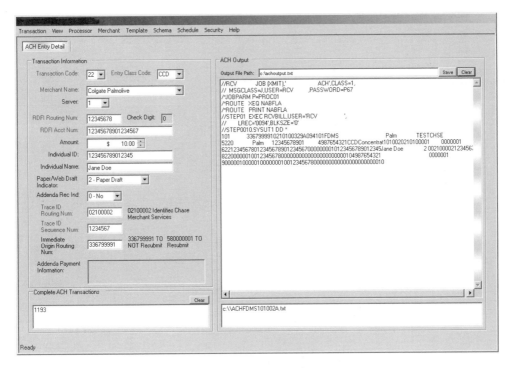

FIGURE 6.5: The framework administrative interface.

cessed. If you have ever used automated bill payment through your bank or had your paycheck automatically deposited, your transaction output would look something like this.

Figure 6.5 shows an example for setting up and testing the ProductX application. The production ProductX application will process information from whatever financial application is used by that particular merchant. The interface depends on the financial package the merchant is using, such as SAP, Great Plains, or CRM, to name a few. From here, the financial packet sends the transaction in a fashion similar to the driver code shown in this section.

Once the ProductX server has the transaction, it can save it and schedule its processing at any time. Typically, ProductX processing is done in batch form on a nightly basis driven by a scheduler, such as the one provided by ProductX. In Figure 6.6, several scheduled items can be seen, such as the action to pick and receive a confirmation file from the bank. This action is automatically generated by the ProductX once a ProductX output file has been successfully sent to a processor.

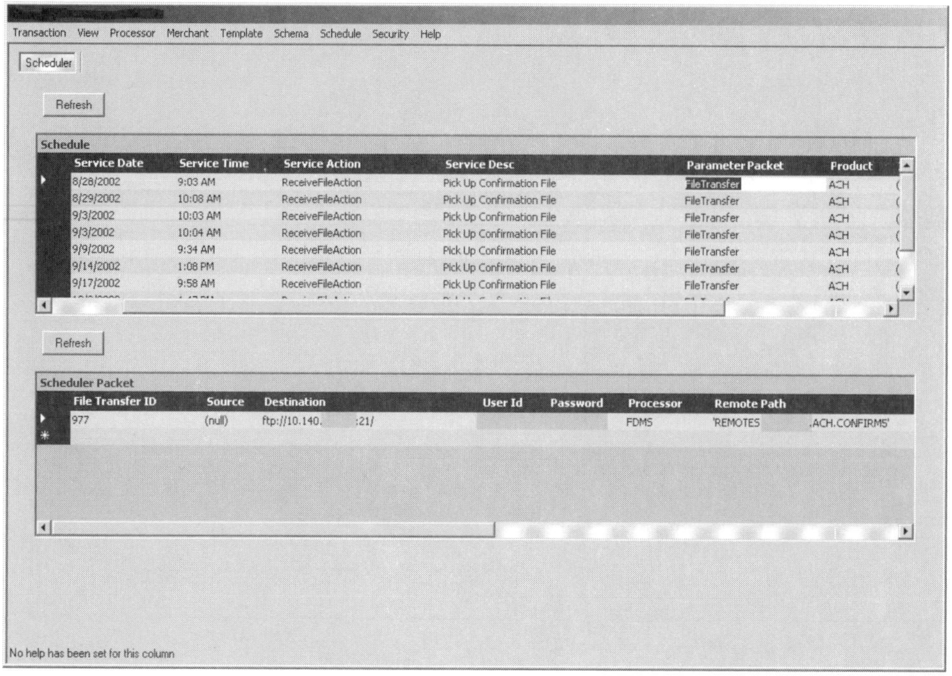

FIGURE 6.6: The scheduling interface used to show which batch files have been to financial processors and are prepared for receiving a confirmation file. A WinForm SmartClient was used here.

This allows any transmission errors to be processed and determines whether it is necessary to resend the ProductX output to the processor.

Figures 6.6 and 6.7 show you configuration screens in the ProductX admin utility. This is used to set up a particular processor's configuration information so that the ProductX transaction can be correctly formatted. It also provides the necessary configuration in order to communicate to the processor, such as FTP IP and security information (because most financial files are actually sent via FTP).

ProductX has its own standard guidelines but how each processor handles a ProductX transaction is somewhat independent of that standard. Even items such as processor configuration, merchant configuration, and general framework setup make use of the basic framework. Creating configuration information allows Company ABC to "eat its own dog food" and use the same facility to set up the application server that is used to actually run the transaction in production at a customer site.

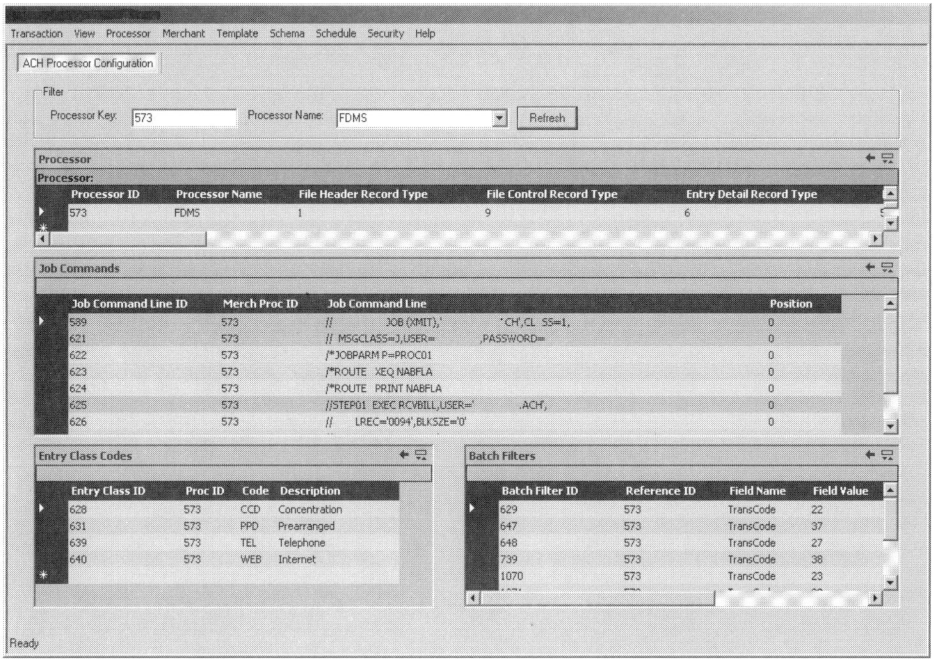

FIGURE 6.7: Another admin screen used for configuring financial processors on the fly.

SUMMARIZING THE SUITE

The power of ProductX and most of the Company ABC product suite is on the server. Once integrated into an existing financial front end, all payment processing happens behind the scenes using the server plumbing provided to each merchant by Company ABC. Here, transactions are managed, sent, received, and reported on. In the end, the merchant saves money transaction by transaction and receives many other benefits awarded by each product in the product suite. For example, if a company uses Microsoft Great Plains to manage customer receivables, ProductX can help automate the receipt and transfer of all necessary funds by providing a means to transfer cash electronically. If that same accounting package is used to manage employee payroll, ProductX can automate the transactions of depositing those funds for each pay period.

Anything that can occur with a check, ProductX can handle electronically and seamlessly, saving the customer money. For credit cards or payment card options, Company ABC offers other product options, as well. With the power and flexibility of .NET, client-based customization is much easier and less expensive for the customer. Using the patterns provided here, I gave the Commercial Framework the ability to respond even more quickly to its customers' needs and to offer the kind of service this company has always dreamed of. Maybe Microsoft's marketing literature for .NET isn't so off base this time. Maybe with the right discipline behind it, we really have reached the programming and technology pinnacle. Only time with tell.

7

Advanced Patterns

OVERVIEW

In Chapters 2 through 5, we discussed some of the mainstream patterns in the architecture catalog when implementing a basic framework in .NET. What this chapter outlines are those patterns that really fall out of any "normally applied" or 80% category, where 80% of the architectures use them as a delivery vehicle. The following patterns deal with more advanced concepts, such as asynchronous processing, caching, interfacing, and pooling. This doesn't mean that these patterns are not needed in 80% of those systems. As you are probably well aware, many tactical applications will not require or have the luxury of time to design these value-added features. These are typically applied as an adjunct to an existing system. In fact, many of the patterns I'm about to discuss can be later added to these systems and are not necessarily required from inception. For some patterns, such as the Loosely Coupled Transactor (LCT), an entire framework gateway could be built around this one pattern or even can be used to wrap a system already in production so that your time to market doesn't suffer up front.

Like the other chapters, most of the following examples keep within the general solution "theme" and use our financial processing application to drive the example code. We cover the following patterns in this chapter:

- Abstract Cache—Abstracted caching framework using .NET caching

- Web Service Interface—Interface-based Web services

- LCT Server—Abstracted asynchronous business transactions (server-based)

- LCT Client—Abstracted asynchronous business transactions (client-based)

- Password Storage—A better way to store passwords to the database

  With mention of the following design patterns:

- Proxy (GoF)

- Factory Method (GoF)

- Façade (GoF)

- Observer (GoF)

ABSTRACT CACHE

Intent

Provide a simple and abstracted means of caching expensive objects. Abstract the container used for holding any of the cached objects (this isolates the architecture from any specific cache container implementation). Place business rules for determining caching semantics (e.g., timeouts) in the objects being cached where they belong. Provide a standard means by which to build a cache and execute cacheable services.

Problem

Improving performance is usually never considered a bad thing. However, those attempts to improve the performance often end up compromising the design.

These attempts include tasks such as denormalizing a database, adding complex thread logic, or using platform-specific caching techniques such as those used in ASP applications. Besides compromising the design, sometimes these "improvements" can have the ill effect of actually slowing down performance. When dealing with the overhead of thread object creation or holding state for caching, the application can sometimes take on the opposite effect from what was intended. Designers should guard themselves from technology- or platform-specific approaches. For threading, this may be more difficult. For caching, however, this can be achieved more readily.

Implementing caching should not slow down a system, nor should the design. Most caching implementations are centralized with some form of "controller." The controller usually takes whatever stateful caching container may be accessible and is in charge of placing content into and out of the cache. Business data must somehow be fed into the cache through the controller, forcing the design to take this into account and thus increasing unnecessary cohesion between the cache controller and the business object that provides the data for the cache. Staying with this scenario, business rules must now be maintained in the cache controller so that the caching semantics can be enforced. These semantics include timeout periods, "stale" data indicators, size restrictions, etc. The cached controller soon becomes an expert in business caching semantics that it should never be aware of.

Most caching implementations utilize a technology-specific means of caching. For ASP applications, the application or session object may be used to cache simple values (although it is not recommended—at least not until .NET arrived). In the MTS and COM+ world, the shared Property Manager (SPM, or "spam") can be utilized to hold cached or stateful data (again, not a recommended practice—the spam has its own issues). Even if the technology is solid, tying an entire framework to one caching technology could become a problem. For .NET applications that wish to be platform-independent someday, using anything technology-specific may not be a good idea.

Caching, at least regarding the performance of critical applications, should become part of the framework at some point. The cached objects themselves should decide how, when, and whether to place objects in the cache. Caching should not itself slow down the system with unnecessary overhead. The container used for holding cached objects should be as technology-agnostic as possible, thus providing a migration path for easily incorporating new containers. Finally, the caching design should be simple enough for all business objects to take advantage of and integrate into the overall architecture.

Forces

Use the Abstract Cache Pattern when:

- Expensive operations can be pre-prepared.

- The application requires performance improvements (when doesn't it?).

- The design cannot tie itself to any one technology-specific caching implementation.

- There are specific rules for caching content, such as expiration, size, etc.

- Several business objects are candidates for caching.

Structure

The following structure (Figure 7.1) shows the pieces of our "caching puzzle" generically. The cache adapter is the driver of the cache object. The cache object is the container itself and will be driven by whatever client code performs the initial caching action. The ConcreteCacheable class contains the element about to be cached and provides the method or methods used to house caching logic within the architecture. This typically will be a key signature method through the architecture typically housed in a base class. The implementation section will go into more detail on the mechanics of this. The structure of the Abstract Cache pattern can be seen in Figure 7.1.

Consequences

The Abstract Cache pattern has the following benefits and liabilities:

1. *Abstracts the cache container implementation.* Using this pattern, any custom cached container can be used. For this example, we use the System.Web.Caching.Cache object for holding all objects and data in the cache. Any custom cache should implement the same interfaces as are provided by .NET's cache object. It should be thread-safe and durable. The only entity that is bound to

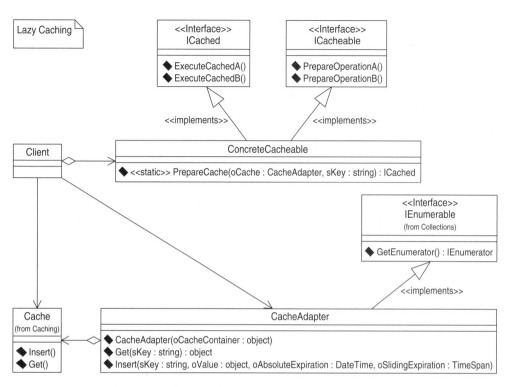

FIGURE 7.1: Abstract Cache class diagram—generic model.

the cache container type is the client (ReportingWebService, in our example) for construction and the CacheAdapter for aggregating the cache container.

2. *Places caching logic with the objects and/or data being cached.* This is probably the best benefit of using this pattern. By passing the cache container in the form of CacheAdapter to a business object that may have data to cache, it allows business rules for caching to be placed where they belong—in the business object. The business object is then given the opportunity to cache data. It also is given the opportunity to specify the necessary rules of the particular cached element.

3. *Provides a simple framework upon which to build all cacheable content.* Caching can become a complex operation if not monitored. Standardizing the way in which all business objects may cache elements is crucial to ensuring a robust framework that can actually utilize the feature. Providing a standard means of controlling a cache also centralizes the cache (great for debugging) without coupling business logic in its container or its aggregator.

4. *Provides a performance improvement for expensive and repeatable operations.* This shouldn't require much explanation and comes under the category of "no kidding." One point to keep in mind, however, is that the last thing you want to do is slow down a system after implementing a caching scheme, so take heed when doing so. Cache only objects and/or data that are very expensive to generate. This includes file I/O, database I/O, or any expensive initialization. Another candidate for the cache is to preinstantiate third-party components. As was mentioned in the Product Manager pattern in Chapter 4, building an unmanaged proxy can become a bottleneck. This usually refers only to custom COM components—components such as those that have been written for a specific business purpose that needs to be leveraged and may contain expensive initializations. COM will take care of most of the caching concerns from a runtime level. This is especially true if the components happened to be COM+ components.

What I am referring to are those custom components that may contain, for example, expensive collections that need to be hydrated, initialized, or whatever. This is where caching from .NET can add benefit. .NET can be leveraged for its advantages because caching was never really addressed as a customizable option (via the Cache object) before .NET or ASP.NET were introduced.

5. *May slow down the system if not applied correctly or if used for single transactions.* Not much more to say here that wasn't said in the above point, except that it would be advisable to perform some form of instrumentation to test for bottlenecks. Instrumentation can help determine whether indeed there really is a performance bottleneck, where it is located, and how you may eliminate it. Instrumentation can take the form of simple a System.Diagnostics.Trace.WriteLine("spit out timespan") or as sophisticated as what a third-party "profiler" tool would provide. Such tools as Compuware's DevPartner Profiler (formerly Numega) for .NET can typically provide enough information to determine what areas of code may be of concern. However, there still may be cases where some form of custom instrumentation will be needed. This is especially true when working with a complex framework driven from Web services that may be located on another machine.

Participants

- Client (ReportingWebService)—This refers to the client of the object containing information to be cached. This is not to be confused with strictly a front-end client, although it could be. For our example, the client is a reporting Web service that acts as a controller to business objects containing expensive operations. Here, the ReportingWebService client will retrieve a reference to the Context.Cache that is accessible from the System.Web.Caching namespace from the Web service code. The client is in charge of creating the CacheAdapter, passing in the cache container (Context.Cache), and calling the business objects preparation method, PrepareCache().

- ConcreteCacheable (ComplexReport)—This is any business object that may contain expensive operations. This is where the magic really happens. For our example, the ComplexReport object must implement a factory method, PrepareCache(), by which it will receive a reference to a CacheAdapter. Using the CacheAdapter, it will determine whether it needs to add items to the cache, determine all caching parameters, or return items from the cache. For this example, we have simplified where the entire business object itself gets cached. This can be easily altered so that only specific items get cached, as long as those items implement a standard interface such as ICache.

- Cache (same)—This is a durable, stateful cache container typically implemented by a technology-specific source. For our example, this is the Context.Cache because it is accessed from the ReportingWebService, or any Web service, for that matter. A custom Cache object can be created as long as it implements similar logic to the out-of-the-box version that comes with .NET. The whole point of implementing the CacheAdapter class is to isolate the framework from whatever cache container is used.

- CacheAdapter (same)—This is the standard class used to aggregate a selected cache container. Its sole purpose is to standardize and control what functionality is exposed from a cache container and to isolate the user of the cache from any technology-specific container. ConcreteCacheable objects speak only to the CacheAdapter, and the CacheAdapter delegates all calls to the cache container.

- ICache (same)—This main interface for all ConcreteCacheable objects will implement what will be executed from the cache. This standardizes the caching framework and abstracts the implementation of how items in the cache are implemented. This is the interface used by the client to execute items from the cache.

- ICacheable (same)—This is implemented by all ConcreteCacheable objects. It contains the framework-specific preparation methods used to "build" the cache once the PrepareCache method is called. This also helps standardize the caching framework so that all business objects with cacheable information can take advantage of it with simplicity.

- IEnumerable (same)—This interface is used so that items in the CacheAdapter can be iterated like the most specific cache containers. This is implemented by the CacheAdapter, and its single GetEnumerator call is delegated to its aggregate (the Cache object, in our example).

Implementation

To implement this pattern, you first need to determine which business operations are sufficient candidates for caching. For our example, the ComplexReport object must retrieve configuration data from an XML file on the local system that will be used to format the report. This configuration information, which will not change from execution to execution, is persisted. It thus requires file I/O and is rather large (well, for our demo purposes it isn't). The ComplexReport object is called numerous times a day by each client wishing to view its report and is expensive. This makes it a great candidate for caching. For our example, we use a Web service to drive the report called, appropriately enough, *ReportingWebService*. Here, the System.Web.Caching.Cache object reference is retrieved, a CacheAdapter is built, and we create the ComplexReport object using the PrepareCache *factory method*. To see my implementation of the Abstract Cache pattern reference Figure 7.2

To determine the key to use for storing the cached object, we use SOAP headers to pass in the key from the client. Using SOAP headers or passing the key from the client is just an option but we found it to be quite useful. Using SOAP headers keeps us from having to pass the key for each method that may drive a cached object. (See the following technology backgrounder for more information on SOAP headers.) If you do not intend to use SOAP headers, will use them strictly from within .NET both from the client and the server, and/or do not wish to have

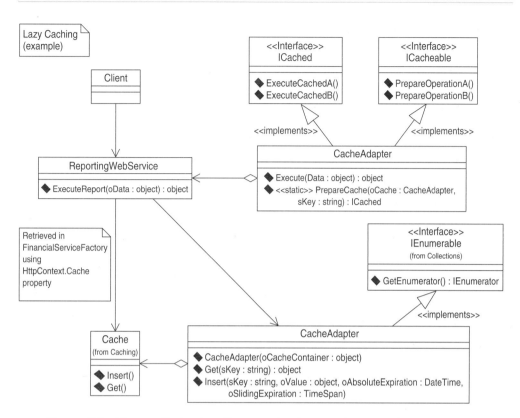

FIGURE 7.2: Abstract Cache class diagram—implementation example.

a deeper understanding of them, you can skip the following technology back-grounder. This is not a book on the details of the SOAP protocol. However, a brief understanding of what SOAP headers are, at least from the SOAP Toolkit Version 2.0 viewpoint, will be very helpful for future debugging.

Technology Backgrounder—A Look at SOAP Headers

Microsoft's SOAP Toolkit allows any message to contain header content in addition to the normal body content. Web service clients may often wish to pass information between a client and a Web service that may not be part of the Web method being requested. For example, a Web service client may request a Web service that first requires login credentials to be passed to its Web methods. This same login method, once authenticating the user, may return a session ID or token back to the Web service client so that return invocations can be authenticated. Without SOAP headers, the client would be required to pass this token into every Web method located on the server, thus forcing each Web method signature to require one or more parameters. With SOAP headers, repeatable parameters such as session tokens can now be sent as part of the header request, thus keeping each public Web method clean from passing this unnecessarily. Your stack will be happier, and the incoming SOAP message will be clearer. When debugging Web methods, this benefit will become all too clear.

If you will not be using .NET for passing SOAP headers to a Web service, you will have a few more steps to perform. This would be the case if your Web service clients could not be guaranteed to have the .NET framework installed on XP or Windows 2000 or if you were not running Windows 2003. Instead, you must rely strictly on XML. This is where the SOAP Toolkit comes into play. The SOAP Toolkit 2.0 allows headers to be accessed and created on both the client and the server. To package and send headers from the client, you must provide a COM component that implements the *IHeaderHandler* interface. Once this component is implemented, it must be passed as the *HeaderHandler* property of the SoapClient component. The SoapClient is the main component used for sending SOAP requests using the toolkit. Pure XML could also be used, as long as it conforms to the SOAP specification, but using the component will save time.

Each time that the client application calls one of the methods of the SoapClient component, it will call the *willWriteHeaders* method of the header handler. If this method returns true, the *SoapClient* will write a SOAP <Header> element to the request message, then will call the *writeHeaders* method of the header handler. This method uses the specified *SoapSerializer* object to write any header content that is desired, such as the VB sample code in Listing 7.1. This client sample happens to work with most Web services written in C#. This is unlike some of the sample code in the SOAP Toolkit or other non-Microsoft toolkits, for that matter, such as Apache.

LISTING 7.1: SOAP Toolkit Visual Basic header serialization example.

```
Private m_Token As String
Private Const HEADER_ELEMENT_NAMESPACE As String = _
"http://www.etier.com/patterns.net"

Private Function IHeaderHandler_readHeader(ByVal pHeaderNode As _
MSXML2.IXMLDOMNode, ByVal pObject As Object) As Boolean

If pHeaderNode.baseName <> HEADER_ELEMENT_NAME Or _
pHeaderNode.namespaceURI <> HEADER_ELEMENT_NAMESPACE Then
```

```
    IHeaderHandler_readHeader = False
    Exit Function
End If

m_Token = pHeaderNode.selectSingleNode("SessionId").Text

IHeaderHandler_readHeader = True

End Function

Private Function IHeaderHandler_willWriteHeaders() As Boolean

    IHeaderHandler_willWriteHeaders = True

End Function

Private Sub IHeaderHandler_writeHeaders(ByVal pSerializer As _
    MSSOAPLib.ISoapSerializer, ByVal pObject As Object)

Dim sElementText As String
Dim sXML As String

    pSerializer.startElement "SessionHeader"
    pSerializer.SoapAttribute "xmlns", , _
      HEADER_ELEMENT_NAMESPACE
    pSerializer.startElement "SessionId"
    pSerializer.writeString "121938123"
    pSerializer.endElement
    pSerializer.endElement

End Sub
```

For more on SOAP serializers, please refer to the SOAP Toolkit 2.0 documentation. Finally, the *SoapClient* writes the body of the request message, sends it to the server, and eventually receives a response. The SOAP message can be captured (traced) in several ways. You can use the MsSoapT.exe trace utility that ships with the SOAP Toolkit 2.0 or you can use a TraceExtension attribute in .NET from the Web service itself. To see all of a service's messages received from all SOAP clients using MsSoapT.exe, perform the following steps on the server.

1. Open the Web Services Description Language (WSDL) file.

2. In the WSDL file, edit the <soap:address> element as part of the service element and change the location attribute to port 8080. (For .NET Web services, you must first save the http://foobarwebservice?wsdl output as a separate file

and invoke the edited version directly.) For example, if the location attribute specifies <http://localhost/pattens.net/webservicefactory.wsdl>, change this attribute to <http://localhost:8080/pattens.net/webservicefactory.wsdl>.

3. Run MsSoapT.exe.

4. Select New from the File Menu and select Formatted Tracing.

5. Accept the default values.

The XML snippet in Listing 7.2 shows what a SOAP header request would look like as sent from a SOAP 2.0 client.

LISTING 7.2: SOAP message header example.

```
<?xml version="1.0" encoding="UTF-8" standalone="no" ?>
<SOAP-ENV:Envelope xmlns:SOAP-ENV="http://schemas.xmlsoap.org/soap/
envelope/">
<SOAP-ENV:Header>
<SessionHeader xmlns="http://www.etier.com/patterns.net">
<SessionId>121938123</SessionId>
    </SessionHeader>
  </SOAP-ENV:Header>
<SOAP-ENV:Body>
...
  </SOAP-ENV:Body>
</SOAP-ENV:Envelope>
```

To use headers on a server not using .NET, you must provide a COM component that also implements the *IHeaderHandler* interface and identify that class in the appropriate <service> element of a suitable Web services meta-language (WSML) file. Unfortunately, I won't be covering the handling of SOAP headers from the server because most Web service development should take place from .NET and is the obvious focus of this book. To access the previous request Session-Header from .NET and C#, keep reading.

In the following code, the service client creates a Web service object (assuming that a Web reference was added) by first instantiating the Etier3.LazyCacheService class. Using this object, it can then set the SoapHeader variable called *sSessionId*. The session ID is a data member of the Etier3.SessionHeader class, which is a nested type of the Etier3.LazyCacheService class. Etier3 just happens to be the name of the machine this Web service is deployed on and is the name of the Web service reference. To set the session ID of the SessionHeader class, you directly create it like any other type and set its data members. The final step in this Web service and SOAP header client is simply to call an operation on oService. The SOAP headers will be passed automatically. Using C# or any other .NET language makes it simple. Using a non-.NET client such as VB6 is possible but more complicated, especially when working with SOAP headers. As mentioned in the previous technology backgrounder, any client that can format and send an XML request can be used. But be forewarned, there is much more work to be done the lower you go in the level of implementation. I suggest using .NET whenever possible, a positive proposition to be sure.

LISTING 7.3: Using .NET to set SOAP headers.

```
Etier3.ReportingService oService = new Etier3.ReportingService();

// bind session id to soap header
oService.SessionHeaderValue = new Etier3.SessionHeader();
oService.SessionHeaderValue.sSessionId = txtSessionId.Text;

// no need to pass session as part of the web service signature,
// it will be included in the soap header
// first call should cache any cacheable objects
oService.Execute(true);

// for demo purposes only -- second call will use cache
oService.Execute(true);
```

From this point, the Web service receives the request along with the any set members of the SOAP headers. Here the SOAP Header class is defined and declared using oSessionHeader, along with the SoapHeaderAttribute declaration. Here we are only passing parameters inward and do not require them. In the execute method, the bCachedObject flag is checked (optional) to see whether caching is desired. From here, the oSessionHeader is used to retrieve our session ID. This will be used as the key for the cache. This provides the flexibility of using different keys for each client in case each cached item should be unique to each client. This also helps with debugging in that it makes it a little easier to mimic multiple clients and/or sessions using something such as a user ID, IP address, etc. From this point, PrepareCache() is called on the ComplexReport object, passing in a newly instantiated CacheAdapter. The CacheAdapter is passed to the Context.Cache object (from the BCL), which acts as our container for this example, and the session ID key. From here, all cacheable items should be cached and the ComplexReport object created. The ICached interface is returned from the newly created ComplexReport and is used to execute the report in a "cache-sensitive" manner.

LISTING 7.4: Lazy Cache Service implementation.

```
[WebService(Namespace="http://www.etier.com/patterns.net")]
public class LazyCacheService : System.Web.Services.WebService
{
   public SessionHeader oSessionHeader;

   /// <summary>
   /// Session Header that contains key for the cache
   /// </summary>
   public class SessionHeader : SoapHeader
   {
      public string sSessionId;


   }

[SoapHeaderAttribute("oSessionHeader",
   Direction=SoapHeaderDirection.In, Required=false)]
   [WebMethod]
   public void Execute(bool bCacheObject)
   {
      if (bCacheObject)
      {
        string sKey = "defaultsessionid";

        // make sure a soap header was sent.
        if (oSessionHeader != null)
           sKey = oSessionHeader.sSessionId;

      // the cacheable object will determine if, when,
      // and how to cache himself
      // we just pass the container wrapper in our
      // CacheAdapter and the lookup key.
      ICached oCachedComplexReport = (ICached)
      ComplexReport.PrepareCache(new CacheAdapter(Context.Cache), sKey);

      // we are cached and prepared either way, now
      // lets run
         oCachedComplexReport.ExecuteCached();
      }
      else
      {
         // interact with object normally...
         ComplexReport oComplexReport = new
      ComplexReport();
```

```
            oComplexReport.ExecuteWithoutCache();
      }
   }
}
```

The implementation of the PrepareCache method and the entire ComplexReport source follows in Listing 7.5.

**LISTING 7.5: Implementation sample of preparing a cache using the Abstract
Cache pattern.**

```
/// <summary>
/// This can be any cacheable business object
/// </summary>
public class ComplexReport : ICached, ICacheable
{
   // declare expensive object
   byte[] m_baConfigData;

   public ConcreteCacheable()
   {
      // perform the usual initialization
   }

   /// <summary>
   /// Property for our configuration data
   /// </summary>
   public byte[] ConfigData
   {
      get { return m_baConfigData; }
      set { m_baConfigData = value; }
   }

   /// <summary>
   /// Factory Method for both object creation and
   /// determining caching semantics (e.g. setting cache or
   /// getting already cached object)
   /// Our CacheAdapter is used to avoid coupling our business
   /// objects with any particular cache
   /// </summary>
   /// <param name="oCache"></param>
   /// <param name="sKey"></param>
   /// <returns></returns>
   public static ICached PrepareCache(CacheAdapter oCache,
      string sKey)
   {
      ICached oCachedObject = null;
```

```
   // if using the cache object check to see if this
   // object is already there
      // any logic could be used here to refresh the cache
      // as well instead of merely checking if not object
      // existing int the cache
      if (oCache[sKey] == null)
      {
      Trace.WriteLine("PrepareCache: Cache object " +
      "inserted into cache\n" +
      "Current Cache Key Used =" + sKey +
      "\n");

         // prepare expensive config buffer
         ComplexReport oCacheable = new
         ComplexReport();
         oCacheable.PrepareConfigData();

            // add any other expensive operation here....
            // ...

      // now insert myself into the passed cache // // object
            // this is where the business object determines
      // expiration etc....
      oCache.Insert(sKey, oCacheable,
      DateTime.MaxValue,
      TimeSpan.FromMinutes(60));

      }

   Trace.Write("Execute: Retrieving Item from Cache\n" +
      "Cache Object Retrieved (By Key) = " +
      sKey + "\n");

   // just return existing cacheable object's interface
// for cached execution....
   oCachedObject = (ICached)oCache[sKey];

   return oCachedObject;
}


/// <summary>
/// This can be an expensive operation, db i/o, file i/o,
/// </summary>
public void PrepareConfigData()
{
   FileStream oFileStream = null;
   int nFileByteLength = 0;

   // create and set expensive objects here
```

```
    // open up our config file and read in the contents
    oFileStream = new FileStream("c:\\config.xml",
FileMode.OpenOrCreate, FileAccess.ReadWrite);
    nFileByteLength = (int) oFileStream.Length;
    ConfigData = new byte[nFileByteLength];
    // save contents into config buffer
    oFileStream.Read(ConfigData, 0, nFileByteLength);

    // close the file
    oFileStream.Close();
}

/// <summary>
/// This can be an expensive operation, db i/o, file i/o,
/// </summary>
public void PrepareWorkers()
{
    // add expensive object initializations here
}

public void ExecuteCached()
{
    // read in configuration data
    if (ConfigData == null)
       PrepareConfigData();

    // use config data for something....
}

public void ExecuteWithoutCache()
{
    // read in configuration data
    if (ConfigData == null)
       PrepareConfigData();

    // use config data for something....
}
}
```

In the PrepareCache method, the "cacheable" object is given the opportunity to cache any data or itself, as is the case here. This is where the cacheable object determines how it will be cached and what data will be a part of that cache. It speaks strictly to the interface provided by the CacheAdapter (Listing 7.6). It first accomplishes this by calling the implemented method on the ICacheable interface methods. For our example, they are PrepareConfigData() and PrepareWorkers(). It does not matter what methods are included in the ICacheable interface, as long as they are implemented correctly for all cacheable objects. This provides the "contract" upon which the drivers of the ConcreteCacheable objects can rely. PrepareConfigData(), for example, happens to be where the expensive operation of reading configuration data from an XML file is performed. Once read, it becomes a data member (a simple byte array, for our example) of the cacheable object. Once all cached preparation methods of the ICacheable interface are called, the main PrepareCache method adds itself to be passed in CacheAdapter by calling Insert(). Here it uses its own business rules for determining the caching semantics, such as expiration. The CacheAdapter interface in our example simply wraps the main features of the System.Web.Caching.Cache object. It then delegates the Insert() call to the aggregated Cache object. If a different cache object were to be added to the framework, only the CacheAdapter would need to change. This isolates the rest of the architecture from changes in the cache container.

LISTING 7.6: Wrapping a cache container—implementation sample.

```
/// <summary>
/// Wraps the existing cache object container used to hold all
/// cached objects, this can be Http Cache or
/// any custom cache object
/// </summary>
public class CacheAdapter : IEnumerable
{
    private Cache m_oCacheContainer;
    private IEnumerable m_oCacheEnum;

    /// <summary>
    /// Main ctor, takes most cache container e.g. Http Cache object
    /// </summary>
    /// <param name="oCacheContainer"></param>
    public CacheAdapter(object oCacheContainer)
    {
        // set generic container object this will be cast for
    // specific cache functionality
    if (oCacheContainer is Cache) CacheContainer =
    (Cache)oCacheContainer;
    // set specific properties that all cached objects should
    // implement
        CacheEnum = (IEnumerable)oCacheContainer;
    }

    /// <summary>
    /// Property for the main cache, should be edited is cached
    /// container type is changed.
```

```
/// </summary>
private Cache CacheContainer
{
   get {return m_oCacheContainer;}
   set {m_oCacheContainer = value;}
}


/// <summary>
/// Property for the enumerable interface which any cache object
/// should implement
/// </summary>
private IEnumerable CacheEnum
{
   get {return m_oCacheEnum;}
   set {m_oCacheEnum = value;}
}


/// <summary>
/// Delegate to cache object's enumerator object to support
/// for/each, etc..
/// </summary>
public IEnumerator GetEnumerator()
{
   return CacheEnum.GetEnumerator();
}


/// <summary>
/// Delegates to cache's count property
/// </summary>
public int Count
{
   get {return CacheContainer.Count;}
}


/// <summary>
/// Delegates to cache's item property
/// </summary>
public object this[string sKey]
{
   get {return CacheContainer[sKey];}
   set {CacheContainer[sKey] = value;}
}


/// <summary>
/// Just delegates to the item property (indexer)
/// </summary>
/// <param name="sKey">see Cache object</param>
/// <returns>see Cache object</returns>
public object Get(string sKey)
```

```
{
    return this[sKey];
}


/// <summary>
/// Just delegates to the insert method of the cache, most cache
/// container should implement a similar object
/// </summary>
/// <param name="sKey">see Cache object</param>
/// <param name="oValue">see Cache object</param>
/// <param name="oAbsoluteExpiration">see Cache object</param>
/// <param name="oSlidingExpiration">see Cache object</param>
public void Insert(string sKey, object oValue, DateTime
    oAbsoluteExpiration, TimeSpan oSlidingExpiration)
{
    CacheContainer.Insert(sKey, oValue, null,
    oAbsoluteExpiration, oSlidingExpiration);
}
```

Implementing a cached solution should by no means tie you to any one specific cache container or implementation. However, it is always nice to leverage code whenever possible. Using ASP.NET and its caching features is just one of those scenarios. When cacheable objects will be primarily driven from either a standard ASP.NET application or a Web service, you have the option of using the CLR and its caching container, as I did in the Abstract Cache implementation. To understand more about the System.Web.Caching.Cache object and ASP.NET caching in general, feel free to read the following technology backgrounder.

Technology Backgrounder—ASP.NET Caching

There are basically two forms of ASP.NET caching, one of which is called *output caching* (e.g., using the @OutputCache directive). I will not be covering output caching in this section. However, I will be covering the second form of caching called dynamic caching. This is the more traditional application caching you have grown to know and love (or should I say hate, in some respects). In this form of caching, you programmatically store any object into memory for the sole purpose of retrieving it at some point during execution. Objects that are cached should be expensive to create; therefore, grabbing them from memory should save you CPU cycles.

Right out of the box, ASP.NET provides you with a simple cache container that allows you to store any objects into the application server's memory. The System.Web.Caching.Cache class data type implements this container and is private to each application. This is a nondurable container, so when the machine shuts down or the application is stopped, the instance of this cache object is re-created. Any items that may reside in the cache in this situation will have to be re-created and cached once more. ASP.NET also provides a form of "scavenging" to ensure the scalability of the application by removing unimportant or seldom-used objects from the cache during low memory states.

You also have the option of controlling how long items remain in the cache by specifying an expiration date and by giving the object a priority to be used during scavenging. You use the CacheItemPriority and optionally the CacheItemPriority-Decay enumeration to set the cacheable object's priority and decay rate while calling Add() or Insert() on the container. You define the object's expiration date by using the DateTime *absoluteExpiration* parameter. You can also use the TimeSpan *slidingExpiration* parameter to allow you to specify the amount of time to elapse before the object expires, based on the time it is accessed. If an object is removed from the cache container, either through expiration or scavenging, it will be removed from the cache. Any future attempt to retrieve the object will result in a null value, and this is what you test for when checking the cache. Determining what expiration or priority to place on a cacheable object should be related to the business data being cached. This is one of the reasons (as mentioned above) for implementing the Abstract Cache pattern. It provides the standard facility to allow the business object to make its own decisions on this policy. For example, you should set the expiration value to keep cached items in the cache as long as the data in the cache remains valid; state data should always expire and recycle.

As a more advanced option, the ASP.NET cache object allows you to define the validity of a cached item based on some external dependency. This includes an external file, a directory, or another relative object in the cache. If the set dependency changes, the cached object will be removed from the cache. For example, if a file dependency is set (for a file that fed the cache's data) and that file is updated, the object will be removed from the cache. This is the perfect scenario to use for large XML files that must be read into memory and may change with regularity. Note that passing large XML files from object to object should be done with some caution, as was mentioned earlier in the book.

Adding Items to the Cache Container

There are a few ways to add objects or values to the Cache object. The Cache object is treated like a dictionary object. It is key-based, and its contents are manipulated using a key value that you provide. A key can be any unique value that will help identify the object in the cache. This can be session ID, generated token, or GUID—it doesn't matter. The key should also be remembered because it will be used to retrieve the added object from the cache. The simplest way to add an object to the cache is simply to specify the key and the object, as follows:

```
Cache["Token Id"] = oCacheableObject;
```

However, this doesn't provide the Cache container with much information regarding the item it just cached. To provide more control over the freshness and priority of the data being added, call Insert() or Add(). This also applies if you want to take advantage of scavenging. To specify dependencies, you must also use one of these two methods. Each has the same signature but the Add method returns an object that represents the item added. The Insert method is overloaded, providing you with a variety of ways to interact with the Cache object. For example, to simply insert an item into the Cache without specifying other parameters such as expiration, use the following:

```
Cache.Insert("Token Id", oCacheableObject);
```

The Add method is not overloaded; however, and you must use a more descriptive signature.

```
OCacheable = (ICache)Add("Token Id", oCacheable, null,
    DateTime.Now.AddMinutes(5),  NoSlidingExpiration,
    priority, priorityDecay, null);
```

As you can see, null values can be passed for some of the parameters whose values do not apply. Both of these methods provide you with the ability to control the caching rules and the conditions under which the item remains in the cache. The Insert method also provides the ability to add dependencies, such as the following example. This adds a dependency based on an XML file:

```
Cache.Insert("Token Id", oCacheableObject, new
CacheDependency(Server.MapPath(c:\\Config.xml)));
```

Both methods can also be used to set expiration policies for an item when you add it to the cache. You cannot set both an absolute expiration and a sliding expiration. One of the policies must be set to zero. There are two fields in the Cache class (NoAbsoluteExpiration and NoSlidingExpiration) that are used to specify the policy not being used. The following code uses the Insert method to add an item to the cache with an absolute expiration of two minutes.

```
Cache.Insert("Token Id", oCacheableObject, null,
DateTime.Now.AddMinutes(2),  NoSlidingExpiration);
```

The following code makes use of a sliding expiration:

```
Cache.Insert("Token Id", oCacheableObject, null,
NoAbsoluteExpiration, TimeSpan.FromMinutes(30));
```

The *priority* and *priorityDecay* parameters are used to set the priority and decay policies, respectively. The following example uses the Add method to add an item to the cache with a *priority* of High and a *priorityDecay* of Never.

```
Cache.Add("Token Id", oCacheableObject, null,
NoAbsoluteExpiration, TimeSpan.FromSeconds(30), CacheItemPriority.High,
CacheItemPriorityDecay.Never, null);
```

Retrieving Cached Items from the Container

Retrieving data from the Cache is simple; you need only to specify the key and value that represent the data. Just like a dictionary object, use the key to find the cached object:

```
ICached oCacheableObject;
oCacheableObject = (ICached)Cache["Token Id <e.g. session id>"];

if(oCacheableObject != null)
{
  oCacheableObject.Execute();
}
else
{
  oCacheableObject = new ConcreteCacheable();
  Cache["Token Id"] = oCacheableObject;
}
```

The previous code shows how to check for whether a cache object exists in the cache by using the key. If it does not exist, a new one is created and inserted into the cache.

Removing an Item from the Cache Container

To control completely when an item is removed from the cache, you can use the Remove method. Otherwise, item "removability" is dependent on the policy rules used when adding the item, as mentioned above. For example, the following code removes an item using the "Token Id" key.

```
Cache.Remove("Token Id");
```

For more information on ASP.NET caching, please refer to the documentation.

Related Patterns

- Adapter (GoF)

- Decorator (GoF)

- Factory Method (GoF)

WEB SERVICE INTERFACE PATTERN

Intent

Provide interface-based client programming to the Web services world. Abstract a Web service class implementation using an interface (interface-based interaction).

Why is this common pattern considered advanced and a part of this chapter?

The structure behind the Web Service Interface (WSI) pattern is simple to implement and could have been discussed in the implementation patterns section earlier in the book. However, this was moved to this chapter for two reasons. First, because most Web service clients will use the facilities provided by Visual Studio .NET, I felt that any implementation that required manual editing of the generated Web service proxy code could be considered an advanced option. This will be explained shortly. Second, this pattern lends itself to a very rudimentary design pattern of interfaced-based programming and thus can also be considered either an architectural pattern or a technology-specific design (implementation) pattern. This is where pattern classification becomes difficult and why I try as much as possible not to classify my patterns. Patterns should not be pigeonholed.

Problem

Implementing a Web service in the .NET is rather simple, even when delving into more advanced functionality. By simply adding the Web service attribute to a System.Web.Services.WebService derived class, along with a Web method attribute marked operation, you can be off and running. Even more advanced Web service functionality, such as tracing input or receiving requestor information, has been made painless by the .NET CLR. However, the out-of-the-box implementation of the Web service framework forces the client to declare a reference of the Web service class when interacting with a Web service class or its generated proxy. For every Web service class implementation, each client must then declare and compile a class-based reference and be coupled to its specific method implementations. Currently, the .NET framework does not a provide means of abstracting a defined Web service, at least not by default.

It would be helpful if there were a way of abstracting Web service implementations so that the Web service client could interact with this abstraction. Those already familiar with interface-based programming have come to appreciate the ability to decouple their clients from method to method implementation details of any server with which they may be interacting. For something as commonplace as interface-based programming, you would think that this would be straightforward in .NET when implementing a Web service. For example, it is more straightforward to trace SOAP messages than it is to abstract a Web service (at least from the Web service client perspective). I guess no framework is perfect, and .NET has come close to providing almost everything else our hearts desire, so cutting Microsoft some slack would not be a bad idea. Fortunately, there is a way to provide an abstract-interface-based programming model to the world of .NET Web services.

Forces

Use the WSI Pattern when:

- Multiple implementations of discrete Web service classes can be abstracted.

- Polymorphism at the Web service level is needed to enhance and standardize functionality.

- Web service classes contain methods with similar signatures but different implementations.

- Implementing Web services in different development teams to standardize Web service development effort.

Structure

The structure of this pattern (Figure 7.3) is very similar to any other Web service class structure, other than the fact that there is an additional Web service class acting as the interface. This additional Web service class is actually an abstract class, and it will never be called. This additional entity represents only the description from which you can then obtain an interface definition. As you will see, it does not matter where you place the client-side interface that represents the abstracted Web service. The interface can go in some shared assembly or can remain local; the choice is yours. There is no trickery to making this work. The point of creating the additional Web service interface abstract class on the server is so that when the WSDL file is accessed and the client proxy code is generated, you now have a "server-controlled" version of this interface contract to work with. However, this entity is optional. As long as the interface is documented, the client can use any implemented interface code, provided that it matches the documented signature. Invoking any Web service class that implements the Web service interface is the same except that the client now casts the return value to the Web service interface. From there, the client can employ any Web service using polymorphism through this interface.

The following class model (Figure 7.3) will be explained more in the implementation section, which should clear up any confusion.

Consequences

The WSI pattern has the following benefits and liabilities:

- *Abstracts the implementation of Web services from their representation.* Using this pattern, Web service implementations can become abstract to Web service clients. This allows Web services to become standardized using the interface defined. Web service clients need only to instantiate the appropriate Web service class and from that point, they can interact with the Web service using the standard interface. Multiple teams can work on different implementations of the interface, abstracting clients from their implementations.

- *Isolates Web service clients from implementation changes.* Using a standard interface to interact with the Web service will protect the client from implementa-

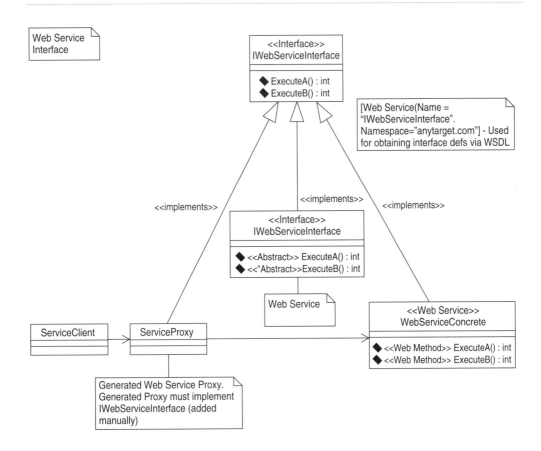

FIGURE 7.3: Web Service Interface generic class diagram.

tion details. It helps protect the Web service client from server-side implementation changes.

- *Adds polymorphism to the Web services architecture.* Polymorphism allows Web service clients to interact with multiple implementations of a Web service in a common fashion. This provides "true" interface polymorphism, using something not typically thought of as polymorphic—Web services.

- *Adds the burden of having to modify the generated proxy code manually for each concrete Web service.* The most annoying implementation of this pattern is the fact that you must manually edit the generated Web service proxy code. If you are automatically generating this from VStudio .NET, this may become some-what repetitive.

Participants

- ServiceClient ()—This represents the Web service client. The service client instantiates the Web service class like any other class but uses the declared Web service interface to interact with it. The Web service interface is declared like any other .NET interface. The interface is made accessible by either including an assembly with it declared as it is declared on the server or by using the *WSDL*-generated proxy as a guide for creating your own. As long as the inter-face signature matches the interface as used on the server (*IWebServiceInter-face*), your code will compile.

- ServiceProxy ()—This is the generated proxy code for all referenced Web ser-vices. This includes the Web service concrete implementations as well as the Web service interface (*WSI* class) itself. The *WebServiceInterface* class is used to generate a proxy that can be used as a guide to create the client-side interface. You can also simply reference the service-side assembly containing the interface or create it manually using the generated Web service interface code as a guide.

- IWebServiceInterface()—This is the actual .NET interface used on the server to implement the interface-based functionality. This is also the external name given to the *WebServiceInterface* abstract class below and is the interface used by the client for interacting with all Web services that implement it. On the client, this can be generated by referencing the *WebServiceInterface* class's *WSDL* and creating it manually. Another option is to reference an assembly containing this interface. Using the *WSDL* method to create it manually on the client keeps you from having to provide the assembly to any Web service clients.

- WebServiceInterface ()—This is actually an abstract Web service class that is externally represented using the *IWebServiceInterface* name (*[WebService(Name = "IWebServiceInterface",...)]*). This class will never directly be instantiated or called. It represents only a means of creating the interface contract on the client so that an interface can be used for interacting with all Web services that imple-ment it on the server.

- WebServiceConcrete()—This is any normal Web service class implementation. It implements *IWebServiceInterface* on the server. Each *WebServiceConcrete* implementation is first directly instantiated by the client, then called using *IWebServiceInterface*'s methods.

Implementation

Listing 7.8 and Figure 7.4 show just one of the many implementation examples that can benefit from the WSI pattern. Sticking with our credit card system, an interface called *IService* has been created that contains a method called *Execute*. This method is passed a DataSet containing the necessary credit card information to authorize a transaction. The Execute method acts as a *factory method* for the remainder of the financial component required to perform the unit of work. This interface is the starting point of this pattern. This becomes the "contract" upon which the abstract Web service interface, called *FinancialServiceFactory*, implements and mimics by externally exposing itself as IService. Using the WSI pattern, we can now abstract all services using the IService as the interface contract with which all Web service clients will interact.

The code in Listing 7.7 shows our simple interface, which happens to be defined in FinancialServiceFactory.asmx.cs.

LISTING 7.7: Sample interface.

```
interface IService
{
    // any signature can be used
    DataSet Execute(DataSet ds);
}
```

Figure 7.4 shows one concrete implementation of the IService interface called *CreditCardService*. The CreditCardService acts like any other Web service class but must implement IService, as shown in Listing 7.8.

LISTING 7.8: One concrete WSI implementation example.

```
[WebService(Namespace="http://www.etier.com/patterns.net",
    Description = "This provides the first implementation of the Web
Service Interface, Any Concrete Implementation will do.")]
public class CreditCardService : System.Web.Services.WebService,
    IService
{
    public CreditCardService()
```

```
{
    InitializeComponent();
}

. . .

[WebMethod(Description = "Implements Execute")]
public int Execute()
{
    . . .
}

. . .
}
```

FinancialServerFactory is the abstract class that is externally represented as the IService interface, as explained in the previous sections. Using the Name property of the WebService attribute, we define IService as what will be represented in the generated WSDL when referencing the FinancialServiceFactory Web service from the client. The FinancialServiceFactory code is shown in Listing 7.9.

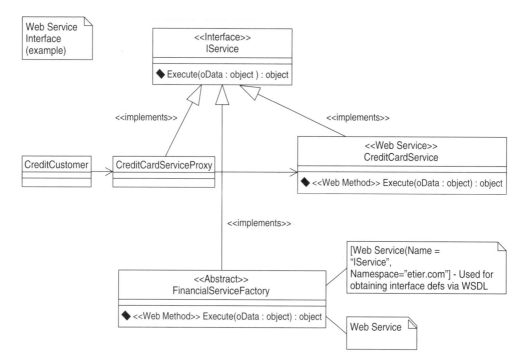

FIGURE 7.4: WSI implementation class diagram.

LISTING 7.9: Web service "piece" of the WSI implementation.

```
[WebService(Name = "IService",
Namespace="http://www.etier.com/patterns.net",
   Description = "This web service is abstract and cannot be
   directly called.")]
abstract class WebServiceInterface : ICanBeAnyInterface
{
   [WebMethod(Description = "Defines as a WebService Interface
      Execute from IService")]
   abstract public int Execute();

}
```

Once these service elements are defined, the client can now interact with the IService interface directly, with one minimal change. The final adjustment that must be made on the client is to modify the generated proxy for each concrete Web service (CreditCardService, in our case). Simply set IService as the implemented interface in the actual proxy code once it is generated from WSDL. Listing 7.10 shows where you must add the IService interface before you can begin interacting with any concrete implementations.

LISTING 7.10: WSDL-generated proxy code—highlighting where to add interface declaration.

```
[System.Diagnostics.DebuggerStepThroughAttribute()]
[System.ComponentModel.DesignerCategoryAttribute("code")]
[System.Web.Services.WebServiceBindingAttribute(Name=
   "CreditCardServiceSoap",
   namespace="http://www.etier.com/patterns.net")]
public class CreditCardServiceSoap :
   System.Web.Services.Protocols.SoapHttpClientProtocol,
IService
{

   /// <remarks/>
   public CreditCardService() {
      . . .
   }


   /// <remarks/>
   . . .


}
```

The interface IService must be defined somewhere on the client. You can define this manually, reference it directly, or infer it from the WSDL generated from the abstract Web service we created earlier (FinancialServiceFactory). Once you've defined the IService interface on the client, you may interact with any Web service using the IService interface. A simple interaction is shown in Listing 7.11.

LISTING 7.11: Client-side implementation sample of WSI.

```
IService oWSI;
DataSet oDsIn = null;
DataSet oDsOut = null;

// instantiate each web service using the interface we are now
externalizing
oWSI = (IService) new localhost.CreditCardService();

. . .

// any interface method calls are polymorphic
oDsOut = oWSI.Execute(oDsIn);

. . .
```

As you can the see, the Web service can now be treated like any other implementation class that implements any interface. Although there are a few hoops to leap through initially, the benefits significantly outweigh the hassles of providing you this useful pattern.

LOOSELY COUPLED TRANSACTOR SERVER

Intent

Provide an asynchronous server-based solution primarily for clients that do not have .NET capabilities and for clients that do not wish to utilize the built-in asynchronous features of .NET and of the Web services proxy-generator tools that come with the framework.

Asynchronous System Design Challenges

Many of you may have already had exposure to asynchronous-based development. If you have ever worked with Microsoft Message Queue Server, TIBCO, or any other asynchronous platform/API, you may already understand the benefits as well as the challenges that coincide with designing such a system. If you have worked with any of these or similar frameworks, you probably have realized that although they may provide the "async" plumbing, the design is still up to you. In fact, it is putting together a sound async design that is the most difficult. The technology behind an async model provides you only with the means of saving state, coordinating action, and possibly notifying the user during state changes. It is this plumbing that your model is designed on top of but it is the overall structure of the objects that are themselves independent of any technology. It seems as though developers initially think that as long as they have TIBCO or MSMQ, the async model will take care of itself. This is contrary to reality, and it is only when complicated async processes are implemented that those issues become plainly apparent. Some typical problems seen in async systems including the following:

- Users do not have TIBCO or another async API installed so that they can receive notifications.

- The business operation returns a very large DataSet.

- An exception occurs after the caller is disconnected.

- A two-phase commit operation must span across multiple async operations.

- Queued business operations continually fail and become stale while remaining in the queue (for those async systems using durable queues).

Many systems have the luxury of being capable of correct design from inception. These systems can take into account the logic necessary to facilitate an async system and are thus better positioned to answer some of these issues above. Typically, however, it seems more common that existing synchronous (sync) systems are those that are targeted to receive async features. Usually, this is a result of poor performance from an existing application and the need to improve scalability. This is indeed more of a challenge. Now you must take existing business logic and retrofit it into an async environment. Most "blocking" or sync methods that must be designed to be async usually must first go through a redesign effort. Usually, you cannot simply put an async wrapper around a sync operation and expect everything to run as before. Not only do such systems undergo a form of technical redesign but they may also undergo a business flow redesign. The amount of refactoring depends on the order of events that must take place within the method logic and what dependencies it may have during execution. Determining these dependencies will help flush out those elements that require attention.

When designing an async function, I suggest first answering some of the following questions:

- What data will be returned to the caller, if any?

- Is the method involved in any distributed transactions?

- Will there be compensating logic required in case of failure (e.g., undo functionality)?

- What exception scenarios will affect the success or failure of the logic?

- How do you communicate to a disconnected caller?

- How many concurrent users must you communicate with or notify?

- Where can you control state? On the server? On the client?

- What form of state management will you use?

- Can transactions go stale? What timeouts, if any, should be employed?

- If using any form of durable queues, what cleanup and/or administration tasks will be required of the system?

- Will storing large result sets in a job table defeat the purpose of calling an operation asynchronously (therefore, will the overall latency between calling and receiving be too lengthy)?

The questions listed above mainly deal with three primary focus areas: *state management, caller communication,* and *disconnected coordination/administration.* State management simply deals with making information durable, whether that be saving data to a database or a file, or using a shared in-memory object. The goal of any asynchronous system is to release callers as soon as possible once the method is invoked so that they may go about their business. Doing so typically involves capturing enough information and continuing the processing of the transaction without blocking the caller. Once the transaction is complete, the response must be made available to the user, either by direct notification or by saving the response. Another use of state management is guaranteeing that what the caller has invoked will indeed eventually run to completion at some point, providing a transaction "status facility." This is typically where message queuing becomes useful by providing a responsive environment for users where once they fire off transactions, they can go about their work and still have the ability to see whether transactions are processing or have completed.

The second area that must be thought out and designed is that of caller communication. This relates to how information will be presented to the user. The user can either be notified of server events directly or may poll the server, seeking status of a previously invoked method. Each has its advantages and disadvantages. Suffice it to say that employing notification is a convenient and efficient means of communication but is very technology-dependent and may not be a scalable option for your application (e.g., Internet applications). Polling is less efficient in that multiple calls may have to be made to assess the state of an async operation but it is beneficial in its simplicity and maintainability. You may also choose to provide notification for simple status messages and polling for large DataSets. This is something I have found to be quite successful as long as a notification and broadcast technology was deployed (e.g., TIBCO). Using MSMQ for broadcasts (one-to-many notifications) will be practical only in smaller environments. For larger environments, I recommend using a third-party message broadcast facility, rolling your own, or using a messaging server, such as Exchange.

The third focus area in asynchronous design is that of disconnected coordination and administration. This relates to the first two in that typically, state must be held to help coordinate a multistep transaction. Also each step of the transaction may require user notification and interaction, depending on how complicated the operation may be. Async models become complicated when many steps require an ordered, coordinated action. You also have to address the freshness of the transaction being invoked. If failure occurs—and it always does—will the transaction be placed back into a queue? If it is, how long should it remain in the queue? Using a message queue system will aid in answering these quandaries through implementation but they are no substitute for a plan that is well thought out. This focus area will probably be the one that requires the most attention. It will also be the one that requires the most administration. For example, when utilizing a message queue environment for transactional multistep processes, there will be instances when transactions never complete. Unless there are administration processes and tools in place, a queue can quickly become overtaken by stale messages. This is where the

K.I.S.S. (keep it simple stupid) principle really needs to be applied. By keeping your async model simple, you will ease your coordination pains in the future.

I hope this won't scare you off from implementing async systems but it should serve as a slight warning. These systems shine in their ability to improve the scalability of most applications immediately and, to the delight of the user, no longer block users from performing other tasks while a transaction is running in the background. However, they can also become quite complicated and warrant significant design attention, especially when operations employ multiple steps or return large DataSets. The LCT Server presents a server-based asynchronous model that employs polling for those clients that do not have the technology for direct callbacks and/or notifications. It also provide a rather simple means of wrapping an existing synchronous system in an asynchronous cover that minimizes those async refactoring challenges mentioned previously.

Problem

The reason for even considering going async is simple—the need for speed and scalability. There is also the added benefit of freeing up the user to do his or her work while a transaction may be running in the background. Not many of us like to see an hourglass while running a lengthy operation when we could be reading email. But for designers and system administrators, the real benefit is improved performance and scalability. With async invocations, the server is free from maintaining long-running connections with what could be hundreds of clients. This frees up memory and other valuable resources, which in turn improves scalability. With freed resources you now have improved performance. This is especially true for Web services applications. In fact, I highly recommend leveraging async processing whenever possible to improve your Web service performance overall.

Much thought was placed in the area of async features as they relate to the .NET BCL, as well as the tools accompanying VS.NET. Instead of an afterthought as it is with some languages, .NET has built into the framework an asynchronous programming model. This programming model is seen in the networking features, such as .NET remoting, sockets, and as you'll see here, XML Web services. In fact, it couldn't be any easier to implement. Simply by instantiating the remote object (or more accurately, its proxy) and calling a remote method, you unblock the caller through async invocation. Microsoft has even taken the asynchronous model a step forward by standardizing the remote method names. For example, if an operation is called *Foo()*, then the remote async version of that will be called

BeginFoo() and *EndFoo()*. With the aid of proxy generators such as WSDL.exe, you do not need to create specific async versions of methods or their signatures. The WSDL.exe tool or VS.NET will generate the async versions for you from the method signature or, more specifically, the WSDL output. Listing 7.12 shows both the Execute method sample from a Chained Service Factory (Chapter 4) and the sample wsdl.exe output generated from VS.NET.

Listing 7.12 is a code snippet from the Chained Service Factory Web method called *Execute*.

LISTING 7.12: Code snippet from a Web Service Factory used by a typical LCT Server.

```
public class ChainedServiceFactory :
System.Web.Services.WebService
    {
        . . .

    [WebMethod]
    public DataSet Execute(DataSet dsData, string sService)
    {
        DataSet ds = new DataSet();
        Facade oFacade = null;

        try
        {
            switch (sService)
            {
                case "Transactor":
                    oFacade = (Facade) new
        TransactorFacade();
                    break;
                case "Report":
        oFacade = (Facade) new
        ReportFacade();
                    break;
                default:
                    return ds;
            }
        }
        catch (Exception e)
        {
        throw new BaseException(. . .);
        }

        // invoke the factory method on the facade
        ds = oFacade.Execute(dsData);
```

```
        return ds;
    }

}
```

Next, the generated proxy code from VS.NET (the Begin and End methods are automatically generated for you):

LISTING 7.13: WSDL-generated output for the code snippet in Listing 7.12.

```
public class ChainedServiceFactory :
    System.Web.Services.Protocols.SoapHttpClientProtocol
{

    /// <remarks/>
    public ChainedServiceFactory()
        {
            . . .
        }

    /// <remarks/>
    [System.Web.Services.Protocols.SoapDocumentMethodAttribute(. . .)]
        public System.Data.DataSet Execute(
        System.Data.DataSet dsData,
        string sService)
            {
                object[] results = this.Invoke("Execute", new object[] {
                    dsData,
                    sService});
                return ((System.Data.DataSet)(results[0]));
            }

    /// <remarks/>
        public System.IAsyncResult BeginExecute(
        System.Data.DataSet dsData,
    vstring sService,
        System.AsyncCallback callback,
        object asyncState)
            {
                return this.BeginInvoke("Execute", new object[] {
                    dsData,
                    sService}, callback, asyncState);
            }

    /// <remarks/>
        public System.Data.DataSet EndExecute(
        System.IAsyncResult asyncResult)
            {
```

```
        object[] results = this.EndInvoke(asyncResult);
        return ((System.Data.DataSet)(results[0]));
    }
```

The same goes for other asynchronous features of the .NET BCL. To create a socket client, for instance, you call BeginConnect() instead of Connect() to make a remote socket connection. You can even build an asynchronous socket server using its built-in async methods. In fact, just by using *Intellisense* from within VS.NET, you can immediately see which class contains async support by looking for methods beginning with *Begin* or *End*. Whether an operation resides as part of a Web service, a socket server, or some other object residing in another app domain on the same machine, .NET gives you the power to call it asynchronously.

Now that your mouth is watering with all of the great asynchronous features of .NET, there will be disappointments. Not every client implementation has the luxury of running .NET. Also there may be instances where changing client code becomes extremely prohibitive. For those cases, the LCT Server may aid in still providing an application with sorely desired async features. The LCT Server provides a server-side async wrapper around existing synchronous applications, and it does so rather unobtrusively. As stated earlier, it is difficult enough to design an async model, but it is considerably more difficult when having to retrofit an existing sync environment to provide async behavior. Does this mean that the LCT Server would never be used for a .NET client to .NET server application written from the ground up? No. In fact, due to its simplicity, it can be a good first design choice for providing async features with minimal headache for your users, as you will see.

Forces

Use the LCT Server pattern when:

- Adding asynchronous services to an existing synchronous system.

- Adding client notification is neither practical nor possible.

- Asynchronously returning large result sets through polling.

- Clients do not have .NET installed or you do not wish to add asynchronous logic at the client level.

- You want to be introduced to asynchronous logic slowly, when a simple introduction to the technology is required.

Structure

The structure begins when any client (does *not* have to be .NET) wishes to execute a synchronous operation *a*synchronously. The client first instantiates the TransactorService object instead of connecting to the original object. The client then calls Execute() on the TransactorService object, passing in any parameters required to send to the original synchronous operation (Figure 7.5). I highly recommend bundling parameters in a flexible, self-describing container, such as a .NET DataSet or XML. For information on how to send DataSets from non-.NET clients, please refer to Chapter 5. In fact, this pattern is a perfect opportunity to use another pattern covered in Chapter 4—Chained Service Factory. By combining the LCT Server with the Chained (or Unchained) Service Factory, you can call any synchronous operation asynchronously.

Once Execute() is called on the TransactorService, an identifier will be generated to identify the async job uniquely. This ID will be used to track and manage the async job once the caller is initially unblocked. The algorithm for generating the ID is up to you. You can use a GUID, an ID column from SQL Server, or as

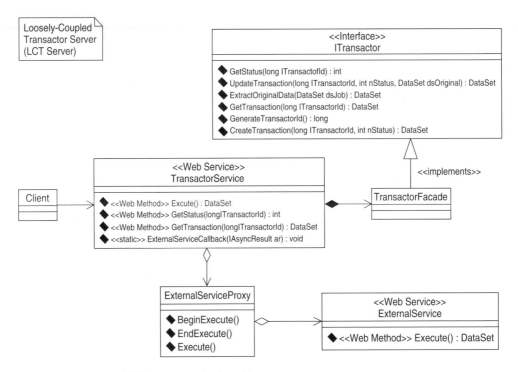

FIGURE 7.5: LCT Server generic class diagram.

you'll see next, a database counter. The only other step before control is returned back to the caller is to save the job. This is where state management comes in. If you are using a formal messaging framework such as MSMQ, you could simply dump the parameterized message to a queue. How the state is held and what transport you use is really implementation-dependent. The only goal you have is to unblock your caller as soon as possible. This, of course, is the whole point of calling something in async fashion—speed. Once the client is free, the server can normally do what it does to finish processing the request. Instead of using MSMQ, this pattern simply abstracts those operations common to all async job management. These operations can be found defined in the ITransactor interface and are implemented in the TransactorFacade. How they are implemented is again up to you. This pattern leverages off of the .NET Web service proxy generated from VS.NET to call the original operation. As shown in the class model, just before Transactor.Execute returns, the BeginExecute is called on the ExternalService. This will invoke the service asynchronously and register a callback method located in TransactorService. Once the operation is complete, the callback method, which is named appropriately enough *ExternalCallback()*, is invoked by .NET. Once invoked, the results of the ExternalService operation can be retrieved. Once retrieved, those results are then stored for later retrieval by the client. The client will use the return job ID from the initial Execute call as the lookup identifier for the both the status and the results of the operation. The LCT Server acts as an async delegate (of sorts) that simply delegates the operation payload but it does so asynchronously. The TransactorService acts as a client to the operation that the caller usually invokes synchronously. In fact, the role of the TransactorService is no different than any client. The only two differences in its role are that it acts as a proxy for the real client and drives the TransactorFacade. The TransactorFacade's role is simply to help manage state.

Consequences

The *LCT Server* pattern has the following benefits and liabilities:

- *Abstracts the implementation of a synchronous model from an asynchronous model.* Using this pattern, the loosely coupled Transactor can be easily added to your existing synchronous system without direct impact on the existing system. This is perfect for those systems that have already been implemented and deployed. This patterns acts as a "wrapper" around synchronous methods by providing

CHALLENGE 7.1

As was mentioned earlier, this architectural pattern can be implemented with several technology variances, including the designer deciding some of the following:

- Should polling be used for determining operation status?
- If so, how often should polling occur?
- Can server-side notification be used to update operation status instead of polling?
- How will state be managed on the server?
- Will messaging be used?
- If the job results are too large, does a buffering mechanism need to be designed?

The implementation section of this pattern covers one particular variance (page 364)

another layer that can be called by non-.NET clients synchronously. The synchronous request is then immediately made into an asynchronous request on the server. The abstraction also acts as a factory for the synchronous services with an interface that does not directly tie itself to any back-end implementation.

- *Eliminates the need for callback interfaces.* When dealing with any asynchronous design, the programmer typically has initially two major choices to make on the model. The first is to employ "callbacks," which will call back to an originating interface when the asynchronous method has completed. The other choice is to poll, and this is what is employed for the LCT pattern. Each has its advantages and disadvantages. Polling is simpler to implement but can be less efficient, depending on how often the server must be polled to obtain a transaction status. On the other hand, callbacks can be more efficient but they require a client system that has the actual ability to receive the callback. This is the biggest

CHALLENGE 7.2

During implementation, what other technologies can be used from the *LCT Transactor Service* to the *external service* while still leveraging the .NET framework's asynchronous features?

The answer lies in the side note in this chapter (page 362).

drawback of callbacks. For simple peer-to-peer activity, this usually isn't an issue. However, even in single-client implementations, the technology must be there to do the broadcast itself.

For non-.NET clients communicating with a .NET server, the choices are more limited. When many clients are involved in an asynchronous system, a more sophisticated model is required. Typically, these systems require something such as TIBCO or other broadcast-oriented callback technologies to scale well. Polling really is the "poor man's" version of implementing asynchronous status codes. Polling may be considered a less sophisticated option but it does work, and it works rather simply. For non-.NET clients, polling is the only simple solution without adding messaging software such as MSMQ or TIBCO. The other option is to implement a threading model on the client that "spoofs" the asynchronous call by simply running the synchronous transaction in a background thread.

- *May affect the scalability of the server due to polling.* The effect polling has on a server's scalability is simply due to the type of request being made and how often it is made. To limit this effect, it is suggested that a simple status request be made and that it be made sparingly. Many applications can be designed so that polling can take place during idle times on the client, when the client starts up, or during some other typically nonimpact event so that the user will not notice. If this is not the case, it would be better to employ some type of callback or threaded event so that a callback can be implemented. Typically, it is better to provide a callback than to call the server continuously more than a few times a minute unless there are only a few clients. These again are design decisions.

- *May force the need for more than one Web server.* Depending on your Web service directory layout and the number of Web servers you can deploy in your architecture or Web forms, this pattern may require an additional server. For larger systems that may have hundreds of calling clients, it may be more effective to employ two Web servers so that the polling and the initial synchronous call to the Transactor Service will *not* affect the scalability of the external service (see Figure 7.5). Each status request made to the Transactor Server may take away from the processing time used by the external service if both services are on the same machine. This should be a concern if there are numerous clients making frequent requests and should be addressed only for large systems or servers with small memory footprints. Again, this is an infrastructure design decision and should be evaluated before deployment.

Participants

- Client (same)—This represents any calling client. The client represents a workstation that does not have .NET installed (e.g., Visual Basic 6.0 fat client). This also is any client that does *not* have messaging software so that polling and the decision to employ the LCT pattern is the best design option. Any existing client will require minor changes to take advantage of this new service. After the client calls the LCT server, it must also poll for status using the same service. How this is implemented is again design-dependent and should be as unobtrusive to the client's normal workflow as possible.

- TransactorService(same)—This is the Web service that will receive all incoming traffic that is called synchronously. Once it receives the invocation (by calling TransactorService.Execute()), its job is to forward the request immediately to an external Web service asynchronously. The implementation of all logic for the TransactorService is implemented in the TransactorFacade to abstract the logic between the Web service and the core business tier.

> **NOTE**
>
> Please note that the external service can be called via ".NET remoting," which may provide better performance, albeit at the cost of some overall system scalability for large implementations. This implementation uses another Web service call but is not tied to this implementation approach. In fact, it is recommended that all controlled server-to-server invocation use .NET remoting, due to its performance benefits. Web services were used here simply for demonstration purposes and ease of implementation.

This service is actually where the callback function is implemented. Upon completion of the external service, the callback is then used to update the original transaction status, using some persistent data store. This status can be queried or polled at any time by the original client. The client polls the TransactorService by calling TransactorService.GetStatus() repeatedly until a completion status or a discrete error status can be obtained. Once a completion status is received by the client, the client can then call GetTransaction() to receive the final results. The GetTransaction() method is the final call made from the client to obtain any results from the original call. For methods that do not return result sets, the asynchronous design is simplified and may keep the client from polling at all. However, for methods that do return data, polling is required, and GetTransaction() must be called at some point. This is where .NET, and more specifically ADO.NET and XML support, really come into play. Instead of requiring the implementation of different data models for each result set from each individual asynchronous method, the developer can leverage XML schemas. With XML schemas and ADO.NET, the developer can store both the schema and the instance data in one table. This allows the developer to represent almost any result set using a single logical database design. For more information how this pattern works, please refer to Chapter 5's dynamic data model pattern called *Poly Model* and the Schema Field pattern.

- ExternalServiceProxy (FinancialServiceFactoryProxy)—This is the generated or manually created proxy between the TransactorService object and the external service itself. This provides the asynchronous logic between these two entities of the pattern and works like any other proxy, representing an external service as though the service were local to the caller. For this implementation, it is the Visual Studio .NET generated proxy from the external service's WSDL file (from its Web service).

- ExternalService (FinancialServiceFactory)—The external service can be any service providing the methods that the client wishes to invoke asynchronously. It can contain any set of method signatures. However, it is recommended that a factory or other standard interface method be used to provide a "contract" between the client and the server so that a single LCT Server can be used. The Execute method is the contract method in this implementation example.

- TransactorFacade (same)—As mentioned in the TransactorService participant, this "houses" all logic used by the TransactorService. This used the Web Service Façade pattern as defined in Chapter 4. It implements all methods from the ITransactor interface and any helper methods used by the TransactorService object.

- ITransactor (same)—All of the standard methods used by the LCT Server are defined here. These methods are implemented by the TransactorFacade, directly called by the TransactorService, and originally delegated from calls originating from the client.

Implementation

One of the primary benefits of this pattern is its ability to be seamlessly added to the existing application. This is especially true for clients that have not yet installed .NET at the desktop. For the Financial Server application, the LCT Server simply "wraps" the FinancialServiceFactory class and is treated as the ExternalService entity. Now the client must now call the TransactorService synchronously and pass identical information as though calling the FinancialServiceFactory (Figure 7.6). The following Visual Basic Service Client calls the Web service method Execute on the TransactorService as though it were the real FinancialServiceFactory, using identical parameters. The difference lies in the methods that may return result sets. All result sets will not be returned synchronously as before but through the invocation of the GetTransaction(), as explained earlier.

Listing 7.14 shows a typical FinancialService non-.NET client (implemented in Visual Basic 6.0) calling the FinancialServiceFactory through the LCT Transactor Service:

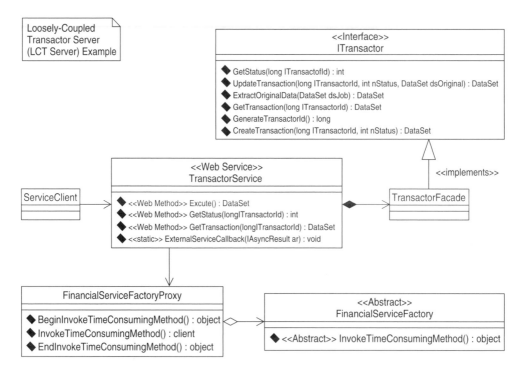

FIGURE 7.6: LCT Server class diagram—implementation example.

LISTING 7.14: Visual Basic SOAP Toolkit client used for calling the LCT Server.

```
Option Explicit

    Dim soapClient As MSSOAPLib.SoapClient
    set soapClient = CreateObject("MSSOAP.SoapClient")
    Dim oNodes As MSXML2.IXMLDOMNodeList
    Dim oDataSet As MSXML2.IXMLDOMNodeList

On Error Resume Next

    . . . 'set up oDataSet

    Call soapClient.mssoapinit(
        "http://localhost/transactorservice.wsdl",
    "TransactorService")

    Set oNodes = soapClient.Execute(oDataSet)
    If Err <> 0 then
        Result = Result & "Err.Number=" & Err.Number
        Result = Result & "Err.Description=" & Err.Description

        Result = Result & "SoapClient.faultcode=" & sc.faultcode
    End If

    . . . 'process oNodes xml return dataset (optional)
```

The Listing 7.14 VB code snippet is just that—a snippet. Most unmanaged clients will most likely be more complex. The LCT server is just another Web service. Calling it from VB can either use the SOAP Toolkit's high-level API as shown in Listing 7.14, or for more control, the low-level API can be used. There are only three calls to be made to the LCT server. The first call invokes the Execute call to initiate the transaction. Once called, the remaining calls consist of any polling invocations and the final call to retrieve the results from the initial request. For those transactions that do not return data, these final two invocations are not necessary. As mentioned, one of the benefits of this pattern is its simplicity. The simpler the client is designed, the better. More complicated clients—such as those that must contain a callback, use multithreading to mimic asynchronous behavior, or utilize a messaging system—all add deployment configuration headaches. Placing more of the design complexity at the server level will increase a developer's control and provide the ability to make future changes in the asynchronous behavior much easier.

Once called, the Transactor service receives the DataSet input parameters and immediately forwards them to the actual service. The only difference is that the

LCT Server becomes a "client" of sorts with that external service, and it is here that the callback must be implemented. The callback, when called, completes the original transaction workflow by updating the status of the transaction from "pending" to "complete" (other status codes can be implemented if needed). The final activity performed by the callback is updating the transaction record with the result set of the external method. The external method, in this case, simply returns a set of records back, and it can contain any data as long as it is encapsulated in a DataSet. The result set is then directly saved to the database by calling TransactorFacade.UpdateTransaction(), as implemented in Listing 7.15.

Listing 7.15 shows the main execution (Execute) call, the callback method, a method for checking the status of the transaction, and the final transaction result set retrieval method.

LISTING 7.15: LCT Server "plumbing" implementation.

```
/// <summary>
/// This is the driver web service for the loosely coupled
///
/// transactor
/// From this web service, another service can be called
///
///
/// asynchronously
/// and its status queried and eventually the transaction results
/// returned
   /// </summary>
   public class TransactorService : System.Web.Services.WebService
   {
   . . .

     /// <summary>
   /// Executes a particular external service asynchronously,
   /// can be easily made to
   /// call chained or unchained service factory (chapter 4)
   /// to launch any external service
     /// </summary>
     [WebMethod]
     public long Execute()
     {
        ITransactor oTransactor = (ITransactor)
        new TransactorFacade();
        long lTransactorId = 0;
        localhost.ExternalService oExtService =
        new localhost.ExternalService();
```

```
   try
   {
      // generate a unique transactor id
      lTransactorId =
   oTransactor.GenerateTransactionId();

         // insert the job into the job table and give
// it a pending status STATUS = 1
         oTransactor.CreateTransaction(
   lTransactorId, 1);  // 1 for pending

         // simply delegate to the
// InvokeTimeConsumingMethod call...
// this can be any call including a
// chainedservicefactory
         oExtService.TransactorHeaderValue =
   new localhost.TransactorHeader();
oExtService.TransactorHeaderValue.lTransactorId
= lTransactorId;
oExtService.BeginInvokeTimeConsumingMethod(
new System.AsyncCallback(
TransactorService.
ExternalServiceCallback), oExtService);
   }
   catch (Exception e)
   {
      throw new
   BaseException(
   Utilities.BuildErrorMessage(
   "LCT Server Exception thrown",
   e.Message), true);
   }

   return lTransactorId;
}

/// <summary>
/// Returns just the status of the original transaction
/// </summary>
[WebMethod]
public int GetStatus(long lTransactorId)
{
   ITransactor oTransactor = (ITransactor)
   new TransactorFacade();
   int nStatus = 0;

   try
   {
```

```
            // insert the job into the job table and give
        // it a pending status STATUS = 1
            nStatus = oTransactor.GetStatus(lTransactorId);

        }
        catch (Exception e)
        {
            throw new
        BaseException(
        Utilities.BuildErrorMessage(
    v    "LCT Server Exception thrown",
        e.Message), true);
        }


            return nStatus;
        }


    /// <summary>
    /// Executes a particular external service asynchronously,
/// can be easily made to
/// call chained or unchained service factory (chapter 4)
/// to launch any external service
    /// </summary>
    [WebMethod]
    public DataSet GetTransaction(long lTransactorId)
    {
        ITransactor oTransactor = (ITransactor)
        new TransactorFacade();
        DataSet ds = null;

        try
        {
            // insert the job into the job table and give
        // it a pending status STATUS = 1
            ds = oTransactor.GetTransaction(lTransactorId);

        }
        catch (Exception e)
        {
            throw new
        BaseException(
        Utilities.BuildErrorMessage(
            "LCT Server Exception thrown",
        e.Message), true);
        }

        return ds;
    }
```

```
/// <summary>
/// Asynchronous Callback method for async ops
/// </summary>
/// <param name="ar"></param>
public static void ExternalServiceCallback(IAsyncResult ar)
{
    DataSet dsOriginal = new DataSet();
    ITransactor oTransactor = (ITransactor)
    new TransactorFacade();

    try
    {
        // Obtains return value from the delegate call
// using EndInvoke.
        localhost.ExternalService oExtService =
        (localhost.ExternalService)ar.AsyncState;
        dsOriginal =
    oExtService.EndInvokeTimeConsumingMethod(ar);

        // update the transaction with a success (==2)
// and the results of the original transaction
        if (dsOriginal != null)
        voTransactor.UpdateTransaction(
    oExtService.TransactorHeaderValue.
    lTransactorId, 2, dsOriginal);

    }
    catch(Exception e)
    {
        throw new
    BaseException(
    Utilities.BuildErrorMessage(
    "LCTServer Exception thrown",
    e.Message), true);
    }
}

}
```

Let's start with Execute(). This is the first method called by the client. The Execute method initially instantiates the external service and later uses its asynchronous interface to invoke its own "contract" method. The external service in this case is another Web service but, as mentioned, can also come in the form of a .NET remoting call. Another Web service was used for simplicity and because the code was already written from the Web Service Factory (Chapter 4). The Web Service Factory Method is named *InvokeTimeConsumingMethod* and is leveraged and invoked through a single call into that external Web service. This call is delegated directly from the Transactor's Execute call, making this pattern relatively simple to implement.

You'll notice that the external service method is actually indirectly called through the Begin version of the call, as generated by the Web service proxy using Visual Studio .NET. Just before calling the asynchronous factory, however, a transaction ID is generated, and a record is created into the database. The transaction ID generation uses a stored-procedure to generate the ID and SQL/ADO.NET to insert the new record in the database, as well as to update the status. The new database record is given a "pending" status code to provide the means by which the client can now track the status of the transaction. Most of the heavy lifting, such as driving the transaction ID generation and the transaction record creation, is done by the TransactorFacade class and its methods. This code is shown in Listing 5.15.

NOTE

I also use SOAP headers to pass the transaction ID. This is completely optional because I decided not to pass any input parameters into the external service.

LISTING 7.16: Sample functional implementation drive by the LCT Server.

```
/// <summary>
/// Main driver for all async (LCT) transaction operations
/// </summary>
public class TransactorFacade : ITransactor
{
    private string m_sConnectionString = string.Empty;

    public TransactorFacade()
    {
        // for SQL Server Test
        m_sConnectionString = "Integrated Security=SSPI;" +
            "Initial Catalog=PatternsDotNet;" +
            "Data Source=DEV06;";
    }

    /// <summary>
    /// Calls the appropriate stored proc to increment a db
/// count and return it
    /// </summary>
    /// <returns></returns>
```

```
public long GenerateTransactionId()
{
    SqlConnection cn = null;
    StringBuilder sbExecSQL = null;
    SqlCommand oCommand = null;
    long lTransactionId = 0;

    try
    {
        sbExecSQL = new StringBuilder(
    "exec sp_DNPatternsIncCounter");
        sbExecSQL.Append(" 'JOB_ID', 1");

        // make the connection
        cn = new SqlConnection();
        cn.ConnectionString = m_sConnectionString;
        cn.Open();

        // call the storeproc sp_DNPatternsIncCounter
        if (cn.State == ConnectionState.Open )
        {
            oCommand = new
    SqlCommand(
    sbExecSQL.ToString(), cn);
                    lTransactionId =
    (long)oCommand.ExecuteScalar();
        }
    }
    catch (Exception e)
    {
        throw new
    BaseException(
    Utilities.BuildErrorMessage(
    "General Exception thrown",
    e.Message), false);
    }
    finally
    {
        cn.Close();
    }
    return lTransactionId;
}

/// <summary>
/// This creates a new transaction
/// as part of a transaction table (uses the specified
/// transactor id)
/// </summary>
/// <param name="lTransactorId"></param>
```

```
/// <param name="nStatus"></param>
/// <returns></returns>
public DataSet CreateTransaction(long lTransactorId,
int nStatus)
{
    DataTable oTable = new DataTable();
    SqlParameter oParam = null;
    string sSelectText = string.Empty;
    SqlConnection cn = null;
    DataSet ds = null;
    SqlDataAdapter da = null;

    try
    {
        // make the connection
        cn = new SqlConnection();
        cn.ConnectionString = m_sConnectionString;
        cn.Open();

        if (cn.State == ConnectionState.Open )
        {
            // build the sql statement and prepare
// the dataset
            da = new SqlDataAdapter(
    "SELECT * FROM JOB", cn);
            ds = new DataSet("JOB");
            da.Fill(ds, "JOB");

            // prepare a data adapter with insert
// statement
            string sInsertCommand = "INSERT INTO JOB
    (JOB_ID, STATUS) VALUES
    (@JOB_ID, @STATUS)";
            da.InsertCommand = new
    SqlCommand(sInsertCommand, cn);

            // bind parms to insert
            oParam = new SqlParameter("@JOB_ID",
    SqlDbType.Int);
            oParam.SourceColumn = "JOB_ID";
            oParam.SourceVersion =
    DataRowVersion.Current;
    da.InsertCommand.Parameters.Add(oParam);

            oParam = new SqlParameter("@STATUS",
    SqlDbType.Int);
            oParam.SourceColumn = "STATUS";
            oParam.SourceVersion =
    DataRowVersion.Current;
```

```
        da.InsertCommand.Parameters.Add(oParam);

            oTable = ds.Tables["JOB"];
            if (oTable != null)
            {
                // insert the new row
                DataRow oNewRow = oTable.NewRow();
                oNewRow["JOB_ID"] = lTransactorId;
                oNewRow["STATUS"] = nStatus;
                oTable.Rows.Add(oNewRow);

                // save it to the database
                da.Update(ds, "JOB");

            }
            else
                throw new
                    BaseException(
        Utilities.BuildErrorMessage(
                    "Inserting Job Failed",
        "Table object was null"),
    false);
            }

        }
        catch (Exception e)
        {
            throw new
        BaseException(
        Utilities.BuildErrorMessage(
        "General Exception thrown",
        e.Message), false);
        }
        finally
        {
            da.Dispose();
            cn.Close();
        }

        return ds;
    }

/// <summary>
/// Updates the transaction with the dataset results
/// of any returned external call
/// </summary>
/// <param name="lTransactorId"></param>
/// <param name="nStatus"></param>
/// <returns></returns>
```

```
public DataSet UpdateTransaction(long lTransactorId,
int nStatus, DataSet dsOriginal)
{
   DataTable oTable = new DataTable();
   SqlParameter oParam = null;
   string sSelectText = string.Empty;
   SqlConnection cn = null;
   SqlDataAdapter da = null;
   DataRow oRow = null;
   DataSet dsJob = null;

   try
   {
      // make the connection
      cn = new SqlConnection();
      cn.ConnectionString = m_sConnectionString;
      cn.Open();

      if (cn.State == ConnectionState.Open )
      {
         // build the sql statement and prepare
// the dataset
         da = new SqlDataAdapter(
            new StringBuilder(
      "SELECT * FROM JOB WHERE JOB_ID = ")
      .Append(lTransactorId).ToString(),
      cn);
         dsJob = new DataSet("JOB");
         da.Fill(dsJob, "JOB");

         // build the update sql command
         da.UpdateCommand = new SqlCommand(
      new StringBuilder(
         "UPDATE JOB SET STATUS = @STATUS, DATA_SCHEMA =
      @DATA_SCHEMA, DATA = @DATA WHERE JOB_ID = @JOB_ID")
      .ToString(), cn);

         // bind the insert parameters
         oParam = new SqlParameter(
      "@STATUS", SqlDbType.Int);
         oParam.SourceColumn = "STATUS";
         oParam.SourceVersion =
      DataRowVersion.Current;
      da.UpdateCommand.Parameters.Add(oParam);

         oParam = new SqlParameter(
      "@DATA_SCHEMA", SqlDbType.Image);
         oParam.SourceColumn = "DATA_SCHEMA";
      voParam.SourceVersion =
```

```
DataRowVersion.Current;
da.UpdateCommand.Parameters.Add(oParam);

     oParam = new SqlParameter(
"@DATA", SqlDbType.Image);
     oParam.SourceColumn = "DATA";
     oParam.SourceVersion =
DataRowVersion.Current;
da.UpdateCommand.Parameters.Add(oParam);

     oParam = new SqlParameter("@JOB_ID",
SqlDbType.Int);
     oParam.SourceColumn = "JOB_ID";
     oParam.SourceVersion =
DataRowVersion.Current;
da.UpdateCommand.Parameters.Add(oParam);

     da.Fill(dsJob, "JOB");

      // grab the table so we can update each
// field as bound by the parameters
     oTable = dsJob.Tables["JOB"];
     if (oTable != null)
     {
         // should be first and only row
   // found
         oRow = oTable.Rows[0];
         if (oRow != null)
         {
             // insert the new row
             oRow["STATUS"] = nStatus;
             if (dsJob != null)
             {
oRow["DATA_SCHEMA"] =
Utilities.ToByteArray(
     DsOriginal
.GetXmlSchema());
             oRow["DATA"] =
Utilities.ToByteArray(
   dsOriginal.GetXml());
             }

         // save it to the database
         da.Update(dsJob, "JOB");
       }
       else
          throw new BaseException(...);
     }
     else
```

```
                    throw new
        BaseException(. . .);
            }


        }
        catch (Exception e)
        {
            throw new BaseException(. . .);
        }
        finally
        {
            da.Dispose();
            cn.Close();
        }


        return dsJob;
    }


    /// <summary>
    /// This will regenerate the original DataSet from the
/// stored schema and data as xml in the job table
    /// </summary>
    /// <param name="dsJob"></param>
    /// <returns></returns>
    public DataSet ExtractOriginalData(DataSet dsJob)
    {
        DataSet dsOriginal = new DataSet("OriginalData");
        string sSchema = null;
        string sData = null;

        try
        {
            // first convert byte array to string
            if (dsJob != null)
            {
                sSchema = Utilities.FromByteArray(
        (byte [])dsJob.Tables["JOB"]
        .Rows[0]["DATA_SCHEMA"]);
                sData = Utilities.FromByteArray(
        (byte [])dsJob.Tables["JOB"]
        .Rows[0]["DATA"]);
                dsOriginal.ReadXmlSchema(
        new StringReader(sSchema));
                dsOriginal.ReadXml(
        new StringReader(sData));
            }
        }
        catch (Exception ex)
        {
```

```
            throw new BaseException(. . .);
      }

   return dsOriginal;

   }

   /// <summary>
   /// Returns the transaction as a dataset
   /// for the transactor id
   /// </summary>
   /// <param name="lTransactorId"></param>
   /// <returns></returns>
   public DataSet GetTransaction(long lTransactorId)
   {
      string sSelectText = string.Empty;
      SqlConnection cn = null;
      SqlDataAdapter da = null;
      DataSet ds = null;
      DataSet dsOriginal = null;

      try
      {
         // make the connection
         cn = new SqlConnection();
         cn.ConnectionString = m_sConnectionString;
         cn.Open();

         if (cn.State == ConnectionState.Open )
         {
            // build the sql statement and prepare
// the dataset
            da = new SqlDataAdapter(
               new StringBuilder(
            "SELECT * FROM JOB WHERE JOB_ID = ")
         .Append(lTransactorId)
      .ToString(), cn);
            ds = new DataSet("JOB");
            da.Fill(ds, "JOB");

            // just so we can see the stored bytes
// array as returned xml data
            dsOriginal = ExtractOriginalData(ds);
         }

      }
      catch (Exception e)
      {
         throw new BaseException(. . .);
```

```csharp
    }
    finally
    {
        da.Dispose();
        cn.Close();
    }

    return dsOriginal;
}

/// <summary>
/// Returns the status of the transaction
/// </summary>
/// <param name="lTransactorId"></param>
/// <returns></returns>
public int GetStatus(long lTransactorId)
{
    string sSelectText = string.Empty;
    SqlConnection cn = null;
    SqlDataAdapter da = null;
    DataSet ds = null;
    int nStatus = 0;

    try
    {
        // make the connection
        cn = new SqlConnection();
        cn.ConnectionString = m_sConnectionString;
        cn.Open();

        if (cn.State == ConnectionState.Open )
        {
            // build the sql statement and prepare
// the dataset
            da = new SqlDataAdapter(
            new StringBuilder(
            "SELECT * FROM JOB WHERE JOB_ID = ")
        .Append(lTransactorId).ToString(),
    cn);
            ds = new DataSet("JOB");
            da.Fill(ds, "JOB");

            // just so we can see the stored bytes
    // array as returned xml data
            nStatus = (int)ds.Tables["JOB"]
    .Rows[0]["STATUS"];
        }


    }
```

```
        catch (Exception e)
        {
            throw new BaseException(. . .);
        }
        finally
        {
            da.Dispose();
            cn.Close();
        }

        return nStatus;
    }
}
```

By placing the logic in this façade, you have the obvious advantage of directly calling that class without going through the Web service (see Web Service Façade pattern in Chapter 4). Each method in this TransactorFacade should be relatively self-explanatory. Each implements one of the ITransactor interface methods and makes up the "heart" of the pattern. UpdateTransaction() requires the most explanation because this is the method that is called by the Transactor Service callback when the asynchronous external service has completed. The two mains items that are updated are the status and the result set that was returned from the original external service call. The dataset is strongly leveraged here in that both the instance data from the data *and* the schema are stored. Each is stored in its own field and allows any data to be stored; the schema can then be retrieved at any time, along with the record. Both the instance data and the schema are stored as "image" fields in SQL Server. If using Oracle, BLOBS could also be used. To store each field, the DataSet XML contents are first converted to a byte array and directly saved using ADO.NET. For more details on using this form of data storage, please refer to Chapter 5 on persistence-tier patterns. The only other method needing explanation is ExtractOriginalData(). This is a helper method used once GetTransaction() is called on the TransactorService, and the database contents are then returned as a complete DataSet.

Like its name, this pattern provides the implementer with a lot of flexibility in the manner in which it is implemented. Using several design variances, it can have many uses and can even function from server-to-server invocation, as well as client to server. It also represents an assembly of several best practices and patterns presented in this book. When it comes to providing any asynchronous solution, the model to live by is "the simpler, the better," and I hope this pattern delivers on that premise.

LOOSELY COUPLED TRANSACTOR CLIENT[1]

Intent

Provide asynchronous services to those systems whose installed clients can be edited or created without the need for .NET on the server or client, or a messaging system of any kind. These clients include Windows 2000 or Windows XP without the .NET runtime. Utilize multithreading to mimic asynchronous behavior on a client.

Problem

The reason for implementing this pattern is that, like the LCT Server, an application can greatly benefit from adding asynchronous-type behavior to a design and can do so in a nonintrusive manner. Fortunately, just as the LCT Server above is a simplified "afterthought," the LCT Client provides the developer with a client-side "add-on" that should not disrupt an existing client implement. However, unlike the LCT Server, this pattern is typically deployed on the client and may require more deployment time. Despite this limitation, this offers a highly controllable means of calling Web services (or any external call) in a loosely coupled fashion. This also provides a solution for those installed applications that do not have the option of changing the server or calling a Web service and do not have .NET installed on the client. Finally, it does not require any messaging software to work.

Forces

Use the LCT Server pattern when:

- Adding asynchronous services to an existing synchronous system.

- Adding client notification through messaging software is neither practical nor possible.

- When clients do not have .NET installed or you do not wish to add asynchronous logic at the server level.

---

1. Portions of the following text are used by permission from Pranish Kumar and Bogdan Crivat, "SOAP: Using ATL Server to Build an Asynchronous SOAP Client in Unmanaged C++," *MSDN Magazine*, April 2002, http://msdn.microsoft.com/msdnmag/issues/02/04/SOAP/default.aspx .

- Client workstations are efficient enough to take advantage of a multithreaded process (not recommended for older desktop footprints).

- Adding multithreaded features is a supportable option for the environment.

Structure

Just like the LCTServer pattern, the structure begins with any client (does *not* have to be .NET) that wishes to execute a synchronous operation *a*synchronously. The class diagram (Figure 7.7) shows this as being the LCTClientMain entity. In the sample code, this is a simple console application written in Visual C++ 7.0. It has two main purposes. First it provides an implementation of a generic callback function whose pointer is passed to the LCTClient during preparation and later called during execution. Second, it calls the Web service using an instantiated object declared as a type, employing a generated ATL template. The ATL template is generated from SPROXY.EXE (Visual C++ 7.0) and provides a custom ATL-based proxy by which to call any Web service method from the client. The details of the implementation are in the following section. Other than that, most of the work is done by the ATL framework, the custom CLCTClientSoapSocket class, and the template it uses, called *CSoapSocketClientT*.

Another feature used in this pattern is that of a ThreadPool object. Although one cannot effectively implement this pattern without the use of mutithreading, employing an actual "thread pool" is optional. However, once again, ATL does most of the work, so why *not*? The ThreadPool object is just like any other object used by the LCTClientMain to create and initialize the pool and add each Web service proxy object to it, just like any array objects. The core of this pattern is rather simple but it's the technology behind it that makes this a more advanced pattern implementation. This pattern acts as hybrid between an architecture *and* an implementation pattern, due to its technological particularities.

CHALLENGE 7.3

Does running an application written in Visual C++ 7.0 require that .NET be installed at runtime?

Even if new ATL features are used from Visual C++ 7.0?
> The answer is no for both. Even though the LCTClient is written in Visual C++ 7.0, this sample will run in an environment without .NET!

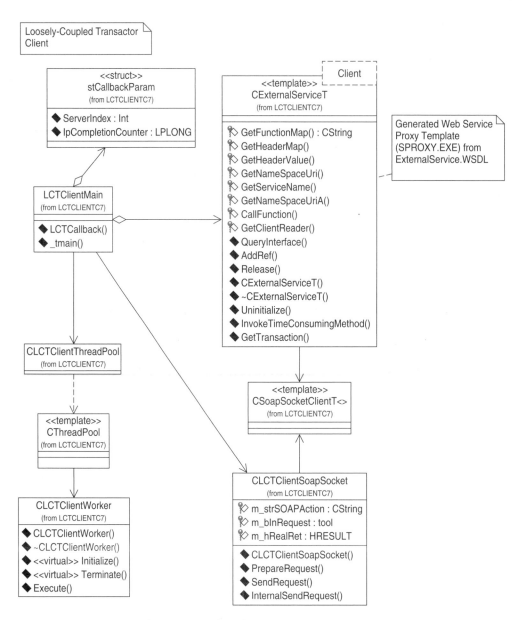

FIGURE 7.7: LCT Client generic class diagram.

Consequences

The *LCT Client* pattern has the following benefits and liabilities:

- *Abstracts the implementation of a synchronous model from an asynchronous model.* Using this pattern, the LCT Client can be easily added to your existing synchronous system without direct impact on the existing system. Like the LCT Server, this is perfect for those systems that have already been implemented and deployed. It also acts as a "wrapper" around client-based synchronous methods by providing another layer that can be called by non-.NET clients synchronously. The synchronous request is then immediately added to a thread pool and called in a background thread that makes the request to the server. Unlike the LCT Server, the abstraction may be limited in the implementation of the callback. Each callback may contain specific business logic, and several callbacks may have to be implemented. The real abstraction lies in the delegated call to the server, using a background thread to mimic asynchronous behavior.

- *Provides a generic facility in which to use callbacks.* When dealing with any asynchronous design, the programmer typically has initially two major choices to make on the model. The first is to employ "callbacks," which will call back to an originating interface when the asynchronous method has completed. The other choice is to poll. This is what is employed for the LCT pattern. Each has its advantages and disadvantages. Polling is simpler to implement but can be less efficient, depending on how often the server must be polled to obtain a transaction status.

  Callbacks can be more efficient but they require a client system that has the actual ability to receive the callback. This is where this pattern fits in. Each call runs in a separate thread from the main process and upon completion invokes the callback passed into the LCTClient during preparation. This provides the most efficient means of communicating from a client to the status of the original transaction without the use of messaging software. The only drawback is that it runs on the client, must be installed there, and is more complicated than simple polling, as explained in the previous pattern.

- *May require more deployment investment.* Because each client that wishes to take advantage of this new feature must install it, it may require more investment for IT support. For large-scale clients, deploying this may not be the best option.

Any client installation has its headache, and this is no exception because each client must have the ability to run multiple threads for it to work.

Participants

- LCTClientMain (same)—This represents any calling client. This client is a simple console application that drives CExternalServiceT by calling GetTransaction() several times to mimic several requests. Each request will then be added to a thread pool and executed asynchronously in a background thread, one by one. As each transaction completes, a callback will be called, which is also implemented here.

- CExternalServiceT (same)—This is the generated ATL proxy for the Web service that will be called using LCTClientMain. It will contain all of the method calls implemented in the Web service. This can be any generated ATL proxy calling any Web service. The GetTransaction() method is implemented here and forwarded to the ExternalService Web service. A call to PrepareRequest() is made on this template but forwarded to CLCTClientSoapSocket, which is passed in during the CExternalServiceT's declaration. It is during PrepareRequest() that the thread pool initializes to be handled later. Fortunately, little work has been put forth in creating this class. To create it, simply use SPROXY.EXE or use Visual Studio .NET to generate it from your workspace environment. Once generated, the namespace declaration is removed, along with two helper methods (at the end of the generated source code) that are created and not used in this implementation.

> **NOTE**
>
> Keep in mind that this application may need to run in an environment that does not have .NET installed. Using the implementation as is will guarantee that.

- CLCTClientThreadPool (same)—This simply represents the thread pool used for this implementation and can be considered optional if pools are not required. However, its implementation is simple enough to keep using it, requiring only initialization and shutdown to be functional.

- CLCTClientWorker (same)—This is the actual worker for the thread invoking the Web service through the LCTClient.

- CLCTClientSoapSocket (same)—This is the heart of the pattern in that it leverages the ATL template CSoapSocketClientT and ATL thread pooling to invoke any Web service in asynchronous threaded-fashion. It is passed as a declaration parameter to the CExternalServiceT template and used for the preparation and actual asynchronous invocations.

- CSoapSocketClientT (same)—A part of ATL, it handles all SOAP-based communications with external Web services and SOAP servers via TCP/IP Sockets. All low-level communications to the Web service use this.

Implementation

One of the primary benefits of this pattern is its ability to be seamlessly added to an efficient asynchronous callback mechanism for any client. However, this pattern does require some understanding beyond just that of C# or VB.NET. For those aching to get their hands dirty with C++, this can be great way to dive in. To start things off, let's first look the LCTClientMain console application (Listing 7.17).

LISTING 7.17: LCT Client C++ console implementation.

```
#include "stdafx.h"
#include "ExternalService.h"

#include "LCTClient.h"

#define CLIENTS_COUNT 8

struct stCallbackParam
{
   int    iServerIndex;
   LPLONGlpCompletionCounter;
};

/*
//This is the callback that is registered with the LCTClient
// class during PrepareAsync
*/
void LCTCallback(LPARAM lParam, HRESULT hRet)
{
stCallbackParam*param= reinterpret_cast<stCallbackParam*>(lParam);
   ATLASSERT(param);
```

```
    // increment the shared counter
    InterlockedIncrement(param->lpCompletionCounter);

    // do something useful with the HRESULT
    printf("\n[Client %d] - Async Result : %s",
        param->iServerIndex,
            SUCCEEDED(hRet)?"SUCCEEDED":"FAILED");
}

/*
// This just drives the LCT Client to execute GetTransaction from
// an external web service pooling up
// several clients in the process.  The number of clients is
// configurable.
*/
int _tmain(int argc, _TCHAR* argv[])

    LCTClientThreadPoolthreadPool;
    tCallbackParam
  paramsExternalService[CLIENTS_COUNT];
    BSTR    bstrRet;
    int        iIndex = 0;
    int        iPoolSize = CLIENTS_COUNT;
    HRESULT  hRet;
    LONG    lCompletionCounter = 0;
    int nCallCounter = 0;

    CoInitialize(NULL);

    // Initialize the tread pool to 4 threads per CPU
    threadPool.Initialize(0, -4);

  {
    // allocate an array of the number of pooled
  // clients you want
    CExternalServiceT<CLCTClientSoapSocket> <- no line break
  proxiesExternalService[CLIENTS_COUNT];

    // loop through each imaginary client, prepare request, and
    // call asynchronously using LCT client for heavy lifting
    for(iIndex = 0; iIndex < iPoolSize; iIndex++)
    {
        // server index can be replaced by some unique
  // cookie/handle for async ops
        paramsExternalService[iIndex].iServerIndex =
  iIndex + 1;
paramsExternalService[iIndex].lpCompletionCounter =
&lCompletionCounter;
```

```
    // pass in an initialized threadpool (the number is
// up to you), the callback and the parameters
    hRet = proxiesExternalService[iIndex].
PrepareRequest(&threadPool,
        LCTCallback,
    (LPARAM)&paramsExternalService[iIndex]);
    ATLASSERT(SUCCEEDED(hRet));

    // just call the sample GetTransaction Web service
    // method, the param will be the return
    // value OUT of that call
    hRet =
proxiesExternalService[iIndex].
GetTransaction(&bstrRet);

    // if E_PENDING things are working..
    ATLASSERT(E_PENDING == hRet);
}

// Request in work, yet
do
{
    Sleep(50);
    printf(".");
}
while(lCompletionCounter < CLIENTS_COUNT);

// call callbacks have been called we can continue and
// receive the operation return values
for(iIndex=0; iIndex<CLIENTS_COUNT; iIndex++)
{
    printf("\nClient %d : ", iIndex + 1);

    // Back from the request
    // Collect the results now
    // Pass only the OUT and IN/OUT params
    // The rest will be ignored
    hRet =
proxiesExternalService[iIndex].
GetTransaction(&bstrRet);

    // now really analyze the results
    if(SUCCEEDED(hRet))
    {
        nCallCounter++;
        printf("Requests Succeeded. Result :\n %ls",
    bstrRet);
        ::SysFreeString(bstrRet);
```

```
        }
        else
            printf("Request Failed");

    }
    if(nCallCounter == CLIENTS_COUNT)
    {
        ::MessageBox(NULL, _T(
    "All async call s completed."),
    _T("Status"),MB_OK);
    }


}

// make sure and clean up the threadpool
printf("\n");
threadPool.Shutdown();
CoUninitialize();

return 0;
}
```

As discussed in the Participants section, any working client can replace this entity. This is only a sample driver of the pattern. Its primary duties are to declare the ExternalServiceT template by passing in the LCTClientSoapSocket class, intializing the thread pool, calling PrepareRequest, executing the Web service iteratively, and implementing a callback to be called upon completion of the original transaction. How this is implemented exactly is up to the developer. The real work happens in the CLCTClientSoapSocket class in Listing 7.18.

LISTING 7.18: LCT Client "plumbing" implementation.

```
#include <atlsoap.h>


#define   LCTCLIENT_EXECUTION   101

class CLCTClientSoapSocket;

typedef void (*SOAP_ASYNC_CALLBACK)(LPARAM lParam, HRESULT hRet);

structstLCTClientRequest
{
   CLCTClientSoapSocket    *pClient;
   SOAP_ASYNC_CALLBACK        pfnCallback;
```

```
   LPARAM                        lpRequestParam;
};

class CLCTClientWorker
{
public:

typedef stLCTClientRequest* RequestType;

   CLCTClientWorker() throw()
   {
   }

   ~CLCTClientWorker() throw()
   {
   }

   virtual BOOL Initialize(void *pvParam) throw()
   {
      // Do any initialization here
      return TRUE;
   }

   virtual void Terminate(void* pvParam) throw()
   {
      // Do any cleanup here
   }

   void Execute(stLCTClientRequest *pRequestInfo,
   void *pvParam, OVERLAPPED *pOverlapped) throw();

};

typedef CThreadPool<CLCTClientWorker>CLCTClientThreadPool;


class CLCTClientSoapSocket : public CSoapSocketClientT<>
{
   protected:

   stLCTClientRequest    m_stRequestInfo;
   bool                  m_bInRequest;

   HRESULT               m_hRealRet;

   CLCTClientThreadPool*m_pThreadPool;
      CStringm_strSOAPAction;
```

```
public:
    CLCTClientSoapSocket(LPCTSTR szUrl) :
    CSoapSocketClientT<>(szUrl)
    {
        m_bInRequest = false;
        m_pThreadPool = NULL;
    }

    // Note : this is not thread safe, the caller should take
// care
    HRESULT PrepareRequest(
    CLCTClientThreadPool *pThreadPool,
    SOAP_ASYNC_CALLBACK pfnCallback, LPARAM lParam)
    {
        // return false, if already in request
        if( m_bInRequest )
            return E_PENDING;

    if( !pThreadPool )
            return E_POINTER;

        m_pThreadPool = pThreadPool;

        m_stRequestInfo.pClient = this;
        m_stRequestInfo.lpRequestParam= lParam;
        m_stRequestInfo.pfnCallback=pfnCallback;

        m_bInRequest = true;

        return S_OK;
    }

    HRESULT SendRequest(LPCTSTR szAction)
{
        HRESULT    hRet;

        if( m_bInRequest )
        {
            // launch the async request
            m_strSOAPAction = szAction;
            ATLASSERT(m_pThreadPool);
            if(m_pThreadPool->QueueRequest(
        &m_stRequestInfo) )
                hRet = E_PENDING;
            else
                hRet = E_FAIL;
    }
    else
    {
```

```
        // post-async request, reading the response.
        // Nothing to do, just return hRet from the
    // real operation
        hRet = m_hRealRet;
    }

    return hRet;
}

HRESULT InternalSendRequest()
{
    m_hRealRet = CSoapSocketClientT<>::SendRequest(
    m_strSOAPAction );

        m_bInRequest = false;
        return m_hRealRet;
    }
};

inline void CLCTClientWorker::Execute(
stLCTClientRequest *pRequestInfo,
void *pvParam, OVERLAPPED *pOverlapped) throw()
{
    ATLASSERT(pRequestInfo != NULL);
    pvParam;    // unused
    pOverlapped;    // unused

    CLCTClientSoapSocket *pClient = pRequestInfo->pClient;
        SOAP_ASYNC_CALLBACK pfnCallBack =
    pRequestInfo->pfnCallback;
    LPARAM lParam = pRequestInfo->lpRequestParam;

    ATLASSERT( pClient );
    HRESULT hRet = pClient->InternalSendRequest();

    if( pfnCallBack )
    {
        pfnCallBack( lParam, hRet);
    }
}
```

This piece of code is rather simple and mainly leverages the use of "thread pools" (see Visual Studio .NET documentation for details on thread pooling) for delegating each synchronous call from the pool onward to the Web service. When a send request is called, what would normally be a synchronous call, instead of immediately calling GetTransaction(), the call is queued using the Thread Pool object. Once on the queue, it will be later called by the Thread worker, using

CLCTClientWork::Execute() (Listing 7.18). From here, all the work has already been performed in relation to this pattern, and it is simply delegated to SoapSocketClient::SendRequest() that sends the transaction as it would during a normal synchronous execution. To see how the LCTClient class is passed into the generated ExternalServiceT proxy, you have to look at the generated code to appreciate what is going on. In Listing 7.19, you'll find the generated ATL template for the ExternalService Web service that contains GetTransaction() and any other method exposed publicly from the Web service.

LISTING 7.19: LCT Client "Plumbing" Implementation – Template Code.

```
#include <atlsoap.h>

struct TransactorHeader
{
   __int64 lTransactorId;
};

template <typename TClient = CSoapSocketClientT<> >
class CExternalServiceT :
   public TClient,
   public CSoapRootHandler
{
public:

       //
       // SOAP headers - used for passed transaction id for ease
       //

       TransactorHeader TransactorHeader0;

protected:

   const _soapmap ** GetFunctionMap();
   const _soapmap ** GetHeaderMap();
   void * GetHeaderValue();
   const wchar_t * GetNamespaceUri();
   const char * GetServiceName();
   const char * GetNamespaceUriA();

   HRESULT CallFunction(
      void *pvParam,
      const wchar_t *wszLocalName, int cchLocalName,
      size_t nItem);
   HRESULT GetClientReader(ISAXXMLReader **ppReader);
```

```
public:

   . . .

   CExternalServiceT(ISAXXMLReader *pReader = NULL)
      :TClient(_T(
"http://localhost/. . ./ExternalService/ExternalService.asmx"))
   {
      SetClient(true);
      SetReader(pReader);

      //
      // initialize headers
      //
      memset(&TransactorHeader0, 0x00, sizeof(TransactorHeader));
   }

   ~CExternalServiceT()
   {
      Uninitialize();
   }

   void Uninitialize()
   {
      UninitializeSOAP();

      //
      // uninitialize headers
      //
      AtlCleanupValueEx(&TransactorHeader0, GetMemMgr());
   }

   HRESULT InvokeTimeConsumingMethod(
      BSTR* InvokeTimeConsumingMethodResult
   );

   HRESULT GetTransaction(
      BSTR* GetTransactionResult
   );
};

typedef CExternalServiceT<> CExternalService;

__if_not_exists(__TransactorHeader_entries)
{
extern __declspec(selectany) const _soapmapentry
__TransactorHeader_entries[] =
```

```
{
     {
         0xC0792CDA,
         "lTransactorId",
         L"lTransactorId",
         sizeof("lTransactorId")-1,
         SOAPTYPE_LONG,
         SOAPFLAG_FIELD,
         offsetof(TransactorHeader, lTransactorId),
         NULL,
         NULL,
         -1
     },
     { 0x00000000 }
};

extern __declspec(selectany) const
_soapmap __TransactorHeader_map =
{
         0x8AA088EA,
         "TransactorHeader",
         L"TransactorHeader",
         sizeof("TransactorHeader")-1,
         sizeof("TransactorHeader")-1,
         SOAPMAP_STRUCT,
         __TransactorHeader_entries,
         sizeof(TransactorHeader),
         1,
         -1,
         SOAPFLAG_NONE,
         0xC2E575C3,
         "http://tempuri.org/",
         L"http://tempuri.org/",
         sizeof("http://tempuri.org/")-1
};
}

struct __CExternalService_InvokeTimeConsumingMethod_struct
{
     BSTR InvokeTimeConsumingMethodResult;
};

. . .

struct __CExternalService_GetTransaction_struct
{
     BSTR GetTransactionResult;
};
```

```
extern __declspec(selectany) const
_soapmapentry __CExternalService_GetTransaction_entries[] =
{

     {
         0xE7350D25,
         "GetTransactionResult",
         L"GetTransactionResult",
         sizeof("GetTransactionResult")-1,
         SOAPTYPE_STRING,
         SOAPFLAG_NONE | SOAPFLAG_OUT | SOAPFLAG_PID
| SOAPFLAG_DOCUMENT | SOAPFLAG_LITERAL | SOAPFLAG_NULLABLE,
offsetof(__CExternalService_GetTransaction_struct,
GetTransactionResult),
         NULL,
         NULL,
         -1,
     },
     { 0x00000000 }
};

extern __declspec(selectany) const _soapmap
__CExternalService_GetTransaction_map =
{
     0x88540AB5,
     "GetTransaction",
     L"GetTransactionResponse",
     sizeof("GetTransaction")-1,
     sizeof("GetTransactionResponse")-1,
     SOAPMAP_FUNC,
     __CExternalService_GetTransaction_entries,
     sizeof(__CExternalService_GetTransaction_struct),
     1,
     -1,
SOAPFLAG_NONE | SOAPFLAG_PID | SOAPFLAG_DOCUMENT |
SOAPFLAG_LITERAL,
     0xC2E575C3,
     "http://tempuri.org/",
     L"http://tempuri.org/",
     sizeof("http://tempuri.org/")-1
};

extern __declspec(selectany) const _soapmap *
__CExternalService_funcs[] =
{
     &__CExternalService_InvokeTimeConsumingMethod_map,
     &__CExternalService_GetTransaction_map,
```

```
      NULL
};

   // cleanup any in/out-params and out-headers from previous calls
   Cleanup();
   __atlsoap_hr = BeginParse(__atlsoap_spReadStream);
   if (FAILED(__atlsoap_hr))
   {
      SetClientError(SOAPCLIENT_PARSE_ERROR);
      goto __cleanup;
   }

. . .

template <typename TClient>

inline HRESULT CExternalServiceT<TClient>::GetTransaction(
      BSTR* GetTransactionResult
   )
{

HRESULT __atlsoap_hr = InitializeSOAP(NULL);
   if (FAILED(__atlsoap_hr))
   {
      SetClientError(SOAPCLIENT_INITIALIZE_ERROR);
      return __atlsoap_hr;
   }

   CleanupClient();

CComPtr<IStream> __atlsoap_spReadStream;
   __CExternalService_GetTransaction_struct __params;
   memset(&__params, 0x00, sizeof(__params));

   __atlsoap_hr = SetClientStruct(&__params, 1);
   if (FAILED(__atlsoap_hr))
   {
      SetClientError(SOAPCLIENT_OUTOFMEMORY);
      goto __skip_cleanup;
   }

   __atlsoap_hr = GenerateResponse(GetWriteStream());
   if (FAILED(__atlsoap_hr))
   {
      SetClientError(SOAPCLIENT_GENERATE_ERROR);
      goto __skip_cleanup;
   }
```

```
   __atlsoap_hr = SendRequest(_T(
"SOAPAction: \"http:// . . ./GetTransaction\"\r\n"));
   if (FAILED(__atlsoap_hr))
   {
      goto __skip_cleanup;
   }
   __atlsoap_hr = GetReadStream(&__atlsoap_spReadStream);
   if (FAILED(__atlsoap_hr))
   {
      SetClientError(SOAPCLIENT_READ_ERROR);
      goto __skip_cleanup;
   }

   // cleanup any in/out-params and out-headers from previousCleanup();
   __atlsoap_hr = BeginParse(__atlsoap_spReadStream);
   if (FAILED(__atlsoap_hr))
   {
      SetClientError(SOAPCLIENT_PARSE_ERROR);
      goto __cleanup;
   }

   *GetTransactionResult = __params.GetTransactionResult;
   goto __skip_cleanup;

__cleanup:
   Cleanup();
__skip_cleanup:
      ResetClientState(true);
      memset(&__params, 0x00, sizeof(__params));
      return __atlsoap_hr;
}

template <typename TClient>
ATL_NOINLINE inline const _soapmap **
CExternalServiceT<TClient>::GetFunctionMap()
{
      return __CExternalService_funcs;
}

. . .

   static const _soapmapentry
__CExternalService_GetTransaction_atlsoapheader_entries[] =
   {
      { 0x00000000 }
   };
```

```
    static const _soapmap
__CExternalService_GetTransaction_atlsoapheader_map =
    {
        0x88540AB5,
        "GetTransaction",
        L"GetTransactionResponse",
        sizeof("GetTransaction")-1,
        sizeof("GetTransactionResponse")-1,
        SOAPMAP_HEADER,
    __CExternalService_GetTransaction_atlsoapheader_entries,
        0,
        0,
        -1,
        SOAPFLAG_NONE | SOAPFLAG_PID | SOAPFLAG_DOCUMENT |
SOAPFLAG_LITERAL,
        0xC2E575C3,
        "http://tempuri.org/",
        L"http://tempuri.org/",
        sizeof("http://tempuri.org/")-1
    };


    static const _soapmap * __CExternalService_headers[] =
    {
        . . .
&__CExternalService_GetTransaction_atlsoapheader_map,
        NULL
    };

    return __CExternalService_headers;
}

template <typename TClient>
ATL_NOINLINE inline void * CExternalServiceT<TClient>::GetHeaderValue()
{
    return this;
}

template <typename TClient>
ATL_NOINLINE inline const wchar_t *
CExternalServiceT<TClient>::GetNamespaceUri()
{
    return L"http://tempuri.org/";
}

template <typename TClient>
ATL_NOINLINE inline const char *
CExternalServiceT<TClient>::GetServiceName()
```

```
{
   return NULL;
}

template <typename TClient>
ATL_NOINLINE inline const char *
CExternalServiceT<TClient>::GetNamespaceUriA()
{
return "http://tempuri.org/";
}

template <typename TClient>
ATL_NOINLINE inline HRESULT CExternalServiceT<TClient>::CallFunction(
   void *,
   const wchar_t *, int,
   size_t)
{
   return E_NOTIMPL;
}

template <typename TClient>
ATL_NOINLINE inline HRESULT
CExternalServiceT<TClient>::GetClientReader(
ISAXXMLReader **ppReader)
{
   if (ppReader == NULL)
   {
      return E_INVALIDARG;
   }

   CComPtr<ISAXXMLReader> spReader = GetReader();
   if (spReader.p != NULL)
   {
      *ppReader = spReader.Detach();
      return S_OK;
   }
   return TClient::GetClientReader(ppReader);
}
```

Although this pattern utilizes ATL and C++ and can be considered advanced for those with primarily C# or VB.NET skills, the generic applicability of this implementation allows any Web service to be represented, threaded, and executed. With the new ATL features, threading and thread pooling have never been easier. This provides the conduit within which to build any asynchronous model using client code. As long as the clients are relatively low in number and simple in complexity, this pattern can be applied to many areas. For those who do not yet have .NET installed, it can provide a tremendous bridge from the "old unmanaged world" to the "new world" of .NET.

PASSWORD STORAGE

Intent

This pattern (actually more of a best practice) provides an easy method of adding some level of encryption for password storage.

Problem

Many applications still store passwords in clear text. Because most of the code is already written to provide at least some level of encryption, there is little excuse for not providing it.

To understand this pattern, you must first understand the concept of a one-way hash. A simple definition of a one-way hash is a scrambled version of a string that cannot be *easily* unscrambled to get the original string back. To store the password, the hash is generated for the password to be stored. We'll call the stored hash value $hash^1$. When the user comes to the site and enters his or her password, the second hash is generated, which we will call $hash^2$. At this point, we don't care what actual passwords are entered, just that $hash^1$ and $hash^2$ match.

I stress that a one-way hash just makes it more difficult to determine the original string because a brute-force method of generating a dictionary of all possible password combinations could be generated for any known hash algorithm. Then, taking the hash and going backward, the original value would be accessible. The obvious ways of making this more difficult would be to expand the number of possible combinations by including numbers and mixed case in the passwords or to keep the one-way hash algorithm (or any keys used) secret. This single table structure can be seen in Figure 7.8.

Forces

Use the Password Storage pattern when:

- Storing passwords. Unless a better method of encryption is used or you have to get access to the original password value.

Structure

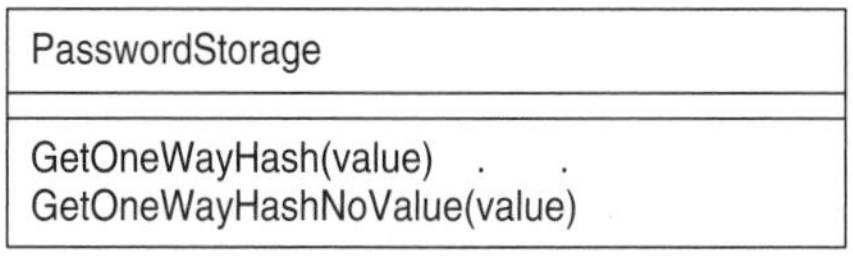

PasswordStorage
GetOneWayHash(value)   .   . GetOneWayHashNoValue(value)

FIGURE 7.8: Password Storage class diagram.

Consequences

The Password Storage pattern has the following benefits and liabilities:

It provides an easy way to add simple encryption to passwords.

Participants

None

Implementation

The Password Storage pattern exposes one main function that, in this example, wraps the MD5 compute hash function to generate the hashes. The only technical details to remember are to convert the string to an array of bytes prior to encryption and to convert the encrypted bytes back to a base-64 string because the string may have embedded nulls or other ugly items that make string handling (and storing them in databases) difficult.

LISTING 7.20: Hashing helper method implementation.

```
public static string GetOneWayHash(string Value)
{
   byte[] data = System.Text.ASCIIEncoding.ASCII.GetBytes(Value);

   // This is one implementation of the abstract class MD5.
   MD5 md5 = new MD5CryptoServiceProvider();

   byte[] result = md5.ComputeHash(data);

   return System.Convert.ToBase64String(result, 0, result.Length);
}
```

It is strongly encouraged that the readers investigate alternate implementations of this method.

Index

A

Abstract Cache pattern, 43, 320–342
    ASP.NET caching, 338–342
    Cache, 325
    cache container:
        adding items to, 339–341
        retrieving cached items from, 341
    CacheAdapter, 325
    class diagram, 327
    Client, 325
    ConcreteCacheable, 322, 325
    consequences, 322–324
    forces, 322
    ICache, 326
    ICacheable, 326
    IEnumerable, 326
    implementation, 326–342
    implementation sample of preparing a cache
        using, 333–335
    intent, 320
    lazy cache service implementation, 332–333
    participants, 325–326
    problem, 320–322
    related patterns, 342
    setting SOAP headers using .NET, 331
    SOAP headers, 327–342
    SOAP message header example, 330
    SOAP Toolkit Visual Basic header serialization
        example, 328–329
    structure, 322
    wrapping a cache container (implementation
        sample), 336–338
Abstract Packet pattern, 42, 142, 178–192, 214,
    257, 260
    benefits/liabilities, 181–183
    boxing/unboxing, 185–184
    consequences, 181–183
    DataSet, 183
    forces, 180
    generic class diagram, 181
    implementation, 183–192
    implementation class diagram, 180
    intent, 178
    Packet, 183
    Packet Translator, 183
    participants, 183
    problem, 179–180
    ProductDataSet, 183
    related patterns, 192
    structure, 181
Abstract Schema, 42, 203
ADO DataSets, 24
ADO.NET, 202–204, 209, 220, 232, 236, 363

Advanced design patterns, 43, 319–401
  Abstract Cache pattern, 320–342
    ASP.NET caching, 338–342
    Cache, 325
    cache container:
      adding items to, 339–341
      retrieving cached items from, 341
    CacheAdapter, 325
    class diagram, 327
    Client, 325
    ConcreteCacheable, 325
    consequences, 322–324
    forces, 322
    ICache, 326
    ICacheable, 326
    IEnumerable, 326
    implementation, 326–342
    implementation sample of preparing a cache
      using, 333–335
    intent, 320
    lazy cache service implementation, 332–333
    participants, 325–326
    problem, 320–322
    related patterns, 342
    setting SOAP headers using .NET, 331
    SOAP headers, 327–342
    SOAP message header example, 330
    SOAP Toolkit Visual Basic header
      serialization example, 328–329
    structure, 322
    wrapping a cache container
      (implementation sample), 336–338
  Loosely Coupled Transactor Client (LCT
     Client), 380–400
    benefits/liabilities, 383–384
    CLCTClientSoapSocket, 385
    CLCTClientThreadPool, 384
    consequences, 383–384
    CSoapSocketClientT, 385
    forces, 380–381
    implementation, 385–400
    intent, 380
    LCT Client C++ console implementation,
      385–388
    LCT Client "plumbing" implementation,
      388–391
    LCT Client "plumbing" implementation
      (template code), 392–399
    participants, 384–385
    problem, 380
    structure, 381
  Loosely Coupled Transactor Server (LCT
     Server), 350–379

    asynchronous system design challenges,
      350–354
    benefits/liabilities, 359–362
    class diagram, 364
    Client, 362
    consequences, 359–362
    ExternalService, 363
    ExternalServiceProxy, 363
    forces, 357
    generic class diagram, 358
    implementation, 364–379
    intent, 350
    ITransactor, 363
    LCT Server "plumbing" implementation,
      366–369
    participants, 362–363
    problem, 354–357
    related patterns, 379
    sample functional implementation drive by,
      370–379
    structure, 358–359
    TransactorFacade, 363
    TransactorService, 362–363
    Visual Basic SOAP Toolkit client used for
      calling, 363
  Password Storage pattern, 400–401
    benefits/liabilities, 401
    consequences, 401
    forces, 400
    hashing helper method implementation,
      341
    intent, 400
    participants, 401
    problem, 400
    structure, 401
  Web Service Interface pattern, 342–350
    benefits/liabilities, 344–346
    client-side WSI implementation example,
      350
    concrete WSI implementation example,
      347–348
    consequences, 344–346
    forces, 343
    implementation, 347–350
    intent, 342
    IWebServiceInterface, 346
    participants, 346–347
    problem, 342–343
    sample interface, 347
    ServiceClient, 346
    ServiceProxy, 346
    structure, 344
    Web service piece of WSI implementation,
      349

WebServiceConcrete, 346
WebServiceInterface, 346
WSDL-generated proxy code, 349–350
Alexander, Christopher, 38–39
American Clearing House Association, 274
Application level, 76
Applying UML and Patterns: An Introduction to Object-Oriented Analysis and Design, 39
.asmx, 20–21
ASP.NET, 63, 278, 338–339
Assembly, System.Reflection namespace, 160
Asynchronous Web services, 286
Authorize method, 170

B
Base Class Library (BCL), 9, 35
Base exception class, 47
BaseException base class, 49, 51
    adding SOAP exception support to, 71–77
        COM exception handling, 75–76
        determining when to log, 76–77
        sample BaseException actor for allowing SOAP Faults, 72–73
        sample SOAP Fault builder for, 71–72
        sample SOAP Fault detail node builder, 74–75
        using XML, 76
    applying the child class, 57
    beginning of, 54–57
    building, 53–63
    features handled by, 51–52
        automated call stack formatting and display, 51
        automated error stack formatting and display, 51
        automated exception chaining, 51
        custom remote exception handling using SOAP, 52
        error logging and message tracing, 52
    logging, 52–53
        environmental information, 60–61
        error stack, building, 61–62
        sample logging routine, 58–59
        what to log, determining, 59–62
        where to log, determining, 58–59
    sample child class, 50
    sample stack builder, 62
    system exceptions, throwing, 62–63
BaseException class, 71, 288
BooleanSwitch, 80–82
Boundaries, 179
Box, Don, 38

Boxing/unboxing, 185–187
BuildDetailNode method, 74–75
BuildErrorStack method, 61
Burgett, David, 298

C
C#, 3, 8, 35, 385
    delegate keyword in, 111
CacheAdapter, 325–326, 331, 335–336
Call stack, 61
Caller communication, 352–353
Categorizing patterns, 39–41
CExternalServiceT, 384
Chained Service Factory pattern, 42, 142, 143–152, 284
    benefits/liabilities, 146–148
    ConcreteFacade, 148
    consequences, 146–148
    Execute method, 144
    Facade, 148
    forces, 145–146
    generic class diagram, 146
    implementation, 149–152
    intent, 143
    participants, 148
    problem, 143–145
    related patterns, 152
    Service, 148
    Service Factory metadata helper method, 150–151
    Service Factory method sample implementation, 149–150
    ServiceClient, 148
    structure, 146
CLCTClientSoapSocket, 384, 385
CLCTClientThreadPool, 384
Client faultcode, 66
COM, 12, 35
COM+, 29, 163, 166
Commercial Framework, 267–270, 278, 304–306
    architectural features, 284–289
        Abstract Data packet, 288
        exception handling and tracing framework, 288
        FTP client/FTP Web services, 286
        instrumentation, 288
        loosely coupled Web services, 284
        managed client framework, 284
        messaging and Message Listening Windows 2000 Service, 286
        network services, 286
        Poly model, 285
        Product Manager, 288

Commercial Framework (cont.)
  remote tracing, 287
  scheduling service, 287
  service facades, 284
  unmanaged client framework, 285
 roles in, 291
 vision statement, 282
Common language infrastructure (CLI), 5
Common language runtime (CLR), 5, 9, 29–31, 35, 75
Common language specification (CLS), 5
Common type system (CTS), 5, 36
ComplexReport object, 331–332
ComplexType element tag, 205
Contract interface, 144
CORBA, 12–13, 24
CreateInstance method, 161
CreditCardDS child class, DataSet, 196
Crivat, Bogdan, 380
CSoapSocketClientT template, 381
Custom SOAP Exception Handler, 41
Custom SOAP trace extension, 288
Custom trace listener, 80, 287

D

Data Access Interface, 285
DataSet, 65, 94, 182–186, 222, 230, 313, 379
DataSet Visual Studio, 207–208
DBGetTransactionBySQL method, 259
DCOM, 12–13, 24
Decision schema, 290
DefaultTraceListener, 78
#define TRACE, 77
DeleteKeys method, 247
Design Patterns: Elements of Reusable Object-Oriented Software, 39
DIME protocol (Microsoft), 24
Disconnected coordination/administration, 352–354
Distributed applications, 6
Distributed garbage collection, 24
Distributed technologies, 11–13
DLL-hell, 7
Document type definition (DTD), 26
DOM, 23
Dump method, 58–59
Dynamic Assembly Loader pattern, 42, 132–134
  benefits/liabilities, 133
  consequences, 133
  constructing an object using Reflection, 134
  forces, 133
  implementation, 134
  intent, 132
  participants, 134

  problem, 132–133
  structure, 133

E

EBInvoke method, 306–308
eBusiness software, and communications management, 7
Edit Relation Dialog Box, constraints available in, 216
Eiffel, 8
Electronic Payments Network, 274
Enterprise Java Beans, 12
Error Cross-Reference Generator pattern, 42, 125–128
  benefits/liabilities, 127
  calling, 128
  consequences, 127
  forces, 126
  implementation, 127–128
  intent, 125
  participants, 127
  problem, 125–126
  related patterns, 128
  structure, 126
ErrorCode set, 75
Essential COM (Box), 38
Etier3.LazyCacheService class, 330
Event log listener, sample for adding to a global collection, 79–80
EventInfo, System.Reflection namespace, 160
EventLogTraceListener, 78
Exception boundaries, 60, 76
  managing, 63–65
Exception chaining, 61
Exception wrapping, 63
Exceptions, throwing from Web services, 63–65
ExceptionThrower.asmx, 68–71
Extensible Markup Language (XML) web services, 5–6
ExternalCallback method, 359
ExtractOriginalData method, 379

F

Faultcode, 70
Faultfactory property, 70
Federal Reserve, 274
  automated check mechanism, 272
FieldInfo, System.Reflection namespace, 160
Filter Builder, 285
FinancialServiceFactory.Execute, 144
Framework patterns, 41, 45–105
  application-specific exceptions, 47–53
  BaseException base class, building, 53–63
  custom trace listener, building, 82–104

exception boundaries, managing, 63–65
exception handling, 47–53
  overview, 45–47
  remote tracing, 82–104
    remote trace receiver, building, 86–87
    remote trace viewer, building, 94–104
    sample business object to be placed on queue, 88–92
    sample Remote Trace Listener viewer (GUI), 94–103
    sample RemoteTraceListener Web service, 86–87
    sample routine for constructing/adding custom listener, 86
    sample socket routine for sending a message, 92–94
    sending races to message queue, 87–92
    sending traces via sockets, 92–94
    Trace Listener template, 84–85
  SOAP Faults, 65–77
    adding SOAP exception support to BaseException class, 71–77
    detail element, 67, 71
    faultactor, 66
    faultcode, 66
    faultstring, 66
    sample SOAP Fault detail block, 67–68
    throwing custom SOAP exceptions, 68–71
  trace listeners, 77–80
FTP, 25, 316
FtpException class, 49–51, 54, 57, 61
FTPMessages string table, 50
FTPWebRequest, 286
FTPWebResponse, 286
Function-specific exception classes, 49

G
Gang of four (GoF), 8, 38
General network libraries, 286
General Responsibility Assignment Software Patterns (GRASP), 39
GetDBType method, 310
GetPlaceList, 16–17
GetSchemaTemplate method, 26–27, 306, 313
GetTransaction method, 262, 362–363, 379, 384, 391

H
Headers, SOAP, 28
HTTP, 25
HTTP GET request, 24
HydrateDataObject method, 194, 195, 198

I
ICacheable interface, 335–336
ICached interface, 332
IErrorInfo interface, 75
  COM, 75
IHeaderHandler interface, 328, 330
Information, and problem solving, 46
InitTraceListeners method, 79–80
Inner exception, 61
Intellisense, 208, 357
Internet protocols, 12
InvokeTimeConsumingMethod method, 369–370
IOException, 63
IService interface, 347
IWebServiceInterface, 346

J
J#, 8, 35
JBuilder, 13

K
Kumar, Pranish, 380

L
Larman, Craig, 39
LBInvoke method, 306–308
LCT Client, 43
LCT Client C++ console implementation, 385–388
LCT Client "plumbing" implementation, 388–391
LCT Client "plumbing" implementation (template code), 392–399
LCT Server, 43
Logging, 76
Loosely Coupled Transactor Client (LCT Client), 380–400
  benefits/liabilities, 383–384
  CLCTClientSoapSocket, 385
  CLCTClientThreadPool, 384
  consequences, 383–384
  CSoapSocketClientT, 385
  forces, 380–381
  implementation, 385–400
  intent, 380
  LCT Client C++ console implementation, 385–388
  LCT Client "plumbing" implementation, 388–391
  LCT Client "plumbing" implementation (template code), 392–399
  participants, 384–385
  problem, 380
  structure, 381
Loosely Coupled Transactor (LTCT), 43

Loosely Coupled Transactor Server (LCT Server)
    pattern, 350–379
  asynchronous system design challenges, 350–
    354
  benefits/liabilities, 359–362
  class diagram, 364
  Client, 362
  consequences, 359–362
  ExternalService, 363
  ExternalServiceProxy, 363
  forces, 357
  generic class diagram, 358
  implementation, 364–379
  intent, 350
  ITransactor, 363
  LCT Server "plumbing" implementation, 366–
    369
  participants, 362–363
  problem, 354–357
  related patterns, 379
  sample functional implementation drive by,
    370–379
  structure, 358–359
  TransactorFacade, 363
  TransactorService, 362–363
  Visual Basic SOAP Toolkit client used for
    calling, 363

M

Macropattern, 202
Managed C++, 8, 35
Message batching, and SOAP, 24
Message routing service, 286
MessageInfo property, 92
Messaging Manager, 286
MethodInfo, System.Reflection namespace, 160
Microsoft Bizatalk, 300
Microsoft CRM, 276–277
Microsoft Message Queue Server, 350–351, 359,
    361
Microsoft Message Queuing, 88
Middle-tier patterns, 42, 142–200
  Abstract Packet pattern, 42, 142, 178–192
    benefits/liabilities, 181–183
    boxing/unboxing, 185–184
    consequences, 181–183
    DataSet, 183
    forces, 180
    generic class diagram, 181
    implementation, 183–192
    implementation class diagram, 180
    intent, 178
    Packet, 183

  Packet Translator, 183
  participants, 183
  problem, 179–180
  ProductDataSet, 183
  related patterns, 192
  structure, 181
Chained Service Factory pattern, 42, 142, 143–
    152
  benefits/liabilities, 146–148
  ConcreteFacade, 148
  consequences, 146–148
  Execute method, 144
  Facade, 148
  forces, 145–146
  generic class diagram, 146
  implementation, 149–152
  intent, 143
  participants, 148
  problem, 143–145
  related patterns, 152
  Service, 148
  Service Factory metadata helper method,
    150–151
  Service Factory method sample
    implementation, 149–150
  ServiceClient, 148
  structure, 146
overview, 141–142
Packet Translator pattern, 42, 142, 192–200
  benefits/liabilities, 194
  ConcreteFacade, 194
  consequences, 194
  DataSet, 196
  forces, 193
  generic class diagram, 193
  implementation, 196–200
  implementation class diagram, 197
  intent, 192
  packet, 196
  PacketTranslator (participant), 195
  participants, 194–196
  problem, 192–193
  ProductDataSet, 196
  related patterns, 200
  sample implementation preparing packets,
    197–198
  sample implementation translating packets,
    199–200
  structure, 193
Product Manager pattern, 42, 142, 163–171
  benefits/liabilities, 166–167
  ConcreteDelegate, 168
  ConcreteProduct, 168
  consequences, 166–167

delegation implementation, 169–170
Facade, 167
forces, 165
generic class diagram, 166
implementation, 168–171
intent, 163
ManagedProduct, 168
method implementation, 169
participants, 167–168
problem, 163–165
ProductManager, 167–168
related patterns, 171
structure, 166
UnmanagedProduct, 168
worker implementation, 170
Service Facade pattern, 42, 142, 171–178
benefits/liabilities, 174
ConcreteFacade, 175
consequences, 174
Facade, 175
forces, 173
generic class diagram, 173
implementation, 175–178
intent, 171
participants, 174–175
problem, 171–173
related patterns, 178
sample implementation, 176–177
Service, 174–175
structure, 173
Unchained Service Factory pattern, 42, 142, 152–162
Activator, 157
Assembly, 157
benefits/liabilities, 146–148
ConcreteFacade, 157
consequences, 155–156
Facade, 157
forces, 154–155
generic class diagram, 155
implementation, 157–162
implementation using Reflection, 158–158
intent, 152
MethodInfo, 157
.NET Reflection services, 159–162
participants, 157
problem, 152–154
related patterns, 162
Service, 157
ServiceClient, 157
structure, 155
Type, 157
Module, System.Reflection namespace, 160
Multisync Thread Manager pattern, 42, 122–125

benefits/liabilities, 124
consequences, 124
DoExecution method, 125–126
forces, 123
implementation, 124–125
intent, 122
participants, 124
problem, 122–123
related patterns, 125
structure, 123

N
NACHA (National Automated Clearing House Association), 270–272, 277, 280
Nested relationships, 212–213
.NET:
components of, 34–37
controllable areas in, 30–31
highlights of, 33–34
interoperability support, 35
base class library (BCL), 35
common language runtime (CLR), 9, 29–31, 35, 75
common type system (CTS), 36
full Web service and SOAP support, 36
object-oriented ASP.NET, 36
simplified deployment, 36
XML at core, 36
libraries, 4
and Microsoft, 43
overview of, 34–36
securing Web services in, 29–30
and XML Web services, 13–18
.NET CLR, 9, 29–31, 343
.NET framework, 268, 281
and a distributed new world, 5–13
major components of, 33–34
and object-oriented languages, 6, 8–11
and objects, 18
and OO, 8–11
and Web services, 18
.NET Framework Configuration snap-in, 30
.NET Reflection services, 61, 159–162
.NET System.Messaging library, 88
Notifying Thread Manager pattern, 42, 108–116
benefits/liabilities, 110
calling Notifying Thread Manager, 113
Client, 109–110
consequences, 110
delegate definitions, 111
DoExecution method notification, 114–115
ExecuteAsync method, 112
forces, 109

Notifying Thread Manager pattern (cont.)
   implementation, 111–115
   intent, 108
   Notifying Thread Manager, 109–111
   participants, 110–111
   problem, 108–109
   related patterns, 116
   structure, 109–110

O

Object references, 24
Object-oriented ASP.NET, 36
Object-oriented languages, 33
   learning, 10
   and .NET framework, 8–11
Originating Depository Financial Institution
      (ODFI), 275
Originator, automated check transaction, 275
OutputDebugString API, 78

P

Packet Translator pattern, 42, 142, 192–200
   benefits/liabilities, 194
   ConcreteFacade, 194
   consequences, 194
   DataSet, 196
   forces, 193
   generic class diagram, 193
   implementation, 196–200
   implementation class diagram, 197
   intent, 192
   packet, 196
   PacketTranslator (participant), 195
   participants, 194–196
   problem, 192–193
   ProductDataSet, 196
   related patterns, 200
   sample implementation preparing packets,
      197–198
   sample implementation translating packets,
      199–200
   structure, 193
Packet.Action property 298:
ParameterInfo, System.Reflection namespace, 160
Password Storage pattern, 400–401
   benefits/liabilities, 401
   consequences, 401
   forces, 400
   hashing helper method implementation, 341
   intent, 400
   participants, 401
   problem, 400
   structure, 401

Patterns:
   categorizing, 39–41
   classifying, 342
   defined, 10, 37, 37–38
   gang of four (GoF), 8, 38
   pattern library, 41–43
      advanced patterns, 43, 319–401
      general framework patterns, 41, 45–105
      how to use, 43
      middle-tier patterns, 42
      persistence-tier patterns, 42, 201–264
      presentation-tier patterns, 42, 107–139
   repeatable, 37
   software design patterns, 38
   usefulness of, 34
Persistence-tier patterns, 42, 201–264
   Abstract Schema, 42, 203
   columns, 215
   keys, 215–217
      keyrefs, 216–217
      primary keys, 215
      unique keys, 215–216
   Poly Model Factory, 203
   Poly Model pattern, 42, 203, 217–231
      benefits/liabilities, 223–226
      consequences, 223–226
      forces, 218–219
      implementation, 226–231
      intent, 217
      participants, 226
      problem, 217–218
      related patterns, 231
      stored procedure used for saving to
         DATALOG table, 229–230
      stored procedure used for saving XML
         instance data to main DATA table,
         230
      StoreTransaction method, 226–228
      storing instance data passed using DataSet/
         passed-in stored procedure, 228–229
      structure, 219–223
   Schema Field pattern, 42, 203, 231–245
      benefits/liabilities, 235–236
      Client, 226
      consequences, 235
      Data Access Object, 226
      forces, 233
      implementation, 235–245
      intent, 231
      problem, 232–233
      related patterns, 245
      structure, 234–235
   Schema Indexer pattern, 42, 203, 245–264
      benefits/liabilities, 250–251

cleaning up lookup keys from INDEX table, 253–254
consequences, 250–251
database-specific helper method for GetTransaction, 263
forces, 247
helper method used to GetTransaction in Poly Model, 260–261
helper method to store lookup key, 254–256
implementation, 251–264
intent, 245
method called to save lookup column, 252–253
method using transaction ID directly, 262
problem, 246–247
related patterns, 264
sample ad hoc query method used for testing queries, 258–259
sample schema generator and sample LOOKUP instance data for convenience, 257–258
sample transaction retrieval method using WhereCollection SQL Builder, 259–260
simple GetTransaction method using transaction ID directly, 261–262
stored procedure source for storing lookup values to INDEX table, 256–257
structure, 247–250
schemas:
and DataSets, 206–208
nested relationships, 212–213
one-to-many relationships, 213
types of, 212–213
XML schema, 204–206
table, 213–214
typed DataSets, creating, 208–212
Pollable Thread Manager pattern, 42, 117–122
AsyncReturn, 118, 119–120
BeginExecution method, 119
benefits/liabilities, 117–118
Client, 118
consequences, 117–118
forces, 116
implementation, 118–122
intent, 116
participants, 118
PollableThreadManager, 118–119
problem, 116
related patterns, 122
structure, 117
WaitForCompletion method, 121–122
Poly Model pattern, 42, 202, 258, 263, 281, 283
Poly schemas, 224

PolyData class, 310
PrepareCache factory method, 326, 333, 335
PrepareConfigData method, 335–336
PreparePacket method, 196, 302, 313
PrepareWorkers method, 335
Presentation-tier patterns, 42, 107–139
Dynamic Assembly Loader pattern, 42, 132–134
benefits/liabilities, 133
consequences, 133
constructing an object using Reflection, 134
forces, 133
implementation, 134
intent, 132
participants, 134
problem, 132–133
structure, 133
Error Cross-Reference Generator pattern, 42, 125–128
benefits/liabilities, 127
calling, 128
consequences, 127
forces, 126
implementation, 127–128
intent, 125
participants, 127
problem, 125–126
related patterns, 128
structure, 126
Multisync Thread Manager pattern, 42, 122–125
benefits/liabilities, 124
consequences, 124
DoExecution method, 125–126
forces, 123
implementation, 124–125
intent, 122
participants, 124
problem, 122–123
related patterns, 125
structure, 123
Notifying Thread Manager pattern, 42, 108–116
benefits/liabilities, 110
calling Notifying Thread Manager, 113
Client, 109–110
consequences, 110
delegate definitions, 111
DoExecution method notification, 114–115
ExecuteAsync method, 112
forces, 109
implementation, 111–115
intent, 108
NotifyingThread Manager, 109–111
participants, 110–111
problem, 108–109

Presentation-tier patterns (cont.)
  related patterns, 116
  structure, 109–110
overview, 107–108
Pollable Thread Manager pattern, 42, 117–122
  AsyncReturn, 118, 119–120
  BeginExecution method, 119
  benefits/liabilities, 117–118
  Client, 118
  consequences, 117–118
  forces, 116
  implementation, 118–122
  intent, 116
  participants, 118
  PollableThreadManager, 118, 119
  problem, 116
  related patterns, 122
  structure, 117
  WaitForCompletion method, 121–122
Stunt Driver pattern, 42, 135–139
  adding items to test parameters, 139
  benefits/liabilities, 136
  building test set the easy way with, 138
  consequences, 136
  forces, 135
  getting test parameters from, 136
  implementation, 136–139
  intent, 135
  ITestable component, 136
  participants, 136
  problem, 135
  related patterns, 139
  structure, 135
  Test Client, 136
  testing Stunt Driver, 138
WebForm Template pattern, 42, 128–132
  benefits/liabilities, 129–130
  consequences, 129–130
  default sample page, 132
  forces, 128
  implementation, 130–132
  intent, 128
  participants, 130
  problem, 128
  related patterns, 131–132
  rendering (complete), 131
  rendering (simple form), 130–131
  structure, 129
Process patterns, 265–318
  applying.NET patterns, 291–313
    Product Manager pattern, 296–303
    Service Facade pattern, 292–296
    Unchained Service Factory pattern, 303–313
  Commercial Framework, 267–270

architectural features, 284–289
  vision statement, 282
.NET technology, as competitive advantage,
    279–291
ProductX, 270–271
Product Manager pattern, 42, 142, 163–171, 296–
    303
  benefits/liabilities, 166–167
  ConcreteDelegate, 168
  ConcreteProduct, 168
  consequences, 166–167
  delegation implementation, 169–170
  Facade, 167
  forces, 165
  generic class diagram, 166
  implementation, 168–171
  intent, 163
  ManagedProduct, 168
  method implementation, 169
  participants, 167–168
  problem, 163–165
  ProductManager, 167–168
  related patterns, 171
  structure, 166
  UnmanagedProduct, 168
  worker implementation, 170
ProductX, 94, 270–271
  automated check payments, 273–275
  checks vs. credit cards, 273
  and consumers/businesses, 271–272
  electronic check Web servicing, 275–279
  Electronic Funds Transfer (EFT)
  invoking framework from ProductX Web client,
      313–317
  summarizing, 317–318
Proof-of-concept (POC) delivery vehicles, 267
PropertyInfo, System.Reflection namespace, 160
Protocols, 12
Public Web services, 14–16

R

Random tracing, 76–77
Real-time logging, 53
Receiver, 275
Receiving Depository Financial Institution (RDFI),
    275
Reference types, 185–186
Referential integrity, 216
Reflection, 134, 156, 281
  Activator class, 158, 161
Reflection services, 61
Reliability protocols, 24
Remote method invocation (RMI) protocol, 12

Remote procedure calls (RPCs), 12, 144
Remote trace errors, 94
Remote Tracer, 41
Remote tracing, 82–104
    remote trace receiver, building, 86–87
    remote trace viewer, building, 94–104
    sample business object to be placed on queue,
        88–92
    sample Remote Trace Listener viewer (GUI),
        94–103
    sample RemoteTraceListener Web service, 86–
        87
    sample routine for constructing/adding custom
        listener, 86
    sample socket routine for sending a message,
        92–94
    sending races to message queue, 87–92
    sending traces via sockets, 92–94
    Trace Listener template, 84–85
RemoteService.RemoteTrace, 85
RemoteTrace class, 80
RemoteTraceService.RemoteTrace, 86
RemoteTraceViewer, 94
RemoveAllKeys method, 253
ReportingWebService report, 326
Rootcause child node, 75

S

SaveTransaction method, 301
Schedule Action Router, 287
Schedule Viewer, 287
Schema Field, 42
Schema Indexer, 42
Schema Indexer pattern, 258, 263
Schemas:
    and DataSets, 206–208
    nested relationships, 212–213
    one-to-many relationships, 213
    types of, 212–213
    XML schemas, 204–206
Server faultcode, 66
Service Facade, 42
Service Facade pattern, 42, 142, 171–178, 292–296
    benefits/liabilities, 174
    ConcreteFacade, 175
    consequences, 174
    Facade, 175
    forces, 173
    generic class diagram, 173
    implementation, 175–178
    intent, 171
    participants, 174–175
    PaymentFacade, 293–294

    problem, 171–173
    related patterns, 178
    sample implementation, 176–177
    Service, 174–175
    structure, 173
Service interface, 292
Service-oriented architecture, 143
SimpleType element tag, 205
Simplified deployment, 36
SMTP, 25
SOAP, 9, 174
    Body tag, 27
    defined, 20
    Envelope tag, 27
    headers, 28
    security in, 28–31
    success of, 26
    Web services, 23–28
    and XML, 24
    and XML Web services, 24
SOAP Exception Fault Builder, 67
SOAP exception handling, 288
Soap Fault Builder, 41
SOAP Fault elements, 65, 74
SOAP faultcodes, 66
SOAP Faults, 65, 65–67
SOAP message, 26–27
    sample captured using SOAP Trace Utility, 27
SOAP Toolkit, 65
SOAP Toolkit (Microsoft), 21–22, 65
SoapException class, 64, 68, 71, 73–74
SoapException.DetailElementName type, 75
SOAP-formatted messages, XML tags essential for
        understanding, 25–26
SoapSerializer object, 328
SoapServer object (SOAP Toolkit 2.0), 67–68
Sound designs, 40
SpDNPatternsUpdateschema, 240
Sproxy.exe, 21
SPROXY.EXE, 381, 384
SSessionId variable, 330
Stack builder, 61
State management, 352
StoreKeys method, 246–247, 253–254
StoreTransaction method, 311
StoreTransactionRecord method, 311–312
Structured exception handling (SEH), 47
Stunt Driver pattern, 42, 135–139
    adding items to test parameters, 139
    benefits/liabilities, 136
    building test set the easy way with, 138
    consequences, 136
    forces, 135
    getting test parameters from, 136

Stunt Driver pattern (cont.)
    implementation, 136–139
    intent, 135
    participants, 136
    problem, 135
    related patterns, 139
    structure, 135
    testing Stunt Driver, 138
System exception classes, 62–63
System Exception Wrapper, 41
System exceptions, 47–48
    throwing, 62–63
System.ApplicationException class, 51
System.Data.OracleClient, 312
System.Diagnostics.Switch, 80–81
System.Diagnostics.TraceListener class, 77–78
System.Exception class, 47, 61
System.Reflection namespace, members of, 160
System.Resources.ResourceManager, 50–51
System.Web.Caching.Cache object, 326, 338
System.Windows.Forms.DataGrid controls, 94
System.Xml.XmlDocument class, 75

T

T+3 settlement period, 273
tblimp.exe, 168, 170
TerraService (Microsoft), 14–15
    main page, 14
    Web methods list form, 15
TextWriterListener, 78
TIBCO, 350–351, 361
TModels (Type Models), 32
Trace listeners, 77–80
    customer, building, 82–104
Trace option, enabling, 77
Trace originator, 92
Trace receiver, 86
Trace switches, 80–82
Trace switching, 287
Trace Viewer, 287
TraceSwitch, 58, 80–82
Trace.WriteLineIf method, 58
Trace.Write/Trace.WriteLine, 78, 80
Tracing, 53–54
TransactorService, 379
TransactorService.Execute, 362
TransactorService.GetStatus, 362
Translate method, 183

U

UDDI, tModels (Type Models), 32
Unboxing, 186, 186–187

Unchained Service Factory pattern, 42, 142, 152–162, 284, 303–313
    Activator, 157
    Assembly, 157
    benefits/liabilities, 146–148
    ConcreteFacade, 157
    consequences, 155–156
    Facade, 157
    forces, 154–155
    generic class diagram, 155
    implementation, 157–162
    implementation using Reflection, 158–158
    intent, 152
    MethodInfo, 157
    .NET Reflection services, 159–162
    participants, 157
    problem, 152–154
    related patterns, 162
    Service, 157
    ServiceClient, 157
    structure, 155
    Type, 157
Uniform Resource Identifier (URI), 66
Universal Discovery Description and Integration (UDDI), 20, 32–33
Universal Resource Identifiers (URIs), 25
Universal Resource Names (URNs), 25
Unrecoverable exception, 47
"Using Data Caching Techniques to Boost Performance and Ensure Synchronization" (Burgett), 298
Utilities.SendSocketStream method, 92

V

ValidatePacket method, 301
Value types, 185
VB.NET, 4, 8, 35, 385
VersionMismatch faultcode, 66
Visa, 274
Visual Basic/Visual Basic C++, 12
Visual Studio .NET, 13, 33–34, 168, 171, 219, 268, 304, 354, 357, 359, 370
    sample Web service WSDL via, 21

W

Web Service, 287
    code, 63
    consumers, issues faced by, 17–18
Web Service Interface pattern, 42, 342–350
    benefits/liabilities, 344–346
    client-side WSI implementation example, 350
    concrete WSI implementation example, 347–348

consequences, 344–346
forces, 343
implementation, 347–350
intent, 342
IWebServiceInterface, 346
participants, 346–347
problem, 342–343
sample interface, 347
ServiceClient, 346
ServiceProxy, 346
structure, 344
Web service piece of WSI implementation, 349
WebServiceConcrete, 346
WebServiceInterface, 346
WSDL-generated proxy code, 349–350
Web service provider, issues faced buying, 18
Web Service Proxy, 285
Web services, 281
Web Services Description Language (WSDL), 7
Web.config, adding a listener using:
WebForm Template pattern, 42, 128–132
benefits/liabilities, 129–130
consequences, 129–130
default sample page, 132
forces, 128
implementation, 130–132
intent, 128

participants, 130
problem, 128
related patterns, 131–132
rendering (complete), 131
rendering (simple form), 130–131
structure, 129
WebServiceInterface abstract class, 346
Windows event log, 58
Windows Event Viewer, 76
WSDL, 7, 9, 31–32
defined, 20
specification, 23
WS-Inspection Language, 33

X

XML, 236
XML namespaces, 25
XML schemas, 26, 204–206, 281, 283, 290
schema element, 204–205
XML Web services, 9, 354
defined, 19–23
and .NET, 13–18
primer, 19–32
XML-formatted system configuration files, 29
XmlNode class, 75
.XSD, 208–209

Other Patterns Resources from Addison-Wesley

Design Patterns
Elements of Reusable Object-Oriented Software
Erich Gamma
Richard Helm
Ralph Johnson
John Vlissides
Foreword by Grady Booch

0-201-63361-2

THE **DESIGN PATTERNS** SMALLTALK COMPANION
Sherman R. Alpert
Kyle Brown
Bobby Woolf
Foreword by Kent Beck
SOFTWARE PATTERNS SERIES

0-201-18462-1

PATTERN HATCHING
Design Patterns Applied
JOHN VLISSIDES
Foreword by James O. Coplien
SOFTWARE PATTERNS SERIES

0-201-43293-5

DESIGN PATTERNS JAVA WORKBOOK
STEVEN JOHN METSKER
Foreword by Rebecca Wirfs-Brock
SOFTWARE PATTERNS SERIES

0-201-74397-3

THE JOY OF PATTERNS
Using Patterns for Enterprise Development
BRANDON GOLDFEDBER
SOFTWARE PATTERNS SERIES

0-201-65759-7

Small Memory Software
Patterns for limited memory systems
JAMES NOBLE & CHARLES WEIR
SOFTWARE PATTERNS SERIES

0-201-59607-5

DESIGN PATTERNS EXPLAINED
A New Perspective on Object-Oriented Design
ALAN SHALLOWAY
JAMES R. TROTT
SOFTWARE PATTERNS SERIES

0-201-71594-5

THE MANAGER POOL
Patterns for Radical Leadership
DON SHERWOOD OLSON
CAROL L. STIMMEL
SOFTWARE PATTERNS SERIES

0-201-72583-5

DATA ACCESS PATTERNS
Using Interaction in Object-Oriented Systems
CLIFTON NOCK
SOFTWARE PATTERNS SERIES

0-13-140157-2